Urban America in Historical Perspective

URBAN AMERICA IN HISTORICAL PERSPECTIVE

EDITED BY

Raymond A. Mohl & Neil Betten

INDIANA UNIVERSITY

WEYBRIGHT AND TALLEY

NEW YORK

Published in the United States by
Weybright and Talley, Inc.
3 East 54th Street
New York, New York 10022

Library of Congress Catalog Card Number: 70-99002

BOOK DESIGN BY VINCENT TORRE

Printed in the United States of America

Contents

PREFACE

The news that American cities are in trouble no longer comes as a surprise. Poverty, slums, crime, racial turmoil, substandard education, inadequate transportation facilities, insufficient tax funds, the flight of business and the middle class, the deterioration of city cores—all these and more trouble municipal officials and urban experts throughout the nation. Even more disturbing to some observers is the way the almost pathological nature of urban life has affected people. Solutions have been proposed in great number and applied with great optimism; but few have succeeded.

The rapid development of urban history as a teaching and research field reflects the scholar's awareness of and concern for the plight of the modern American city. In response to the multiple problems of urban America, historians have begun describing the origin and the process of urbanization in the United States. Long the prerogative of amateurs and antiquarians, urban history has now become the province of professionals—a coming of age symbolized by the establishment in 1954 of an Urban History Group within the American Historical Association.

The purpose of this volume is to provide a source of important writings to aid in understanding urbanization and its consequences. It is intended especially as supplementary material for courses in urban history, but urban materials can be incorporated in general American history courses as well. Students in urban sociology, urban politics, and city planning would likewise benefit from historical insight. Without proper understanding of historical background, governmental officials, city planners, urban experts in various disciplines, and concerned citizens are limited in their understanding of the crisis of the modern city. Historical perspective, we suggest, can heighten the potentiality for urban accomplishment.

R.A.M.
N.B.

Gary, Indiana
June 1969

Urban America in
Historical Perspective

I

Introduction

———

For many decades after the emergence of professional historical writing in the United States in the late nineteenth century, the frontier hypothesis remained the dominant interpretive theme. Set forth by Frederick Jackson Turner in his famous 1893 essay on "The Significance of the Frontier in American History," this interpretation stipulated that the existence of the frontier and the constant westward movement of people shaped the American character and much else besides. In Turner's words, "the existence of an area of free land, its continuous recession, and the advance of American settlement westward, explain American development." The Turner thesis captured the imagination of a whole generation of historians and, despite Turner's later qualifications, diverted attention from other important influences and causal forces in American history.

The American city, one of these neglected areas of inquiry, was left behind in the intellectual migration of historians to the frontier. But by the end of his distinguished career, Turner had begun the backward trek, writing of the possibility of an "urban reinterpretation" of American history and collecting materials for an essay on "The Significance of the City in American History." Turner never completed this project, but the urban dimension of the American past began to interest other scholars by the 1930's. In 1932 the American Historical Association noted twenty opportune topics demanding study and research; urban life and urbanization topped the list.

The turmoil of the modern city has given the historical perspective of urban America new importance and contemporary relevancy. Thus, after many years of comparative neglect, urban history has now achieved academic respectability. But, as in most developing areas of scholarly inquiry, the nature and character of this historical endeavor have been matters of controversy; methods and techniques have remained undefined and attempts at interpretation have failed to satisfy. Advocates and critics alike have been unable to answer the question "What is urban history?" with any degree of certitude or satisfaction. Is it, asks historian Charles Glaab, "the history of cities, the history of urbanization, or the history of anything that takes place in an urban setting?"

THE DIVERGING PATHS

OF

AMERICAN URBAN HISTORY

DWIGHT W. HOOVER

The ambiguities of urban history can be seen in its numerous historiographical trends. Dwight W. Hoover, Professor of History at Ball State University, surveys the varied work of urban historians.

The years following World War II have been characterized by an increased interest in urban themes. As succeeding census reports show growing metropolitan areas and as urban problems attract America's attention, the city looms larger and larger. Historians share in the increased awareness of the city; in the years since 1945 the number of urban histories has increased and the number of historians specializing in urban history has grown commensurately.[1] The trend at the present seems irreversible; more not less effort will be devoted to the history of the American city.

However, urban historians have not yet agreed upon an all embracing theory, one that would provide an organizing prin-

From Dwight W. Hoover, "The Diverging Paths of American Urban History," *American Quarterly*, XX (No. 2, Part 2, Summer Supplement, 1968), 296–317. Copyright 1968, Trustees of the University of Pennsylvania. Reprinted by permission of the University of Pennsylvania.

[1] For bibliographical data see Allen F. Davis, "The American Historian vs. the City," *Social Studies*, LVI (Mar.–Apr. 1965), 91–96, 127–35; and Charles N. Glaab, "The Historian and the American City: A Bibliographical Survey," in Philip M. Hauser and Leo F. Schnore, eds., *The Study of Urbanization* (New York, 1965).

ciple upon which the history of the city could be based. Several approaches have been suggested; each approach has had its disciples. No single theory has gained the universal approbation of urban historians. Each is based upon different assumptions and value systems; each has its drawbacks and its virtues. The purpose of this essay is to explore the paths that are now most heavily used by scholars of the city.

Part of the dilemma of the urban historian is the dilemma of the recent historian, whether to remain a humanist or become a social scientist, whether to turn to aesthethics or to sociology. More specifically, the problem of the urban historian begins with the subject to be studied. Is the historian to study the city or urban civilization? [2] Is urban history to attempt the formulation of a general law of urbanization, or is it to essay a comparative study of persisting institutions? Is the city itself the source of social change or is it only part of a larger source? What element in the cities is crucial to development? As scholars search for answers, the projection of Kenneth Boulding concerning the future ought to haunt us all. When 90% of the population becomes urban, Boulding says, the city will have no separate meaning. An Iowa farmer at present is an exurbanite who is part of an occupational subculture.[3] If urban culture becomes the only standard, will urban history become the only history? Perhaps the historical future belongs to the urban historian and urban interpretations.

Any consideration of a theory of urban history must start with A. M. Schlesinger. Channing's fifth volume [4] in his *A History of the United States* had hinted at the importance of the city, but the bold claims of an urban historian were initially made by Schlesinger. In 1933 he wrote *The Rise of the City* in which he attempted to place the American city in its proper perspective; and in the *Mississippi Valley Historical Review* (June 1940), his article "The City in American History" blazed a trail which many urban historians have followed. Schlesinger claimed to have found the key to social change in America in

[2] John Burchard, "Some Afterthoughts," in Oscar Handlin and John Burchard, eds., *The Historian and the City* (Cambridge, 1963), p. 254.

[3] *Ibid.*, "The Death of the City," p. 143.

[4] W. Stull Holt in his article, "Some Consequences of the Urban Movement in American History," *Pacific Historical Review*, XXII (Nov. 1953), 337–51, vividly recounts how he discovered that what he thought was an original idea had been anticipated by Channing.

the city. For him, the city was the frontier where new ideas, revolutionary in impact, were originated, and where social practices, under pressure by problems generated by people living in close proximity, changed to fit new experiences. Innovation, hence change, in both social and intellectual spheres was a product of city life. On the basis of this assumption, Schlesinger proposed a program for historians. From colonial times to the present, the city should be the prime object of study. The major elements within the city to be investigated should be the characteristic economic institutions and social practices of the citizens. Thus, Schlesinger wished to change both the locus and the focus of American historians.

The claims of Schlesinger for an urban centered history did not go unchallenged. William Diamond the following year commented devastatingly upon some of the weaknesses of the Schlesinger thesis. His criticisms are still apropos for urban historians today. Schlesinger failed, according to Diamond, to define either the city or urbanization clearly, to take cognizance of Mumford's work which showed the city to be more than one entity, to distinguish between the cultural traits that were permanent in the city and those that were merely transitional, and to demonstrate that an urban-rural division of history was more significant than others in explaining behavior. Above all, Diamond insisted that Schlesinger's concept of the city was ambiguous, just as the Turnerian concept of the frontier had been. All Schlesinger had done was to substitute one broad generalization for another.[5] Since neither the city nor the frontier was rigorously enough defined, no light was shed on the problem of cause in history.

Diamond's criticisms, appropriate and convincing as they appear to be, did not dim the hopes of urban historians who found the concept of the city as originator of social change appealing. Indeed, the analogy of the city with the frontier proved too compelling to discard. A decade later, W. Stull Holt explicitly thought of the city in these terms while reviewing studies done of individual cities: Bessie Pierce's *A History of Chicago*, Bayrd Still's *Milwaukee*, and Constance McLaughlin Green's *Holyoke, Massachusetts*. The histories of these specific cities, Holt said, "are like the various histories of sections of the frontier such as

[5] "On the Danger of an Urban Interpretation of History," in Eric J. Goldman, ed., *Historiography and Urbanization* (Baltimore, 1941), pp. 67–108.

Roosevelt's *Winning of the West* before Turner in his famous essay saw the forest as well as the trees." [6] (One might wonder whether the comparison with Roosevelt would be considered complimentary by these historians.) Holt, however, was not completely satisfied with the generalizations of Schlesinger and tried to add to the description of the urban experience. Several consequences of living in cities were significant to Holt. These included an older population, a lowered birth rate, more freedom for women and a change in the conception of the function of the state from a negative to a positive one, necessitated by problems of public health, education and sanitation.[7] These characteristics of an urban population, both demographic and ideological, were the ones that had made the city the innovator in the American past. The quality of city populations and the necessity to regulate the environment in order to survive had produced the welfare state which is most characteristic of American life.

Two comments are in order here. Using Diamond's insight that there are trends in the city that are short rather than long range, two of Holt's city population characteristics, an older population and a lowed birth rate, are temporary. Again much depends upon the definition of the city. Does the city include the suburbs? If so, the population is not noticeably older than the aging rural population. If only the inner city is used, the Negro migration to and the white flight from the center still tends to weaken the generalization. The population age is more a function of socio-economic class than residence, and the demographic features of the city reflect the social make-up of the times. Secondly, the change in political theory attributable to urban condition discounts the cries for federal regulation by farmers in the nineteenth century and the considerable federal aid to rural interests in the twentieth. One could well argue that farmers, although retaining a Jeffersonian anti-governmental ideology, were among the first to enter a planned society; and city dwellers, although not averse to aid, among the last.

Despite the demurrers, the Schlesinger thesis has persisted. Carl Bridenbaugh in *Cities in Revolt* (1955) and *Cities in the Wilderness* (1938) traced the role of cities in the American Revolution and in frontier settlement, attributing to the cities

[6] "Some Consequences of the Urban Movement in American History," p. 339.
[7] Diamond had pointed to a lower birth rate in the city twelve years before.

considerable credit for both these movements. Richard C. Wade has also continued the tradition in *The Urban Frontier: The Rise of Western Cities* (1959) and *Slavery in the Cities: The Antebellum South* (1964). Despite the rural nature of both the trans-Appalachian West and the South in the pre-Civil War period, Wade portrayed cities as important transforming forces. In the South the rural institution of slavery underwent a noticeable transformation into a kind of urban segregation under the liberalizing influence of urban living conditions. In the West Wade concludes that "Cities represented the most aggressive and dynamic forces."[8] Both Bridenbaugh and Wade center the city in the middle of political, intellectual and social developments from the beginning of the Republic.

In addition to specific studies of American cities Wade has, perhaps, made the best summation of the claims for urban innovation. Among the contributions made by cities to American life Wade lists are the origin of settlement, particularly in the West; the responsibility for triggering the revolution, especially in Boston; the promotion of economic growth through city rivalry in the nineteenth century; the coming together of North and West in the Civil War because of Chicago's triumph over St. Louis as a railroad center; the degeneration of slavery in the South; the development of techniques of political manipulation such as boss rule; and the reactions to this manipulation such as progressive reform.[9] With Wade, as with Schlesinger, the cities are where social change originated.

Another urban historian, Blake McKelvey, studying the period after the Civil War, 1865-1915, made as great claims for the role of the city. McKelvey explicitly tied the city to the frontier, stating that the unexploited potential of older established cities or of hamlets near them provided a substitute for the closing of the frontier in 1890.[10] That McKelvey's book is in the Schlesinger tradition is evident in the topics he considered; economic growth, especially in banking and credit facilities; the development of regional centers with outlying tributaries; the expansion of transport facilities; and technological change. These all are cited as having been advanced by urbanization.

---

[8] *The Urban Frontier* (Chicago, 1964), pp. 341–42.
[9] "The City in History—Some American Perspectives," in Werner Z. Hirsch, ed., *Urban Life and Form* (New York, 1963), pp. 59–77.
[10] *The Urbanization of America, 1865–1915* (New Brunswick, 1963), p. 32.

A corollary theme was the interaction between social forces and the city, especially in education, public health, recreation and the arts. McKelvey gave much credit to the urban atmosphere for the changing of American attitudes in the social realm and economic institutions in the economic sphere.

Perhaps the most prolific woman historian in America is Constance McLaughlin Green, who, like McKelvey, came to consider the broader theme of the city in American development through the biography of individual cities.[11] Green's two volumes on American urban history, *American Cities in the Growth of the Nation* (1957) and *The Rise of Urban America* (1965), viewed the city as an important factor in the development of an American way of life.[12] In the earlier book Green had a series of vignettes, four involving cities of a particular type—seaboard cities of the nineteenth century, river cities, New England manufacturing cities and cities of the great plains—and four individual cities—Chicago, Seattle, Detroit and Washington. As can be seen, this division was socio-economic, reflecting an interest in unique social and economic development of particular cities. In *American Cities in the Growth of the Nation*, there was not the concerted attempt to tie city growth in the United States together as in the later book, *The Rise of Urban America*, but Mrs. Green's second effort at a larger urban history is quite inferior to her first. *American Cities in the Growth of the Nation* has many valuable insights in it while *The Rise of Urban America* seems slim by comparison. It is essentially a conventional social and economic history placed in an urban setting, and suffers from the lack of any overall conceptual framework. While Mrs. Green assumes that cities have shaped American life, she is never as explicit as Schlesinger or Wade, making her synthesis disjointed and weak.

The kind of urban history that Wade, McKelvey and Green write is obvious. Taking the themes already extant in American history—sectionalism, the growth of public education, reform and reaction—these historians search for the roots in movements in the city. With varying degrees of sophistication, they switch

---

[11] McKelvey studied Rochester while Green has written histories of Holyoke, Naugatuck and Washington, D. C.

[12] McKelvey in his review of *The Rise of Urban America* in the *American Historical Review*, LXXI (Jan. 1966), 680, criticized Green for not emphasizing the importance of the city enough.

the locale of historical change from the frontier to the city. Unlike Schlesinger, they are modest and less willing to make sweeping claims for the place of the city in American history, although implicitly they believe that place has been severely undervalued by earlier historians. For this group of urban historians, urban history is social history drawn from the city.

Urban history following this path does reveal a number of possibilities for further research, particularly in recent history. The role of city in civil rights movement, as Green suggests, the attraction of McCarthyism in the city, the city origins of the New Deal, isolationism in the cities, modern Republicanism in the cities, all could be studied in depth. However, the substitution of the city for the frontier as an organizing principle has pernicious as well as fruitful results. By explaining too much, the city as a cause of social change blocks other, better explanations.

Still, the use of the Schlesinger thesis gave some differentiation to urban history which biographies of individual cities or collective biographies seemed to lack. But all of the histories considered so far suffer, as Roy Lubove says, from the same difficulty: "The main point is that all the publications in this category deal with cities, or life in cities, but rarely with urban history as distinguished from social, economic or political history in the context of the city." [13] The need for a unique framework for urban history remains unmet in this approach.

Possibilities other than social history became evident in the post-World War II period. Earlier definitions of urban history by historians proved too gross and the need to be more precise was obvious. In addition, the work being done by social scientists seemed to offer a theoretical basis for a study of the city as a process of urbanization. Urban historians, like other historians, were not unaware of the prestige attached to scientific enterprises. The discipline that offered the most promising insights was sociology, which had had a continuing interest in

[13] "The Urbanization Process: An Approach to Historical Research," *Journal of the American Institute of Planners*, XXXIII (Jan. 1967), 33. Lubove sees three categories in urban history: social, cultural, economic and political studies; the formation of the urban environment studies, or urban history as the process of city building over time; and urbanization as a broad societal process. Lubove believes the second category is the most promising one, since it focuses on city building and makes possible a connection between technology and social organization.

community studies, and not political science, which had become involved elsewhere.[14]

For years the center for urban sociology was located at the University of Chicago from which sociologists fanned out to study the city. The most productive theory also came from Chicago. Robert Park, one of the pioneers of urban sociology, had derived an ecological model from biology and seemed to regard human ecology like plant and animal ecology with "social equivalents."[15] Park proposed to study population movements and land values in the aggregate and to deny the possibility of the planned urban environment. The city environment, rather, was a natural, unplanned one which determined interdependence between individuals. Park's associate, Burgess, developed an ecological map of Chicago in the 1920s which was composed of five concentric circles, each representing a different environment or natural area. The crude ecology of Park and Burgess soon came under attack as being inadequate. In the 1930s the retreat from the original ecological presumption began and the strict determinism softened, as Louis Wirth, Park's student, shifted Park's ecological emphasis somewhat in order to meet the criticisms. Starting with ideal types of cultures, urban-industrial and rural-folk, similar to the distinction between *Gemeinschaft and Gesellschaft* and to the urban-rural dichotomy of Schlesinger, Wirth attributed the difference between the two types to urbanization. Urbanism was:

that cumulative accentuation of the characteristics distinctive of the mode of life which is associated with the growth of cities, and finally to the changes in the direction of modes of life among people, wherever they may be, who have come under the spell of influences which the city exerts by virtue of the power of its institutions and

[14] R. T. Daland's "Political Science and the Study of Urbanism: A Bibliographical Essay," *American Political Science Review*, LI (June 1957), 491–509, reports on the dearth of interest in urban studies in political science in the 1950s.

[15] Leonard Reissman, *The Urban Process: Cities in Industrial Society* (Glencoe, Ill., 1964), p. 98. Reissman's book contains an excellent, short description of various urban sociologists with a corresponding typology into which each is placed. Park and Burgess are called ecological empiricists, Wirth and Redfield theoreticians. This should be compared to Gideon Sjoberg's chapter, "Theory and Research in Urban Sociology," in *The Study of Urbanization* where Park and Burgess are identified as the Chicago school and Wirth and Redfield as the urbanization school.

personalities operating through the means of communication and transportation.[16]

From Wirth's statement it is apparent that while ecological considerations are still important, other influences on the creation of an urban type also must be taken into account. A theory of urbanization followed with three necessary factors: physical structure (population, technology, ecology); social organization (status-groups, institutions); and collective behavior (group attitudes, ideologies). Wirth's theory has been quite fruitful; but, like many other seminal ideas, has rarely been taken whole. The diverging paths of urban history lead out from Wirth.[17] The first category, physical structure, has appealed primarily to sociologists who have emphasized ecology and population aggregates and to historians who have visualized communications as the key to the cities in naturalistic, reductionist fashion. Still others have concentrated upon the second category and traced the evolution and influence of social stratification and institutions in the growth of the city. Still others see the third as most meaningful and have written about the mutual interaction of ideas and the city. Finally, there are those historians who attempt to use all three categories in an explanation of the process of urbanization, which for these individuals, is urban history.

The first group, the ecologists, are still physically located in Chicago. The death blow to the original ecology of Park seemingly was struck by a book written by Walter Firey, *Land Use in Central Boston* (1946), which showed that community and society were inseparable and that urban land value was a function of cultural demands set by community sentiment as well as by location. Yet old ideas are hard to kill. The same year in Chicago the Chicago Community Inventory was created by a grant from the Wiebolt Foundation. In 1951, Philip M. Hauser, a sociologist interested both in studies of population and comparative urbanization, became director. Hauser has collaborated

---

[16] "Urbanism As a Way of Life," *American Journal of Sociology*, XLIV (July 1938), 1–24. Wirth's article is a landmark in the field of urbanization. Perhaps Wirth's greatest strength lay in his ability to project into the future. Reissman characterizes Wirth as a deductive theorist, a characterization that is basically sound.

[17] This is not to argue that present day urban historians, or sociologists for that matter, recognize their debt to Wirth or call themselves disciples of Wirth. While his framework is a suggestive one, the fitting of individuals into that framework is an arbitrary act. Nor is the framework to be considered as a completely satisfactory one.

with Leo F. Schnore, a Wisconsin sociologist, also interested in population theory. Schnore and another sociologist, Otis D. Duncan, have attempted to revive ecology as a respectable explanation for the structure of cities, and hence are in a direct line from Robert Park. Using Amos H. Hawley's *Human Ecology* (1950) as a base, these sociologists continue to insist that population aggregates are the most important element in the study of the city and that statistical manipulation is the necessary tool. A typical ecological statement by Duncan and Schnore is contained in a 1959 issue of *American Journal of Sociology*, published by the University of Chicago. Duncan and Schnore argue that ecology offered the best insights into the perennial problems of sociologists emanating from social organization—bureaucracy and stratification. In addition the ecological approach provided a theory of social change which the cultural and behavioral schools could not do. Finally, ecology was the best base for interdisciplinary cooperation. After presenting a case for ecology, Duncan and Schnore then constructed a modified ecological complex consisting of population, environment, technology and organization.[18] The relationship between men and their environment combined with social organization and technology made up all the necessary ingredients for urbanization. Wirth's third division was ignored and the first expanded to occupy almost the whole of urban studies.

The ecological approach has not converted a great number of sociologists. Duncan and Schnore were immediately challenged for distortion of the cultural and behavioral assumptions of sociologists and for attempting to include all of sociological endeavor under one great imperial network.[19] In addition, their belief that more orthodox methodologies were inadequate for studying social organization was not matched by a completely convincing methodology of their own. Duncan and Schnore opted for a quantitative method, deliberately incomplete (an abstract model), and for comparative analysis of aggregates.[20] For Duncan and Schnore, the greatest asset was the statistical mani-

[18] "Cultural, Behavioral and Ecological Perspectives in the Study of Social Organization," *American Journal of Sociology*, LXV (Sept. 1959), 132–46. Schnore has elaborated on this thesis in *The Urban Scene: Human Ecology and Demography* (New York, 1965).

[19] Peter H. Rossi, "Comment," *American Journal of Sociology*, LXV (Sept. 1959), 146–49.

[20] "Rejoinder," *American Journal of Sociology*, LXV (Sept. 1959), 149–53.

pulation of increased sophistication possible in the ecological approach.[21]

More recently the assumptions of the ecologists have been specifically attacked. While admitting that ecology is the "closest we have come to a systematic theory of the city," [22] Reissman argues that ecologists are still biological determinists. The study of population aggregates and the principles that keep these aggregates operative is undertaken as analogous to animal ecology. Thus, the environment in ecological discussions assumes the causative function; adaption to the environment by man includes culture, social stratification and institutions. In finding this cause for social change the ecologists have returned to a Spencerian figure of a social organism.[23]

The rehabilitation of ecology by sociologists like Duncan and Schnore came during the 1950s when urban historians were casting about for an organizing theory. One individual in particular, Eric Lampard, has tried to promote the ecological principle as the framework for urban history.

Lampard explicitly uses the ecological ideas of Duncan and Schnore in his framework for the study of urbanization.[24] For Lampard, as for the ecologists, community structure is the result of a changing equilibrium between population and environment mediated by technology and organization. Lampard urges the adoption of the ecological complex of Amos Hawley, Otis Duncan and Leo Schnore, as well as the study of urbanization as a societal process without committing the past errors of confusing the pathological aspects of the process with the normal.

Lampard not only urges historians to be ecologists; he also dissects the failures of urban history.[25] Tracing the backgrounds of urban history, Lampard finds the difficulty in this past. Coming out of social history, urban history concentrated on

[21] Otis Dudley Duncan does recognize inherent statistical problems in the theory of ecological correlations as seen in his article written with Beverly Davis, "An Alternative to Ecological Correlation," *American Sociological Review,* XVIII (Dec. 1953), 665–66.

[22] *The Urban Process,* p. 93. Reissman uses the term neo-ecologists for these sociologists.

[23] Roy Lubove has the same criticism in "The Urbanization Process: An Approach to Historical Research." Ecologists err in ignoring the role of values, small groups, interpersonal relations and cultural traits in shaping the city.

[24] "American Historians and the Study of Urbanization," *American Historical Review,* LXVII (Oct. 1961), 49–61.

[25] "Urbanization and Social Change," *The Historian and the City.*

social problems rather than social change, on conflicts of interest and ideas rather than social organization and social structure.[26] Because of these preoccupations, urban history lacks both a general, theoretical framework and relevant data to that framework.[27] Lampard proposes to remedy both deficiencies. "At stake in a broader view of urban history is the possibility of making the societal process of urbanization central to the study of social change. Efforts should be made to conceptualize urbanization in ways that actually *represent* social change." [28] Basic to social change is ecology—population, its changing composition and its distribution in space and time.[29] The theoretical framework for the urban historian, then, should be the study of population change. The necessary social data is to be found in migration and social mobility, which includes both occupational shifts and changes in social status.[30] Of the salient ways to advance on the city—structural, behavioral and demographical—the demographic is best, according to Lampard.[31]

Lampard represents a bridge between the neo-ecological sociologists and the urban historian. At a time when the study of population movements and ecology are out of favor with the majority of sociologists, Lampard attempts to make ecological assumptions palatable to historians and to convince historians that they must study population change. While no historian has become an avowed ecologist, certainly there is a noticeable tendency to make population studies on a quantified basis.[32]

That the study of population mobility can be instructive is illustrated by a pioneer work of Stephan Thernstrom. Thernstrom was connected with another center for studying urban and regional affairs, the Joint Center for Urban Studies of Harvard University and Massachusetts Institute of Technology. Begun in 1959, the Joint Center has been interested in basic research in a variety of disciplines including aesthetics, architectural history and urban planning. Its basic orientation was not

[26] *Ibid.*, pp. 226–27.
[27] *Ibid.*, p. 232.
[28] *Ibid.*, p. 233.
[29] *Ibid.*, p. 236.
[30] *Ibid.*, p.235.
[31] *Ibid.*, p. 238.
[32] For bibliographical material see "The Historian and the American City: A Bibliographical Survey."

sociological, as was Chicago's, so its studies have ranged more widely. Indeed, the ecological tradition was never strong at the Joint Center because of the considerable impact of *Land Use in Central Boston*.

Thernstrom's book, *Poverty and Progress*, did utilize criteria for studying Newburyport similar to those proposed by Lampard. Using manuscript census schedules and local records of the 1850-1880 period, Thernstrom analyzed occupational, geographic and inter-generational mobility among laborers and their sons, as well as property accumulations and other evidence of increased affluence. All of this was designed to discover social mobility in mid-nineteenth century Newburyport. Thernstrom's conclusions were that social mobility was minimal, that occupational shifts upward were slight, and that property accumulations seldom amounted to more than a house. On the basis of these conclusions, Thernstrom hazarded an opinion that the open class system of the nineteenth century was largely mythical. As he put it, "The findings of the present study, however, when coupled with scattered evidence concerning social mobility in several twentieth-century American cities, permit a more definite verdict: to rise from the bottom of the social scale has not become increasingly difficult in modern America: If anything it appears to have become somewhat less difficult." [33]

Thernstrom's work cut in several directions. On the one hand, it opened the door for other urban historians to study further social mobility in other American cities to see if Thernstrom's results obtain. (Curiously enough, Thernstrom indicates that his findings are not too divergent from Curti's study of Trempealeau County.) In particular, those communities that had been already studied without much consideration of the time dimension by sociologists or anthropologists provide a base from which to work. Not only Yankee City, but Middletown and Elmtown, could be examined; and since some of the census data is now being programmed for computers, the possibility of machine assisted research also obtains. Thernstrom presently is engaged in just such a study of Boston under a grant from the American Council of Learned Societies. Furthermore, the study of mobility could be extended to other than the laborer category; studies of middle and upper class mobility might well be

[33] *Poverty and Progress* (Cambridge, 1964), p. 216.

assayed. Perhaps Thernstrom, more than any other urban historian, has shown the way for further statistical attacks on the
city.

On the other hand, Thernstrom's work is a devastating criticism of the ahistorical social scientist, and of W. Lloyd Warner,
in particular. After giving Warner due credit for the magnitude
of his efforts, Thernstrom listed his major failures: not coming
to grips with social mobility, not seeing changes in population
composition or in the character of institutions, and unwillingness to use objective criteria for classes. From these failures
Thernstrom derives an unequivocal theorem: "The distortions
of the Yankee City volumes should suggest that the student of
modern society is not free to take his history or leave it alone.
Interpretation of the present requires assumptions about the
past." [34] The choice is between an assumed past and a studied
one. Warner had been guilty of holding romantic assumptions
about Newburyport's past; he had not bothered to examine that
past, and, as a result, had produced a distorted study. Equally
important with the critique of Warner was Thernstrom's insistence that a community study be done over a span of time.
The urban historian becomes an indispensable part of a community study, not an unnecessary luxury. Because of its opening
of new areas of investigation and reassertion of the value of
historical methods, Thernstrom's book is a landmark in urban
history.[35] But Thernstrom's position is not an ecological one; it
does not operate with aggregates or mathematical models.

[34] *Ibid.,* p. 239.

[35] *Poverty and Progress* has aroused much opposition as might be expected
from its temerity in attacking a giant like Warner. Reviewers of the book
had a number of qualifications both about Thernstrom's methods and conclusions.

The necessity of history in community studies is not a position solely held
by historians, however, as several sociologists testify. These sociologists—John
R. Seeley, Morris S. Schwartz, Kurt H. Wolff and Maurice Stein—have opted
for the older tradition of humanistic, historical sociology instead of the middle
range theories of Merton and the structural-functional bifurcation of the majority of sociologists of the day. For representative essays see Maurice Stein
and Arthur J. Vidich, eds., *Sociology On Trial* (1963), and Arthur J. Vidich,
Joseph Bensman and Maurice Stein, eds., *Reflections on Community Studies*
(1964). Perhaps the most vocal and impressive individual in this group, to the
author, is Maurice Stein. As early as 1960, Stein's *The Eclipse of Community*
traced the history of twentieth-century sociology, focusing upon the reasons
for the switch of interest from community to small groups studies. His major
conclusion was that the change from the study of cities to a study of peer
groups was a reflection of new attitudes and tensions in sociologists themselves.
Stein even spoke kindly of Park and the Lynds, at a time when such praise
was quite out of fashion. To further his heresy, Stein recommended the use

Another approach is to use one particular category in the study of communities as Seymour Mandelbaum has done with communications in New York in the era of Boss Tweed.[36] Rather than study population characteristics as Thernstrom did, Mandelbaum studied technology in the form of communications networks in Tweed's New York. Mandelbaum has returned to Park, who held that the key to the city is communication. However, the theoretical basis here is much more sophisticated. While Mandelbaum has not become involved in the mathematical methods of Karl W. Deutsch in *The Nerves of Government* (1963) or Richard L. Meier in *A Communications Theory of Urban Growth* (1962), he does suggest that these have promise for the future. The central theme of Mandlebaum's book is the primitive state of communication networks in New York City in Tweed's time. Basic to Tweed's ascendancy was the failure of information to be exchanged in any kind of adequate manner. Mandelbaum does effect a limited rehabilitation of Tweed, arguing that he was a product of a system of decentralized decision making and narrow, insufficient communication between decision centers. In a sense Mandelbaum suggests a theory of social change; when the price of ignorance becomes too high, citizens demand better information. When better information is had, political organizations change. When more sophistication in communications is desired, social evolution results.

There is an obvious difficulty in using communications theory as a basis for urban history. Once again a kind of naturalistic determinism permeates this theory. Communications theory shares the same real problem of neo-ecology, the use of organic

---

of some of Collingwood's insights by sociologists. (Indeed, the burden of Stein and his ilk is that the participant-observer must attain a kind of empathy with the community he is studying.) Stein, in relating how he came to a position of appreciating "how much was lost when historical contexts were abandoned in favor of historical generalizations whether these took the form of structural-functional propositions or survey reports," shows some of the characteristics of an urban historian. After learning middle range theories at Columbia from Merton, Stein had to teach urban sociology and sociology of community. In order to accomplish this Stein returned to Park, Warner and the Lynds and from them arrived at a working theory of urbanization. For Stein, sociology in the western tradition combines history, system and drama. Orthodox sociology has become interested only in system, neglecting both history and drama. To return to a wider, more vital sociology, it is necessary to turn back to history and to poetic metaphors. The polemic nature of Stein's argument from the left has stimulated much reaction, but may also serve as a corrective to sociological orthodoxy.

[36] *Boss Tweed's New York* (New York, 1965).

analogy. Deutsch's book uses a figure that is singularly Spencerian, nerves of government; and the conception of a city ham-
pered in social development by channels of communication can
easily become the city as a biological organism. Despite this
demurrer, the use of the model may be expected to increase.

Another possibility emerging from Wirth's third category this
time is the study of group attitudes and ideologies regarding the
city. The organizing principle in this approach might well be
called, as several schools have already done, the image of the
city. The image of the city involves, not necessarily simultaneously, intellectual history, a theory of aesthetics, history of
planning, perception theory and social psychology. In all cases
the interest of the historian is in the concept of the city, whether
that concept be a rational construct, an aesthetic reaction or a
trained perception. Moreover, this approach has the virtue of
being humanistic and nondeterministic.

Perhaps the most traditional way to undertake urban history
in this fashion is through intellectual history, the study of the
concept of urbanism and anti-urbanism. The antagonisms between rural and urban ways of life and thought have long been
noted by historians as well as by those involved in popular
culture. Almost every student of Jefferson has mentioned his
anti-urban sentiments, and the reaction to the urbanization in
the last half of the nineteenth century has been well documented.[37] However, the generalization was crude; urbanization
and industrialization were sometimes used synonymously and
the assumptions that anti-urbanism was a single, unchanging
strand in American thought remained relatively unexamined.

An attempt to analyze some of the ideas of leading American
theorists concerning the city was made, not by intellectual historians, but by a philosopher and a social worker, Morton and
Lucia White. Operating from the institutional impetus of the
Joint Center for Urban Studies, as well as the Center for Advanced Study in the Behavioral Sciences, the Whites gleaned
selective attitudes toward the city and published them in *The
Intellectual Versus the City* (1962).[38] The title gives away the
plot; the opinions of the city considered are largely negative.

[37] From Schlesinger's *The Rise of the City* (1933) to McKelvey's *The
Urbanization of America* (1963) the theme persists. Thirty years is only a
short time and the step is small.

[38] The thesis of *The Intellectual Versus the City* is contained in an essay by
Morton White entitled "Two Stages in the Critique of the American City"
in *The Historian and the City*.

In the individuals whose ideas were presented, from Benjamin Franklin to Frank Lloyd Wright, from the early republic to the twentieth century, anti-urbanism was a constant theme. However, the Whites were able to distinguish two varieties of anti-urbanism, one romantic and the other nonromantic. The earliest critique of the city, the romantic one, shared by Jefferson and Emerson, held that the city was overcivilized and distorted nature. Since nature was the repository of virtue, the city was evil. The romantic view of the city is most often the one cited in anti-urban views, but it is not the most recent or persistent. Commencing after the Civil War, the second critique of the city, one shared by Robert Park and Henry James, made an opposing point, the city is undercivilized. The city had failed to achieve the kind of community necessary for human development, whether that development be intellectual as it was for Henry Adams and Henry James, or emotional as Robert Park and Jane Addams envisaged in their hopes for improved small group relationships. The Whites professed to find anti-urbanism even in persons most intimately connected with the city in a time when the city was becoming the dominant form of American life; the concept of sophisticated anti-urbanism is perhaps their most original contribution.

While *The Intellectual Versus the City* is a compelling book, it is at the same time unsatisfactory. On the one hand, anti-urbanism is demonstrated; but, on the other, the nagging question persists as to whether the two views (or, for that matter, the many views in the book) belong in the same category, springing as they do from different premises. The romantic view could not countenance the city; the nonromantic could and did. The romantic would wish to destroy the city; the nonromantic to transform it. In addition, the growth of American cities in the period after the Civil War, the period that the Whites treat most extensively, poses the question of how this was possible without considerable intellectual energy behind it.[39]

[39] I am indebted to Charles N. Glaab for this insight. He has proposed to do a study of pro-urban thought which is badly needed. See his "The Historian and the American Urban Tradition," *Wisconsin Magazine of History*, LXVII (Autumn 1963), 12–25, reprinted in A. S. Eisenstadt, *The Craft of American History* (Harper Torchbook, 1966), which elaborates some pro-urban sentiment. Also in opposition to the Whites is Frank Freidel, whose chapter, "Boosters, Intellectuals, and the American City," in *The Historian and the City* suggests many nonintellectuals and even some intellectuals, Benjamin Franklin for one, were pro-city. Boorstin's *The Americans: The National Experience* (New York, 1965) is supportive of Freidel.

Furthermore, the twofold division of anti-urbanism is admittedly too simple; even the Whites suggest this. Hence, the investigation of anti-urban themes in American thought has continuing possibilities.

Not only could such a study be made of intellectuals, but also of leaders of popular culture. A case can be made that there is and was considerable uneasiness about urban life on the level of popular culture. One recent example of the possibility is Robert H. Walker's study of popular verse between 1876 and 1905. After studying six thousand volumes of verse (one wonders at Walker's strength and persistence after scanning some of the poems), Walker concludes that the poetical images of the city were negative, portraying the city as an ugly place where economic inequities were the rule, where crime, drunkenness, sexual excesses, amorality prevailed, where existence was characterized by craftiness, overcompetitiveness and artificiality.[40] The view of the city as immoral and threatening on a less rarefied level of abstraction does seem to support the Whites' thesis, although the poetical critique of the city is a romantic one in the nonromantic era. This, of course, does not demolish the Whites' categories; one might suppose that a poetic image would always be romantic.

A much broader approach toward the images of the city comes from Anselm Strauss, a sociologist. Recognizing Park's dictum that the city is a state of mind, Strauss tried to identify the many minds that have conceived of the city and the many cities that have been seen.[41] Strauss' book, *Images of the American City*, shows some of the possibilities in the conceptualization of the city. For richness of suggestions for further study this book must rate high in the historiography of urban studies. Strauss is impressed with the symbolic imagery of the city and treats aesthetic dimensions left out by quantifying sociologists.

Strauss began with a premise that multiplies the images of the city. He argued that the city cannot be comprehended as a whole; that, at best, only parts can be visualized. Therefore, symbolic representation of the city is necessary and such sym-

---

[40] "The Poet and the Rise of the City," *Mississippi Valley Historical Review*, XLIX (June 1962), 85–99.

[41] *Images of the American City* (New York, 1961). However, Strauss' work has serious flaws in it primarily because of the lack of historical perspective. Had Strauss been more familiar with historical method, the book would have been sounder.

bolism is a function of physical, social and perceptual factors. As Strauss put it:

> The city, I am suggesting, can be viewed as a complex related set of symbolized areas. Any given population will be cognizant of only a small number of these areas: most areas will lie outside of effective perception; others will be conceived in such ways that will hardly ever be visited, and will indeed be avoided.[42]

For each group in each area in every age there is a city. Strauss only begins to show the possible images of the city inherent in this approach. Among those he does treat are those views of the city found in ethnic groups, in urban novels, in visiting tourists, in city boosters, in mediators between towns and cities, in planners and in suburbanites. Not that these are by any means all new views of the city; some of them were used by the Whites, Park and Wirth. The accomplishment of Strauss is to collect all of the views together as examples of the multifaceted nature of the city, to suggest the barrenness of a single image of the city, and to use literature in an imaginative way.

Strauss in the case of Chicago shows how varying images of the city, over a period of time, can coalesce into one image. However, the thrust of his work is in two other directions. One is the direction of the positive image of the city. The negative concept of the city must certainly be qualified in order to meet Strauss' suggestions. Particularly intriguing is Strauss' discussion of the image of the city held by ethnic groups and the image of the city as the country. Strauss shows how it is possible for the city to be an urban village, which leads to the question of why the city could not be also an extension of Europe or of the countryside.[43] In the second place, the insistence upon the human necessity of symbolically representing the city is thought provoking. Projected into the past, several areas for investigation become obvious. In addition to studying the city in literature, the novel and the poem, why not study the city in painting? Or why not combine the two as Leo Marx did in *The Machine in the Garden* (1964), detailing the impact of technology on

---

[42] *Ibid.*, p. 59.

[43] Herbert Gans, another sociologist, in his study of Italian-Americans in Boston, *The Urban Villagers* (1962), concludes that the populace did live in a symbolically bounded village. There is no logical reason why the city, contrary to Tönnies and Redfield, could not be an extension of village or folk culture. Oscar Lewis has shown that this is possible in Mexico and New York City.

American imaginations? Indeed some form of middle landscape might be as typical of views of the city as views of industrialization. Or symbolic representation of a particular section of a city might be studied as Allan Trachtenberg has done for the Brooklyn Bridge, *The Brooklyn Bridge* (1965).

Basic to the theoretical underpinning of the visual concept of the city is a book from the Joint Center for Urban Studies. That book is Kevin Lynch's *The Image of the City* (1960). In *The Image of the City* Lynch holds that cities must provide an image for their inhabitants. While some cities are more manageable than others, having parts more easily recognized and organized into a coherent pattern, all cities are represented symbolically by their citizens.[44] To prove this thesis Lynch analyzed three rather disparate cities—Boston, Jersey City and Los Angeles—using interviews as well as field reconnaissance.

In each city a form emerged; each city had the requisite identity, structure and meaning.[45] To be sure, Lynch has a message; in order to enhance the ability of Americans to learn the images of their cities a concerted attempt to operate directly on the external physical shapes of the cities must be made.[46] Lynch's book is a plea for a new kind of urban design to create the kind of city that can be easily managed into an image. As Lynch sees the problem, the question is not whether a city has an image; it is how can designers aid the image-making process? In support of his major thesis of environmental images Lynch cites material from psychology and anthropology. Using data gathered from studies of perception and from studies of primitive tribes, Lynch holds symbolic representation of environment is found everywhere in man. At M.I.T., Lynch is striving to improve visual education through training perception for city planners.[47] Much of the image of the city approach to urban history lies in the area of design of American cities and Lynch has outlined both a method and a philosophy to come to terms with urban design.

The history of the design of American cities considered in a holistic way has been the province of Christopher Tunnard. Predating Strauss and Lynch, and yet anticipating them both,

[44] (Cambridge, 1960), pp. 2–3.
[45] *Ibid.*, p. 8.
[46] *Ibid.*, p. 12.
[47] Jerome Bruner in "Education as Social Invention," *Saturday Review* (Feb. 19, 1966), mentions Lynch's project with favor. Of course, the idea of underlying structure is one of Bruner's favorites, so the praise is not unexpected.

Tunnard is an ardent proponent of the city as an aesthetic whole and of city planning as a humanistic experience. Like Lynch's, Tunnard's books [48] are pleas for better civic design and for a recognition that cities do have some basic image. Tunnard asserts that American townscapes in the past, as in the present, reflect American values. As values have changed, the purposes for which cities of the past were built have become foggy or even lost. Tunnard suggests in *American Skyline* a kind of topology for American city architecture. In America there have been seven eras of city development. There are: 1609-1775, colonial; 1775-1825, young republic; 1825-1850, romantic; 1850-1880, the age of steam and iron; 1880-1910, expanding city (the city as a way of life, the city beautiful); 1910-1933, city of towers; 1933—the regional city. Each of these eras had distinctive city designs, reflecting changing values. This periodization is as satisfactory, it seems to me, as more conventional political ones; and the study of cities as architectural entities is as viable as the study of images expressed by poets.

The impressionistic studies of Tunnard were followed by two others which were pioneering in their own ways. John Burchard and Albert Bush-Brown produced *The Architecture of America: A Social and Cultural History* (1961). Although including more than city architecture, Burchard and Bush-Brown do consider the city as occupying a central role in American art forms. Another approach to urban history through aesthetics is John W. Reps' *The Making of Urban America: A History of City Planning in the United States.*[49] In the first full-scale study of planning, Reps ranges from European backgrounds to 1910 when two-dimensional concern of width of street and spatial patterns gives way to a three-dimensional interest in design, location and mass of buildings.[50] Voluminously illustrated, *The Making of Urban America* dispels the myth that American city planning was unimaginative and undeviatingly based upon a gridiron pattern. In this, Reps and Tunnard agree. They also agree on the historical importance of the Chicago World's Fair of 1893 as a watershed for the image of the city. The arrangement of the fair made possible a visualiza-

[48] *The City of Man* (New York, 1953) and with Henry H. Reed, *American Skyline* (Cambridge, 1953). The first is more general, treating both European and American cities; the second is specifically oriented to the design history of American cities.
[49] (Princeton, 1965).
[50] *Ibid.*, p. 524.

tion of architectural arrangement that was most significant in stimulating the imaginations of the American public.[51] Perhaps the aesthetic history of the city could be periodized thusly, before the Chicago World's Fair and after.

The image of the city approach to urban history offers many possibilities. A history of the American concept of the city in painting, by city boosters, in immigrant letters, in school textbooks, in expositions and fairs, in popular magazines, requires more detailed exploration. The idea of community in American cities has yet to be done. These are only a few of the avenues that branch off the main path of the image of the city. However, just as the urban historians of the neo-ecological approach lean toward sociology, the core of the image of the city seems to be aesthetics, particularly city design.

Not that this approach is free of danger. Attempts to derive images must necessarily be tenuous, unless concrete plans are used, as in Reps, and the deviation could be highly subjective. The emphasis upon quantification is unlikely to intrude (although this cannot be dismissed as a possibility). Rather the necessary qualifications seem to be artistic training and sensibility, plus an ability to go behind the obvious. Urban history as a history of the images of the city will also entice another clientele, those persuaded that history is art.

Beyond those scholars who can be subsumed under one or two Wirthian categories are those who attempt a synthesis of physical structure, social organization and collective behavior. Among such urban historians are individuals such as A. Theodore Brown, Charles N. Glaab and Roy Lubove. Brown and Glaab were influenced by R. Richard Wohl who collaborated with the sociologist Anselm Strauss, and who, while teaching at the University of Chicago, was also assisting in the study of the community of Kansas City. Wohl, who had a wide-ranging mind and competencies in history, economics and sociology, did stimulate Glaab and Brown at Kansas City.[52] Another in-

[51] The earlier views of the fair as an artistic disaster seem to be disappearing, perhaps as the proponents of Sullivan and Wright lose some of their popularity. One suspects that the denial of design that Reps, Tunnard and Lynch attack is in part a product of the rejection of nineteenth-century art and artistic values. If Victorian furniture becomes more popular (as it seems to be), this may herald further change.

[52] For an article reflecting the conjunction, see R. Richard Wohl and A. Theodore Brown, "The Usable Past: A Study of Historical Traditions in Kansas City," *Huntington Library Quarterly*, XXIII (May 1960), 237-59.

dividual prominent in the attempt to fit these categories together has been Roy Lubove. Lubove, who has done some theoretical work, prefers to call this attempt a study of "the formation of the urban environment." [53] Such a title reflects the volitional aspects of city building, which is an important part of Lubove's theory.

All three of these historians share certain assumptions. They emphasize city building as interaction between decision-making individuals and groups—holding certain ideological views and under social and economic pressures—and technological and population change. They focus attention on city planning and city promotion.[54] While these historians are sympathetic with social science and behavioral approaches, they object to the determinism of the ecological sociologists which leaves out elements of value. The human and accidental aspects of city building are emphasized, the study of rational as well as nonrational forces operating upon men and communities:

for the history of many American cities, if closely examined, demonstrates a decidedly undeterministic pattern of false starts, fundamental changes in the direction of community policy, and discernible turning points.[55]

The kind of urban studies these historians view as most promising centers upon areas and periods where technological innovation occurs, where social change is obvious and where decison-making can be found. Two works that illustrate the possibilities of this approach are Julius Rubin's *Canal or Railroad? Imitation and Innovation in the Response to the Erie Canal in Philadelphia, Baltimore, and Boston* (1961), and Sam B. Warner Jr.'s *Streetcar Suburbs: The Process of Growth in Boston, 1870-1900* (1962). In the first book, Rubin, an economist, argued that the response of three communities, Philadelphia, Baltimore and Boston, to the Erie Canal was quite different and that the different responses were products not of

[53] "The Urbanization Process: An Approach to Historical Research," p. 33.
[54] *Ibid.*; A. Theodore Brown and Charles N. Glaab, "Nature and Enterprise: Two Studies in the Culture of 19th Century Midwestern City Growth," *Bulletin of the Central Mississippi Valley American Studies Association*, II (Fall 1958), 1–19; Charles N. Glaab, "Visions of Metropolis: William Gilpin and Theories of City Growth in the American West," *Wisconsin Magazine of History*, LXV (Autumn 1961), 21–31.
[55] "Visions of Metropolis: William Gilpin and Theories of City Growth in the American West," p. 31.

differences in physical characteristics, nor in economic development, but rather of attitudinal differences. As Rubin put it:

If so, the differences in behavior are to be explained by attitudinal rather than situational factors; by divergencies in the history and traditions of the three regions which produced differences in the attitudes that the decision-making groups brought to the common problem rather than by differences in the problem itself.[56]

In the second book, published by the Joint Center for Urban Studies, Warner studied suburban growth in Roxbury, West Roxbury and Dorchester, Massachusetts, through the examination of 23,000 building permits issued from 1870 to 1900. He was able to derive from this examination a process of growth which included technological change, the introduction of the streetcar; decisional factors, where to locate the lines; social mobility, the rise in occupational status of those moving to the suburbs; and an attitudinal factor, the view of the suburbs. Warner's work tied all of the Wirthian categories together into one neat package; and, since his effort was quantitative, Warner could claim to be as scientific as any ecologist. It is no surprise then that Lubove calls Warner's study one of the most satisfactory of the environmental analyses.[57]

The urban historians who operate with the definition of urbanization as the creation of a city through time stress both planning and technology, both social organization and change. Two of Lubove's books, *The Progressives and the Slums: Tenement House Reform in New York City, 1890-1917* (1962), and *Community Planning in the 1920's: The Regional Planning Association of America* (1963), reflect his connection of the image of the city with environmental change and social reform, as does his book of readings, *The Urban Community: Housing and Planning in the Progressive Era* (1967). Lubove also emphasizes the changes in ideas from regarding the city as a product of natural forces to the view of the city as a creation of man. Lubove does not ignore technology either; his volumes add this consideration also.

Perhaps more than Lubove, A. Theodore Brown and Charles N. Glaab emphasize the connection between technology and decision-making. Brown's *Frontier Community: Kansas City to*

[56] (New York, 1961), p. 9.
[57] "The Urbanization Process: An Approach to Historical Research," p. 38.

1870 (1963) and Glaab's *Kansas City and the Railroads: Community Policy in the Growth of Regional Metropolis* (1962) attempt to answer the question as to how Kansas City was able to become a successful regional center despite challenges from more promising sites. In both cases the answers are complex, involving city promoters, railroad and bridge development and theories of city growth. Moreover, the answers are not deterministic. Glaab and Brown also collaborated to write a general history, *A History of Urban America* (1967). In it, the authors attempt to apply the same conceptual structure which they used in their monographic studies of Kansas City. They concentrate on the process of urbanization and on the factors, physical, social and ideological, that bear on this process. They do not regard the city as a fixed environment initiating social change but treat the city as Lubove says it should be treated, as an "artifact." While *A History of Urban America* has some weaknesses, among them a tendency to overstate the role of the city in America, it is, I think, the most satisfactory urban history to date.

The younger generation of urban historians represented by Brown, Glaab and Lubove are characterized by considerable sophistication, energy and reach. They are not content to concentrate upon one part of urbanization but instead opt for a more comprehensive approach. Neither are they sympathetic with a deterministic, mechanical explanation of urbanization; they prefer humanistic explanations of city development. Because of these qualities, they are the true heirs of Louis Wirth.

For the purpose of this essay, a number of approaches to urban history have been delineated and historians have been arbitrarily placed in one or another category. The author recognizes the injustices done and admits that some urban historians belong in more than one category. McKelvey includes images of the city; Stein is very interested in the symbolic representation of communities. However, the concern has been for the major thrust of each person's ideas.

Urban history will certainly become increasingly important as people concentrate more and more in cities. The paths already laid out will be traveled, improved, widened and made more or less beautiful, but perhaps the really significant organizing principle for urban history has yet to be found. Perhaps it will come from a center for urban or behavioral studies; perhaps it will come from another discipline; or perhaps some historian, out of his past experience or present inspiration, will hit upon a more satisfactory way of depicting the impact of the city upon American life.

II

The Colonial City

─────

In an age increasingly characterized by chaotic suburban sprawl and massive urban disorder it is easily forgotten that the American city is an old and established institution. American urban society traces its origins to the first European colonies in the New World. Urban attitudes and aspirations formed an integral part of the cultural baggage of many seventeenth- and eighteenth-century migrants to British America. The earliest settlements assumed the form of towns and villages and performed all the functions of traditional urban communities, serving as centers for the exchange of goods, services, and ideas.

During the seventeenth century American colonists established a dynamic, aggressive, and expansive urban culture. These small urban centers, extending the length of the Atlantic coastline, were founded for a variety of reasons. For many early English and European immigrants, the need for mutual defense and protection from Indians, French and Spanish enemies, as well as pirate raiders, stimulated the growth of closely settled communities. Others found economic endeavors sufficient reason for the establishment of town society; thus, fishing villages, mining and lumber centers, Indian trading posts, and commercial entrepôts sprouted throughout the colonies. Similarly, English-based joint-stock companies often sponsored town development in efforts to more efficiently exploit the resources of the newly discovered continent. Religious enthusiasm also attracted Puritans, Quakers, Anglicans, and others to settlements with churches, ministers, and regular services.

Clearly, the British government encouraged urban develop-

ment. The formation of active seacoast communities not only
stimulated mercantilist profits but also brought the colonies under
closer supervision and imperial regulation. The emerging cities
of the American colonies served essentially as outposts of
empire—the political and administrative nerve endings of a
highly complex imperial system. Thus, multiple forces fostered
the growth of colonial towns.

The colonial seaport cities were small by present standards.
The population of Boston, largest of the seventeenth-century
towns, hardly surpassed 7000 in 1700. In the same year, Philadelphia and New York were bustling ports of 4000. Boston's
population leveled off around 15,000 after 1750, while Philadelphia surged ahead as the economic and cultural center of the
American colonies. Indeed, with 40,000 inhabitants on the eve
of the American Revolution, the Quaker City ranked as the
second largest city in the British Empire. A population of 25,000
in 1775 placed New York second only to Philadelphia, although by 1800 the Hudson River port had replaced its
southern neighbor as the American metropolis. Rising rapidly
after 1750 on an economic base of wheat exportation, Baltimore
became America's first "boom town." In the Southern colonies,
Charlestown emerged by the Revolution as a dominant and
sophisticated center of 12,000. By the end of the eighteenth
century, 5 per cent of Americans, about 200,000 people, lived
in twenty-four urban places of 2500 or more. But despite their
relative smallness, the colonial cities wielded an influence far
out of proportion to their size and numbers.

Commerce provided the measure of urban importance. At
first colonial entrepreneurs established profitable trade connections with the products of an extractive economy—fish and furs,
wheat and rice, tobacco and indigo, naval stores, lumber, and
minerals. Later, as more sophisticated trade routes developed
with Europe, Africa, and the West Indies, returns from commerce encouraged supportive industries. Flour milling, for
example, early became a major industry in New York, Philadelphia, and Baltimore. Norfolk, Virginia, thrived on the processing of naval stores. New England port towns dominated
the shipbuilding industry; by 1720, some fourteen shipyards in
Boston produced more than two hundred ships annually. And
in each of the colonial towns, a variety of trades developed
which supplemented the mercantile base, particularly shops pro-

ducing sails, rope, barrels, ship fittings, and provisions. These advances in craft and commerce brought money into the economy, stimulated the domestic market, and promoted urban growth.

Urban growth brought typical urban problems. Fire and police protection, water supply, poor relief, construction and repair of streets and harbor facilities—all these and more occupied the attention of the rising commercial communities. Drawing from English precedent, municipal corporations adopted mercantilistic regulatory policies and displayed paternalistic concern for the welfare of town dwellers. The prosperity of the colonial city depended on orderly economic activity; thus the medieval doctrine of the "just price" guided municipal supervision of the market. As the colonial period progressed, urban problems and demands were met with an increasing degree of sophistication by civic leaders.

Additional evidence reveals the emerging maturity of colonial urbanism as well. The development of schools, colleges, libraries, theaters, and newspapers fostered an active cultural and intellectual life. Urban taverns and clubs became the focus of social activity. An added measure of the importance of major colonial cities was their function as centers of provincial politics. The spirit of innovation, perhaps symbolized by the endeavors of Benjamin Franklin in Philadelphia or of Cotton Mather in Boston, seemed to thrive in the seaport communities.

Unquestionably, urban maturity provided impetus to imperial breakup, for the cities became centers of revolutionary activity. Britain's new colonial policy seemed to threaten urban prosperity. Boycotts were implemented in the port towns. The Sons of Liberty drew upon the discontent and radicalism of urban workers. City newspapers spread revolutionary propaganda through the countryside. British troops stationed in the cities stimulated added hostility. And colonial urbanities, in confronting community problems over many years, had acquired "training in collective action," which served in good stead during the War for Independence.

COLONIAL PHILADELPHIA:
THE ENVIRONMENT OF
PRIVATE OPPORTUNITY

SAM BASS WARNER, JR.

Sam Bass Warner, Professor of History at the University of Michigan, analyzes the urban dynamics of eighteenth-century America's largest city.

American cities have grown with the general culture of the nation, not apart from it. Late eighteenth-century Philadelphia was no exception. Its citizens, formerly the first wave of a Holy Experiment, had been swept up in the tides of secularization and borne on by steady prosperity to a modern view of the world. Like the Puritans of Massachusetts and Connecticut, the Quakers of Pennsylvania had proved unable to sustain the primacy of religion against the solvents of cheap land and private opportunity. Quaker, Anglican, Presbyterian, Methodist, Pietist—each label had its social and political implications—but all congregations shared in the general American secular culture of privatism.

Already by the time of the Revolution privatism had become the American tradition. Its essence lay in its concentration upon the individual and the individual's search for wealth. Psychologically, privatism meant that the individual should seek happiness in personal independence and in the search for wealth;

socially, privatism meant that the individual should see his first loyalty as his immediate family, and that a community should be a union of such money-making, accumulating families; politically, privatism meant that the community should keep the peace among individual money-makers, and, if possible, help to create an open and thriving setting where each citizen would have some substantial opportunity to prosper.

To describe the American tradition of privatism is not to summarize the entire American cultural tradition. Privatism lies at the core of many modern cultures; privatism alone will not distinguish the experience of America from that of other nations. The tradition of privatism is, however, the most important element of our culture for understanding the development of cities. The tradition of privatism has always meant that the cities of the United States depended for their wages, employment, and general prosperity upon the aggregate successes and failures of thousands of individual enterprises, not upon community action. It has also meant that the physical forms of American cities, their lots, houses, factories, and streets have been the outcome of a real estate market of profit-seeking builders, land speculators, and large investors. Finally, the tradition of privatism has meant that the local politics of American cities have depended for their actors, and for a good deal of their subject matter, on the changing focus of men's private economic activities.

In the eighteenth century the tradition of privatism and the social and economic environment of colonial towns nicely complemented each other. Later as towns grew to big cities, and big cities grew to metropolises, the tradition became more and more ill-suited to the realities of urban life. The tradition assumed that there would be no major conflict between private interest, honestly and liberally viewed, and the public welfare. The modes of eighteenth-century town life encouraged this expectation that if each man would look to his own prosperity the entire town would prosper. And so it had.

Founded in 1682 under William Penn's liberal instructions, and settled first with Quaker artisans and a few Quaker merchants, the town had since prospered as the capital of a thriving colony. By 1720 Philadelphia was said to have 10,000 inhabitants; by 1775 it had more than doubled to 23,700. The townsite bordered the Delaware and Schuylkill rivers, both of which tapped rich forests and excellent farm lands. The line of north-south trade ran nearby, and Philadelphia also lay within reach of the Susquehanna and Potomac rivers openings to the west. Philadelphia, thus, soon excelled in most of the staples of colonial trade, exporting furs, lumber, staves, iron, wheat, and flour, and importing rum, sugar, wine, and English manufactures.

Conditions outside the colony encouraged a heavy immigration of new settlers. Because Pennsylvania had been founded late, by comparison to other Atlantic colonies, west-bound space abounded on ships sailing from Great Britain and the Low Countries. Quakers, of course, fleeing persecution in England came to the colony in large numbers, but by the early eighteenth century their group came to be rivaled by Scotch-Irish and German immigrants. The Act of Union joining Scotland to England opened up the entire British Empire to poor Scots, while Irish wars and famines, and rack-renting landlords drove their fellow Presbyterians from Ulster. On the continent west German peasants fled the destruction of Louis XIV's repeated wars. Finally, in America the Indian control of upstate New York deflected the flow of westward settlers south to Pennsylvania. The result of all these outside events was a boom in the colony and the town; Pennsylvania and Philadelphia had everything, settlers, natural resources, capital, religious freedom, and comparatively little government.

Within the town three conditions confirmed its privatism— its individualized structure of work, its general prosperity, and its open society and economy. When eighteenth-century Philadelphians spoke of the individual and his search for wealth as the goal of government they were simply basing their political arguments on the commonplace facts of town life. The core element of the town economy was the one-man shop. Most Philadelphians labored alone, some with a helper or two. A storekeeper tended his shop by himself or with the aid of his family or a servant. Craftsmen often worked with an apprentice, or more rarely with another skilled man.

More than at later times, this Philadelphia was a town of entrepreneurs. Artisans sewed shoes, made wagons, boiled soap, or laid bricks for customers who had already placed an order. Workers did not labor under the close price and time disciplines of manufacture for large-scale inventories or big speculative wholesale markets. Most Philadelphians were either independent contractors hiring out on a job-by-job basis, or they were artisan shopkeepers retailing the products of their work. Even the establishment of a large merchant more resembled a small store than a modern wholesale house. Such a merchant frequently had a partner and the two partners carried on the business with the aid of a full-time clerk and an apprentice or servant to help with errands. When a cargo arrived at the pier the partners would hire some laborers to unload the goods and move them to the storehouse. Thus, a very large proportion of the town's men—artisans, shopkeepers, and merchants—shared the common experience of the individual entrepreneur.

In later years the work groups of factories, offices, stores, and construction crews would have enormous significance for the discipline, acculturation, and education of Philadelphia's residents. Such groups were almost entirely absent from the eighteenth-century town. Shipyard, ropewalk, and distillery workers labored in groups of five and even ten, but theirs were exceptionally large urban production units. In the colonial era the plantation, whether for agriculture or manufacture, was the characteristic place of large work gangs. In 1775, associated with Philadelphia's general run of family enterprises were only about 900 indentured servants, 600 slaves, and perhaps 200 hired servants who lived with their employers. These helpers shared the discipline of family life and work; they did not live by the modes of the work gang. Taken all together the eighteenth-century exceptions to the entrepreneurial role had but little significance for the functioning of the town's society.

A German visitor of 1750 wrote: "Pennsylvania is heaven for farmers, paradise for artisans, and hell for officials and preachers." By the same token, Philadelphia on the eve of the Revolution was a town of freedom and abundance for the common man. For young persons there was a great demand for apprentices in all lines of work. An unskilled laborer without connections could find work with board and wages to begin accumulating a little money for tools. An artisan who wanted to carry a few shopkeeping goods in his shop, or a storekeeper with a good reputation, could get his stock from the merchant and settle for his advance a year later.

The ordinary artisan or shopkeeper, if his health was good, could be assured of a comfortable, if frugal, living. To be sure, houses were small and rents high, and furnishings were spare compared to later levels of living: no carpets, no upholstered furniture, a sand-scrubbed floor, and whitewashed walls. Stoves and fireplaces only partially heated drafty rooms, and in severe winters the cost of firewood or imported coal was a major item of family expense. Nevertheless, at the city's markets food was cheap and plentiful. The earnings of the ordinary artisan and shopkeeper could support a wife and children without their having to take outside employment. The rapid growth of the town and its trade meant regular work and good earnings for artisans and easy business, if not wealth, for shopkeepers.

Although the customary hours of work were long, sunrise to sunset, the pace of work was often easy and varied with the season. Those who worked outside their homes, like men in the building trades, took an hour for breakfast, a break in the middle of the day, and an hour for dinner in the afternoon. Coopers, shoemakers, smiths, and men who practiced their craft in their own houses and yards must have stopped work as customers and friends came in, and a trip or two to the local tavern must also have been usual. Although there were no formal vacations, the traditional English holidays and frequent *ad hoc* town celebrations provided about twenty days off each year.

Franklin's *Autobiography* abounds with injunctions for regular habits, and the reputation for diligence he established by staying at his bench for the entire formal working day suggests that his was an extraordinary pace. For most workers rush seasons of hard work and long hours alternated with slack times. These variations meant days for fishing or spare moments for gossip on the streets and visits to the tavern.

Such a commonplace prosperity, generous at least by eighteenth-century standards, confirmed the privatism of the town and its age. As important a confirmation came from the openness of its economy and society. The failure of the craft guilds to control the trades of the town gave newcomers and resident artisans alike an occupational freedom unknown in Europe. Shopkeepers and artisans—and often one man was both—could take up any craft or open any line of business they wished. Although Philadelphia had inherited English regulations favoring the "freemen" of the town, established artisans could not maintain their control of the town's businesses against newcomers. The carpenters and cordwainers managed to form associations to set prices for their work, but failed when they attempted to close the membership of their trades. In Philadelphia men added trades and lines of goods as they thought demand justified. Although this freedom undoubtedly produced a great deal of incompetent craftsmanship, the importance to the individual artisan or shopkeeper of open trades and plentiful work cannot be overestimated. It meant for the common man that there was always a chance for a fresh start. This chance for a new beginning was the urban equivalent of the contemporary farmer's chance to pick up and try again in the West.

Already in these years the American pattern of social mobility by property obtained. No invidious distinction between land and trade favored some occupations over others. As eighteenth-century Philadelphians grew rich they kept their original occupations, whether they were carpenters, distillers, printers, or lawyers. Whatever a man's occupation, there were only a few channels for investment open to the rising man. Since there were no banks, private money lending was the most important investment opportunity in the town. Houses and land were also a favorite way of using savings both among the rich and those with a little capital. Only 19 percent of the families of Philadelphia owned their houses and therefore home rentals offered a safe investment. Other opportunities were shares in voyages, marine insurance, and, of course, land and farms outside the town.

The prosperity and abundant opportunity of the town should not be confused with an even distribution of wealth. According to the published tax list for 1774 the upper tenth of the taxpaying households owned 89 percent of the taxable property. In this respect late eighteenth-century Philadelphia resembled the later Philadelphias—it was a pyramid of wealth in which about five hundred men guided the town's economic life. Its unique quality lay in the general prosperity of the common artisan and shopkeeper, and the widely shared entrepreneurial experience and goals of the artisan, shopkeeper, and merchant.

The wealthy presided over a municipal regime of little government. Both in form and function the town's government advertised the lack of concern for public management of the community. The municipal corporation of Philadelphia, copied from the forms of an old English borough, counted for little. Its only important functions in the late eighteenth-century were the management of the markets and the holding of the Recorder's Court. A closed corporation, choosing its members by co-option, it had become a club of wealthy merchants, without much purse, power, or popularity.

By modern standards the town was hardly governed at all.

The constable in each ward and a few watchmen provided an ineffective police, the safety of the house and shop being secured by citizens' helping each other to drive away intruders or pursue thieves. Most streets went unpaved, the public wharves little repaired. There were no public schools, no public water, and at best thin charity.

The enduring contribution of the colonial era to Philadelphia government lay in its inauguration of the committee system of municipal government. This system, if system it may be called in the eighteenth century, consisted of placing the administration of specific tasks in the hands of independent committees, or commissions. The Pennsylvania Provincial Assembly, lacking faith in the municipal corporation, created a number of commissions. First came the Board of Assessors established to raise money to pay the debts of the corporation and to require that wharves and streets be repaired and a workhouse erected. Then came separate street commissioners, next the City Wardens to manage the night watch and the lighting of the streets, and, still later, a Board of Overseers of the Poor. None of these commissions' performance would satisfy modern municipal standards. The commissioners were elected officials, chosen under the colonial fifty-pound, freehold qualification by the voters of Philadelphia. Like the town's fire companies, lending libraries, and tavern clubs these commissions helped train Philadelphians to the habits of committee government, a form of management they would have to call upon when creating a new independent government during the Revolution. Like many of the laws and forms of the colonial era which passed into the usage of the subsequent Commonwealth of Pennyslvania, the committee system of government was the legacy of colonial municipal life to later Philadelphias.

The real secret of the peace and order of the eighteenth-century town lay not in its government but in the informal structure of its community. Unlike later and larger Philadelphias, the eighteenth-century town was a community. Graded by wealth and divided by distinctions of class though it was, it functioned as a single community. The community had been created out of a remarkably inclusive network of business and economic relationships and it was maintained by the daily interactions of trade and sociability. Because it was small and because every rank and occupation lived jumbled together in a narrow compass the town suffered none of the communications problems of later Philadelphias.

At most, 23,700 people lived in Philadelphia on the eve of the Revolution, 16,500 in the city proper, 7,000 in the adjacent districts of Northern Liberties and Southwark (Table I). The town crowded next to its shore. Its wharves and warehouses stretched a mile and a half along the Delaware River, but the built-up blocks of houses at their deepest point, along Market Street, reached back from the river at most half a mile to about Seventh Street.

The settlement pattern of the town combined two opposing social tendencies. The clustering of marine trades and merchants next to the Delaware suggested the beginnings of the specialized industrial quarters then characteristic of European cities. On the other hand, the rummage of classes and occupations found in many Philadelphia blocks continued the old tradition of mixed work and residence characteristic of American and English country towns.

Ship carpenters, ship joiners, ship smiths, and sail makers lived and worked along the Delaware River shore. Sailors and stevedores dwelt among the yards and wharves along the entire shore, but they gathered especially on the south side of town (Dock Ward and Southwark). Mixed among them were many of the houses and shops of the merchants which were concentrated one block back from the riverfront. Together the shipbuilders, the marine trades, and the merchants pre-empted the narrow strip of frontage between the river and Second Street.

The crowding of marine trades and commerce next to the port also influenced the location of other Philadelphians. Tailors, hatters, tinsmiths, and silversmiths clustered in the central wards of town (Walnut, Lower Delaware, and Middle Wards) to be near, if not in, the portside concentration of customers. Conversely, those who needed large lots, or those who could not afford expensive land, drifted toward the edge of town. Here on the fringes the building trades, weavers, dyers, tanners, distillers, and laborers dwelt in more than normal proportions.

The differential pricing of land seems to have affected the laborers more than any other occupational group in the colonial town (Table II). Surprisingly enough, they were more segregated in this period than in the mid-nineteenth century, when the immigrant laborer was such a prominent element of the city. In 1774 the special locations of the laborers were the northern and southern edges of town—the Northern Liberties and adjacent parts of the Mulberry Ward, and Southwark.

A slight ethnic clustering also existed in eighteenth-century Philadelphia, but by no means of the same intensity as later twentieth-century ethnic and racial ghettos. German immigrants and their descendants had concentrated north of Market Street, over half of them living in the North, High, and Mulberry wards of Philadelphia and in the adjacent Northern Liberties Districts. This was also the Quaker side of town. Such ethnic and religious clusters, however, did not seem to have important effects upon the functioning of the town.

One can get some idea of the quality of urban life imposed by this settlement pattern by looking at one ward in a little detail. The Constable in making his enumeration of the residents of the Middle Ward left notes on his list showing when he turned the corner of a street. This record, plus some material from tax ledgers make it possible to reconstruct the settlement pattern of this ward in 1774.

As its name suggests, the Middle Ward lay in the center of town, bounded on the north by Market Street, then the highway connecting Philadelphia to Chester and the south and to Lancaster and the west. The ward also was next to the market traffic. The sheds of the farmers' market in these years stretched up Market Street from the Delaware River only as far as Fourth Street. The Middle Ward was not a crowded dockside ward, but began just behind the dockside wards at Second Street. Its well-filled section covered five blocks to Seventh Street, Market to Chestnut. Beyond these blocks of houses the farms of the ward extended all the way west to the Schuylkill River.

Many famous Philadelphians lived within the ward. The old-fashioned Quaker radical, Anthony Benezet, the Proprietors John and Richard Penn, two opponents of the British who later turned Tory, Joseph Galloway, and James Allen, and the steadfast revolutionaries Benjamin Franklin and Daniel Clymer all lived in the center of the ward. The State House Yard (now Independence Square) stood across Chestnut Street between Fifth and Sixth streets. Such distinction, however, did not create the solid blocks of *haut bourgeois* fashion that they would today; rather it embroidered the commonplace fabric which was the revolutionary town. In 1774 the Middle Ward was the home of at least 1,401 men, women, and children of every degree and condition from Proprietor to slave (Table III).

The physical arrangements of the ward reflected the high cost of eighteenth-century housing and the crowding of Philadelphians near their port. Each of the Middle Ward's five settled blocks contained slightly less than five acres of land. On the first block of the ward (between Second and Third streets, the area nearest the Delaware River) there stood 137 dwellings, on the next 65, on the next 67, on the next 29, and on westernmost 39. To accommodate so many families in so little space some of the blocks of the ward had been cut by alleys so that little houses might be crowded onto the back lots of the houses facing the main streets. Strawberry Alley and Elbow Lane cut through the first block, Petty's Alley divided the third block, and Benjamin Franklin had begun the alley process with his house lot off Market Street in the second block of the ward. He had built a row of three houses on Market Street, thereby turning his home yard into an interior lot. His son-in-law Richard Bache, a merchant, rented one of the new row houses, Eden Haydock, a plumber, rented another, and Frederick Stonemetz, a cooper, took the third. In the early nineteenth century Franklin's home parcel became Franklin Court, an alley lot which opened up the interior of the block.

Such density of housing and such methods of land division had by 1774 destroyed the hopes of Penn and his surveyor for a "Green Town." The practice of subdividing blocks and alleys and jamming tiny houses on vacant rear yards continued strongly for the next ninety years. By 1860 the density of population in Philadelphia's inner wards reached its all-time peak. Then, in the second half of the nineteenth century the street railway opened up vast tracts of cheap suburban land and thereby destroyed the market for new alley construction. The old alleys with their dark and cramped houses, however, did not disappear at once. Rather they remained standing for years, giving discomfort to Philadelphia's poor for many generations, and the history of some alleys is not yet closed.

Already in the 1770's the crowding of the land exceeded the sanitary capabilities of the town. The streets and alleys reeked of garbage, manure, and night soil, and some private and public wells must have been dangerously polluted. Every few years an epidemic swept through the town. In the 1790's the city would pay a terrible price in deaths from recurring yellow fever.

Though dangerous to health the eighteenth-century pattern of settlement guaranteed every citizen a knowledge of town life. At such density and small scale no generation could be raised ignorant of the other side of town, of the ways of life of the working class, or of the manners of the *haut bourgeois*. Within the Middle Ward at least 346 families with 469 children, 17 hired servants, 65 indentured servants, 78 Negro slaves, and 80 tenants share the settled 25 acres (Table III). Those who left a record carried on seventy different occupations (Table IV).

Although merchants and shopkeepers, hatters, innkeepers, and tavernkeepers concentrated more heavily in this ward than in most others, variety best characterizes the occupational structure of the ward as it did all the other wards of the first Philadelphia. The Proprietors, the merchants, and the doctors shared the narrow compass of the Middle Ward with such ungenteel occupations as laborer, porter, carter, skinner, watchman, crier, paver, grazier, and even goatkeeper. The outer three blocks of the ward also housed several breweries and a distillery, and every one of the five blocks contained one or more of those notorious enemies of sweet residential air—the stable.

One cannot, at this late date, reconstruct in detail the communications patterns of eighteenth-century Philadelphia, but the crowded living of the age encouraged a street and tavern life which more resembled the social habits of the later nineteenth and early twentieth-century immigrant ghettos than the isolated private family life of today's working class and middle class.

The high cost of building kept houses small, cramped, and in short supply. The common artisan's or shopkeeper's house was a narrow structure, about seventeen feet wide and twenty-five feet deep. A story-and-a-half high, it offered about eight hundred square feet of floor space on its ground floor and attic. Most often the owner plied his trade in the largest front room. The Middle Ward records show that although some families had five to seven children, most had few. The average number of children per household was 1.3, and counting servants and slaves the average household was four persons. The small houses, thus, were cramped but not severely crowded. If the artisan or shopkeeper prospered he would add a kitchen ell or more likely move to a house of similiar proportion with a kitchen ell at the rear. The house of an ordinary merchant or even a craftsman who had grown rich, would be like the artisan's house with the ell, but would be two and one-half stories instead of one and one-half. Such houses of the prosperous also possessed deep lots for gardens, a shed for a cow and some chickens, and perhaps a horse.

A town of small houses, where most houses also served as stores, offices and workshops, encouraged people to live out upon the streets. Moreover, the pace of work, most of it governed by the seasons or advance orders from customers, was irregular, what one would call today a rural pace. Both the physical structure of the town and the pace of its work thus encouraged a more public, gossipy style of life than could later be sustained when a steady pace of work and larger interiors drove people into sharply defined spaces for work and residence.

The ordinary housewife shopped daily, going to the baker's for her bread, and taking her meat and pies to the baker's oven to be cooked. Street peddlers called her out for fish, eggs, and produce, and twice a week the farmers of Philadelphia County held a full market at the public stalls. As in the nineteenth century with its dark tenements and crowded row houses, sunlight must have been a great source of pleasure for women sewing and spinning and many must have worked at these and other household chores out on their doorsteps, as their tenement sisters did years later.

For the husband the eighteenth-century custom of men's gossip at the tavern provided the first Philadelphia's basic cells of community life. Every ward in the city had its inns and taverns. The 1774 tax list recorded 93 tavernkeepers and 72 innkeepers in the city of Philadelphia, Southwark, and the Northern Liberties, approximately one neighborhood drinking place for every 140 persons in the city (23,000/165). The Middle Ward, alone, held 18 inns and taverns. Some must have served purely a neighborhood custom; others, like the London Coffee House or the City Tavern, served as central communications nodes for the entire city.

Then, as now, each one had its own crowd of regulars and thus each constituted an informal community cell of the city. Out of the meetings of the regulars at the neighborhood tavern or inn came much of the commonplace community develop-

ment which preceded the Revolution and proved later to be
essential to the governance of the city and the management of
the ward. Regular meetings of friends, or men of common occupations, led to clubs of all kinds and of every degree of formal-
ity from regular billiard sessions to fire companies and political
juntos. Benjamin Franklin and the many community innovations
of his junto showed the potential of these informal tavern
groups. They provided the underlying social fabric of the town
and when the Revolution began made it possible to quickly
gather militia companies, to form effective committees of corres-
pondence and of inspection, and to organize and to manage mass
town meetings.

At the center of the town's communications system stood
the merchants' coffee houses. On the eve of the Revolution
Philadelphia had two such major meeting places—the old London
Coffee House (established 1754), run by William Bradford, the
newspaper publisher, and the new City Tavern (established
1773), just founded by a syndicate of merchants. The London
Coffee House, located at Front and Market streets, adjacent to
the town's principal market stalls and overlooking the Delaware,
had been for many years the place where merchants gathered
every noon to read incoming newspapers, to discuss prices, and
to arrange for cargoes and marine insurance. These noon meetings in time ripened into the specialized institutions of exchanges, banks, and insurance companies. As yet, Philadelphia
had but one insurance company and its merchants' business depended on the variety of functions of these daily tavern gatherings. For many years ship captains and travelers first stopped
at the London Coffee House when they arrived in town, messages were left, auction notices posted and auctions held. Frequently on market days, after a parade through the streets,
horses were auctioned in front of the tavern doors. Slaves and
indentured servants stood before the same block.

As the town grew the importing merchants no longer had a
need to be near the market dealers. The merchant community
split into at least two parts. The new City Tavern surpassed
the old London Coffee House as a place of fashion with the
importing merchants, though its function remained that of its
competitor. On May 19, 1774, Paul Revere brought his news of
the closing of the Port of Boston to the City Tavern, and here
numerous Revolutionary committees gathered. The still extant

Philadelphia Assemblies were held at this new tavern, as was the endless series of banquets and balls which served the town with high entertainment.

Because the merchants' tavern was a public place in a small town it escaped the limitations of later Philadelphia merchant centers—the exchanges, the Chamber of Commerce, and the gentlemen's clubs. These later gatherings were either meeting places of specialists and thereby encouraged only the brokers' or downtown merchants' view of the city, or they were closed organizations which directed their members' attention inward toward the sociability of the group. The eighteenth-century tavern, however, opened out to all the life of the street and it did not shield the leaders of the town from contact with the life that surrounded them.

It was the unity of everyday life, from tavern, to street, to workplace, to housing, which held the town and its leaders together in the eighteenth century. This unity made it possible for the minority of Revolutionary merchants, artisans, and shop-keepers to hold together, run the town, and manage a share of the war against England, even in the face of Quaker neutrality and Tory opposition.

TABLE I
POPULATION OF URBAN PHILADELPHIA 1775

WARD	MAXIMUM POPULATION			INDENTURED SERVANTS			SLAVES			FREE	
	ADULTS	CHILDREN	TOTAL	ADULTS	CHILDREN	TOTAL	ADULTS	CHILDREN	TOTAL	ADULTS	CHILDREN
Dock	2,064	1,985	4,049	90	179	269	63	105	168	1,911	1,701
Walnut	268	218	486	16	6	22	30	7	37	222	205
South	432	315	747	18	27	45	19	15	34	395	273
Middle	945	740	1,685	41	61	102	49	22	71	855	657
Chestnut	337	248	585	10	32	42	23	7	30	304	209
Lower Delaware	312	304	616	17	33	50	35	19	54	260	252
High Street	391	391	782	12	29	41	22	14	36	357	348
North	947	829	1,776	37	63	100	60	16	76	850	750
Mulberry	2,699	2,087	4,786	81	101	182	44	32	76	2,574	1,954
Upper Delaware	574	474	1,048	20	33	53	18	12	30	536	429
Sub Total, City of Philadelphia	8,969	7,591	16,560	342	564	906	363	249	612	8,264	6,778
East Northern Liberties			2,340								
West Northern Liberties			1,758								
Southwark			3,081								
Total Urban Philadelphia			23,739								

TABLE II

INDEX OF DISSIMILARITY
INDUSTRIAL GROUPINGS AND
SOME ADDITIONAL CATEGORIES
PHILADELPHIA, NORTHERN LIBERTIES, AND
SOUTHWARK, 1774;
PHILADELPHIA COUNTY, 1860

1774	INDEX	1860	INDEX
Laborers	37.2	Negro, free, native born	47.3
Metalworking, ex. iron,		Miscellaneous textiles	40.3
steel	32.5	Germany, foreign born	34.1
Iron, steel, shipbuilding	29.4	Bakeries	30.7
Paper & printing	29.4	Iron, steel, shipbuilding	29.0
Transport, ex. rail, transit	24.7	Hotels, laundries, domestic	25.9
Misc. textiles	24.3	Metalworking, ex. iron,	
Clothing	22.3	steel	25.6
Building trades	21.2	Professional,	
Wholesale & retail	20.5	ex. entertainment	25.4
German surnames	19.7	Laborers	21.9
Professional,		Clothing	21.8
ex. entertainment	19.7	Ireland, N S, for. born	19.8
Bakeries	16.7	Transport, ex. rail, transit	19.6
Hotels, laundries, domestic	15.1	Paper & printing	19.0
Homeowners	6.1	Britain, ex. Ireland,	
		for. born	17.5
		Building trades	16.4
		Pennsylvania, native born	10.1
		Wholesale & retail	9.6

TABLE III

THE MIDDLE WARD OF PHILADELPHIA
APRIL 8, 1774

Free Adults (346 households x 2 for wives)	692
Children	469
Negro Slaves	78
Bound Servants in Residence	65
Hired Servants in Residence	17
Inmates (other free adults living in households)	80
Population	1401
Homeowners	80
Houserenters	266
Taxpayers living with other families	102
Total Taxpayers	448

TABLE IV

275 PERSONS WHOSE OCCUPATIONS CAN BE IDENTIFIED
MIDDLE WARD, APRIL 8, 1774

23	Shopkeepers	2	Druggists
19	Merchants	2	Livery stables
17	Laborers	2	Silversmiths
15	Cordwainers	2	Stablekeepers
13	Hatters	2	Staymakers
13	Tailors	2	Stockingweavers
13	Tavernkeepers	2	Tobacconists
11	Innkeepers	1	Boatbuilder
10	Bakers	1	Breechesmaker
10	Carpenters	1	Cheesemonger
7	Joiners	1	Crier
7	Saddlemakers	1	Distiller
6	Coopers	1	Engraver
5	Colonial Officers	1	Ferryman
5	Schoolmasters	1	Goatkeeper
4	Brewers	1	Grazier
4	Hucksters	1	Grocer
4	Porters	1	Harnessmaker
4	Skinners	1	Heelmaker
3	Barbers	1	Lawyer
3	Blacksmiths	1	Minister
3	Carvers	1	Painter
3	Coppersmiths	1	Paver
3	Curriers	1	Plumber
3	Mariners	1	Printer
3	Potters	1	Reedmaker
3	Smiths	1	Ropemaker
3	Tinkers	1	Scrivener
3	Watchmen	1	Sheriff
2	Bookbinders	1	Snuffmaker
2	Brushmakers	1	Threadmaker
2	Butchers	1	Upholder
2	Carters	1	Watchmaker
2	Chaisemakers	1	Wheelwright
2	Cutters	1	Workhouse keeper
2	Doctors		

ECONOMIC DEVELOPMENT
AND SOCIAL STRUCTURE
IN COLONIAL BOSTON

JAMES A. HENRETTA

*Princeton historian James A. Henretta argues that increased so-
cial stratification accompanied the development of a commercially oriented economy in pre-Revolutionary Boston.*

A distinctly urban social structure developed in Boston in
the 150 years between the settlement of the town and the
American Revolution. The expansion of trade and industry
after 1650 unleashed powerful economic forces which first distorted, then destroyed, the social homogeneity and cohesiveness
of the early village community. All aspects of town life were
affected by Boston's involvement in the dynamic, competitive
world of Atlantic commerce. The disruptive pressure of rapid
economic growth, sustained for over a century, made the social
appearance of the town more diverse, more complex, more
modern—increasingly different from that of the rest of New
England. The magnitude of the change in Boston's social composition and structure may be deduced from an analysis and
comparison of the tax lists for 1687 and 1771. Containing a
wealth of information on property ownership in the community, these lists make it possible to block out, in quantitative
terms, variations in the size and influence of economic groups

From James A. Henretta, "Economic Development and Social Structure in
Colonial Boston," *William and Mary Quarterly*, XXII (January 1965), 75–92.
Copyright 1965 by James A. Henretta. Reprinted by permission of the author.

and to trace the change in the distribution of the resources of the community among them.

The transformation of Boston from a land-based society to a maritime center was neither sudden nor uniform. In the last decade of the seventeenth century, a large part of the land of its broad peninsula was still cultivated by small farmers. Only a small fraction was laid out in regular streets and even less was densely settled. The north end alone showed considerable change from the middle of the century when almost every house had a large lot and garden. Here, the late-comers—the mariners, craftsmen, and traders who had raised the population to six thousand by 1690—were crowded together along the waterfront. Here, too, in the series of docks and shipyards which jutted out from the shore line, were tangible manifestations of the commercial activity which had made the small town the largest owner of shipping and the principal port of the English colonies. Over 40 per cent of the carrying capacity of all colonial-owned shipping was in Boston hands.

Dependence on mercantile endeavor rather than agricultural enterprise had by 1690 greatly affected the extent of property ownership. Boston no longer had the universal ownership of real estate characteristic of rural Massachusetts to the end of the colonial period. The tax list for 1687 contained the names of 188 polls, 14 per cent of the adult male population, who were neither owners of taxable property of any kind nor "dependents" in a household assessed for the property tax. Holding no real estate, owning no merchandise or investments which would yield an income, these men constituted the "propertyless" segment of the community and were liable only for the head tax which fell equally upon all men above the age of sixteen. Many in this group were young men, laborers and seamen, attracted by the commercial prosperity of the town and hoping to save enough from their wages to buy or rent a shop, to invest in the tools of an artisan, or to find a start in trade. John Erving, a poor Scotch sailor whose grandson in 1771 was one of the richest men in Boston, was only one propertyless man who rose quickly to a position of wealth and influence.

But many of these 188 men did not acquire either taxable property or an established place in the social order of Boston. Only sixty-four, or 35 per cent, were inhabitants of the town eight years later. By way of contrast, 45 per cent of the polls assessed from two to seven pounds on the tax list, 65 per cent of those with property valued from eight to twenty pounds, and 73 per cent of those with estates in excess of twenty pounds were present in 1695. There was a direct relation between permanence of residence and economic condition. Even in an expanding and diversifying economic environment, the best opportunities for advancement rested with those who could draw upon long-standing connections, upon the credit facilities of friends and neighbors, and upon political influence. It was precisely these personal contacts which were denied to the propertyless.

A second, distinct element in the social order consisted of the dependents of property owners. Though propertyless themselves, these dependents—grown sons living at home, apprentices, and indentured servants—were linked more closely to the town as members of a tax-paying household unit than were the 188 "unattached" men without taxable estates. Two hundred and twelve men, nearly one sixth of the adult male population of Boston, were classified as dependents in 1687. The pervasiveness of the dependency relationship attested not only to the cohesiveness of the family unit but also to the continuing vitality of the apprenticeship and indenture system at the close of the seventeenth century.

Yet even the dependency relationship, traditionally an effective means of alleviating unemployment and preventing the appearance of unattached propertyless laborers, was subjected to severe pressure by the expansion of the economy. An urgent demand for labor, itself the cause of short indentures, prompted servants to strike out on their own as soon as possible. They became the laborers or semiskilled craftsmen of the town, while the sons of the family eventually assumed control of their father's business and a share of the economic resources of the community.

The propertied section of the population in 1687 was composed of 1,036 individuals who were taxed on their real estate or their income from trade. The less-skilled craftsmen, 521 men engaged in the rougher trades of a waterfront society, formed the bottom stratum of the taxable population in this pre-industrial age. These carpenters, shipwrights, blacksmiths, shopkeepers owned only 12 per cent of the taxable wealth of the town. Few of these artisans and laborers had investments in shipping or in merchandise. A small store or house, or a small farm in the south end of Boston, accounted for their assessment of two to seven pounds on the tax list (Table III).

Between these craftsmen and shopkeepers and the traders and merchants who constituted the economic elite of the town was a middle group of 275 property owners with taxable assets valued from eight to twenty pounds. Affluent artisans employing two or three workers, ambitious shopkeepers with investments in commerce, and entrepreneurial-minded sea masters with various maritime interests, bulked large in this center portion of the economic order. Of the 275, 180 owned real estate assessed at seven pounds or less and were boosted into the third quarter of the distribution of wealth by their holdings of merchandise and shares in shipping (Table III). The remaining ninety-five possessed real estate rated at eight pounds or more and, in addition, held various investments in trade. Making up about 25 per cent of the propertied population, this middle group controlled 22 per cent of the taxable wealth in Boston in 1687. Half as numerous as the lowest group of property owners, these men possessed almost double the amount of taxable assets (Table I).

Merchants with large investments in English and West Indian trade and individuals engaged in the ancillary industries of shipbuilding and distilling made up the top quarter of the taxable population in 1687. With taxable estates ranging from twenty to 170 pounds, this commercial group controlled 66 per cent of the town's wealth. But economic development had been too rapid, too uneven and incomplete, to allow the emergence of a well-defined merchant class endowed with a common outlook and clearly distinguished from the rest of the society. Only eighty-five of these men, one third of the wealthiest group in the community, owned dwellings valued at as much as twenty pounds. The majority held landed property valued at ten pounds, only a few pounds greater than that of the middle group of property holders. The merchants had not shared equally in the accumulated fund of capital and experience which had accrued after fifty years of maritime activity. Profits had flowed to those whose daring initiative and initial resources had begun the exploitation of the lucrative colonial market. By 1687, the upper 15 per cent of the property owners held 52 per cent of the taxable assets of the town, while the fifty individuals who composed the highest 5 per cent of the taxable population accounted for more than 25 per cent of the wealth (Table I).

By the end of the seventeenth century widespread involvement in commerce had effected a shift in the locus of social and political respectability in Boston and distinguished it from the surrounding communities. Five of the nine selectmen chosen by the town in 1687 were sea captains. This was more than deference to those accustomed to command. With total estates of £83, £29, £33, £33, and £24, Captains Elisha Hutchinson, John Fairweather, Theophilus Frary, Timothy Prout, and Daniel Turell were among the wealthiest 20 per cent of the population. Still, achievement in trade was not the only index of respectability. Henry Eames, George Cable, Isaac Goose, and Elnathan Lyon, the men appointed by the town to inspect the condition of the streets and roads, had the greater part of their wealth, £105 of £130, invested in land and livestock. And the presence of Deacon Henry Allen among the selectmen provided a tangible indication of the continuing influence of the church.

These legacies of an isolated religious society and a stable agricultural economy disappeared in the wake of the rapid growth which continued unabated until the middle of the eighteenth century. In the fifty years after 1690, the population of the town increased from 6,000 to 16,000. The farms of the south end vanished and the central business district became crowded. In the populous north end, buildings which had once housed seven people suddenly began to hold nine or ten. Accompanying this physical expansion of Boston was a diversification of economic endeavor. By 1742, the town led all the colonial cities in the production of export furniture and shoes, although master craftsmen continued to carry on most industry on a small scale geared to local needs. Prosperity and expansion continued to be rooted, not in the productive capacity or geographic position of the town, but in the ability of the Boston merchants to compete successfully in the highly competitive mercantile world.

After 1750, the economic health of the Massachusetts seaport was jeopardized as New York and Philadelphia merchants, exploiting the rich productive lands at their backs and capitalizing upon their prime geographic position in the West Indian and southern coasting trade, diverted a significant portion of Euro-

pean trade from the New England traders. Without increasing
returns from the lucrative "carrying" trade, Boston merchants
could no longer subsidize the work of the shopkeepers, craftsmen, and laborers who supplied and maintained the commercial
fleet. By 1760, the population of Boston had dropped to 15,000
persons, a level it did not exceed until after the Revolution.

The essential continuity of maritime enterprise in Boston from
the late seventeenth to the mid-eighteenth century concealed the
emergence of a new type of social system. After a certain point
increases in the scale and extent of commercial endeavor produced a new, and more fluid, social order. The development of
the economic system subjected the family, the basic social unit,
to severe pressures. The fundamental link between one generation and another, the ability of the father to train his offspring
for their life's work, was endangered by a process of change
which rendered obsolete many of the skills and assumptions of
the older, land-oriented generation and opened the prospect of
success in new fields and new places. The well-known departure
of Benjamin Franklin from his indenture to his brother was
but one bright piece in the shifting mosaic of colonial life.

The traditional family unit had lost much of its cohesiveness
by the third quarter of the eighteenth century. The Boston tax
lists for 1771 indicate that dependents of property owners accounted for only 10 per cent of the adult male population as
opposed to 16 per cent eighty-five years earlier. Increasingly
children left their homes at an earlier age to seek their own way
in the world.

A second factor in the trend away from dependency status
was the decline in the availability of indentured servants during
the eighteenth century. Fewer than 250 of 2,380 persons entering Boston from 1764 to 1768 were classified as indentured
servants. These were scarcely enough to replace those whose
indentures expired. More and more, the labor force had to be
recruited from the ranks of "unattached" workers who bartered
their services for wages in a market economy.

This laboring force consisted of the nondependent, propertyless workers of the community, now twice as numerous relative to the rest of the population as they had been a century
before. In 1687, 14 per cent of the total number of adult males
were without taxable property; by the eve of the Revolution,
the propertyless accounted for 29 per cent. The social conse-

quences of this increase were manifold. For every wage earner who competed in the economy as an autonomous entity at the end of the seventeenth century, there were four in 1771; for every man who slept in the back of a shop, in a tavern, or in a rented room in 1687, there were four in the later period. The population of Boston had doubled, but the number of property-less men had increased fourfold.

The adult males without property, however, did not form a single unified class, a monolithic body of landless proletarians. Rather, the bottom of society consisted of a congeries of social and occupational groups with a highly transient maritime element at one end of the spectrum and a more stable and respected artisan segment at the other. Although they held no taxable property, hard-working and reputable craftsmen who had established a permanent residence in Boston participated in the town meeting and were elected to unpaid minor offices. In March 1771, for instance, John Dyer was selected by the people of the town as "Fence Viewer" for the following year. Yet according to the tax and valuation lists compiled less than six months later, Dyer was without taxable property. At the same town meeting, four carpenters, Joseph Ballard, Joseph Edmunds, Benjamin Page, and Joseph Butler, none of whom was listed as an owner of taxable property on the valuation lists, were chosen as "Measurers of Boards." That propertyless men should be selected for public office indicates that the concept of a "stake in society," which provided the theoretical underpinning for membership in the community of colonial Boston, was interpreted in the widest possible sense. Yet it was this very conception of the social order which was becoming anachronistic under the pressure of economic development. For how could the growing number of propertyless men be integrated into a social order based in the first instance on the principle that only those having a tangible interest in the town or a definite family link to the society would be truly interested in the welfare of the community?

Changes no less significant had taken place within the ranks of the propertied groups. By the third quarter of the eighteenth century, lines of economic division and marks of social status were crystalizing as Boston approached economic maturity. Present to some degree in all aspects of town life, these distinctions were very apparent in dwelling arrangements. In 1687,

85 per cent of Boston real estate holdings had been assessed within a narrow range of two to ten pounds; by the seventh decade of the eighteenth century, the same spectrum ran from twelve to two hundred pounds (Table II). Gradations in housing were finer in 1771 and had social connotations which were hardly conceivable in the more primitive and more egalitarian society of the seventeenth century. This sense of distinctiveness was reinforced by geographic distribution. Affluent members of the community who had not transferred their residence to Roxbury, Cambridge, or Milton built in the spacious environs of the south and west ends. A strict segregation of the social groups was lacking; yet the milieu of the previous century, the interaction of merchant, trader, artisan, and laborer in a waterfront community, had all but disappeared.

The increasing differences between the social and economic groups within the New England seaport stemmed in part from the fact that craftsmen, laborers, and small shopkeepers had failed to maintain their relative position in the economic order. In the eighty-five years from 1687 to 1771, the share of the taxable wealth of the community controlled by the lower half of the propertied population declined from 12 to 10 per cent (Table II). If these men lived better at the end of the century than at the beginning, it was not because the economic development of Boston had effected a redistribution of wealth in favor of the laboring classes but because the long period of commercial prosperity had raised the purchasing power of every social group.

The decline in the economic distinctiveness of the middle group of property holders, the third quarter of the taxable population in the distribution of wealth, is even more significant. In 1771, these well-to-do artisans, shopkeepers, and traders (rising land values had eliminated the farmers and economic maturity the versatile merchant-sea captain) owned only 12½ per cent of the taxable wealth, a very substantial decrease from the 21 per cent held in 1687. These men lived considerably better than their counterparts in the seventeenth century; many owned homes and possessed furnishings rarely matched by the most elegant dwellings of the earlier period. But in relation to the other parts of the social order, their economic position had deteriorated drastically. This smaller middle group had been assessed for taxable estates twice as large as the bottom

50 per cent in 1687; by 1771 the assets of the two groups were equal.

On the other hand, the wealthiest 25 per cent of the taxable population by 1771 controlled 78 per cent of the assessed wealth of Boston. This represented a gain of 12 per cent from the end of the seventeenth century. An equally important shift had taken place within this elite portion of the population. In 1687, the richest 15 per cent of the taxpayers held 52 per cent of the taxable property, while the top 5 per cent owned 26.8 per cent. Eighty-five years later, the percentages were 65.9 and 44.1 (Tables I and II and Chart A).

Certain long-term economic developments accounted for the disappearance of a distinct middle group of property owners and the accumulation of wealth among a limited portion of the population. The scarcity of capital in a relatively under-developed economic system, one in which barter transactions were often necessary because of the lack of currency, required that the savings of all members of the society be tapped in the interest of economic expansion. The prospect of rapid commercial success and the high return on capital invested in mercantile activity attracted the small investor. During the first decade of the eighteenth century, nearly one of every three adult males in Boston was involved directly in trade, owning at least part of a vessel. In 1698 alone, 261 people held shares in a seagoing vessel. Trade had become "not so much a way of life as a way of making money; not a social condition but an economic activity." This widespread ownership of mercantile wealth resulted in the creation of a distinct economic "middle class" by the last decades of the seventeenth century.

A reflection of a discrete stage of economic growth, the involvement of disparate occupational and social groups in commerce was fleeting and transitory. It lasted only as long as the economy of the New England seaport remained under-developed, without large amounts of available capital. The increase in the wealth and resources of the town during the first half of the eighteenth century prompted a growing specialization of economic function; it was no longer necessary to rely on the investments of the less affluent members of the community for an expansion of commerce. This change was slow, almost imperceptible; but by 1771 the result was obvious. In that year, less than 5 per cent of the taxable population of Bos-

ton held shares in shipping of ten tons or more, even though the
tonnage owned by the town was almost double that of 1698.
Few men had investments of less than fifty tons; the average
owner held 112 tons. By way of contrast, the average holding at
the end of the seventeenth century had been about twenty-five
tons. Moreover, on the eve of the Revolution ownership of
shipping was concentrated among the wealthiest men of the
community. Ninety per cent of the tonnage of Boston in 1771
was in the hands of those whose other assets placed them in the
top quarter of the population. With the increase in the wealth
of the town had come a great increase in the number of propertyless men and a bifocalization of the property owners into
(1) a large amorphous body of shopkeepers, artisans, and laborers with holdings primarily in real estate and (2) a smaller,
somewhat more closely defined segment of the population with
extensive commercial investments as well as elegant residences
and personal possessions.

A similar trend was evident in other phases of town life. In
the transitional decades of the late seventeenth and early eighteenth century, the fluidity inherent in the primitive commercial
system had produced a certain vagueness in the connotations of
social and economic status. Over 10 per cent of the adult males
in Boston designated themselves as "merchants" on the shipping
registers of the period from 1698 to 1714, indicating not only
the decline in the distinctiveness of a title traditionally limited
to a carefully defined part of the community but also the feeling
that any man could easily ascend the mercantile ladder. Economic opportunity was so evident, so promising, that the social
demarcations of the more stable maritime communities of
England seemed incongruous. By the sixth decade of the eighteenth century, however, rank and order were supplanting the
earlier chaos as successful families tightened their control of
trade. The founding in 1763 of a "Merchants Club" with 146
members was a dramatic indication that occupations and titles
were regaining some of their traditional distinctiveness and
meaning.

An economic profile of the 146 men who composed this self-
constituted elite is revealing. Of those whose names appeared
on the tax and valuation lists of 1771, only five had estates which
placed them in the bottom three quarters of the distribution
of wealth. Twenty-one were assessed for taxable property in

excess of £1,500 and were thus in the top 1 per cent of the economic scale. The taxable assets of the rest averaged £650, an amount which put them among the wealthiest 15 per cent of the population.

That 146 men, 6½ per cent of the adult male population, were considered eligible for membership in a formal society of merchants indicates, however, that mercantile activity was not dominated by a narrow oligarchy. The range of wealth among the members of the top quarter of the propertied population was so great and the difference of social background so large as to preclude the creation of a monolithic class or guild with shared interests and beliefs.

Yet the influence of this segment of society was pervasive. By the third quarter of the eighteenth century, an integrated economic and political hierarchy based on mercantile wealth had emerged in Boston to replace the lack of social stratification of the early part of the century and the archaic distinctions of power and prestige of the religious community of the seventeenth century. All of the important offices of the town government, those with functions vital to the existence and prosperity of the town, were lodged firmly in the hands of a broad elite, entry into which was conditioned by commercial achievement and family background. The representatives to the General Court and the selectmen were the leaders of the town in economic endeavor as well as in political acumen. John Hancock's taxable wealth totaled £18,000; James Otis was assessed at £2,040, while Colonel Joseph Jackson had property valued at £1,288. Other levels of the administrative system were reserved for those whose business skills or reputation provided the necessary qualifications. Samuel Abbot, John Barrett, Benjamin Dolbeare, John Gore, William Phillips, William White, and William Whitewell, Overseers of the Poor in 1771, had taxable estates of £815, £5,520, £850, £1,747, £5,771, £1,953, and £1,502 respectively. All were among the wealthiest 7 per cent of the property owners; and Barrett and Phillips were two of the most respected merchants of the town. John Scollay, a distiller with an estate of £320, and Captain Benjamin Waldo, a shipmaster assessed at £500, who were among those chosen as "Firewards" in 1771, might in an earlier period have been dominant in town affairs; by the seventh decade of the century, in a mature economic environment, the merchant prince had replaced the man of action at the apex of the social order.

Gradations continued to the bottom of the scale. Different social and occupational levels of the population were tapped as the dignity and responsibility of the position demanded. It was not by accident that the estates of the town assessors, Jonathan Brown, Moses Deshon, and John Kneeland, were £208, £200, and £342. Or that those of the "Cullers of Staves," Henry Lucas, Thomas Knox, and Caleb Hayden, totaled £120, £144, and £156. The assumption of a graded social, economic, and political scale neatly calibrated so as to indicate the relation of each individual to the whole was the basic principle upon which the functioning of town-meeting "democracy" depended. William Crafts, with a taxable estate of £80, was elected "Fence Viewer." Half this amount qualified William Barrett to be "Measurer of Coal Baskets," while Henry Allen and John Bulfinch, "Measurers of Boards," were assessed at £80 and £48. The design was nearly perfect, the correlation between town office and social and economic position almost exact.

As in 1687, the distribution of political power and influence in Boston conformed to the standards and gradations of a wider, more inclusive hierarchy of status, one which purported to include the entire social order within the bounds of its authority. But the lines of force which had emerged on the eve of the American Revolution radiated from different economic and social groups than those of eighty-five years before, and now failed to encompass a significant portion of the population. The weakening of the "extended" family unit and the appearance of a large body of autonomous wage earners, "proletarians" in condition if not in consciousness, had introduced elements of mobility and diversity into the bottom part of society. Equally significant had been the growing inequality of the distribution of wealth among the propertied segment of the community, notably the greater exclusiveness and predominance of a mercantile "elite." Society had become more stratified and unequal. Influential groups, increasingly different from the small property owners who constituted the center portion of the community, had arisen at either end of the spectrum. Creations of the century-long development of a maritime economy in an urban setting, these "merchant princes" and "proletarians" stood out as the salient characteristics of a new social order.

TABLE I
DISTRIBUTION OF ASSESSED TAXABLE WEALTH IN BOSTON IN 1687 *

TOTAL VALUE OF TAXABLE WEALTH	NUMBER OF TAXPAYERS IN EACH WEALTH BRACKET	TOTAL WEALTH IN EACH WEALTH BRACKET	CUMULATIVE TOTAL OF WEALTH	CUMULATIVE TOTAL OF TAXPAYERS	CUMULATIVE PERCENTAGE OF TAXPAYERS	CUMULATIVE PERCENTAGE OF WEALTH
£ 1	0	£ 0	£ 0	0	0.0%	0.0%
2	152	304	304	152	14.6	1.8
3	51	153	457	203	19.5	2.7
4	169	676	1,133	372	35.9	6.8
5	33	165	1,298	405	39.0	7.8
6	97	582	1,880	502	48.5	11.3
7	19	133	2,013	521	50.2	12.1
8	43	344	2,357	564	54.4	14.2
9	22	198	2,555	586	56.6	15.4
10	45	450	3,005	631	60.9	18.1
11	17	187	3,192	648	62.5	19.2
12	30	360	3,552	678	65.4	21.4
13	13	169	3,721	691	66.6	22.4
14	12	168	3,889	703	67.9	23.4
15	22	330	4,219	725	69.9	25.4
16	21	336	4,555	746	72.0	27.5
17	1	17	4,572	747	72.0	27.6
18	18	324	4,896	765	73.8	29.5
19	1	19	4,915	766	73.9	29.6
20	30	600	5,515	796	76.8	33.2
21–25	41	972	6,487	837	80.7	39.0
26–30	48	1,367	7,854	885	85.4	47.3
31–35	29	971	8,825	914	88.2	53.1
36–40	21	819	9,644	935	90.2	58.1
41–45	19	828	10,472	954	92.1	63.1
46–50	16	781	11,253	970	93.6	67.8
51–60	16	897	12,150	986	95.1	73.2
61–70	19	1,245	13,395	1,005	97.0	80.7
71–80	7	509	13,904	1,012	97.8	83.8
81–90	3	253	14,157	1,015	97.9	85.3
91–100	7	670	14,827	1,022	98.6	89.3
100–	14	1,764	16,591	1,036	100.0	100.0

* Money values are those of 1687. Many of the assessments fall at regular five pound intervals and must be considered as an estimate of the economic position of the individual. No attempt was made to compensate for systematic overvaluation or undervaluation inasmuch as the analysis measures relative wealth. The utility of a relative presentation of wealth (or income) is that it can be compared to another relative distribution without regard to absolute monetary values. See Mary Jean Bowman, "A Graphical Analysis of Personal Income Distribution in the United States," *American Economic Review*, XXXV (1944–45), 607–628, and Horst Mendershausen, *Changes in Income Distribution during the Great Depression* (New York, 1946).

TABLE II
DISTRIBUTION OF ASSESSED TAXABLE WEALTH
IN BOSTON IN 1771 *

TOTAL VALUE OF TAXABLE WEALTH	NUMBER OF TAXPAYERS IN EACH WEALTH BRACKET	TOTAL WEALTH IN EACH WEALTH BRACKET	CUMULATIVE TOTAL OF WEALTH	CUMULATIVE TOTAL OF TAXPAYERS	CUMULATIVE PERCENTAGE OF TAXPAYERS	CUMULATIVE PERCENTAGE OF WEALTH
£ 3–30	78	£ 1,562	£ 1,562	78	5.0%	0.3%
31–40	86	2,996	4,558	164	10.6	0.9
41–50	112	5,378	9,936	276	17.9	2.2
51–60	74	4,398	14,334	350	22.6	3.5
61–70	33	3,122	17,456	383	24.7	3.8
71–80	165	12,864	30,320	548	35.4	6.5
81–90	24	2,048	32,368	572	36.9	7.0
91–100	142	13,684	46,052	714	46.1	10.0
101–110	14	494	46,546	728	47.1	10.1
111–120	149	17,844	64,390	877	56.7	13.9
121–130	20	2,570	66,960	897	58.0	14.5
131–140	26	4,600	71,560	923	59.7	15.5
141–150	20	2,698	74,258	943	60.9	16.1
151–160	88	14,048	88,306	1,031	66.6	19.1
161–170	11	1,846	90,152	1,042	67.4	19.6
171–180	18	3,128	93,280	1,060	68.6	20.3
181–190	10	1,888	95,168	1,070	69.2	20.7
191–200	47	9,368	104,536	1,117	72.2	22.7
201–300	126	31,097	135,633	1,243	80.4	29.4
301–400	60	21,799	157,432	1,303	84.2	34.1
401–500	58	24,947	182,379	1,361	88.0	39.6
501–600	14	7,841	190,220	1,375	88.9	41.3
601–700	24	15,531	205,751	1,399	90.4	44.6
701–800	26	19,518	225,269	1,425	92.2	48.9
801–900	20	17,020	242,289	1,445	93.4	52.6
901–1,000	16	15,328	257,617	1,461	95.4	55.9
1,001–1,500	41	48,364	305,963	1,502	97.1	66.4
1,501–5,000	37	85,326	391,289	1,539	99.5	84.9
5,001–	7	69,204	460,493	1,546	100.0	100.0

* The extant tax list is not complete. In ward 3, there are two pages and 69 polls missing; in ward 7, one page and 24 polls; in ward 12, an unknown number of pages and 225 polls. Only the total number of polls (224) is known for ward 11. The missing entries amount to 558, or 19.3 per cent of the total number of polls on the tax list. Internal evidence (the totals for all wards are known) suggests the absent material is completely random. Nevertheless, it should be remembered that this table represents an 80 per cent sample.

The value of shipping investments and of "servants for life" was not included in the computation of the table as it was impossible to determine the assessor's valuation. For the law regulating the assessment, see *The Acts and Resolves, Public and Private, of the Province of the Massachusetts Bay* . . . , IV (Boston, 1881), 985–987. Money values are those of 1771.

TABLE III
REAL ESTATE OWNERSHIP IN BOSTON IN 1687 AND 1771 *

1687			1771		
ASSESSED TOTAL VALUE OF REAL ESTATE	NUMBER OF OWNERS	CUMULATIVE TOTAL OF OWNERS	ASSESSED ANNUAL WORTH OF REAL ESTATE	NUMBER OF OWNERS	CUMULATIVE TOTAL OF OWNERS
£ 1	0	0	£ 1	0	0
2	168	168	2	1	1
3	75	243	3	9	10
4	203	446	4	49	59
5	85	531	5	22	81
6	167	698	6	79	160
7	3	701	7	0	160
8	54	755	8	115	275
9	2	757	9	3	278
10	107	864	10	91	369
11	0	864	11	4	373
12	24	888	12	43	416
13	0	888	13	163	579
14	3	891	14	10	589
15	25	916	15	3	592
16	8	924	16	148	740
17	0	924	17	6	746
18	7	930	18	7	753
19	1	931	19	5	758
20	46	932	20	236	994
21–30	25	1,003	21–25	41	1,035
31–40	11	1,014	26–30	163	1,198
41–50	2	1,016	31–35	93	1,291
			36–40	92	1,383
			41–45	5	1,388
			46–50	42	1,430
			51–60	32	1,462
			61–70	10	1,472
			71–80	9	1,481
			81–90	3	1,484
			91–100	3	1,487

* The assessed annual worth of real estate in the 1771 valuation must be multiplied by six to give the total property value.

CHART A

LORENZ CURVES SHOWING THE DISTRIBUTION OF
WEALTH IN BOSTON IN 1687 AND 1771
(DRAWN FROM DATA IN TABLES I AND II)

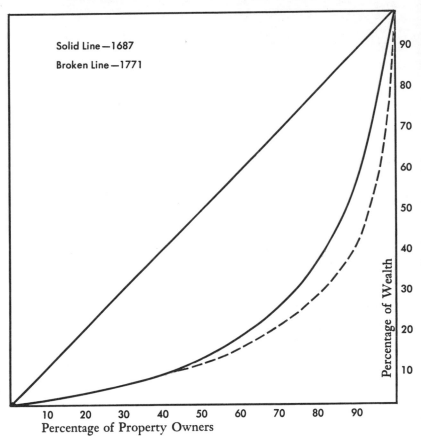

Solid Line—1687

Broken Line—1771

Percentage of Wealth

Percentage of Property Owners

POVERTY IN COLONIAL
NEW YORK CITY

RAYMOND A. MOHL

*Assistant Professor of History at Indiana University, Raymond
A. Mohl uses New York City as a test case in contradicting
the traditional assumption of widespread economic opportunity in colonial America.*

Colonial America often has been described as a land of opportunity, an open and mobile society composed largely of the
"middling sort" and devoid of extremes of poverty and wealth.
Land was cheap, labor scarce, and wages high, the argument
runs. The colonies had no beggars, no poor, not even a genuine
lower class. Unlimited economic opportunity created political
democracy, and both together made America the "ideal spot for
the common man." With few exceptions, this view of colonial
society has dominated recent American historical writing. Historians have remarked on poverty in early America only to deny
that it existed, or to assert it to be an exception rather than the
rule. The most recent historical study of poverty in America's
past dates the emergence of the poor relief problem at 1830,
when the United States began to experience heavy immigration, rapid urbanization, and the turmoils of industrialization.
The implication remains that American society escaped such
evils in the pre-industrial period.

From Raymond A. Mohl, "Poverty in Early America, a Reappraisal: The Case
of Eighteenth-Century New York City," *New York History*, L (January
1969), 5–27. Copyright © 1969 by the New York State Historical Association.
Reprinted by permission of the New York State Historical Association,
Cooperstown, New York.

Abundant evidence, however, casts serious doubt upon the validity of these popularly accepted propositions, evidence which indicates that poverty in early America may have been substantially more widespread than previously believed. Colonial poor laws, restrictive immigration policies, heavy municipal relief expenditures, overcrowded institutional facilities, extensive private benevolence and mutual aid, occasional preventive measures—all these affirm the reality of poverty. And while some historians have attempted to disprove the existence of poverty in the colonial period by stringing together quotations from travel accounts, colonial boosters, and royal governors, equally impressive quotations can be gathered from more reliable sources which support the contrary position. The experience of eighteenth-century New York City in coping with poverty and poor relief supplies a test case for these generalizations.

The New York response to poverty stemmed from British precedent and example, especially the Elizabethan Poor Law of 1601 and the Settlement Act of 1662. This legislation charged the parish—the unit of local government—with care of the poor, prescribed public taxation to support poor houses and work houses, and defined the status of legal settlement as the eligibility requirement for parish assistance. Soon after the conquest, the British in New York, acting on orders from the colony's new proprietor, devised and implemented a comprehensive legal code called the "Duke's Laws." Among other things, the new code divided the New York City area (called Yorkshire) into parishes, called for the selection of eight overseers of the poor and two church wardens within each parish, and stipulated public taxation to support the poor. Provincial legislation of 1683, passed at the meeting of New York's first assembly, extended the principle of local responsibility for the poor throughout the colony, but on a county rather than a parish basis. The law also established legal residence requirements, directed ship masters to furnish local magistrates with lists of immigrants within twenty hours of arrival, and authorized the removal of potential paupers and public charges—that is, newcomers without "Visible Estate, . . . manuall craft or occupacon." Additional legislation in the eighteenth century elaborated or slightly modified these early laws but retained the basic structure.

Although provincial legislation established the framework for poor law administration, handling the relief problem became the responsibility of town or county officials. Within their jurisdictions, local overseers of the poor determined methods of relief, investigated applicants for assistance, distributed aid to the needy, and enforced the settlement clauses. In New York City the elected aldermen of each ward performed the duties of overseers until 1691, when vestrymen and church wardens assumed such functions. Despite the delegation of authority, the city magistrates (the mayor and aldermen) continued to exercise relief powers concurrently.

Most municipal assistance during this early period consisted of outdoor relief—aid to the indigent and needy within their own homes. The records of the mayor's court and the minutes of meetings of the vestrymen and church wardens reveal that this relief took many forms: money, firewood, food and provisions, shoes and clothing, funeral expenses, and nursing or medical care for the sick poor (a physician was maintained as "Doctor of the Poor"). The municipality even supplied funds to finance return trips to Europe or to some other American colony. Church wardens and aldermen also apprenticed poor children as a method of poor relief; occasionally adult paupers, too, were bound out as indentured servants. Local officials required paupers to wear badges of blue or red cloth with the large letters "N:Y" sewn on their clothing, without which no assistance would be granted. Such symbols, designating dependent status, indicate the social stigma attached to recipients of early public poor relief.

By present standards, the number of public charges seems small. According to extant records, the permanent poor list of the church wardens in January 1700 numbered 35; by 1725 the list totaled 42 adults and numerous children; in 1735 the overseers recorded at least 58 adult paupers and an indeterminate number of children. These records are incomplete, however, because they fail to include grants of temporary assistance, often necessary during winter months when cold weather and an ice-filled harbor suspended most forms of business and economic activity. Nor do the records indicate the large numbers of city residents who received no relief but lived on a subsistence level.

Even in the early eighteenth century, poor relief costs were surprisingly high; occasionally the church wardens, to relieve distress, dispensed more money than authorities appropriated from municipal taxes. The poor tax for the period November 1697 to July 1698 totaled £250; by 1714 the annual levy for the poor had increased to £438. A complete set of church wardens accounts for the years 1723-1735 reveals average annual relief expenditures of £523. In an era of limited municipal services, poor relief expenses consistently comprised the largest single item in the annual budget of New York City.

Yet these funds hardly sufficed, and church wardens continuously had to plead with the Common Council for additional support. In September 1700, for example, they requested supplementary funds because "the Crys of the poor & Impotent for want of Reliefe are Extreamly Grevious." During the winter of 1713 they reported the poor of the city to be "in great Want & a Miserable Condition & must inevitably perish unless some speedy Method be taken for their support." In the face of such pressures, the Common Council usually took action. When the Council petitioned the provincial assembly in 1702 for permission to levy additional taxes for the poor "soe often as their shall be Occasion," the assembly complied by raising the ceiling on the city's poor rates. The aldermen frequently borrowed against future tax revenues to maintain the poor relief program, or sold municipal land to increase relief funds, and occasionally they resorted to general public subscriptions. Fines of various kinds supplied additional financial support. Provincial settlement laws failed to prevent the arrival of pauper immigrants, so the Common Council adopted more rigid regulations of its own, requiring not only immigrants but visitors and other "strangers" as well to register with the mayor upon entering the city.

The municipal government also provided some institutional care for the poor in this early period. As early as 1696 the Common Council rented a small house as a hospital for the sick poor; by 1700 it also served as a house of correction "for the punishing of Vagabonds & Idle Persons that are a Nuisance & Common Grievance of the Inhabitants." A committee of aldermen considered the possibility of a general poor house in 1714, but without result. In February 1734 the *New-York Gazette* printed the complaint of a citizen about rising poor taxes and the "many Beggarly people daily suffered to wander about the Streets." The only solution to these undesirable conditions, suggested the anonymous correspondent, lay in the construction of public buildings for the helpless poor, for the unemployed, and for "Sloathful . . . disobedient, and Stragling Vagabonds"—the fulfillment, in other words, of the Elizabethan poor law establishment. By the 1730's the need for permanent institutional facilities for the urban poor had become clear.

That governmental officials thought along the same lines is apparent from the new city charter, granted by the assembly in 1731, which authorized the municipality to build a poor house. The Common Council studied the proposal once again and in December 1734 decided to go ahead with the building project. The Council's report on the subject described the condition of the poor in the city and revealed an awareness of the social problems created by poverty:

Whereas the Necessity, Number and Continual Increase of the Poor within this City is very great and Exceeding burthensome to the Inhabitants thereof for want of a Workhouse and House of Correction AND WHEREAS there is not yet any Provision made for the Relief and setting on Work of Poor Needy Persons and Idle Wandering Vagabonds, Sturdy Beggars and Others, who frequently Committ divers misdemeanors within the Said City, who living Idly and unimployed, become debauched and Instructed in the Practice of Thievery and Debauchery. For Remedy whereof . . . Resolved that there be forthwith built . . . A good, Strong and Convenient House and Tenement.

The two-story brick structure completed in 1736 received the all-inclusive title of "Poor House, Work House, and House of Correction."

Insufficient funds obviously prevented separate facilities at this early date, but the several compartments or divisions of the institution did suggest some differentiation among the inmates: an infirmary for the sick poor; a cellar for the "unruly and obstinate"; and a room for "Carrying on Trades, Occupation and Manufactures," especially spinning, weaving, and shoemaking. A large garden laid out around the house supplied employment for some and fresh vegetables for all. Poor children acquired the elements of education and preliminary training in trades to qualify them as apprentices. Unruly slaves or servants could be sent to the house by their masters upon payment of fees for entrance, support, and whipping. An elaborate set of rules adopted by the Common Council required paupers to attend regular prayer readings, prohibited smoking in bed and begging, and even set forth the weekly menu for poor house residents—an unappetizing diet of bread and cheese, beef broth, and milk or pease porridge. A keeper appointed by the aldermen at an annual salary of £30 maintained order within the institution and enforced regulations.

The poor house rapidly became an important and indispensable public institution. When the facility opened in the spring of 1736, a total of 12 adults and at least seven children found immediate refuge; others soon followed, and by March 1772 the house contained some 425 paupers. Because the building had been designed only for the most extreme cases of indigence and sickness, the church wardens continued to supply relief to large numbers of outdoor poor each year. Expanded and enlarged on several occasions, the alms house with its three-fold function, remained the central agency of public poor relief in New York City throughout the eighteenth century.

Despite the provision of institutional facilities, municipal relief seemed insufficient. The problem of poverty became more serious in the four decades between the construction of the poor house and the outbreak of the Revolution. A writer in the *New-York Weekly Journal*, for example, complained in February 1737 about the increasing number of young beggars in the streets and saw a solution in public education for indigent children. Economic depression in 1737 caused a decline in trade and commerce, "whereby the honest and industrious tradesmen are reduced to poverty for want of employ." During the winter of 1741 a private subscription raised more than £500 to supplement inadequate public relief funds. On several different occasions small pox epidemics brought calls for increased aid for the sick poor.

The demands of war intensified the relief problem in New York. Militia service imposed burdens upon the laboring people of the city, while wartime disruption of colonial trade brought added poverty in its wake. Municipal relief expenditures rose during the French and Indian War, amounting in 1759 to £1,200, considerably above the pre-war average. In January 1760 the church wardens made special collections in each ward to supplement tax funds for the poor, and in 1762 the editor of the *Weekly Post-Boy* complained about the growing "Number of Beggars and wandering Poor" in the streets of New York. And post-war depressions had observable results as well. "A Citizen" who described the city in 1749, at the close of King

George's War, adopted a pessimistic tone: "We already begin to experience the Effects of idle Hands; some of the Inhabitants have been robbed, others knocked down; many Beggars troubling our doors, and our Poor-House full; our Taxes high, our Provisions dear, and all Trade at a Stand at present. . . ."

The rapid population growth of New York City from about 7,000 in 1720 to more than 25,000 in 1775 indicates another important cause of increasing poverty. That the city fathers recognized immigration as a source of paupers and public charges is evident in the numerous provincial laws and municipal regulations setting forth requirements for legal residence. Legislation and enforcement, however, are two different things. William Livingston, editor of New York's *Independent Reflector*, criticized municipal officials in 1752 for failing to guard the city against "foreign Invasions of Beggary and Idleness." Under pretext of increasing the industry and productivity of the colony, promoters had imported large numbers of Germans. But the *Independent Reflector* characterized these immigrants as "useless and insignificant Drones"—a group of poverty-stricken beggars and paupers lacking in skills and trades who taxed the benevolence of the community and drained the municipal treasury. On another occasion editor Livingston attacked the transportation of British felons to the colonies on the same grounds.

Urban poverty became especially apparent during the 1760's and indeed, as one historian has suggested, may have contributed to the growing radicalism of New York's lower classes. Post-war depression, followed by a series of boycotts of British goods, disrupted the city's commerce and produced a decade of crisis for the poor. The newspapers of the period, most often during the winter months, filled their columns with editorials and letters detailing the hardships of unemployed laborers and low income people. Petitions for benevolence and relief demanded the attention of municipal officials and the community at large. In January 1765 the Common Council resorted once again to borrowing, for "the distresses of the Poor being at Present so Extremely Great that unless some Expedient Can Be fallen on for their Relief many . . . must unavoidably perish." Throughout the decade and into the 1770's New Yorkers made extra collections of taxes and charity for the poor, and in 1774 the provincial assembly made a half-hearted effort to increase relief funds by authorizing church wardens to tax dogs at the rate of one shilling each! But this additional humanitarian assistance seemed "insufficient for the numerous Objects that Stand in need of it." By February 1771 the poor house supported 339 paupers; during the following year the church wardens admitted 372 new public charges. Substantial outdoor relief payments continued simultaneously, amounting to as much as £67 per month. In the years just prior to the Revolution, overall poor relief expenditures averaged £5,000 annually.

In response to growing poor lists and rising relief costs in the pre-Revolutionary period, New Yorkers attempted to devise solutions to their most serious social problem. The municipal government adopted a partially negative approach, emphasizing reduction of public expenses rather than attacking the causes of poverty. Thus the Common Council tried to shorten the poor list by renewing efforts to apprentice pauper children and by rounding up vagrants for transportation from the city. A new provincial poor law of 1773 revamped the settlement clauses and set forth detailed procedures for removing paupers without legal residence. On the positive side the Council ordered the construction of a bridewell, or house of correction, completed in 1775, to separate vagrants and disorderly people from the alms house poor. And in addition to the normal relief program, aldermen occasionally assisted particular distressed groups, such as war refugees or imprisoned debtors.

If the efforts of the municipal government seemed sadly lacking in purpose and result, the proposals of private individuals and the activities of benevolent groups and *ad hoc* organizations were more productive. The movement for home manufactures, for example, represented at the same time an attack on poverty. Reacting in 1764 to declining trade, unemployment, high prices, scarcity of specie, restrictions on paper money, and new commercial regulations such as the Sugar Act, New York merchants formed a Society for the Promotion of Arts, Agriculture, and Economy. The Society encouraged domestic industries and farm products with the promise of premiums, bounties, and prizes. It established a linen factory which employed more than 300 indigent workers for 18 months during 1766 and 1767. In addition, the organization lent spinning wheels to poor women and founded a trade school for pauper children. With the passage of the Townshend Acts in 1767, the activities of this society were supplemented by a special committee of citizens, appointed "to consider of the Expediency of entering into Measures to encourage Industry and Frugality, and employ the Poor." Similarly, New York's Revolutionary Committee of 100 selected a subcommittee in 1775 to collect charitable donations and find work for indigent and unemployed laborers, for which purpose they established a company called the "New York Society for employing the Industrious Poor, and Promoting Manufactory."

Numerous other suggestions addressed themselves to the plight of New York City's poor, and while few produced results, all are indicative of urban poverty. Schemes for employment abounded: ideas for putting idle craftsmen to work; plans to send inactive seamen and vessels to the Greenland whale fisheries; proposals for manufacturing silk, paper, wool, nails, and other products. One commentator in 1768 recommended the establishment of a bank and loan office to ease the hardships of "infectious" poverty. Others made a determined attack on the theater as an obstacle to charity, for "the money thrown away in one night at a play" would support many poor families "in tolerable comfort" during a long and severe winter. Another observer, perhaps viewing poverty and distress in the city more pessimistically, asserted the only remedy to be "that old-fashioned but prevailing weapon, Prayer."

Religious benevolence maintained a variety of programs for the poor. Early in the century the Society for the Propagation of the Gospel in Foreign Parts established charity schools in New York City for Indian, Negro, and poor white children. The Anglican Church supported a charity school of its own with annual church collections. Other churches, notably the Presbyterian, Dutch Reformed, and French Huguenot, held charity sermons each winter to raise relief funds for the poor of their congregations, for imprisoned debtors, and similar purposes. As the eighteenth century progressed, Quakers turned from "in-group" charity to more general humanitarian objectives. In 1773 a group of pious New Yorkers formed an American Society for Promoting Religious Knowledge among the Poor. Undoubtedly the religious ferment of the Great Awakening promoted the benevolent spirit, and George Whitefield himself appeared in the city in 1754 to support worthy causes.

Private charity supplemented the relief activities of municipal government, *ad hoc* committee, and organized religion. Mutual benefit societies and immigrant aid associations provided care for sick or distressed members, their families, and newly arrived countrymen. The earliest of these groups, the Scots Charitable Society founded in 1744, went beyond mere relief by employing poor Scots women to spin cotton, linen, and wool. Occupational groups also formed for mutual relief, a trend especially apparent in the 1760's when organizations such as the Society of House Carpenters (1767) and the Marine Society (1769) appeared. In imitation of neighboring Philadelphia, New Yorkers, led by Dr. Samuel Bard and assisted by an annual subsidy from the assembly, founded the New York Hospital in 1771 to care for the sick poor. Benefit theater performances supplied funds for charity schools and poor prisoners. Individual donations and bequests encouraged other humanitarian causes, as did groups as varied as Free Masons and Sons of Liberty. Successful candidates for public office often became charitably inclined; on the day following his election to the assembly in 1752, for example, Mr. John Watts distributed £70 among "the most indigent Families" in the city. And while New Yorkers toiled to combat poverty in their own community, they found energy and resources in 1774 to make donations for the poor of Boston, who suffered under limitations imposed by the Coercive Acts.

The American Revolution created new hardships for the poor of New York. As the imperial crisis neared climax in 1775 and 1776, the city's Committee of Safety assumed overall responsibility for relief administration, distributing firewood, provisions, and, where possible, employment among the needy. When British forces began seven years of occupation in September 1776, thousands of patriots fled the metropolis—among them about 400 alms house poor who were assisted to havens of safety and refuge in Westchester, Dutchess, and Ulster counties, where local committees provided for them at state expense. Legislation of 1778 made a special appropriation for these and other pauper refugees, and authorized appointment of a board of commissioners to supervise their maintenance.

Meanwhile, the British found themselves burdened with a growing population of indigent loyalist refugees in New York City. The military command established a new relief structure in January 1778 with the selection of 19 overseers to supervise the alms house and the outdoor poor. In the absence of regular tax collections, these men energetically tapped other sources of income—rents from houses and businesses abandoned by patriots, tavern and liquor license fees, Brooklyn Ferry rents, fines for violation of local ordinances, charitable subscriptions, and lotteries. According to one estimate, the overseers collected and disbursed more than £45,000 in public charities between 1777 and 1783. The social and economic dislocations produced by the Revolution, therefore, aggravated poverty and relief problems in early New York.

The evacuation of New York by British forces on November 25, 1783, symbolized the achievement of victory and independence, but also imposed heavy responsibilities upon the new city government. Among early municipal actions, relief provisions for returning refugees assumed high priority, a function handled temporarily by a special commission until regular city positions were filled. Legislation of 1784 abolished offices of vestrymen and church wardens for New York City, and after a short period of administrative confusion, a new set of municipal appointees—Commissioners of the Alms House and Bridewell—absorbed duties formerly exercised by church wardens. The passage of new state poor laws in 1784 and 1788 strengthened the important features of pre-war legislation and completed the post-Revolutionary transition.

The last two decades of the eighteenth century witnessed further intensification of urban poverty in America. In February 1784, when New York City's population totaled about 12,000, one newspaper estimated that more than 1,000 families were supported by public and private charity. Outdoor relief assisted thousands of indigent persons, especially during periods of epidemic or depression, and during winter months when unskilled day laborers could find no employment. The seasonal character of employment for seamen, longshoremen, cartmen, and most craftsmen who worked out of doors contributed to swollen poor lists. Heavy immigration in the post-Revolutionary period bears a direct relation to increasing relief burdens. The Commissioners of the Alms House reported in 1795, for example, that 44 per cent of poor house residents came from immigrant stock. Besides immigrants and unemployed, the public charges of the city included widows, orphans, and abandoned infants, the sick, aged, and insane, and disabled Revolutionary War veterans. Officials described the alms house in 1795 as full of paupers "subject to Rheumatisms, Ulcers and Palsies and to Fits which impair their Reason and elude all the force of Medicine."

Many agricultural laborers from neighboring counties migrated to New York each winter to live on the public bounty. Although some of the poor were transients and received relief only a short time, many became long-term charges. Not uncommon was the case of John Sullivan, born blind in the poor house in 1759 and a resident of the institution until his death in 1819. Alms house records reveal that numerous other blind, crippled, and infirm paupers of pre-Revolutionary years remained public pensioners well into the early national period. That some families stayed on relief for more than one generation is suggested by the comment of one of the alms house commissioners to the visiting duc de la Rochefoucauld in 1797, that "the poor-house of New York produces paupers."

Municipal officials, especially mayors James Duane and Richard Varick, expressed constant concern and alarm at urban poverty and its social manifestations. Demands for relief forced the Common Council to build a new and larger alms house in 1796 at a cost of $130,000; by the end of the decade more than 900 poor crowded the new institution. Relief expenses remained the largest item in the municipal budget, totaling more than $42,000 in 1800. In an effort to reduce costs, the city government revamped poor relief administration at the turn of the century with passage of new local ordinances and appointment of a new set of expert alms house commissioners. But these measures had little effect, largely because the Common Council failed to implement preventive solutions concurrently.

The associative pattern of private humanitarianism became more pronounced in post-Revolutionary years. New immigrant aid groups such as the Friendly Sons of St. Patrick (1784), the German Society (1784), and St. George's Society (1786) appeared, while an informal French Benevolent Society became active in the 1790's when several thousand refugees from Santo Domingo arrived in New York City. After 1794 a Society for the Information and Assistance of Persons Emigrating from Foreign Countries helped newcomers of all nationalities. Occupational and trade associations proliferated as the eighteenth century drew to a close, providing not only benevolence but also the nucleus of nascent labor organizations. One of the most important of these groups, the General Society of Mechanics and Tradesmen, founded in 1785, had its own overseers of the poor and a loan committee to assist needy members and families.

Patriotic and political organizations such as the Tammany Society and the Order of Cincinnati also engaged in some charitable work, as did social and fraternal societies like Free Masons. Further manifestations of the humanitarian spirit of the age can be found in the Society for the Relief of Distressed Debtors (1787), which became the Humane Society in 1803; the City Dispensary (1791), which provided free medical care for the indigent; the Manumission Society (1758), which in addition to other activities opened an African Free School in 1787; and the Society for the Relief of Poor Widows with Small Children (1797). Education for poor children flourished with the development of new religious charity schools, alms house schools, and, by 1805, the Free School Society. Although it is impossible to determine the total amount of assistance furnished by these organizations, private charity certainly supplemented public relief in a most important way.

Although the humanitarian spirit of the eighteenth century generated new energy for the alleviation of human misery, although the municipal government accepted extensive responsibility for the poor, neither public nor private benevolence succeeded in eliminating or even reducing poverty in New York City. By the end of the century poor relief and charity had proved inadequate as preventive measures. Contemporary conceptions of society help to explain this failure, for few thought of poverty in other than moral terms. Intemperance, immorality, irreligion, voluntary idleness—New Yorkers fastened on vices such as these to explain poverty in their community. With the exception of occasional employment schemes, few proposals aimed at solving the social and economic problems of the urban environment; most programs concentrated in purging the poor of their supposed vices. Education might have helped had its promoters abandoned the idea that schooling should serve primarily as the agent of morality and social control. The tendency of New Yorkers to moralize about the poor prevented reforms and real solutions, and poverty remained a serious social problem as urbanization of the city progressed rapidly during the nineteenth century. One is tempted at this point to ask how all of this differs from our approach to poverty in 1969. Are we attacking the real problems through preventive measures, or are we still merely relieving, and thus perpetuating, poverty and indigence? Do we still moralize about the poor? Is the modern

attitude toward poverty and relief really much different from
that of the eighteenth century?

Clearly poverty in eighteenth century America bears a close
relation to urbanization. The poor became observable in New
York after 1730 as immigration speeded population growth. A
doubling in the city's population during the last decade of the
century, from about 33,000 in 1790 to more than 60,000 in 1800,
brought unexampled poverty and distress. What was true of
New York was, in large measure, true also of other seaport
cities in colonial America. One recent study of the social structure of colonial Boston finds the class of propertyless laborers
increasing twice as rapidly as population as a whole. Philadelphia,
the largest colonial city after 1750, similarly felt the undesirable
social effects of rapid urban growth.

This paper has attempted to qualify some current opinions
about early American society. Those who find widespread economic opportunity, who see very little poverty, who generalize
about an open and mobile society have seemingly overlooked a
portion of the evidence. If there were no poor, why the elaborate
legislation and administrative machinery for a problem which
did not exist? If there were no poor, how does one explain heavy
relief expenditures and overcrowded alms houses? If none were
in need, why the proliferation of mutual aid societies and humanitarian organizations? If economic opportunity was a reality
for all, how does one account for large numbers of unemployed
on the poor lists? And certainly the class of poor persons included a much larger group than just those assisted by public and
private charity, for many urban workers remained precariously
perched on the nether edge of subsistence. Slaves, free Negroes,
and most indentured servants fall into the same category. Indeed, as Jackson Turner Main has suggested in his recent study,
The Social Structure of Revolutionary America, the poor comprised perhaps as much as one-third of the population in the
northern colonies and states. Surely colonial society, and especially the urban ingredient of that society, requires closer
scrutiny before the cliché of America as the land of opportunity
can be accepted at face value.

THE MECHANICS OF REVOLUTIONARY CHARLESTON, 1760-1776

RICHARD WALSH

Richard Walsh, Professor of History at Georgetown University, places Charleston's skilled craftsmen within the context of the urban community and describes their active role in the Revolutionary movement.

Among the three influential classes in Charleston during the colonial and Revolutionary periods were the mechanics. These artisans were the first to move in the direction of revolution in 1765. Here were the men who with their retinue of apprentices, journeymen, and slaves formed the advanced guard of rebellion. . . .

The Mechanics in Business

As the small businessmen of the colonial and Revolutionary periods, the mechanics may be divided into two classifications. One was the manufacturing shopkeepers, like the saddlers, cabinetmakers, and shoemakers, who fashioned wares and placed them directly on sale at the shop. Rarely did they sell to merchants of the town who, as in England, then resold elsewhere.

From Richard Walsh, "The Charleston Mechanics: A Brief Study, 1760–1776," *South Carolina Historical Magazine*, LX (July 1959), 123, 132–144. Copyright 1959 by the South Carolina Historical Society. Reprinted by permission of the South Carolina Historical Society.

Charleston makers of goods, with the exception of tanners, chandlers, and coopers, did not usually export nor—like the Philadelphia or New York artisans—enter the coastal trade. The other mechanics, though masters, were essentially laborers. These included such groups as carpenters, bricklayers, carvers, joiners, and tinsmiths. They did not keep shop, except as headquarters for an extensive establishment—for example, a master house-wright or shipbuilder.

Two business forms were employed, the sole proprietorship and the partnership. Almost invariably the former was used, but it was not uncommon for the mechanic to take in a partner, by which means additional capital, a good name, or skill was gained, or perhaps a competitor eliminated. Such must have been the case in the partnership of John Fisher and Thomas Elfe. Elfe was one of the opulent mechanics of Charleston, who loaned money at interest. Some of the most prominent inhabitants, including the artisans, were indebted to him. Another partnership combining skills was that of Edward Weyman, a glazier and upholsterer, and John Carne, who advertised himself as a cabinet and chair-maker. An advertisement of the painter Hawes, the wheelwright Laughton, and the coachmaker Bookless, refers to a "Company of Coachmakers." But this was not a company in the modern sense. The three were merely partners, the establishment unin-corporated, and probably only skill the chief offerings of the trio. By means of the newly joined company, they write:

They can now advertise the publick, that they have brought all branches of the coach making business to such perfection, as not to exceed in quality the materials, goodness of the work or neatness, by any importation; so that they can make and finish, without any assistance, out of their own shop all sorts of Coaches, Chariots, Phaeton, Post Chaises, Landau, Currices, Sedans, Sleighs, in the most complete and elegant manner, and afford them at more reasonable rates than can be imported. . . .

There were no business corporations in Charleston. However, mechanics in the same trade and with similar economic interests united. The tailors combined in 1760, and the Grand Jury com-plained that Negro apprentice chimney sweeps had joined to-gether to raise their wages. The latter probably represents one of America's oldest labor unions, but unfortunately nothing more is known about it than the Jury's grievance. After the Revolution, the Carpenters', the Barbers', and the Master Coopers' Societies were formed, and in 1794 various tradesmen began the Mechanics' Society, which admitted "any number of free white Mechanics, Manufacturers, and Handicraftsmen." These organizations tried to increase their wages or the prices of their wares, for which the legislature was reluctant to incorporate them. Only when it was convinced that they were not combinations for "forestalling and monopoly" and were benevolent and charitable societies were charters granted. Thus were the Master Tailors' and the Mechanics' Societies finally incorporated, the first in 1784, the other at its inception.

The mechanic of this day was ambitious, ever watchful of his interests, and always ready to improve and extend them. Sometimes his shop was the center of several activities which had nothing whatever to do with his trade but gave additional income. Thomas Nightingale, advertised as a saddler, serves as a case in point. He augmented his earnings by keeping a race track at which was run the "Mechanicks Purse," and prizes were also awarded for the fastest mounts owned by planters and merchants. Besides this, Nightingale also conducted cock fights, loaned money at interest, auctioneered, rented wagons for carting, "entertained Indians" for the province. A shop was also a family concern. For example, when Edward Weyman became immersed in Revolutionary politics, his wife conducted business as usual. Upon the illness of the blacksmith Bricken, his wife continued his work. As proof that not all of the mechanic businesses remained small, there were from time to time notices in the gazettes offering to bring to date and balance the books of tradesmen as well as merchants.

As with all colonists, land was the chief investment. If the artisan was only fairly prosperous, he speculated in town lots— often to a fault during the Revolution, when property changed hands repeatedly because of inflation. But if the mechanic were more cautious, he built on his land and rented the buildings. Buying plantations was also common among the artisans. Such a purchase was sound not only monetarily but also socially, affording entrance into the planter class, the pinnacle of Southern society.

Shipowning was another avenue of investment. To illustrate, Benjamin Hawes and George Flagg, the painters, bought a fifteen-ton vessel in 1763 with which to enter the West Indian trade in rice. Another of several shipowners was Walter Mansell, who with George Sheed, a plumber, acquired a sixty-five-ton vessel. They operated with such success that they rose to the rank of merchants. When the economy became rocky during the war, Jonathan Sarrazin quit silversmithing and with his son, Edward, used his ship to eke out a living. The examples of ship-buying were by no means few.

In his shop the artisan employed apprentices. These supplied him with cheap labor for at least four years, and each apprentice brought a fee of £20 sterling, in payment for which he was faithfully taught the craft. Apprenticeship had its disadvantages, however. As a worker the apprentice was but an irresponsible learner, usually beginning training at the ages of twelve to fourteen years. He found the town gaming houses more intriguing than the shop, and so pressing was this problem that in 1762 the legislature acted to prevent "excessive gaming" of servants, apprentices, and journeymen. By the frequency of such notices in the gazettes, runaways also plagued masters. Weyman, the glazier, once advertised in digust for the return of a persistent perambulator: "Whoever shall deliver him to the master, shall receive a reward of Two Large Hand Fulls of Pine Shavings for their trouble."

Use was made of indentured servants. Evidently these repeated all the woes of apprentices—running away, idleness, stealing, and whatnot. But often the "servant man" was as skilled as the master himself and having availed himself of one or more, the master might advertise that he had added another "branch" to his shop. For example, Alexander Learmouth, a tanner, boasted that since he had supplied himself with tanners and curriers from England, he could sell leather cheaper than any yet done. The servant, like the apprentice, was impermanent and after his period of service, about five to seven years, departed. He then could, and frequently did, become his master's competitor.

Journeymen and masters lacking tools or wealth to enter trade on their own account were also hired. One master often employed another, for there existed no agency, such as a guild, to set standards of workmanship or the rank of artisans. The customer determined quality and capital, rank. As soon as the free laborer saved sufficient funds, he began his own enterprise, making free labor so scarce that the newspapers record tradesmen sending as far as England to engage experienced workmen.

Because of this apparent scarcity of labor, and its instability, the artisan resorted to slavery. He gained from this system permanent workers whose wages and skill belonged to the owner. Among the numerous slave-holding artisans was Thomas Elfe, whose account book illustrates the system. Elfe kept six slaves valued at £2,250 sterling. They were trained as house-painters, cabinetmakers, and carpenters for use in the shop and for hire by town and countrymen. Elfe's income from the latter employment amounted to £632:16:2 in 1768, £405:19:00 in 1769, and £279, in 1770.

His is not the only example. A court record indicates that Nathaniel Scott, a carpenter and housewright, used himself, some white carpenters, and his Negroes Ben, Cudgoe, and Harry in building for one of the townsmen. David Saylor, the cooper, worked as many as thirty slaves in his packing house. At one time Hawes entered a typical advertisement in the *Gazette*, saying that he could undertake any job of house painting by the use of his white apprentices and Negroes. In 1785 a visitor to the city commented, though in somewhat exaggerated terms: "I have seen tradesmen go through the city followed by a negro carrying their tools—Barbers who are supported in idleness and ease by their negroes who do the business; and in fact many of the mechanics bear nothing more of their trade than the name."

The census of 1790 listed 1,933 heads of families in Charleston, of whom 1,247 owned one or more slaves. Of the 79 mechanics who left wills between 1760 and 1785, 37 specifically mentioned ownership of slaves. Of the 194 artisans who worked during these years and who could be identified in the census of 1790 there were 159 slaveholders. In other words, the percentage of slaveholders stood at 80% of the total number. Slaves were trained for sale to the planters or townsmen at great profit. Sometimes he was chattel kept as a legacy for the family. In case of the death of the master, the Negro became the wage earner or maintained the shop while some member of the family supervised the business, as was very probably the case with the lady blacksmith, Sarah Bricken.

Thus were the tradesmen of Charleston saddled with slavery. They were not happy with it and found that "jobbing Negroes" worked at low rates for some non-artisan townman, merchant, or planter, at times making employment scarce for whites. They had fashioned their own dilemma, however. Journeymen and poor masters hated the system more than the shop-keeping tradesman. It meant for labor only ruinous competition and low wages. In 1796, after the incorporation of the city, free labor secured a law to force masters to employ at least one white apprentice or journeyman for every four Negroes; yet the have-nots displayed human inconsistency. Upon acquiring enough capital to set up for themselves, they joined the slaveholders with a purchase or two. Such was the condition of Southern society.

Mercantilism aided many groups of mechanics. Hemp makers were given British bounties, and coopers were subsidized. Manufactories of potash were assisted by the removal of duties on the product upon its importation to Great Britain. The London Society of Arts also aided the fertilizer makers. Shipbuilders and those who produced naval stores were encouraged by the Empire with grants of money.

On the other hand, the spirit of mercantilism was an absolute discouragement to the artisan who competed with his counterpart in England. Artisans of Charleston daily saw English-made furniture, silver, guns, iron, coaches, saddles, and shoes unloaded at their port for sale to the provincials. English merchants consistently flooded the market with wares, thereby depriving Charleston artisans of customers and profits. Indeed, at times they were the forgotten men of the colony as their manufactures were passed over for English importations.

There were no laws passed by Parliament directly to curtail their manufacturing. The Hat Act did not, for example, immediately affect them, nor did the Iron Act. There is no record of a hatter in Charleston, and there was only one manufactory of iron, in York County, which was in a very poor condition. But the attitude which brought about such acts, the favoritism shown for Englishmen over Americans by the Parliament, did not sit well with the mechanics.

The Charleston artisan, mainly interested in the invasion of the local market by English mechanics, was very favorably disposed toward the boycotts and embargoes erected on the eve of the Revolution. Such antimercantilistic weapons brought the mechanic new and willing customers. The phrases in so many Charleston newspaper advertisements, "as good as imported," "as cheap as imported," were not written idly; these were aimed at England.

Monetary difficulties were also the result of the imperial system, affecting every mechanic industry. In general, acting in the role of creditor to the colonies, the British consistently tried to keep the value of money at a high level, forbidding or only grudgingly assenting to issues of Carolina paper money. The province employed the subterfuge of issuing certificates or bills of credit, to be used for the payment of taxes only but which circulated readily. When the province spent heavily, as during the war with France, money was plentiful and times were good. Correspondingly when less was spent and a large number of certificates were retired, times were exceedingly bad. Debtors and creditors were at one another's throats.

The mechanics and planters were in agreement over the merits of cheap money, which they wanted for buying tools, materials, and labor, and for expansion and payment of debts. On the other side, the merchants, being creditors, naturally leaned toward the hard-money policies of the British and were for this reason very hesitant to move against the crown on the eve of the war. They carried on little or no clandestine trade, unlike their brothers in New England, and were only mildly annoyed at the political harpies, the customs collectors, who descended on their port as a result of the acts of trade of the 1760's.

But there were occasions when the mechanics could sympathize with the advocates of hard money, for they too were sellers of wares and services. During difficult times, unable to collect their dues from the planters, they were in turn squeezed by the merchants from whom they had purchased materials or borrowed money. At such times a mechanic might call "to those who have open accounts with him, to discharge the same immediately, else, when the courts open, their neglect may prove fatal to him," or as Sarrazin, the silversmith, warned his debtors, not to "take it amiss if I call often upon them, as I must keep up my credit." He added: "my worthy friends must also consider that the sun is very hot to walk in . . . I spend more time in collecting . . . money than earning it."

The Mechanics in Revolutionary Politics

Before the Revolution, the mechanics were apparently contented with their political situation in provincial society. To translate economic and social desires into legislative action, they employed the petition or the ballot. Most of them were property

owners, and the suffrage act of 1721 required merely the ownership of 50 acres of land or the payment of 20 shillings taxes in
currency in order to vote. They also used the Grand Juries of the
two parishes which made up the town, St. Philip's and St.
Michael's, to make their sentiments more directly known to the
Commons House of the Assembly.

They also played a minor role in parochial affairs. As elected
Anglican vestrymen together with two wardens, always planters
and merchants, they oversaw the orphanage, pest house, the
parish schools, and the securing of clergymen. Artisans served in
the fire department, such as it was, and frequently performed as
constables. Sometimes one was appointed by the Commons
House as a wood and coal measurer of the market.

But no mechanic ever sat in the Commons House of Assembly
representing the town and their interests, even though many
could meet the necessary property qualifications. Before the
Revolution, in aristocratic British and Charleston society they
were regarded as socially inferior to merchants and planters
and unfit to manage affairs of state. The attitude of William
Drayton was typical: mechanics were "a useful and essential
part of society . . . but every man to his trade: a carpenter would
find himself put in an awkward situation on a cobbler's bench.
When a man acts in his own sphere, he is useful in the community, but when he steps out of it, and sets up for a statesmen
[*sic*], believe me he is in a fair way to expose himself to
ridicule. . . ."

And on the very eve of the Revolution, the assistant rector of
St. Michael's church declared from the pulpit that "every silly
Clown, and illiterate Mechanic [takes it upon himself] to cen-
sure the conduct of his Prince and Governor, and contribute,
as much as in him lies, to create and foment those misunder-
standings which . . . come at last to end in Schisms in the
Church, and sedition and rebellion in the State. . . .There is no
greater Instrument or Ornament of Peace than for every man to
keep his own rank, and to do his own duty in his own station
. . .," all of which created an uproar leading to the minister's
dismissal.

Lower class though they were, the mechanics became more
articulate during the years of revolution. In 1762, the upholsterer Edward Weyman founded the Fellowship Society, a
benevolent organization chiefly composed of mechanics and

concerned with building a hospital and other charitable works. Although the founders were the very same group who supported Gadsden at the time of the Stamp Act, no political pronouncements emanated from the society—at least nothing like this is contained in the earliest records of the organization. Yet to conclude that not a word of politics was uttered in their meetings would be unwise. The founder was one of the leading radical townsmen. Later in the 1760's, merchants of more conservative temperament gained admittance, but by then the mechanics appear prominently in such revolutionary societies as the John Wilkes Club or the Palmetto Society.

The mechanics vigorously opposed the Stamp Act. It was at this time that they cemented an alliance with Christopher Gadsden (the first man in the province to advocate independence), which lasted until 1778, when he broke with them for their continued rioting and other disturbances.

That they were enthusiatic followers of the program of the radicals of New England was reflected by Gadsden when he wrote Sam Adams that during the early days of the revolt many Charlestonians looked upon the "New England States with a kind of Horror, as artful designing Men altogether pursuing selfish purposes." "How often," he related, "I stood up in their Defence and only wish'd we would imitate instead of abusing them. . . . I thank'd God we had such a Systematical Body of men as an Asylum that honest men might resort to in the Time of their last Distress, supposing them driven out of their own States. I bless'd God there was such a People in America. That for my part I never look upon any danger from them. . . ."

In 1768, the mechanics supported John Wilkes for his *North Britain* No. 45 and the ninety-two anti-rescinders of Massachusetts Bay for their resistance to Royal authority. At a meeting which has been described as America's earliest political convention, they chose their political candidates for the Commons House, Gadsden among those selected, and then in the words of Peter Timothy, the rebel editor of the *South Carolina Gazette:*

. . . the company partook of a plain and hearty entertainment that had been provided by some upon whom this assembly will reflect lasting honour. About 5 O'Clock they all removed to a most noble LIVE OAK, in Mr. Mazyck's pasture, which they formally dedicated to LIBERTY, where many loyal, patriotic, and constitutional toasts were drank, beginning with the glorious NINETY-TWO Anti-Rescinders of Massachusetts-Bay, and ending with, unanimity among the members of our ensuing Assembly not to rescind from the said resolution [to boycott England], each succeeded by three huzzas. In the evening, the tree was decorated with 45 lights, and 45 sky-rockets were fired. About 8 O'Clock, the whole company, preceeded by 45 of their number, marched in regular procession to town, down King-street and Broad-street, to Mr. Robert Dillon's tavern; where the 45 lights being placed upon the table, with 45 bowls of punch, 45 bottles of wine, and 92 glasses, they spent a few hours in a new round of toasts, among which, scarce a celebrated Patriot of Britain or America was omitted; and preserving the same good order and regularity as had been observed throughout the day, at 10 they retired.

As indicated in the above, they were the first party to take steps against the Townshend Acts. Their influence grew as America and Britain moved toward war. So great had their power grown in 1769 that they were given equal representation with the planters and merchants when thirteen mechanics were elected to the Committee of Enforcement of the boycott. During this struggle they were adamant proponents of action prohibiting importation of British manufactures. When the merchants offered a program of non-importation which did not contain this prohibition, it drew the prompt response of: "A Mechanic": "How can it be expected, that any Planter, Mechanic, or other inhabitant . . . will subscribe to their Resolution . . . when THEY do not contain a single syllable *Encouraging American Manufactures*." The mechanics, with Gadsden's assistance, finally won their point at a meeting of the inhabitants under "Liberty Tree," and a non-importation program was accepted which satisfied them.

In 1775, with the colonies on the brink of war, and a British task force lying off Charleston harbor, the provincial radicals hoped to provoke attack. Two Tories were tarred and feathered by a mob turned loose by the rebellious aristocrat William Henry Drayton and upholsterer Edward Weyman. Gunner Walker of the British army received a "suit of Cloathes . . . without the assistance of a single Taylor," and as the mob carted its victim through the streets of the city, as a warning to everyone of royalist leaning, it passed by the Governor's house. There a bag of feathers was tossed to his balcony, and the mob "desired he would take care of it till his turn came." The unfortunate Gunner was forced to drink "Damnation to Lord North" with grog demanded of the chief magistrate. Walker was afterwards deposited at the door of his Majesty's surgeon general to Carolina forces, one Dr. Johnston-Milligan who had been pressed to declare his loyalty to the Americans by Weyman, Cannon, Johnson, and the carpenter, Fullerton. Artisans were also prominent in attacking the royal arsenals.

Why were the mechanics so enthusiatic in the cause of independence? In 1769, Gadsden answered this question:

> There are not wanting wealthy men amongst the . . . mechanics; yet in common their circumstances are but low; and oppression, when at its height, generally falls heaviest upon men, who have little beforehand, but depend, almost altogether upon their daily labour and industry, for the maintenance of themselves and families; it is no wonder, that throughout America, we find these men extremely anxious and attentive to the cause of liberty.

He continued that there was in America no great danger of starvation and that the mechanic here finds himself in a more comfortable situation than his European counterpart. "The distinctions . . . between the farmer and the rich planter, the mechanic and the rich merchant, being abundantly *more* here in imagination, than reality," but

> When oppression stalks abroad, then the case is widely different: For in arbitrary governments, tyranny generally descends, as it were, from rank to rank, through the people, til' almost the whole weight of it, at last, falls upon the honest, laborious farmer, mechanic, and day labourer. When this happens, it must make them poor indeed! And the very apprehension thereof, can not but cause extreme uneasiness. This, therefore, naturally accounts for these people, in particular, being united and steady, everywhere to prevent, if possible, being reduced to so dismal a situation: Which should it be unhappily the case, they can not but know, they must then see it out, and feel it out too, be it what may.

It was not entirely a question of forestalling poverty that motivated the ambitious Revolutionary mechanic, particularly the master. He wanted his man in the Assembly; this he won. When the first Provincial Congress convened, George Flagg, William Johnson, Edward Weyman, and Daniel Cannon were

therein seated, active in guiding the rebellion with radical planters and merchants. He desired "encouragement" for his manufactures. This he achieved in the form of a tax exemption on
his profits in trade. The Revolution, it seemed to him, eliminated
his overseas rival in London, Glasgow, Manchester, and other
English cities. In later years, he found himself again forgotten,
as cotton tied the South to the factories of England. But during
the Confederation, the Charleston mechanic identified himself
with fellow artisans in Boston, Philadelphia, and New York in
their intensive program for the support of manufactures, just as
he had agreed with the associations emanating from those cities
on the eve of the war. In 1788, at the ratifying convention for
the Constitution, the delegates Johnson, Cannon, and Sarrazin
voted for the Constitution. One suspects they were as favorably
disposed toward tariffs as Hamilton himself.

Thus were the Charleston mechanics a very important element. To the economy and to society in general, they were
essential, and in the history of the period they are significant.

III

The Pre-Industrial City

────────────

The years between the American Revolution and the Civil War witnessed the remarkable growth of cities in the United States. New urban centers sprang up in the trans-Appalachian West, matching the established seaport cities of the Atlantic coast in influence and importance. Stimulated by the combined impact of commercial prosperity, transportation innovations, new sources of population, and the beginnings of manufacturing, urban dominance spread throughout the nation.

Existing cities expanded at an astounding rate. During every decade from 1790 to 1860, with one exception (1810–1820), New York City's population increased by more than 50 per cent; it rose from about 33,000 at the beginning of the period to more than 800,000 by 1860. Likewise, Philadelphia rose from 42,000 in 1790 to above 565,000 by the Civil War. Brooklyn, a suburban village of less than 5000 in 1790, had become a bustling port of 280,000 by 1860, the nation's third largest urban center. Between 1790 and 1830 the population of Baltimore increased 497 per cent. With a more circumscribed hinterland than its competitors, Boston nevertheless maintained fifth place among American cities by mid-nineteenth century. In no other period did the seaport cities grow as rapidly.

Even more startling was the rise of new cities. The river towns—Pittsburgh, Cincinnati, Louisville, St. Louis, and New Orleans—"spearheaded" the westward movement, became regional market and manufacturing centers, and facilitated settlement of surrounding farmlands. With the completion of the "transportation revolution" the lake ports developed rapidly as well. Utilizing canal, and later railroad, connections to the East, cities like Buffalo, Cleveland, Detroit, Milwaukee, and Chicago quickly became important processing and distribution centers. These ten interior cities, which by 1860 ranged in size from about 45,000 to nearly 170,000, belie the rural nature of the westward movement and affirm the reality of urban importance in early America.

A variety of forces shaped the pre-Civil War American city. Clearly, commerce sustained urban growth in the early nineteenth century. Before 1830 participation in the world carrying trade and the export of American foodstuffs and cotton stimulated economic prosperity. Taking full advantage of a fine natural harbor and imaginative mercantile innovations (an economically efficient auction system and regularly scheduled shipping service to Europe), New Yorkers dominated overseas trade. New York merchants and insurance brokers aggressively won control of disposal of Southern cotton and thus came to monopolize the coastal carrying trade as well. And the success of the Erie Canal in tapping the produce of a vast hinterland securely established the commercial primacy of New York City.

The opening of the Erie route also set off a wave of transportation improvements which fostered urbanization east and west. Boosters in Boston, Baltimore, and Philadelphia, assisted in each case by municipal and state investment, reached into the interior with turnpikes and rival canal systems. The canal craze also captured town-site speculators and investors in the West, who laced Ohio, Indiana, and northern Illinois with man-made waterways which linked with the Great Lakes and the eastern routes. As urban competition intensified, railroads supplemented canals as agents of urban imperialism. Promoters in Charleston had built by 1833 the world's longest railroad, extending 136 miles into the cotton country of South Carolina and Georgia. Between 1840 and 1860 rails criss-crossed the Northeast and the West as urban rivalries facilitated the growth of a domestic market.

The completion of the transportation network turned cities increasingly toward production for internal consumption. After 1830 manufacturing began to replace commerce as the major activity of the coastal cities. By 1860 New York and Philadelphia had become the largest manufacturing centers in the nation, concentrating on production of cotton textiles, woolen goods, finished clothing, boots and shoes, and leather goods. Entrepreneurs in western cities processed local products and area resources, dominating particularly the flour milling, meat packing, and lumber industries. By the Civil War, Cincinnati ranked third in manufactures. The factory organization of work stimulated the growth of numerous smaller urban places as well. Lowell, Lawrence, Waltham, and Chicopee in Massachusetts, Bridgeport and Hartford in Connecticut, Rochester and Syracuse in New York, Newark, New Jersey, Richmond, Virginia, and Lexington, Kentucky, all grew on a manufacturing base. Specialization, division of labor, and the concomitant decline of household manufactures and locally oriented handicraft industries marked the end of the pre-industrial city by the 1850's.

While this economic transition took place, the social complexion of urban America changed as well. Immigration, for example, only a small stream at the beginning of the century, hit flood tide between 1840 and 1860, when more than four million newcomers arrived. Many immigrants, particularly those of German and Irish background, remained in the cities, where they added ethnic diversity and provided a pool of cheap labor. So powerful was this trans-Atlantic migration that by 1860 the foreign-born comprised 50 per cent or more of the populations of New York, Chicago, Milwaukee, St. Louis, and San Francisco. Reacting to both new industrial trends and rising numbers of immigrants, native artisans and craftsmen supported a strong trade union movement in the late 1820's and early 1830's. Its demise in succeeding depression years intensified economic stratification and lessened social mobility. When social, ethnic, religious, and racial tensions boiled over, the platitudes of "Jacksonian democracy" failed to prevent urban mobs from rioting in the streets of major American cities.

Other unsavory developments also reflected the growing disorder of the American city. Municipal governments failed to cope with a multiplicity of urban problems, city services lagged far behind residential demand. The urban poor crowded tenements, cellars, and shacks as racial and immigrant slums characterized the expanded, but unplanned, physical city. Inadequate facilities for sewage and garbage disposal made cities like New York, as former mayor Philip Hone said in 1832, "one huge pigsty." Indeed, in the absence of real municipal responsibility, roving pigs provided the most efficient method of urban street sanitation. Poor water supply and distorted medical conceptions rendered public health measures useless, and epidemics of yellow fever and cholera periodically ravaged the cities. Crime, prostitution, pauperism, alcoholism—all seemed to affirm the validity of Jeffersonian anti-urbanism.

Yet, if city life intensified, as Jefferson argued, "all the depravities of human nature," it displayed many attractive features as well. That urban centers fostered cultural and intellectual development provided part of the "lure of the city." "There can be no question," wrote New Yorker Henry P. Tappan in 1855, "that the association of men in cities is favorable to the highest development of humanity." An even more important urban magnet, economic opportunity, drew rural population and immigrants to the cities in large numbers. By the end of the pre-industrial period, Horace Greeley could write, "We cannot all live in cities, yet nearly all seem determined to do so."

THE WORKING CLASSES
OF THE
PRE-INDUSTRIAL CITY

DAVID MONTGOMERY

Labor historian David Montgomery examines the social history of the American worker in the seaport cities of the Northeast between 1780 and 1830. The author is Associate Professor of History at the University of Pittsburgh and Senior Lecturer in the History of American Labour at the University of Warwick, England.

In the years since Raymond W. Goldsmith submitted to Congress his statistical findings on the rise of per capita income in the United States many economic historians have come to date the beginnings of sustained industrial growth at some time during the 1830s. This chronology has provided historians of the working class with a significant bench-mark to guide their own research and analysis. Among other things it raises questions concerning the sources, size, and character of the labor supply which was at hand before the acceleration of economic growth and the ideological baggage (attitudes, customs, institutions) which the available workers carried with them when they entered the industrial era. The objective of this article is to suggest some parameters for both sets of questions derived from an examination of the working classes in the young nation's

From David Montgomery, "The Working Classes of the Pre-Industrial American City, 1780–1830," *Labor History*, IX (Winter 1968), 3–22. Copyright © 1968 by the Tamiment Institute. Reprinted by permission of the editor of *Labor History*.

four northern cities: Boston, New York, Philadelphia, and Baltimore.

During the five decades before 1830 these cities were essentially depots for trans-oceanic shipping, and their labor force
was largely tied to maritime commerce. Surrounding each of
them was "a vast scene of household manufacturing" where,
wrote Alexander Hamilton, country folk produced clothing,
shoes, and other necessities, "in many instances, to an extent not
only sufficient for the supply of the families in which they are
made, but for sale, and even, in some cases, for exportation."
Such a countryside Albert Gallatin found twenty years later in
New Hampshire, where the average farmer's house had at least
one spinning wheel, and every second house boasted a loom on
which from 100 to 600 yards of saleable cloth were woven
annually (at a time when journeymen weavers in their homes
averaged only 829 yards per year and factory looms, 1,111
yards). Most manufacturing, in other words, was carried on
outside of the major cities. By 1820 some 12 percent of the
nation's labor force was engaged in manufacturing and construction, and 28 percent in all non-agricultural occupations,
but at that time the residents of these cities and their contiguous
suburbs totalled only 356,452, or 3.7 percent of the American
people.

The merchant elite of these communities, furthermore, was
concerned not so much with hiring labor as with vending the
produce of labor, both agricultural and mechanical. Mathew
Carey went so far as to accuse the merchants of hostility toward
manufacturing interests, of striving "to impress upon the public
mind, that the national prosperity depended almost altogether on
commerce; that the protection of manufactures by duties on
imports was impolitic and unjust." Understandably the broad-
sides of Carey, Gallatin, Tench Coxe, and other promoters of
manufacturing bore the aspect of appeals to the dominant agricultural and commercial interests of the land to pay some heed
to the needs of industry and to believe that the growth of
domestic manufactures could take place without depriving
farmers and merchants of either manpower or customers.

But Carey's conception of the merchant as industry's relent-
less foe slighted the encouragement offered manufacturing by
the commercial city itself. The concentration of population in
seaports required by a growing flow of commerce prevented

urban residents from producing their own necessities in the fashion of farm families. It generated a social division of labor within the city itself and hence a need for sedentary artisans. The accumulation of merchant fortunes, furthermore, created a demand for luxury goods and thus for expert craftsmen: for silversmiths, goldbeaters, clockmakers, wig and peruke makers, printers of books and journals, tailors, and cordwainers familiar with European fashions and capable of reproducing them. By the end of the eighteenth century, moreover, seaboard merchants had opened a substantial oceanic trade in shoes, clothing, barrels, and ironwares with the regions of slave plantations. This trade encouraged the development of both the putting-out system and the early efforts toward factory organization of production.

Although most manufacturing was carried on outside the great urban centers, the seaport itself, therefore, generated a demand for labor in production as well as trade. In the eighteenth century most manufacture had been performed in the workshops of mechanics who, with the aid of family apprentices, and occasional journeymen, made the wares they vended themselves. The printer, for example, was usually a bookseller and a journalist as well, in the manner of Mathew Carey, who in the 1790s composed his own editorials in type and then hawked the paper about Philadelphia. Only after 1810 did urban newspapers gravitate into the hands of publishers who were not printers but, in the language of the journeymen, "speculators on the labor of printers" who installed "hireling editors" to write the columns printers now set in type.

The colonial conception of a journeyman as tomorrow's master mechanic was neither dead nor fully obsolete by 1820, for vertical mobility was still remarkable. Among the early members of the Franklin Typographical Association of New York, a trade society of journeymen founded in 1799, were David Bruce, the future owner of the city's largest printing shop and a pioneer typefounder; Thurlow Weed, a future boss of state politics; Samuel Woodworth, the poet of "Old Oaken Bucket" fame; and Peter Force, America's most eminent historical archivist. Two of the master shoemakers who testified against the cordwainers union in Philadephia's 1805 conspiracy trial were former journeymen and union members, as were two of the employers at the similar Pittsburgh trial ten years later.

But by the first two decades of the nineteenth century the emergence of distinct societies of journeymen and of masters among printers, tailors, shoemakers, carpenters, stone cutters, and other trades in every seaport indicated a new awareness of distinct class interests. The seventeen benevolent societies of Philadelphia carpenters, ship masters, stone cutters, and other trades listed by James Mease in 1811 were clearly organizations of master mechanics. Their initiation fees ranging from $10 up and their annual dues of four or five dollars contrast remarkably with the one dollar initiation and the 25 cents monthly dues (waived after ten years' membership) charged by that city's printers union. Societies of journeymen that sought to combine benevolent functions with the enforcement of union wage scales ultimately found it necessary to either expel members who had risen to the rank of employers, or to succumb to the urgings of "alimoners" in their midst and abandon the effort to regulate trade conditions. Thus the printers' organizations in Philadelphia and Boston during the 1820s converted themselves into friendly societies open to employers and workmen alike, while the New York society, bent on controlling wages and aware that "the interests of the journeymen are separate and in some respects opposite to those of the employers," resolved in 1817 "that when any member of this society shall become an employing printer he shall be considered without the limits of this society."

The myth of harmonious personal relationships among masters, journeymen, and apprentices in a setting of domestic paternalism may be quite anachronistic when applied to post-Revolutionary decades. Ian Quimby's study of apprentice contracts in eighteenth century Philadelphia revealed a persistent erosion of filial duties and loyalties by the emerging ethos of commercialism. The mutual moral obligations of apprentices and masters in such matters as work expected of the boy, and the education and clothing due him were converted over the course of the century into money values and specified in ever-increasing detail in the contracts. The experience of cabinetmakers, furthermore, suggests that journeymen seldom remained long enough with any master to develop a sense of personal attachment. The journeymen of Samuel Ashton's Philadelphia cabinet shop between 1795 and 1803 averaged scarcely six months in his employ. So rapid was the turnover of craftsmen that, though

Ashton rarely needed more than five workmen at a time, forty-nine different men worked for him during those eight years. Under such circumstances class antagonisms based on chronic disputes over wages could be quite consistent with a high level of upward social mobility.

By the 1820s, therefore, the urban working classes comprised recognizable and self-conscious elements of urban society. The "classes . . . who are wholly dependent upon wages," wrote Reverend Joseph Tuckerman, "are very numerous" and, he continued:

would, indeed, be numerous, if we looked for them among only those who have no trade, and who are generally distinguished alone, as labouring men. This large division includes shop, market, and other porters; carmen; those who are employed in lading, and un-lading vessels; wood-sawyers; hod carriers; house servants; those employed by mechanics in a single branch of their business; and multitudes, who are men and women of any work, occasionally required in families, as washing, scouring, etc.; or on the wharves, or in the streets of the city. Besides these, the number is great of those, who are journeymen, and many of whom will never be anything but journeymen, in the various mechanic arts; and considerable numbers are also employed in the different departments of large manufactories, who possess no capital; and who know, and will continue to know, little or nothing in any other department of these establishments, except that in which they are themselves employed. All these, in the strictest sense, and in the common acceptation of the term, are dependent on the wages which they obtain for their services.

Tuckerman's definition of the wage earning classes suggests that journeymen, mechanics, casual laborers, and factory operatives must be analyzed separately. Even though many mechanics would "never be anything but journeymen," they enjoyed the highest incomes and status of any wage earners and were psychologically the most firmly wedded to the social values and practices of the traditional artisan. Apprenticeship was the historic route of access to "the art and mysteries" of any trade, and the journeymen of this period strove to bar any other avenue of entry. The Philadelphia Typographical Society, which sought with occasional success to reserve all printing positions in town for its own members, excluded from membership anyone "who shall not have served an apprenticeship satisfactory to

the board of directors" of the union, and subsequently tried to
keep from the presses anyone who had "broken into the trade"
after he was twenty-one years old. Both the income and the
honor associated with the printer's art were thus to be reserved
to those who elected to ply it when they first attained the age
of productive manhood at fifteen or sixteen years old. Altogether Philadelphia's complete records of apprentices bound
between October 1771 and October 1773 revealed 1,075 youths
apprenticed to sixty-eight trades (including many girls indentured to learn "housewifery"). Ten percent of them were to
learn the cordwainer's art, and the trades of tailor, mariner,
carpenter, and cooper followed shoemaking in order of preference.

Sons of mechanics apprenticed to trades were supplemented
by those of farmers who, for example, constituted the bulk of
Massachusetts' supply of shoemakers, and in Baltimore by young
slaves. The emancipation of northern slaves meant the eclipse
of Negro apprenticeship in most urban trades elsewhere. Because the training of slave craftsman had rarely been complete,
freed Negro artisans, who faced intense animosity from white
craftsmen and had lost the protection of their masters, rarely
survived in positions where they could train apprentices of their
own race, and even fewer whites would engage black youth
for training. The influx of white farm boys to urban trades, on
the other hand, was inhibited by that "desire of being an independent proprietor of land" which Alexander Hamilton believed
would always keep small the number of those "who would be
diverted from it towards manufacturers." Youth who did elect
urban trades, furthermore, often fled their apprenticeships after
only a year or two of service and, to the great distress of established journeymen, easily found employment as half-trained
workmen at substandard wages. The supply of labor was thus
rapidly increased at the expense of its quality. The founding of
mechanics' institutes (vocational schools) in every major northern city in the 1820s bears witness to the breakdown of traditional apprenticeship training.

The fact remains that residents of rural areas in the Northeast
were being lured toward the city, just as others were migrating
westward, and frequently such migrants had been craftsmen,
rather than (or as well as) farmers. In every decade between
1790 and 1840, the population of all four cities under review

grew at a rate substantially above the 33 percent to 36 percent growth for the nation as a whole, with two exceptions: both Philadelphia and New York grew at less than the national rate between 1810 and 1820, and Baltimore's increase after 1820 was chronically below the national pace. This urbanization of native Americans was supplemented by the arrival of European immigrants, but the extent of the trans-oceanic contribution to the growth of these seaports is difficult to measure. Although newcomers to America totalled 400,000 between 1790 and 1830, with 1801-1807, 1816 and 1828-1830 being the years of greatest influx, the bulk of them came not to the American seaport but through it. It was the demand for farm laborers in the hinterland which produced, for example, the large scale trafficking in redemptioners Frances Wright witnessed in the Philadelphia of 1818.

Among the immigrants who tarried in the city, however, were many skilled mechanics. British emigrants and British trade union practices (complete to the oaths sworn over union scales and the trappings of secrecy necessitated in the old country by the Combination Acts but retained here as a matter of custom) showed up in every conspiracy trial of union journeymen. When the prosecutor charged Philadelphia cordwainers in 1805 with "crimes" committed by union members a decade earlier, the defense replied with only slight exaggeration that none of the journeymen on trial had been in America when those acts were committed. Stocking weavers in Germantown and Kensington outside of Philadelphia had almost all learned their trade in Leicester or Nottingham or the Rhineland. Linen weavers had poured out of northern Ireland in the early 1770s and again at the close of the American Revolution, many of them coming to the new republic. In 1784 alone 11,000 passengers embarked from Dublin, most of them emigrants of this type.

An extreme case of immigrants' providing an industry with its skilled labor was offered by the thousand or so carpet weavers in the country in the early 1830s, at least nine-tenths of whom were Scots, largely from Kilmarnock and Ayr. So well did these mechanics know each other that when sixty-three of them struck the Thompsonville Carpet Manufacturing Company in Connecticut, they quickly assembled, compiled from memory a list of the eleven other principal carpet manufactories in the nation, wrote personal letters to friends in each of them explaining the dispute, notified the Blue Bonnet Tavern in New York City, which served as the country's hiring hall for carpet weavers, to divert men from the struck plant, and dispatched an appeal to the *Old Countryman* in that city to warn off any Scots not reached by the other methods.

Such incidents suggest the hypothesis that America was then a land of opportunity for handicraftsmen whose skills were being undermined by the industrial revolution in England but still in high demand in the more backward American economy. True, the number of handloom weavers and stockingers working in England continued to grow rapidly down to 1820 and perhaps beyond, despite the unmistakeable deterioration of income and status in those trades. Many older craftsmen, Arthur Redford found, moved to manufacturing cities in England, there continuing to ply their obsolete trade while depending increasingly on the earnings of their factory-employed children. The Scottish carpet weavers brought to trial in Connecticut for their strike, however, were remarkably young men, twenty-two years of age or less. The presumption is that the craftsman-immigrant tended to be neither the daring innovator nor the veteran artisan who could not quit his obsolescent trade, but the mobile youth who spurned Britain's factory for the possibility of plying the (to him) preferable family trade in a new location.

This hypothesis is consistent with Hamilton's belief that "the disparity" between the "dearness of labor" in America and that in England was "much less in regard to artificers and manufacturers, than in regard to country labourers," a belief recently concurred in by H. J. Habakkuk and Stuart Bruchey. During the first two decades of the nineteenth century skilled tradesmen in England engaged in "hounourable work" (a high quality work not yet subjected to a division of labor and deterioration of apprenticeship standards) looked upon 30s. weekly ($7.50) as an expected income, while some earned £3 and over. Such a 30s. standard fell below the $8.25 of an American shoemaker or the $9 a more seasonal carpenter might ordinarily have expected when working at union standards by precisely the differential of 12 percent-20 percent in America's favor which J. Leander Bishop found for glass workers. True, American workmen paid considerably fewer taxes than their English counterparts, and as D. B. Warden observed of Philadelphia,

"Smiths, shoemakers, weavers, and tailors have generally one or two acres of land, which afford pasture for a cow, fuel, and esculent plants." But such bucolic benefits were by no means unknown to English weavers, croppers, and shoemakers, most of whom still worked in their cottages in rural villages.

Far more extreme was the contrast between the American municipal or canal laborer's expectation of some $4.50 a week (often paid partly in board) and the earnings of the English casual laborer, which then ranged from perhaps 11s. weekly in cotton factories to 1s. a day for wheelbarrow men in Birmingham. Taking 10s. (i.e., $2.50) as good weekly pay for such laborers in the second decade of the century, the unskilled American enjoyed a premium of 80 percent over his British counterpart. That the wage differential was less rather than greater for the artisan than for casual labor is thus evident even without investigation of the real values of money wages in the two countries. Yet British craftsmen did migrate, spurred by the deteriorating conditions in their trades at home and lured, as one emigrant manual declared, by the openings in American trades left by "the strong emulation of the *cute* native Yankee to elevate himself above the common labour class."

Whether graduates of American or British apprenticeships, urban tradesmen were both geographically mobile enough and sufficiently well informed about the state of the labor market elsewhere to maintain rather uniform wage standards throughout the northeastern cities. When Philadelphia shoemakers demanded a schedule of prices based on $4 a pair for back strap boots in October 1805, they were aware that the New York union had established precisely that scale in March. Similarly, when Pittsburgh shoemakers unionized at the end of that decade, they quickly drove up their prices from 75 cents below the Philadelphia wage to parity with it—but when they sought a scale higher than Philadelphia's, they were roundly defeated by their masters. Both the New York and Washington societies of printers undertook—by correspondence with their counterparts in Philadelphia, Baltimore, Boston, and Albany—to establish uniform scales, and all these societies exchanged "rat lists" with each other, so that typographers who violated union rules and standards could not find refuge in other communities. At times employers cooperated with these efforts of the journeymen, as did master printers in New York in 1815, or, more dramatically,

the master weavers of Baltimore, who in 1829 did everything in
their power to ostracize a fellow employer for slashing his
journeymen's wages below the city norm.

Although the mechanic was ranked by Tuckerman within
the wage-earning classes, there is little evidence that prior to
the 1830s he either identified himself with "the poor" or felt in
any way alienated from the existing social order. Despite the
absence from common American parlance of the rigid British
distinction between "honourable" and "dishonourable" work,
only the scale of the New York shoemakers out of all the union
price lists which have been preserved from that period (mainly
those of printers, shoemakers, tailors, and weavers) included a
specified wage for coarse work, partially completed work, or
the work of helpers. While the Pittsburgh shoemakers union
did explicitly deem coarse work "out of society" and posed no
objections to non-members performing such tasks, there is no
such clear evidence from any of the seaport cities. It is remarkable, however, that the prosecutor in the New York shoemakers'
trial, while conceding that many journeymen were not members, insisted that "all the best workmen were in the society."
Similarly Philadelphia shoemakers considered themselves fully
unionized between 1798 and 1804, when their society had 100
to 150 members, while the city directory for 1798 listed 292
shoemakers and cordwainers. A plausible inference is that cheap
shoes for slaves and for auction sale, which did not appear in the
union's scale of prices, were deliberately relegated to inferior
workmen whom the society made no effort to recruit.

The mechanics proudly preserved an ideological heritage
blended of Ben Franklin's maxims and Tom Paine's "rights of
man." The best local legal talent defended their societies in the
several conspiracy trials to which they were subjected, as witness Philadelphia's shoemakers enlisting Caesar Rodney, whom
President Jefferson was soon to appoint Attorney General of
the United States. When seventeen years earlier that city's
mechanics had paraded with their masters in joyous celebration
of the ratification of the federal constitution, they had borne
such emblems as "the weavers' flag, a rampant lion in a green
field, holding a shuttle in his dexter paw—motto—'*may the
government* protect us,'" the boat builders' flag (atop the
thirty-three foot schooner *Federal Union* drawn down Market
Street for the occasion) bearing "an axe and an adze crossing

each other—motto, 'by these we live,' " or the bricklayers' flag, with "the federal city rising out of a forest, workmen building it, and the sun illuminating it," motto, *both buildings and rulers are the works of our hands.*' " At the close of the procession, bakers distributed bread to the poor, victuallers slew their "two stately oxen" and gave away the meat, and millers provided the needy with flour. The best printers could do was to read the destitute a poem, but clearly the citizen craftsmen were dispensers, not recipients, of charity.

Very different was the outlook of the impoverished residents of the Rittenhouse Square vicinity, who petitioned the Philadelphia city council in 1830 to halt the dumping in the square of offal swept from neighboring streets, "which being in heaps, occasions numerous ponds of stagnant and putrescent water in the immediate spots, which in summer send forth pestilential vapours wafted by every breeze to the dwellings of your petitioners, whose only comfort, health, is thus destroyed." These poor argued that "being of the working class, their whole time is indispensably employed in various labour to maintain their families," so that sickness is "a scourge the most severe." Here was a group whose annual incomes ranged far closer to $200 than to $400 or $425 expected by craftsmen, a group who Reverend Tuckerman feared "have lived, and to a great extent are living, as a *caste*,—cut off from those in more favoured circumstances; and doomed to find their pleasures, and sympathy in their sufferings, alone among themselves."

The seaport poor were by no means a new phenomenon at the end of the 1820s. James Henretta has clearly traced their emergence in eighteenth-century Boston as a function of the growth of overseas commerce. He discovered from the Boston tax rolls of 1687 that only 14 percent of the adult male population of the city, that is, 188 men, were neither "dependent" nor owners of property. In contrast to them stood the 17 percent of the adult males who as servants, apprentices, or participants in family home enterprise were classified as dependent. The propertied classes numbered 1,036 (69 percent of the adult males) and included 521 poor craftsmen, 275 artisans of the "middling sort" with two or three journeymen apiece, and the wealthier tradesmen, professionals, and merchants. By 1771 only 10 percent of the adult males were dependent in the traditional sense, while 29 percent were neither dependent nor propertied.

These were wage earners in the full meaning of the term, and while the city's population had doubled between the two counts, their number had increased fourfold. They ranged in occupation from seamen and longshoremen at one end of the scale to journeymen at the other, but, while the latter ranked close to the small property-holding mechanic, the division of wealth between the upper and lower halves of property owners was far sharper than had been the case in the seventeenth century.

Most day laborers participated directly in transportation and commerce. It was the demand for seamen, longshoremen, carters, and domestic servants which absorbed unskilled wage earners already in the eighteenth century. By the early nineteenth century, construction work, wood cutting, and road building employed many, while thousands of Philadelphia's poor, Mathew Carey found, "travel hundreds of miles in quest of employment on canals at 62½, 75 and 87½ cents per day, paying a dollar and a half or two dollars per week for their board, leaving families behind, depending on them for support." By 1830 Carey estimated "labourers, hodmen, seamstresses, families of workmen on canals and rail-roads" at 40 percent of the working classes and 25 percent of the total population of Philadelphia.

Many laborers reached the city from the farm by way of the sea. The merchant fleet of Massachusetts, wrote Samuel Eliot Morison, "was manned by successive waves of adventure-seeking boys, and officered by such of them as determined to make the sea their calling." The great majority on the crew lists professed "to be native-born Yankees, and probably were." Seamen would register with federal revenue agents after 1796 and receive, for a fee of 25 cents, papers certifying their United States citizenship. Between that year and 1812, 106,757 seamen collected their papers, and of them only 1,530, or 1.4 percent, were naturalized citizens. The registrations reported for the years after 1808 were certainly still incomplete, for district revenue collectors were very tardy in submitting their reports to Washington. The fact that registration was heaviest in years such as 1797 and 1805, when the danger of British impressment was most severe, indicates that enrollment was never very thorough. These figures, nevertheless, can suggest the large number of native Americans who took to the sea.

So high were the rates of promotion, death, and desertion that the man who spent more than twelve years before the mast was rare indeed. No other occupation offered an unskilled farmboy so great an opportunity to rise quickly in wealth and standing— or to topple from yardarm into the cold Atlantic. Few seamen dwelt long in any port, but while ashore they augmented the local casual labor supply significantly. Illustrative of their role was young Charles Erskine, whose mother moved to Boston in the early 1820s after his father (a currier) had deserted her. Playing about the docks, Erskine heard the tales of sailors and through them was lured to sea. Between voyages he and his mates earned their keep ashore by whatever employment was available wherever they happened to be. He once helped construct an aqueduct in Washington and at another time worked in a Philadelphia hook and eye factory.

In marked contrast to the artisan's tendency to ply for life the trade he had learned in his adolescence, the laborer was the epitome of versatility. To move from sea to canal digging to hod carrying to factory work was well within the realm of possibility. Many of the half-trained journeymen and "botches" who bedevilled mechanics' efforts to retain high quality and wage standards were of this sort. New England's first factory to use cotton spinning machinery, founded in Beverly, Massachusetts, in 1787, wasted precious quantities of material in training its workmen, then was driven close to ruin when it had to raise wages to prevent its partly-taught employees from deserting to rival firms. Mercifully, perhaps, the factory burned down in 1808. A happier experience with such labor was reported by a cotton mill near Providence, which employed fifty-three workers in the factory and 125 on putting-out by 1810. The owners, reported Albert Gallatin, at first suffered "in being put to much expense by English workmen, who pretended to much more knowledge in the business than they really possessed." But the phony Samuel Slaters were discharged, "and Americans, as apprentices, &c. are getting the art very fast," though the company did not anticipate dividends "for a considerable time."

The fact that machine operatives could be trained made the "factory controversy" of this period focus not on the fate of the workers, as was to be the case in the 1830s and 1840s, but on the potential impact of manufacturing upon the nation's supply of farm labor. Wages of farm hands, Henry Carey re-

ported, were higher in the vicinity of the cities than in more
rustic settings. Whether this differential in money wages was a
sign of competition from urban employments or simply an
indication that the market economy was more mature near the
cities (that a smaller portion of the farm laborer's income was
paid in kind and more in cash than was the case to the West) is
not clear. Whichever it meant, advocates of governmental aid
to manufactures fom Coxe through Carey felt obliged to echo
Hamilton's famous assurance that manufacturing would not
attract able-bodied men away from the land, that it would rather
"afford occasional and extra employment to industrious individuals and families," through which farmers could profit by
the home produce of their wives and daughters, and provide
steady employment for "persons who would otherwise be idle,
and in many cases a burthen on the community," and render
women and children "more useful, and the latter more early
useful . . . than they should otherwise be."

At this period, therefore, it was impossible to speak of the
factory labor force without directing attention to women, children, and charitable institutions. This was the case long before
the mills of Lowell arose. Philadelphia's first large-scale use of
spinning jennies were undertaken by the United Company of
Philadelphia for Promoting American Manufactures, founded
by patriotic subscriptions in 1775. By the late 1780s it employed 400 women, most of them recruited from the city's
poor rolls. Despite the pride with which the Society displayed
a jenny of eighty spindles in the Federal Procession of 1788, and
boasted that the woman operating it was "a native of and instructed in this city," the company's building was destroyed by
an arsonist only two years later. Newly inaugurated President
Washington found a similar labor force when he visited a Boston
sail duck factory. Here pairs of little girls spun and wove flax
from eight in the morning until six at night, but their demeanor
favorably impressed the President, who described them as
"daughters of decayed families" and "girls of character—none
others are admitted."

Two decades later the Secretary of the Treasury reported
that eighty-seven cotton mills then in operation or about to
commence operations in the United States needed a labor force
of about 500 men and 3,500 women and children. Such a work
force was for Gallatin proof positive that manufacturing need
not lure men from the farm. Tench Coxe agreed:

Female aid in manufactures, which prevents the diversion of men and boys from agriculture, has greatly increased. Children are employed, as well as the infirm and the crippled. The asylums of the poor and unfortunate, and the penitentiaries of indiscretion and immorality are improved and aided by the employment and profits of manufactures.

The markets of seamstresses were especially crowded with unmarried and widowed women, not to speak of those whose husbands were "travelling"—in the informal divorce procedure of the day. When such women bid on sewing work, they competed with both married women trying to supplement their own families' meager incomes and recipients of work relief. While female operatives in Philadelphia factories earned two or three dollars a week in the 1820s, seamstresses rarely surpassed $1.25, and the city's home relief system helped keep those earnings low. In slack seasons so many women applied to the Provident Society and other charities for work to tide them over that the scale offered by almshouses became, during the 1820s, the standard price offered by private firms. Thus the U.S. War Department offered seamstresses 12½ cents a shirt, the very wage given by the Provident Society. In reply to a plea that such a price reduced the seamstress "to the degradation of pauperism," the Secretary of War termed the subject "of such delicacy, and so intimately connected with the manufacturing interests and the general prices of this kind of labour in the city of Philadelphia" that he dared not change his Department's practice.

While the seamstress stood with one foot in the poor house, this was not the case with the weaver, for in the urban areas most cloth was still put out to families with handlooms. The city and county of Philadelphia in 1809 produced 65,326 yards of cloth in its six factories on both hand and power looms, but its home production amounted to 233,232 yards. Furthermore, the spinning mills, while they continued to be staffed primarily by women and children, tended to free themselves by the second decade of the century from dependence on public charities. The reason is that unmarried women, widows, and orphaned families gravitated toward them by free choice.

Especially was this the case in New England, where the textile mill became a means of emancipation for the "maiden aunts" who lived with so many of the region's families. In Massachusetts the 1810 male population under the age of sixteen outnumbered females of the same age in the ratio of 104 to 100. Between the ages of sixteen and forty-five, however, the proportions were reversed. During the marrying season (ages sixteen through twenty-five) there were 103 women for every 100 men, but in the post twenty-six age of the spinster, women outnumbered men by a ratio of 107 to 100. And Massachusetts had 3,335 more women of that age than it had men. Theirs was the choice, at best, of boarding with parents, or a married sister, or entering a mill. Since the loss of males was a result of the westward movement, it would seem that, as far as New England's early textile industry is concerned, the famous "safety-valve" worked in reverse. The migration of men to the West created a surplus of female labor in the East.

Neither New York State nor Pennsylvania exhibited such an imbalance of the sexes, for both were receiving substantial immigration, and considerable westward movement still occurred within their boundaries. But within the cities of New York and Philadelphia free white women between the ages of sixteen and twenty-five sharply outnumbered the men of the same age. The New York ratio in 1820, for example, was 119 women to 100 men in that age bracket, while in Philadelphia women of this marriageable age outnumbered men 122 to 100. Similarly, the Boston ratio was 127 to 100, and that of Baltimore 108 to 100. Although the terrible toll of childbirth, among other hazards, more than corrected the balance of the sexes in all four cities after the age of twenty-six, each of the seaports was naturally provided with a sizeable force of women for whom there was no prospect of marriage and for whom entry into the labor market was a necessity.

Each of these groups of city workers of the pre-industrial epoch (journeymen mechanics, male laborers, and women) merits careful historical study. Little new work has been done in this area since David J. Saposs contributed his chapters to John R. Commons' *History of Labour in the United States* in 1917, and because of this deficiency the labor historian's view of this period has fallen seriously out of phase with that of the economic historian. For example, Saposs' contention that "the wages of the unskilled were going up while those of the skilled were kept down by the merchant-capitalist" in the century's first two decades finds no support in the wage data of this article or in recent economic studies.

The problem assumes considerable significance in the light of George Rogers Taylor's hypothesis that per capita income in America declined rather steadily between 1807 and the early 1830s. The impact of such a trend could logically have been different for mechanics, for factory operatives, for casual laborers, and for women sewing in their rented rooms. Only specific studies of particular groups of workers can yield conclusive data on the standard of living. Jackson Turner Main and James Henretta have shown that enough evidence exists in tax rolls, judicial records, and the press of the eighteenth century to enable the historian to reconstruct patterns of property and income distribution quite clearly. Their work challenges other historians to trace the evolution of these patterns in early nineteenth century city life and to reduce their reliance on impressionistic evidence.

Still greater is the need for research into the cultural and intellectual life of the working classes of this period. We need to know what the urban poor expected of life, how they reacted to the commercial ethos of their cities, and how they conceived their relationship to the governing merchant elites. Were they, as some historians have recently portrayed the poor of Naples or London, simultaneously devoted to the traditional social order, aware of their power as a mob, confident the city would care for them in times of want, and profoundly hostile toward the emerging impersonal and amoral market economy? Was it such a mentality which made some 200 assembled New York sailors, idled by the embargo, respond obediently when Mayor Marinus Willet commanded them to disperse, with assurances that the embargo was "the *Captain's Orders*," and that the city would "do everything possible for your relief"? Such questions cannot yet be answered because a fixation on the clash of "agrarian" and "industrial" values has distracted us from exploring pre-industrial urban values and customs.

Similarly American historians have yet to probe the culture of the American mechanic as, say, E. P. Thompson did for his British counterpart. Our concern has been either with the journeyman's economic circumstances (where there is still much to be learned) or with whether he voted for Andrew Jackson (and may we be spared that debate for a while). Because the mechanics were frequently organized and far more articulate than the urban poor, research into the mind of the journeyman should prove relatively easy. The ideas suggested in this article need careful testing, to begin with, and beyond them lie several major issues for research. How open was economic mobility for the journeymen, and what changes did the post-Revolutionary generation experience in this regard? Why did this class provide most of the country's early nineteenth century adherents to deism, and just how widespread and significant was infidelity among them? What new circumstances made craftsmen in every major city between 1827 and 1837 expand the horizons of their concern beyond the limits of their own trades, create city Trades' Unions as new institutions to fuse the efforts of the several crafts, undertake unprecedented united action with the unskilled laborers, giving rise to something worthy of the name labor movement?

These problems suggest that we have rushed ahead to evaluate labor's response to industrialism without first ascertaining labor's pre-industrial behavior and attitudes. In exploring the shock of change after the Civil War our attention has been directed half a century too late, and our concern with the fate of agrarian values has led us to ignore the impact of the spreading factory system on the cultural heritage of urban America's lower orders.

IMMIGRANTS AND
TENEMENTS IN
NEW YORK CITY, 1825–1863

ROBERT ERNST

Robert Ernst, Professor of History at Adelphi University, describes social consequences of urbanization which particularly affected the living conditions of Irish and German immigrants in the middle years of the nineteenth century.

As New York's wharves became crowded with warehouses amid a scene of noisy and ceaseless activity, the wealthier inhabitants moved elsewhere, and their homes passed into the hands of boardinghouse keepers and of real estate agents. White-collar employees and workingmen, finding it necessary to live near the docks, warehouses, stores, and workshops, occupied these old dwellings and found them a blessing. However, as property values rose in the lower wards, rents were raised, and those tenants who could afford it followed their former proprietors into the upper wards. The rest sought cheaper quarters in the old neighborhood.

To meet the demand for rooms and apartments, owners and agents converted old homes into tenements by erecting partitions for the accommodation of three or more families. Unscrupulous owners made room for more by dividing their space into "the smallest proportions capable of containing human life within four walls." Beginning in the thirties, immigrant families

From Robert Ernst, *Immigrant Life in New York City, 1825–1863* (New York: King's Crown Press, 1949), pp. 48–60. Copyright 1949 by Robert Ernst. Reprinted by permission of the author. Footnotes omitted.

poured into these reconstructed buildings, the Irish becoming their principal occupants, although in some houses Negroes crowded "from cellar to garret." Thus appeared the first stage in the development of the modern New York slum.

Housing facilities could not keep pace with the incoming tide of foreign workingmen and their families, and the insistent demand for shelter at low rentals resulted in the development of a second type of tenement. When owners discovered that converted dwellings yielded substantial profit in rents, they constructed new buildings designed especially as tenement houses. Usually such a building contained a narrow hall opening from a street or court; on each floor, including the cellar, two suites of rooms opened into the hall. Front and rear rooms of the building contained windows, but the bedrooms and closets in the middle were dark. In most cases there was another tenement in the back yard, frequently altogether enclosed and accessible only through an alley. Alongside these buildings and in the yards were many little, irregular frame structures, some in dilapidated condition, serving partly as sheds and partly as homes for the overflow of the tenements. Such haphazard combinations of front and rear buildings on the same lot created an intricate array of rear courts and alleys, notoriously dark, foul-smelling, and encumbered with accumulations of filth.

As immigration intensified the housing shortage, the insistent demand for rooms and apartments induced owners to rent basements, attics, and even lofts and stables to eager but poor homeseekers. In the seven wards below Canal Street, the gross density of population per acre climbed from 94.5 persons in 1820 to 163.5 in 1850, while the average block density increased from 157.5 to 272.5 in the same period. In the Seventh Ward, with a large Irish population, and the Tenth Ward, which included many Irish and Germans, the average block density rose from 54.5 persons per acre in 1820 to 170.9 in 1840.

A considerable number of immigrants moved into cellars, where rents were cheaper and where, consequently, diverse ages, sexes, races, and nationalities crowded together. In 1843, 7,196 persons were living in cellars. During the great waves of Irish and German immigration, the basement population expanded so that by the middle of the century about twenty-nine thousand persons were living underground. Thereafter, the number of cellar residences decreased as newer and larger tenements were built, and by 1863 it was estimated that only eighteen thousand persons lived in cellars. Typical of overcrowded cellars was a house in Pike Street which contained a cellar ten feet square and seven feet high, with one small window and an old-fashioned inclined cellar door; here lived two families consisting of ten persons of all ages. The occupants of these basements led miserable lives as troglodytes amid darkness, dampness, and poor ventilation. Rain water leaked through cracks in the walls and floors and frequently flooded the cellars; refuse filtered down from the upper stories and mingled with the seepage from outdoor privies. From such an abode emerged the "whitened and cadaverous countenance" of the cellar dweller.

Population could expand only northward on Manhattan Island. This limitation increased the competition for apartments in an area of already inflated property values and drove rentals upward. Immigrants who had lived in cities in the Old World resented the high rents which they were forced to pay and cried out bitterly against the rapacity of landlords. Disillusioned about the city's living conditions, an English workman grumbled that for a New York room with bare, whitewashed walls and no sanitary facilities, the rent was double that in London. As middle-class private dwellings disappeared, the clerical workers and artisans also relapsed into tenement lives.

Tenement houses were rented by the week or month. Many an owner was enriched by charging $3.00 to $13.00 per month for apartments, and seventy-five cents to $1.25 per week for single rooms twelve feet square. In this system of rent gouging, the chief figure was an agent, or sublandlord, who leased a house or group of houses for several years. The owner thereby was assured of an income and relieved of responsibility for direct supervision of tenants, while the agent collected the rents and sometimes saved enough money to purchase the property in a short time. Since the agent was a speculator whose interest was to make as large a profit as he could, he thought in terms of risk and reimbursement, not of tenant welfare. "He measures rooms, and estimates—not their capacities for accommodating human life in health and comfort—but their capability of containing human life to pay the rent."

Despite the fact that many poor tenants frequently moved about in response to changing employment conditions, they were conscientious about paying their rent. The reason was fear of eviction. This possibility placed the tenant at the mercy of the landlord and put rent before fuel and clothing. For those who had acquired a small amount of personal property, the consequences of eviction were disastrous. A wife's property could be seized as well as her husband's and sold on execution for his nonpayment of rent. Only such items as necessary food and clothing, cooking utensils and tableware, fuel for sixty days, a few pieces of furniture, the family pictures, and a few books, including the Bible, were exempt from levy or sale. To insure that rents would be paid, some landlords maintained blacklists of delinquent tenants; evicted persons thus found it difficult to rent new homes.

Newspapers, both native and foreign-language, were full of protests against evictions and high rents. They reported spontaneous meetings of lodgers to combat the inhumanity of the landlords and the raising of rents. At a mass meeting in 1848, tenants demanded that the legislature limit profit in rents to 7 per cent on assessed valuation and put a stop to the practice of ejecting one paying tenant in order to rent to another. They called for a city tax of 3 per cent on all unimproved lots. A proposition before the legislature was condemned as tending to encourage the combination of capital for the suppression of the poor. Finally, the formation of a lodgers' league was urged to protect the interests of the tenants against property owners and their agents.

The wide gulf between tenants and owners was emphasized by the unhealthy physical aspects of tenement life. To the immigrant who had been a city dweller in Europe it was no novelty to settle in apartments which lacked proper lighting and ventilation, but the peasant from rural Ireland or southern Germany was forced to make a difficult adjustment to living conditions in New York. Instead of the fresh country air, he breathed the foul miasma of cramped and insalubrious quarters; instead of the surrounding daylight of farm and field, there was little but gloom and darkness. Daylight rarely entered more than one of the two or three rooms in the apartments of the poor, and cross ventilation was usually an impossibility. Samuel Gompers, the immigrant cigar maker and future labor leader, wrote:

Our apartment in Sheriff Street was a typical three-room home. The largest, the front room, was a combined kitchen, dining-room, and sitting-room with two front windows. There were two small bedrooms back, which had windows opening into the hall. We got water from a common hydrant in the yard and carried it upstairs. The toilet was in the yard also.

When water for bathing and washing had to be fetched from street pumps or near-by wells, bodily cleanliness was more of an ideal than a reality. Not only was it impossible to bathe, but insufficient space and air hindered home laundering. To overcome this situation, private philanthropy erected a "People's Washing and Bathing Establishment" in Mott Street in the early fifties. A few years later a *Verein* was formed to crusade for free baths for the German working population. All such ventures failed, however; it is likely that most immigrants bathed in the Hudson, East, or Harlem rivers. One of the chief attractions of Sunday excursions was a swim in the ocean, in Long Island Sound, or in the Hudson above the city, where bathers were free of the polluted waters of lower Manhattan.

The deficiency of water in the tenement areas was largely responsible for the accumulation of filth. Nearly all the old buildings, and many of the newer ones, lacked toilet facilities. Back-yard, wooden privies were common, but they could not accommodate the large number of inhabitants they were intended to serve. Through overuse and improper care, the privies remained a constant menace to health, and their contents, instead of being drained or carried away, frequently overflowed to the surface and created breeding places of disease.

Had the city maintained adequate inspection and control of tenement sanitation, New York might have avoided its reputation for dirtiness. City ordinances provided for the regulation of privies, cesspools, sewers, gutters, and cemeteries, but these laws were poorly enforced, particularly in tenement localities, where complaints proved ineffective. The lack of official supervision was largely the result of maladministration, employment of incompetent health officers, and the fear of infringing upon the presumed rights of private property. Owing to the paucity of sewers, the question of sanitation was of city-wide concern. As late as 1857 only 138 miles of sewers had been constructed in nearly 500 miles of streets, leaving unsewered "nearly three fourths of the city, including some of the most densely populated and filthy portions." Waste water drained into yards and alleys, filled the sinks, and broke into cellars and foundations;

some 24,000,000 gallons of sewage matter daily accumulated in such areas and in the gutters and streets of the city.

The streets were cleaned under a contract system which resulted in neglect and avoidance of responsibility. In the absence of a paid municipal street-cleaning force, contractors vied to receive "the highest compensation for the smallest discharge of duty." Imperfectly drawn contracts provided loopholes for evasion, and the spirit of the law was repeatedly violated. The contractors usually subcontracted for the cleaning of several wards, the subcontractors often letting out further subcontracts; meanwhile, the low wages, uncertainty of pay, and harsh treatment of the laborers who did the actual cleaning contributed to the ineffectiveness of the system. The haphazard removal of garbage forced even cleanly inhabitants to violate the law. They dumped into the streets the contents of their unemptied refuse containers. Since poor women were the usual offenders, sympathetic policemen hesitated to tear them from their families by hauling them off to jail.

In New York, where it was asserted that overcrowding was greater and that there was less concern and expenditure for the welfare of the slum population than in any other large city, the lower wards became the scene of frequent accidents among workingmen and their families. The concentration of shipyards, docks, and manufacturing plants in lower Manhattan exposed the laborer to collisions in cluttered streets, falling timber and brick, and collapsing walls. This peril was likewise an ever present possibility in the tenements and boardinghouses wedged amid factories, slaughterhouses, stables, and lumber and coal yards. When inadequately inspected buildings crumbled on their foundations and antiquated firetraps suddenly were consumed in flame, the danger became real. Where front doors and windows were the only fire escapes, the inhabitants were compelled to "roast or break their necks." Typical of such catastrophes were the $600,000 fire in the Woolsey sugar factory at Clinton and South streets and a frightful explosion in Hague Street, both in the winter of 1849-1850.

Life in the slums was a continual struggle with illness and death. The high incidence of disease in New York was directly related to the sanitary condition of tenement dwellers, of whom a large number were the foreign born or their children. In the crowded immigrant quarters quarantine was an impossibility, and communicable diseases suddenly erupted into epidemic proportions. The Sixth Ward was a center of contagion, typhoid breaking out among the Irish and Germans in 1837, typhus in 1842, and cholera in 1849. Respiratory diseases likewise took their toll. Tuberculosis, pneumonia, and bronchitis were common, and scrofula was called "the great scourge of the pauper population."

That immigrants suffered more heavily from disease than the native population was well known. During the ten years from 1849 to 1859, of all persons admitted to Bellevue Hospital, a public institution, 83.9 per cent were foreign born. According to the unusually complete report of the city inspector for 1857, three of every five deaths from cancer in that year occurred among the immigrants; tuberculosis took the lives of 656 more immigrants than natives. Deaths from all causes were always proportionally higher among the foreign population than among the natives. More than half of the persons over ten years of age who died in 1840 were immigrants. In the latter fifties aliens accounted for 36.6 per cent of all deaths, but had the city statisticians considered parentage, the number of deaths in immigrant families would have produced a far higher percentage. The mortality of children of foreign parents showed a great excess over those of American parents, an eloquent proof of their poverty and lack of proper medical care. Nearly two thirds of New York City's total mortality in 1857 were children under the age of five, the majority undoubtedly of foreign parentage. A physician of Providence, Rhode Island, wrote:

It is well known that the foreign population, as a class, in this city, and in other cities in this country, are under entirely different sanitary influences from the American population. The greater portion of the foreign population live in a miserable class of tenement houses, with all the want of conveniences, and positively injurious influences of such houses; their social habits are not calculated to preserve health; and a knowledge of the laws of hygiene is entirely wanting among them. Of course, the children of foreign parents are subject to the same injurious influences upon health, and suffer from them more than the parents themselves.

Despite the hospital facilities of the port of New York, diseases were introduced by newly arriving immigrants, and their spread was inevitable in the densely populated tenement districts. The largest annual number of deaths from typhoid, typhus, dysentery and diarrhea occurred during the periods of the greatest influx of immigrants—from 1847 to 1855. Fleeing the famine in their native land, many starving and diseased Irish left the emigrant ships, spread their diseases, and died shortly afterward.

Among the immigrants, the Irish were the chief victims of disease, and Irish-born patients of city institutions were nearly always in the majority. Natives of Ireland comprised 53.9 per cent of New York City's foreign-born inhabitants in 1855, but at Bellevue Hospital, 85 per cent of all the foreign born admitted from 1849 to 1859 were born in Ireland. The comparatively good health of the Germans is in striking contrast with the Irish. While 29.4 per cent of the city's foreign-born population were natives of Germany, only 6.25 per cent of admissions to Bellevue were German-born. Thus the proportion of Germans admitted to the hospital was only one fifth of the proportion of Germans in the total immigrant population of New York. In explanation it was asserted that the Germans were more cleanly and orderly in their living habits, but it is more likely that their generally superior economic status enabled them to live in comparatively comfortable surroundings. Moreover, the German immigrants, as a rule, were not so physically debilitated as were the poorer Irish, particularly those escaping famine in their native land and fortunate enough to survive the horrors of the voyage in tightly packed emigrant ships from Liverpool. The greater financial resources of the Germans were indicated by the statistics of the German Society relating to the annual immigration of Germans at the port of New York. Perhaps for similar reasons other nationalities sent proportionally few persons to Bellevue. The English comprised 6.9 per cent of the foreign born, yet only 4.56 per cent of admissions to the hospital were natives of England; the Scotch accounted for 2.6 per cent of the alien population, yet only 1.78 per cent of the Bellevue admissions were born in Scotland.

As in the case of other diseases, the insanity rate among the foreign born was considerably higher than that of the native Americans, and that of the Irish was by far the highest of the foreign born. Over three fourths of the admissions to the city lunatic asylum on Blackwell's Island from 1849 to 1859 were of alien birth; two thirds of these were natives of Ireland. The resident physician at the asylum admitted his inability to account satisfactorily for the high proportion of foreign insane. "Very few of the indigent insane of this city," he asserted, were

sent to the State Asylum at Utica, and none to Flushing, Hudson, or the Bloomingdale Asylum. Either the ratio of insane is very much less among the natives, or they are kept at their homes. Probably the first supposition is true, and this may arise in part from the shipment of the insane from Europe during a lucid interval.

Nevertheless, it is also likely that many natives had better means of taking care of their insane and at the same time were unwilling that their kin associate with the foreign-born insane at a public institution.

Insanity, apparently, was common among newly arrived immigrants. This phenomenon was attributed to the "privations on shipboard," "the changes incident to arriving in a strange land," and to "want of sufficient nourishment." In 1854 thirty-five of the hundred patients admitted to the Lunatic Asylum and chargeable to the Commissioners of Emigration had been in New York City less than one year, although many were only temporarily deranged and soon recovered. Insanity was prevalent especially among young women, according to one physician, who ascribed it to "the combined moral and physical influences of their leaving the homes of their childhood, their coming almost destitute to a strange land, and often after great suffering."

If physical and mental illness could be traced to the conditions of immigration or to existence in New York's slums, ignorance, lack of cleanliness, and inadequate medical care also played their part. Attracted by cheap prices, many poor families bought impure food from hucksters and basement storekeepers. Medical advice was ignored by many, the Irish being the chief offenders. While the Irish exposed their children to inclement weather, the Germans went to the other extreme, confining their sick to overheated rooms and excluding fresh air. Superstition and home remedies were applied to all sorts of common ailments and disabilities. To her bald and toothless son in New York an English mother wrote, "You can have false teeth that is a very common thing and you must get some Castor Oil and rum and rub your head every morning."

Credulous persons were fair targets for the army of charlatans

who offered a pill for every ill. Advertisements for patent medicines appeared in nearly every newspaper, particularly in the
German papers. For twenty-five cents one could buy a box of
Dr. Fubarsch's *Vegetabilische Lebenspillen* for the cure of fever,
colds, scrofula, worms, hemorrhoids, and "all delicate female
ailments." Van Pelt's Indian Vegetable Salve, costing fifty cents,
was for the treatment of "breast ailments," burns, and car-
buncles; *Pastilles de Paris* were good for colds and bronchitis;
Tarrant's Cordial Elixir of Turkey Rhubarb for indigestion and
dyspepsia; "innocent-pills," "blood-cleaning pills," "family
pills," and "anti-diarrhea pills" vied with "syrup of naphtha,"
"lung balsam," and "marshmallow drops" as specifics or cure-
alls. At one dollar a box, "Ladies Silver Pills" were "the rich
man's friend and the poor man's need."

Despite insufficient medical care, poor immigrant families were
not completely without the services of doctors. European
physicians, surgeons, dentists, specialists, and midwives offered
consultation and aid either free of charge or at nominal fees.
Occasionally, these doctors co-operated with immigrant aid
societies. In 1843, for instance, thirteen German physicians
agreed to treat the poor gratis upon presentation of a certificate
of need from the German Society. Besides employing doctors
for the free treatment of needy Germans, the society also spent
several hundred dollars annually for medicines and paid the bills
of the dispensaries which leading Germans founded in the lower
part of the city. Ultimately, a German hospital was established
in 1866, but only after a long agitation by community-conscious
German businessmen, physicians, and philanthropists. Likewise,
the dream of a Jewish hospital was slow of realization, and it was
not until 1855 that the Jews' Hospital was opened to patients.
A Jewish clinic, however, was organized a few years earlier to
meet the crying need for free medical service. The Irish failed
to develop such a degree of medical cooperation. Overburdened
with work among the poor, the relatively few Irish physicians
faced an insuperable task of giving medical attention to the
multitude of Irish immigrants who could not pay for it. When
the Irish fell sick and home remedies did not avail, they sought
admission to the city dispensaries and hospitals, where they were
nearly always in the majority. The only organized medical aid
among the Irish was through their benevolent and fraternal associations, a form of mutual aid common to all immigrant
groups.

The helplessness of the immigrant poor was reflected in the large proportion of foreign-born paupers. City almshouse statistics prior to 1849 were unreliable, but during the next decade detailed figures revealed that fully three quarters of all persons admitted to the almshouse were born outside the United States. After the middle of the century, extensive immigration coincided with rising living costs to aggravate the already precarious existence of the newcomer, and in 1852 more than half the needy in all the Atlantic seaboard cities were Irish and German immigrants, mostly day laborers. In the Empire City alone, half of the persons relieved by the Association for Improving the Condition of the Poor were Irish; three eighths, Germans and other nationalities; while only one eighth were born in the United States. Then depression struck. In 1854 and 1855, and again in 1857, the number of indigent poor mounted to unheard-of figures as unemployment stalked the city and mass meetings demanded public works to feed the starving. It was an ominous sign that in the year of Lincoln's election fully 86 per cent of the paupers in New York City were of foreign birth.

Huddled together in teeming tenements, in squalid alleys and courtyards, immigrants came into frequent conflict with the law, particularly in the extremely poor neighborhoods of the Fourth and Sixth wards. Panel thieves operated in the "Dutch" groceries of Duane, Thomas, and Anthony streets and in West Broadway, hardened murderers and harbor thieves congregated in Cherry and Water streets and on the wharves, and gangs of criminal hoodlums like the "Kerryonians" and the "Dead Rabbits" haunted the Five Points and the Bowery. Most immigrant lawbreakers, however, were individuals incapable of organized crime. In the vast majority of cases, they were arrested by the police on charges of petty thievery, drunkenness, or disorderly conduct. Family worries involving illnesses and deaths, the monotony and uncertainties of work in New York, and the isolation and friendlessness of the immigrant were relieved by frequent trips to the tippling shop. Love of liquor, fostered in Ireland by the hopeless outlook of the Irish peasantry, was further encouraged in New York by innumerable bartenders. Nor was hard drinking limited to the children of Erin, for the English and Scotch liked their whiskey too, and the French and Germans, traditionally wine and beer drinkers, included lovers of rum, brandy, and schnapps. Under the influence of drink, desperate and reckless individuals forgot their sufferings and their sorrows, committed assault or robbery, and wound up in jail. Of the total number of persons committed to the city prison during the nine years 1850-1858, seven eighths were recorded as "intemperate," most of them immigrants, unmarried, and between the ages of twenty and forty.

Immigrants were easy prey for policemen who, unwilling to risk their jobs by raiding gambling dens, brothels, and criminal hideouts, kept a sharp eye for slight misdemeanors committed by persons of no political influence. Because of alien habits or unfamiliarity with the English language, some foreigners unintentionally violated city ordinances; others, who happened to be present at brawls and riots, were subjected to arbitrary arrest. As common among the poor as the boisterous conduct of the intemperate was the addiction to petty stealing. The culprits apparently stole needed goods more often than money, and sometimes they were arrested merely on suspicion, as is evidenced by this press report:

ARRESTS—John McGorty and Michael Dowd were arrested for stealing a keg of white lead; John McKeeney on suspicion of having stolen $34; Jane Mullen for stealing a wash tub; Mary Donahan stole 34½ yards of calico from the premises of Mr. Taylor, 31 Catharine st.

After their apprehension, the guilty and innocent alike were herded into the overcrowded city prison. Petty offenders mingled with confirmed felons, the sane with the insane, and children with jaded adults reeking of alcohol. During 1859, 23 per cent of the persons arrested in New York City were native Americans, 55 per cent were born in Ireland, 10 per cent in Germany, 7 per cent in England and Scotland, and 5 per cent in other countries. These figures are less significant, however, than the rate of criminal convictions for each nationality. In the courts of special sessions, slightly less than one per cent of the native American population of New York City were convicted in 1859, while 5.5 per cent of the Irish, 3 per cent of the Scotch, 2.5 per cent of the English, 2 per cent of the Canadians, 1.5 per cent of the French, and 1.2 per cent of the Germans were convicted. The high proportions of foreign-born criminals are misleading, however, for the vast majority of crimes were committed by persons between the ages of twenty and forty, and it was this age group which was so largely filled with the foreign born. Among the immigrant groups, the Germans were known for their law-abiding qualities, and the Jews, most of whom were Germans, appear to have had the lowest incidence of criminality. "There are far less charges of crime alleged against the Jews as a class, than against any other equal portion of citizens in our city," reported the *National Police Gazette*. Yet when a Jew was arrested, the newspapers noted that he was a Jew, whereas the creed of others was rarely given.

Dens of gambling and vice dotted lower Manhattan. Despite the ban on lotteries passed by the state legislature in 1832, New York gamblers bought tickets for lotteries in other states, in Cuba, or in Europe, or they turned to the policy game. Negroes were the main victims of this numbers racket, but many immigrant women were also "daily won to its infatuation." There is no evidence, however, that the foreign born gambled more than the natives; Jonothan Green's curious "Report on Gambling" hardly mentioned foreigners.

Prostitution appears to have been almost as common among American women as among immigrants, but in either case poverty was the chief inducement to vice. In their failure to make ends meet, immigrant girls, devoid of family life, walked the streets in despair or drifted into dance halls and brothels, where in some instances they were exploited by women of their own nationality. Of 2,000 prostitutes examined in 1858 at the Penitentiary Hospital on Blackwell's Island—in effect, the city's venereal hospital—762 were natives of the United States and 1,238, or five eighths of the total, were immigrants. The largest proportion was born in British territory: 706 in Ireland, 104 in England, 63 in British North America, 52 in Scotland, and one in Wales, while 257 were natives of the German states, 17 of Switzerland, and 13 of France. More than 45 per cent of these foreign-born prostitutes had lived in the United States less than five years, and of these, 21 per cent were residents of less than one year. Of the 2,000 women, native and immigrant, three eighths were between the ages of fifteen and twenty, and fully three quarters were younger than twenty-six.

Forced by circumstances to spend their formative years amid poverty, vice, and crime, children of the poorest immigrants grew up without family guidance and the restraining influences of church and school. Parents, who were subject to definite social controls in Europe, were unable to assert authority over

children whose views of life were gained from experiences with
" 'flash-men,' engine-runners, cock-fighters, pugilists, and pick-
pockets . . . and . . . low theaters." For the boys of the streets,
the Golden Rule was an altogether impossible precept, especially
when they were "stuck and short" and "had to live." Girls,
pitiable and deserted, sometimes the daughters of prostitutes,
made a scant living as fruit, nut, and candy peddlers, by petty
thievery, or "by more questionable means." Drifting loose upon
society, the homeless, friendless, and lawless youth created serious problems of juvenile delinquency in New York as early as
the 1820's. The vagrant and criminal children of foreign parentage admitted to the House of Refuge over a period of three
decades were far more numerous than those of native parentage.
Although specific offenses committed by children were not
reported before 1863, nearly all the children sent to the House
of Refuge during the four years 1863-1866 were charged with
petty larceny and vagrancy; but some were accused of disorderly conduct, assault and battery, manslaughter, rape, arson,
forgery, and other crimes.

Such were the living conditions of the foreign born. The New
York tenement houses appeared in response to the needs of a
growing population in congested lower Manhattan. Crowding
into the hurriedly reconstructed dwellings or, later, into especially designed tenements, immigrant families occupied the
poorest districts of the city, where life and limb were jeopardized by the failure to enforce housing regulations, the presence of factories and other industries in their midst, the un-
cleaned streets, the ineffective sewage system, the absence of
bathing facilities, the futility of quarantining diseased persons,
the widespread ignorance and lack of medical care, and the high
incidence of pauperism, crime, vice, and juvenile delinquency.
Persons of middle age or older, having little opportunity to rise
to a comfortable living standard, eked out a bare existence in
the forgotten streets of the lower wards. Younger men and
women, more often their children, improved their status and
moved to cleaner, safer neighborhoods, vacating their former
rooms and flats for occupancy by more recent immigrants. As
this process was repeated year by year, the foreign settlements
acquired a fluidity made possible by the immigrants' occupational skills and their adjustment to the employment opportunities in New York.

CANALS, RAILROADS,
AND URBAN RIVALRIES

JULIUS RUBIN

The Erie Canal stimulated urban imperialism and served as a catalyst for the "transportation revolution." Julius Rubin, Associate Professor of History and Economics at the University of Pittsburgh, analyzes the response to the New York innovation in Boston, Philadelphia, and Baltimore.

One of the great American technological feats of the early nineteenth century, one that revolutionized the transportation system and soon became a dominant factor in the rapid development of the interior of the country, consisted of a 364-mile canal between Albany and Buffalo, begun in 1817 and completed in 1825. The Erie Canal was a true innovation. Of the American canals preceding it only three were more than two miles long and the longest of these, the Middlesex, was hardly 28 miles in length and in severe financial difficulties by 1816. So new to the United States was the type of work required that the state had to depend upon untrained persons, chiefly lawyers, to plan and supervise construction. Furthermore, the Erie was built largely through unsettled territory, and its economic justification lay not in current traffic but in the expected development of a wilderness when provided with a cheap, long-range transportation line. Hence, George Rogers

From Julius Rubin, "Canal or Railroad: Imitation and Innovation in the Response to the Erie Canal in Philadelphia, Baltimore, and Boston," *Transactions of the American Philosophical Society*, 51, Part 7 (1961), 5–14. Copyright © 1961 by the American Philosophical Society. Reprinted by permission of the American Philosophical Society.

Taylor refers to the building of the Erie as "an act of faith, the demonstration of a spirit of enterprise by an organized government that has few parallels in world history."

The Canal was not simply another success; it was an enormous, astounding, almost unbelievable success. Throughout the country, the press printed and reprinted astonished accounts of the size of the toll revenues, which were impressive as early as 1823, when large sections of the Canal were open to traffic. Just as impressive were the descriptions of the marvelously rapid development of the affected regions of western New York. Inevitably, the Erie Canal sparked a national canal craze.

The Canal's success vitally affected the rivalry of the major eastern seaboard cities. Up to the 1820's, New York's competitors to the south had confidently relied upon their turnpikes to maintain their position in the western trade. That policy had been successful, for the shortest route to the west led across Pennsylvania, Maryland, and Virginia and the two principal east-west roads favored Philadelphia and Baltimore. It is estimated that in the early 1820's the Pittsburgh Pike carried about 30,000 tons of goods annually, the National Road about 10,000 tons. As a result, Pittsburgh, Cincinnati, and Wheeling became important commercial centers at a time when Buffalo, Cleveland, and Detroit were mere frontier settlements. In this respect, New York City was at a disadvantage during the turnpike era.

The turnpikes' advantages, however, were severely limited. Those tons of goods were overwhelmingly manufactures shipped westward. The bulky agricultural produce of the west continued to use the Mississippi route to New Orleans. Furthermore, the growing use of the steamboat for up-river carriage on the Mississippi and Ohio rivers threatened to deprive the turnpikes of even their westward trade. New Orleans was still a dangerous rival of the eastern seaboard cities.

This situation was transformed by the construction of the Erie Canal. Here was a transportation method far superior both to the turnpike and to the river, with or without steamboats. The Canal immediately took over from the turnpikes a part of the westward trade and, when the immigrants it transported had built up the northern midwest, it carried their agricultural produce back to the east. For the first time, east and west were linked by a direct two-way trade. New York, already in the lead in other fields because of its geographic advantages and superior enterprise, seemed now in a position to dominate the trade of the northern midwest and to extend that domination southward. Her major rivals—Boston, Philadelphia, and Baltimore—were left in the rear facing a most difficult problem. One way out was to imitate the innovation. But the Appalachian barrier stood in their way; it granted a relatively water-level route only to New York State.

Nevertheless, the temptation to imitate New York's project was almost irresistible. For if New York's rivals did not get competing lines across their mountains, they would be shut out, it seemed forever, from the western trade. This danger appeared precisely at the time when the center of economic interest was shifting from the ocean to the developing interior, from foreign to internal commerce. A failure to achieve a line to the west, therefore, meant stagnation, even decline; this was the view of the advocates of internal improvement in all the rival cities. . . . Their agitation was imbued with a sense of desperate urgency; to them it was a case of expand or die. On the other hand, the achievement of a line to the west would bring with it enormous prizes; they would participate in the expansion of a continent. And the magnitude of the Erie's financial success seemed to guarantee the success (even though a lesser success) of any canal connecting the Atlantic with the river and canal system of the west. It is not surprising, therefore, that all three of New York's rivals placed their hopes, at least for a time, in that technological monstrosity, a canal over the mountains.

Coincidentally, at the very time that New York's rivals were casting about for some way of overcoming those mountains, the long-run solution to their problem appeared on the horizon. The railroad, still a very primitive thing, was going through a rapid evolution in England during the first quarter of the nineteenth century. In rails, the edge-rail replaced the flat plate, the flange was transferred from rail to wheel, and malleable iron began to replace cast iron. The first locomotive was used in 1804, there was constant improvement in the following two decades, and by the early 1820's Stephenson's locomotives were attracting attention all over England. In 1821 a charter was obtained for a horse-drawn freight railroad between Stockton and Darlington, but the amended charter of 1823 gave the road permission to carry passengers (an innovation) and to use locomotives (but stationary engines were used on the steep inclines).

The Stockton and Darlington opened on September 27, 1825, and was a resounding success. Its locomotive was able to draw up an easy incline a train weighing eighty tons at ten to fifteen miles per hour.

Thus, by 1825 all the essential elements required to make the railroad the answer to the transportation problems of continental areas had been discovered and tried out on a limited scale in England and Scotland. Furthermore, the rapidity of technological development in this field was a clear indication to many that it was the coming mode of transportation; that soon it would be far superior to the canal because of its flexibility of location, its speed of conveyance, its simpler means of handling grades, and its year-round use. Here was the answer to the Erie Canal, here was the technique that would free New York's rivals from the accidents of nature and would allow them once again to compete for the western trade. This was understood by the railway advocates of the 1820's in all the rival cities; and the expectation was of course fully borne out by events.

But there was another side to the question. The railroad of 1825 was sufficiently developed to indicate its potentialities, but it was not yet adequately tested. The British railroads were all extremely short and almost all were special-purpose lines carrying coal, usually down an incline, from a mine area to a waterway. Only the Surrey Railroad, built in 1804, carried a general line of miscellaneous goods, and it was not a financial success. Even the Stockton and Darlington carried mostly coal and did not develop much of a passenger traffic until the 1830's. But it was not only that the railroad was inadequately tested in Britain; it was nonexistent in the United States before 1826. As many Americans were willing to point out, everything was bigger, better, and deeper in America; the mountains were higher, the frosts more intense, the snows deepers, the spring freshets more violent. Obviously, the railroad had to be tested under American conditions. Since the interregional lines contemplated by the three rival cities required an enormous investment, there was great danger in proceeding before a series of smaller American railroads had been constructed.

The uncertainty associated with the railroad confronted New York's rivals with a difficult choice. Should they use the tried and tested method of canals in a geographical situation entirely unsuited to that method or should they turn to the new and

untried? Should they imitate or innovate? Of course, a third
alternative was possible: they could postpone a decision, avoid
investment in either railroad or canal, and wait for the railroad
to prove itself. But in the meantime New York was monopoliz-
ing the western trade. Delay required coolness and great ob-
jectivity. The pressure was for immediate action in a deteriorating situation. Consequently, a bitter debate developed in all three
cities during 1825 and 1826.

It is of particular interest that each of the rival regions
reacted differently. The Pennsylvania improvement movement
demanded immediate state construction of a canal to the Ohio
and succeeded in obtaining passage of a law authorizing construction of the first segments of such a line in February, 1826.
But the great technical difficulty of crossing the mountains by
water forced a railroad portage over the summit; then the inadequacies of the existing Union Canal in the east forced construction of another railroad there. Pennsylvania, therefore,
ended up with a cumbrous mongrel line requiring three trans-
shipments and incapable of competing successfully with the Erie
Canal. Baltimore at first also thought of linking its fortunes to
a canal by means of a difficult canal feeder to the projected
Chesapeake and Ohio Canal. But in February, 1827, a Baltimore
merchant group, uninterested in government enterprise, decided
upon immediate construction under private auspices of a full
railroad line to the Ohio. Massachusetts, however, delayed.
There was talk of a canal over the Berkshires, surveys were
taken, and in 1826 a canal to the Hudson was recommended by
the state commissioners and a nationally known engineer; but
by the end of 1826 the leaders of the state's internal improvement movement had realized that the railroad was the answer to
Boston's competitive problems. However, they did not call for
immediate construction. Only in 1829, when experience and
the progress of railroad technique in England had fully proven
the advantages of the general-purpose railroad, did they demand
state construction of a railroad to the Hudson; and only in
1836, after the failure of intensive efforts to obtain state construction, did a private corporation launch, with great trepida-
tion, a railroad over the Berkshires.

These striking differences in behavior seem completely out of
proportion to the small divergencies in the situation of these
three closely similar regions. For these were all commercialized

coastal areas of the same country; all were subject to the competitive pressure created by the success of the Erie Canal; all were confronted with the problem of crossing a mountain range; all had access to almost identical technical information on canals and railroads; and all made their decisions at almost the same time. Is it possible that extremely small disparities in situation, information, and timing could have produced such large differences in response? I shall try to demonstrate that this is highly improbable. If so, the differences in behavior are to be explained by attitudinal rather than situational factors; by divergencies in the history and traditions of the three regions which produced differences in the attitudes that the decision-making groups brought to the common problem rather than by differences in the problem itself. Since that common problem involved a choice between a tried and untried method and between immediate action and postponement, differences in attitudes toward uncertainty and delay must account for those remarkable differences in behavior. This is the thesis of the following pages.

The thesis requires a good deal of discussion and qualification. Firstly, was the situation actually so similar for all of them? Certainly the mountains were somewhat different for each—in grade, height, hardness and permeability of the soil, and volume of water available. Furthermore, their geographic relation to the west differed. Boston, for example, was off in a corner, with hopes of reaching directly, not the west, but only the Erie Canal at Albany; Baltimore, unlike the others, had to depend on a branch canal to a route that ended at the doorsteps of her competitors, the Potomac cities, if she chose the canal method. Finally, the technical information available to each may have differed in important respects because the crucial decisions were taken at slightly different times. Would railway developments between February, 1826, when Philadelphia decided in favor of the canal, and February, 1827, when Baltimore chose the railroad, explain the differences in the decisions?

The differences in the physical characteristics of the mountain barrier are, to my mind, the least of the difficulties in the way of the thesis. For all the cities were confronted with the same alternatives. All were assured by competent governmental commissions that a canal over the mountains was technically practicable at varying but not impossible costs, and all had to decide whether the railroad could efficiently overcome a mountain range. The fact that, to take the two extreme cases, the merchants of Baltimore were confronted with a summit height of 2,680 feet while the Massachusetts railroad advocates were confronted with two summits, one of 1,480 feet, the other of approximately 900 feet; that the distance from Boston to the Hudson was approximately 200 miles while the distance from Baltimore to the Ohio was about 380 miles; that of the extremely steep grades confronting all of the cities, one grade was somewhat more steep than another; these are differences, but they fade to insignificance in relation to the overwhelming fact that, in contrast to New York, they all had to climb the Appalachian mountain range. This common factor produced . . . substantially the same arguments for and against the two modes of transportation in all the cities. . . .

The differences in the various cities' geographic relation to the west constitute a more important limitation upon my attempt to isolate the influence of attitudes. While Baltimore and Pennsylvania could project independent lines to the Ohio River, the great artery of the west of the time, Boston's goal was the Hudson River at the eastern end of the Erie Canal; from that point on the city would use its adversary's route to the west. This gave New York an important advantage: its ships reached the Erie by means of the wide and navigable Hudson River, while Boston's trade would reach the Erie by means of an expensive canal or railroad over the Berkshires. Consequently, while Boston could hope to participate in the trade of the west, it could never hope to replace New York as the great entrepôt of the Atlantic coast.

. . . It is important to emphasize that we do not have to assume that any of the rivals of New York had a chance of surpassing New York, nor that they believed in so remote a possibility (despite some euphoric declarations to the contrary). The thesis is that the rivals differed in their ability to take full advantage of the potentialities of their position; that when confronted with an almost identical problem, one city adhered to a by then traditional method entirely unsuited to the situation, another rushed forward with an appropriate but untried method, a third postponed all action until the new method was fully tested elsewhere. That the potential expansion of each city's trade differed is relevant only to the extent that it may have influenced attitudes; a lesser potentiality, for example, might have produced a less inspired, more deliberate attitude. But this effect is not evident in the Massachusetts case. Just as improvement leaders in Pennsylvania and Baltimore envisaged their lines to the Ohio as a link to an expanding continent, leaders in Massachusetts conceived of their line to the Hudson as a link to the continental hinterland of the Erie Canal: to the Great Lakes, to the Ohio canals and the Ohio River, ultimately to the Mississippi and the Gulf of Mexico. And in the eyes of the improvement leaders of all three areas, a failure to build such a line meant stagnation. Thus, the problems, the dangers, and the perceived opportunities were closely similar, if not identical.

Baltimore's relation to the Potomac cities raises a more difficult problem. A canal from Boston or Philadelphia would not have led to a competing coastal city before it headed west; but a canal from Baltimore would have had to go to Georgetown before it went up the Potomac valley. This disadvantage undoubtedly produced in Baltimore a more realistic and sceptical attitude toward the canal method. . . . Two considerations . . . reduce the importance of, though they do not eliminate, this factor. Firstly, before the appearance of the railroad alternative, Baltimore did place its hopes in the canal method, despite the competitive disadvantage. Secondly, the city could have projected a railroad to a point far up the Potomac valley (something impossible with a canal); from that point it could have used the Chesapeake and Ohio Canal as its route to the west without fear of competition from Georgetown. Hence Pennsylvania's mongrel-line method was available to Baltimore; the circumstances of the two cities were similar.

Finally, there are the differences in the timing of the decisions. The leaders of the improvement movement in Pennsylvania rejected the alternative of a full railroad late in 1825, and the legislation for state construction of the first canal segments passed in February, 1826; the leaders of the Massachusetts improvement movement rejected the canal method at the end of 1826; the merchants of Baltimore began their discussion of the railroad alternative in the fall of 1826 and decided to build the railroad in February, 1827. It is important to determine whether the development of technique and the acquisition of further experience in the railroad field between late 1825 and February, 1827, can explain the differences in the decisions. . . . Pennsylvanians rejected the railroad on the ground that it had never been tested adequately in its general-purpose form; and the railroad was thus tested only in 1830 with the operation of the world's first true general-purpose railroad, the Liverpool and Manchester. Furthermore, . . . the experience upon which the Baltimore decision was based was the same as that to which the Pennsylvanians had referred and found inadequate, with but one exception. That exception was the specialized, primitive, three-mile Granite Railroad constructed during 1826 at Quincy, Massachusetts. This railroad did not answer the objections of the Pennsylvanians, for it did not test the general-purpose railroad; indeed it was far more primitive than the current English examples known to them. But as the first American railroad, it did have an impressive demonstration effect. This is the extent to which the difference in the timing of the decisions interferes with the attempt to isolate the effects of the attitudinal factors.

If we may conclude that the differences in the decisions reflected certain differences in the attitudes of the decision-making groups of the three areas, then two questions arise: How may we define these characteristics? And what causes these differences among groups residing in a very similar general environment? This study cannot hope to answer these questions because of two limitations in its scope. Firstly, it does not investigate in detail the decision-making groups; indeed the entire history, traditions, and social and political structure of the three areas lie outside its view. Secondly, it deals with but a single decision in each region; a comparative analysis of many such decisions, both within and outside the field of internal improvements, would be required in order to be able to draw definitive conclusions regarding the nature and causes of those differences in attitudes. Nevertheless, tentative hypotheses are possible, and these may suggest directions for further comparative investigations.

This work deals with decisions of large scope involving the use of new technical means; they therefore involved a good deal of the kind of uncertainty that prevents careful estimates of the probable effects of alternative courses of action. It has often been pointed out that the assumption of rational and prompt decision-making by all economic agents—which means of course identical behavior in relation to the same problem—cannot be applied to such cases. As Joseph Schumpeter has put it:

. . . the assumption . . . works tolerably well only within the precincts of tried experience and familiar routine. It breaks down as soon as we leave those precincts and allow the business community under study to be faced by—not simply new situations, which also occur as soon as external factors unexpectedly intrude but by—new possibilities of business action which are as yet untried and about which the most complete command of routine teaches nothing.

Schumpeter was here writing of the problems of the firm. But in our cases, the decision-makers, except for Baltimore, were larger, more decentralized bodies—legislatures, large internal improvement societies, or less formally organized leaders of state-wide opinion—for whom rational and prompt decision-making under conditions of uncertainty is far more difficult. Furthermore, when the society is democratic and the decision-making unit is political, even larger groups must be convinced of the wisdom of any decision. The private entrepreneur, Schumpeter thought, has a great advantage here. He operates,

. . . not by convincing people of the desirability of carrying out his plan or by creating confidence in his leading in the manner of a political leader—the only man he has to convince or to impress is the banker who is to finance him—but by buying . . . their services, and then using them as he sees fit . . . he renders a service, the full appreciation of which takes a specialist's knowledge of the case. It is not so easily understood by the public at large. . . .

In the comparison of the Pennsylvania and Baltimore decisions . . . we have the opportunity of comparing a decision made, on the one hand, by a large internal improvement movement and a legislature; on the other hand, by a relatively small group willing to invest its own capital. But the situation in Baltimore differed considerably from Schumpeter's description. In these large decisions affecting the long-range economic fates of whole areas, it is impossible for the entrepreneurial group to consider only its "banker." The merchants of Baltimore had to win over a large group of potential investors to the railroad idea and certainly must have felt it important to create a climate favorable to state and city subsidies. In all of our cases, then, great uncertainty as to technical means was combined with the problem of convincing large numbers. A decision on purely rational grounds was therefore ruled out: are other principles of behavior discernible?

The hypothesis here suggested is that the uncertainty associated with these projects must be eliminated by non-rational means before the support of a large sector of the population can be obtained. . . . In the Pennsylvania and Baltimore cases an emotion-charged symbol that seemed to guarantee success exorcised uncertainty from people's minds and produced a mania that made possible a project whose immediate construction had little objective justification. In Baltimore it was the reputation of a wealthy, decisive, and remarkably optimistic merchant group that overcame doubt and hesitation; in Pennsylvania it was the triumphant New York canal policy that was put forward as a guarantee of success to whoever would imitate it. The difference between the Philadelphia and Baltimore decisions, then, reflected a difference in the quality of leadership. The businessmen of Baltimore, by risking their own capital and proceeding on their own, themselves provided the faith that created a railroad mania in Baltimore; but the businessmen of Philadelphia, unwilling to invest and dependent upon a legislature, could obtain action only by appropriating a symbol created by the leadership of another state, a state whose geographical conditions had produced technical means which were entirely inappropriate to the geographical situation of Pennsylvania.

But a mania does not always occur. Massachusetts presents us with a case in which, evidently, both the leadership of the improvement movement and the population were immune to the magic of symbols of great success. In this case, the canal was rejected—the symbol of the Erie Canal did not take hold—and the railroad project was postponed for a decade despite a need for a trans-Appalachian line that was felt at least as urgently in Massachusetts as in the other two areas.

The utter dependence upon a "foreign" symbol in Pennsylvania makes the railroad-canal debate there an extraordinarily interesting one. Fortunately, it is available in the daily newspapers in great detail, for it was public, unlike the debate in Baltimore, and it was long drawn out, unlike the debates in both Baltimore and Massachusetts. . . . The Pennsylvania leaders managed almost to ignore the mountains in drawing a remarkably crude analogy between Pennsylvania's situation and that of New York, and used the argument, based on the Erie Canal's effects in New York state, that any long-range transportation project through undeveloped regions yields enormous developmental benefits that cannot be measured by toll-gate receipts. The potential applicability of this "economic development argument" to all such large political decisions reinforces Schumpeter's emphasis upon the difficulty of rational behavior in these cases. For, together with the rejection of the measurable profit criterion, the Pennsylvanians were able to reject all the complex technical criteria that should have been involved in the choice between railroad and canal. Since all such projects could succeed, their one criterion became that of experience—this gave them certainty. They, therefore, chose the canal, for the canal had been tested, especially in New York, while the railroad was new and untried. The Pennsylvania case suggests too that an imitation of advances made in other areas that on the surface seems dynamic and enterprising may in reality represent a passive abdication of independent thought, action, and leadership. Both Pennsylvania and Baltimore experienced a mania for improvements. But in Pennsylvania it was a mania involving imitation while in Baltimore it was a mania for innovation.

Thus, the severe limitation on the scope of this investigation has not prevented some flickering insight into the nature of those divergent attitudes that were produced by the differing histories and traditions of the three regions. But it is of value, I believe, merely to demonstrate the existence of attitudinal differences important enough to have a decisive influence upon decisions that may have determined the long-run economic fates of communities. For it indicates that what is known as "national character"—that little-understood complex of habits and attitudes so important to an understanding of comparative economic development but so difficult to define and investigate—can be investigated on a relatively small scale, among communities which are otherwise quite similar in economic function, in social structure, and in general environment. This may be especially true of the early nineteenth century. For this was the period of the "parochial point of view," when the scope of businessmen's decisions was local or regional and when they could not easily change the locus of their activities. Their fortunes were largely tied to their city's economic development, just as later they were to be tied to their country's development. This period of "municipal mercantilism," therefore, provides us with an opportunity to study on a small scale that which later can only be studied on the large. If our aim is to isolate the casual factors in economic development by means of the comparative method, then the comparison of similar cities and regions in one country during this early period may yield results impossible to obtain in national comparisons, where the scale is so formidable and the differences of all kinds are so great. The present study presents some preliminary evidence for this belief.

SLAVERY IN THE CITIES

RICHARD C. WADE

*University of Chicago historian Richard C. Wade surveys the
urban dimension of the antebellum South and reveals a
neglected aspect of black bondage.*

By 1860 slavery was disintegrating in Southern cities. Forty
years earlier, the institution had seemed as stable and vigorous
in town as in country. Slaves comprised at least 20 per cent of
the population of the major cities. In most places the proportion
was much higher, and in Charleston blacks outnumbered whites.
Slaves handled the bulk of domestic drudgery; worked in shops
and factories; built the streets, bridges, and municipal installa-
tions; some even acquired mechanical skills. Within four
decades, however, the picture had changed dramatically. In
the border cities the institution had nearly disappeared altogether; farther south it had diminished in extent and vitality.
Everywhere proportionately, and in many places absolutely,
the number of town slaves declined. In the countryside slavery
still appeared stable and successful, but wherever it touched
urban conditions it was in deep trouble.

A Kentuckian observed in 1848 that "slavery exists in Louisville and St. Louis only in name," for "there are two things that
always, and under all circumstances, abrogate slavery. The first
is a dense population, . . . the next [is] the intelligence of slaves.
Both of these are silently and imperceptibly working their
legitimate results." A Louisiana planter, who was also a frequent
visitor to New Orleans, had noticed this same process: "Slavery

is from its very nature eminently patriarchal and altogether agricultural. It does not thrive with master or slave when transplanted to cities." Probably the best Northern student of the South, Frederick Law Olmsted, made the same point in 1857. "Servile labor must be unskilled labor," he wrote, "and unskilled labor must be dispersed over land, and cannot support the concentrated life nor amass the capital of cities." And those Negroes who had known bondage in both town and country perhaps understood the problem best. One of them, Frederick Douglass, stated it simply, "Slavery dislikes a dense population."

But what became clear in 1860 was not apparent forty years earlier. In 1820, slavery was as much a part of life in the city as on farm and plantation. In fact, some municipal officials expressed anxiety over the rapid increase in colored townspeople. And surely no one questioned the adaptability of slavery to the urban milieu. Yet experience ultimately proved this assumption mistaken. For, as the cities grew, they produced conditions which first strained, then undermined, the regime of bondage in the South's metropolises.

II

Though the South was primarily rural before the Civil War, it did not lack important cities. Resting on its irregular perimeter were New Orleans, Mobile, Savannah, Charleston, Richmond, Baltimore, Louisville, and St. Louis. These seaports and river towns sent Dixie's produce to the outside, distributed necessary imports to the countryside, and formed enclaves of cosmopolitan life in a generally agricultural society. Scattered across the interior were smaller places, usually state capitals or trading towns, with more than local importance. Then, too, there was Washington, the nation's capital but still very much a regional city. In fact, on the eve of the Civil War the census listed 30 places of over 8000 inhabitants throughout the South.

Taken together, these urban centers contained only a small part of the South's population, yet their influence was much greater than their numbers. De Bow, writing in 1860, was impressed by their constantly widening significance: "Within the last forty years country life has quietly and almost imperceptibly undergone great changes." These changes consisted "in the country having become more and more dependent on the town. Whether in pursuit of business, pleasure, or information, men leave the country and visit some neighboring city." "Our bodies," he concluded somewhat wistfully, "are in the country, our souls in town."

New Orleans was the largest city of the deep South. It also seemed to many the least American. Founded by the French in 1718, it retained an intensely European flavor even a half century after the Louisiana Purchase. The "old quarter" in 1860 still reminded people of parts of Paris, with its "French noises and French smells, [and] French signs." But beyond Canal Street, dubbed by residents "the Rubicon," was the newer and American section. There Southern architecture suggested native dominance; but the large number of Germans, Irish, and Spanish gave the area a cosmopolitan complexion. "It is unlike any other city in the Union, being foreign in air, in customs, and mainly in population," wrote one visitor. Or, as an early gazetteer put it, "it is a world in miniature."

New Orleans's initial growth under the American flag had been modest, but by the late 'twenties it began an extraordinary expansion. In 1831 William Gilmore Simms could observe that it had "grown prodigiously—perhaps its increase in wealth, population, and business generally, since 1825, is without parallel in the United States." The census figures confirmed this enthusiasm as the population surged from nearly thirty thousand to over one hundred thousand. A decade later, an exhilarated De Bow could predict that New Orleans "will be indeed to the Father of Rivers, 'as London to the Thames, and Paris to the Seine.'" On the eve of the war, the city counted 168,675 residents.

New Orleans owed its success to its location at the foot of the great river system that drained half the continent. From this strategic spot it handled most of the sugar from Louisiana, cotton from the Southwest, and grain and livestock from the interior. To its wharves came goods from the North, from Europe, Latin America, and the Orient. At the busy season the docks seethed with activity. "The very air howls with an eternal din and noise," a visitor remarked with wonder in 1847. "Drays and wagons of all descriptions, loaded with the produce of every clime, move on continually in an unbroken chain. Ships from every nation, whose masts tower aloft in a dense forest for five miles. . . . Steamboats, and crafts of every make and shape, from every river which empties into the Mississippi are here mingling in the strife of commerce." Another Southerner rhapsodically pronounced the scene as without historical parallel. "Tyre nor Carthage, Alexandria not Genoa," he wrote, "those aforetime imperial metropoles of merchant princes, boasted no quay like the Levee of New Orleans."

By the late 'twenties the town's exports were second largest in the nation, and for a few years in the late 'thirties and early 'forties it actually surpassed New York. "No city in the world has ever advanced as a mart of commerce with such gigantic and rapid strides, as New Orleans," wrote De Bow, the town's leading booster, in 1846. "In 40 years she has become the fourth city of the world . . . for the magnitude and value of her commerce." And the future seemed unlimited. George Washington Cable, who grew up there in these years, remembered how this development bred "an overweening confidence in the ability of the city to become speedily and without exertion the metropolis of America, if not eventually of the world."

These expansive dreams, however, were dashed in the next decade. The rate of growth slackened, and though population and trade continued to rise, New Orleans could not match the pace of its competitors across the country. Nevertheless, on the eve of the Civil War, the city ranked sixth in the nation's urban sweepstakes.

One hundred and fifty miles to the east was Mobile, a few years older but considerably smaller than New Orleans. Situated on a bay between the mouth of the Alabama River and the Gulf of Mexico, it had been transformed by cotton from a drowsy little town into a bustling port. French and Spanish at the beginning, it remained so for almost a century, and despite its transformation a visitor occasionally could be struck by the colonial legacy. "The names of the streets are Frenchy," a visitor from Ohio wrote in his diary in 1858. "Dauphin, Royal, Conti, St. Joseph, St. Louis, St. Michael and plenty of other saints." Continuity, too, could be found in a few old families and a sprinkling of creoles and in the "mingled traces of the manners and language of the French and Spaniards." But fundamentally Mobile's population, appearance, and spirit were thoroughly American, if not peculiarly Southern.

The Alabama port's progress dated from its annexation to the United States. Watching its advance, *Niles' Register* asserted in 1822 that "*Mobile* is becoming a place of great importance" and "may soon be one of the most populous of our Southern cities." In just nine years it has grown from "less than 300 inhabitants" to 2800. "We have never witnessed such an influx of strangers as is now pouring into our city," boasted the *Commercial Register* in 1833. And the people kept coming. Two years later, the same editor reported that "the city is at this moment one-fourth larger than it was twelve months since." In 1840 the census showed over twelve thousand residents, and two decades later it had reached nearly thirty thousand.

The city's ante-bellum boom sprang from the immense productivity of the cotton hinterland. "The great business of the town," Olmsted observed, "is the transfer of cotton, from the producer to the manufacturer, from the wagon and steamboat to the seagoing ship." Indeed, the crop seemed to command every aspect of Mobile's life. A sojourning Briton spoke of the port as a place where "people live in cotton houses and ride in cotton carriages. They buy cotton, sell cotton, think cotton, eat cotton, drink cotton, and dream cotton. They marry cotton wives, and unto them are born cotton children. . . . It has made Mobile, and all its citizens." The crop, another visitor asserted, was "the mighty pivot upon which the business of this city of 30,000 inhabitants revolves."

Built on commerce, too, though facing the Atlantic rather than the Gulf, was Savannah, Georgia's major port and one of the South's most enterprising entrepots. Founded in 1733 by James Oglethorpe, it sood sixteen miles up the river from the ocean, and was English in background and experience. A unique plan had fixed the development of the city around a series of charming little parks which gave the place "a curiously rural and modest aspect." Its sandy streets, kept unimproved presumably for reasons of health, fortified the impression. But the small-town flavor could not conceal the intensely commercial character of a people who prided themselves on their industry and aggressiveness. Occupying, as a traveler noted, "the primal and efficient seat . . . of the energy of Georgia," they advertised themselves as "plain, old fashioned, hard working men and women, who . . . transact business before 8 o'clock a.m."

Though an old city, Savannah rose to importance in Dixie in the years just before the war. In 1820 Savannah had only

7523 residents, very gradually increasing in the following decade. But by 1840 the figure climbed to over eleven thousand, moved beyond fifteen thousand at the next census, and reached over twenty thousand by 1860. While this growth seemed modest by the lusty Western standards of the time, it nonetheless was a notable achievement to triple population within forty years.

In fact, its aggressiveness had brought it early fame. In 1818 Savannah sent a steamship bearing the city's name on a pioneer, if unprofitable, trip to Liverpool. Fifteen years later, the city started a railroad venture into the uplands. A visiting New Yorker who watched this project remarked years later that it demonstrated "a spirit of enterprise that could honor any place in the country. While containing less than eight thousand people, black and white," he concluded, "it projected and completed . . . a railroad 190 miles in length, to Macon, at that time the longest railroad in the country."

This mercantile audacity paid off. Not only did it sustain a growing population, but the inland trade strengthened every aspect of the city's economy. By 1860 the value of cotton exports alone amounted to over $17 million. Manufacturing, too, felt the stimulus, but without the fanfare of commerce. A municipal official observed in 1848 that "this increase of steam power has been so noiseless" that most residents "will be surprised to learn that of the *eighteen* establishments propelled by steam, *fourteen* of them have been erected within the last ten years." Nearly every indicator carried good news. "Her growing population—the great increase of the mechanical arts— the extended use of steam as applied to mills, presses, and other useful employments—" the same source asserted, "are all evidence of a healthful state of the body politic." "She has both the power and inclination," a visitor contended, "to maintain her position in the struggle for commercial supremacy now going on among Southern cities."

Savannah depended on cotton no less than Mobile. The great staple came to the docks from nearly every direction and in every kind of conveyance. The river, of course, brought most, but by the 1850's other carriers shared the commerce. "Daily," said one observer, "nine trains came down the Central Railroad . . . with from twenty to thirty cars in each train, loaded mountain high with this article. The depots and plank yards, covering several acres, were groaning constantly under the immense burden, while long trains of horse teams" moved to the commission houses. The "spacious and elegant" homes of successful merchants and factors combined with "large and well filled" stores to demonstrate that many Savannahians profited considerably by this activity. Indeed, as cotton-growing moved to the interior, mercantile leaders chased the trade with railroads and river steamboats.

One hundred miles up the coast was Charleston, oldest and proudest metropolis in Dixie. By 1860 it was no longer the largest and richest, but it still claimed to be the "capital of the South." Acutely conscious of a colonial past that stretched back to 1680 and of earlier days when it ranked among the nation's most important cities, Charleston sought to preserve its supremacy through political and cultural leadership. This was no easy task, for the competitors, old and new, proved many. Yet Charleston had substantial assets. Set on a tongue of land between the Ashley and Cooper rivers, it had easy access to the back country. Its spacious harbor could accommodate most of the Atlantic's shipping at one time. Its climate and beauty, moreover, made it the favorite resort of the rice and cotton planters, who built expensive and tasteful town houses on the blue bay and gave a special polish and sophistication to Charleston society.

The celebrated ease and leisure of aristocratic life, however, could not conceal the growing difficulties of the city. De Bow, who had lived in both Charleston and New Orleans, could not help but contrast the development of the two places. "When the Crescent City consisted of a few huts on the low lands of the Mississippi, her sister of the Palmetto State was reveling in the riches of foreign commerce, and in all affluence and prosperity," he wrote in 1846. "But now the vision is changed. The noble city on the banks of the Cooper and Ashley looks back to the past with lingering regret," as the Louisiana port forged ahead. From being the nation's fifth largest metropolis in 1810, Charleston dropped to twenty-second in 1860. Its supremacy in the South, moreover, slipped away with the rise of other urban centers.

This descent was relative, not absolute. In the forty years after 1820 the city nearly doubled its population, reaching forty thousand by the Civil War. By 1850 it had annexed the "Neck," a suburb on its only land boundary, which opened up possibilities of further expansion. Yet the growth was never substantial or sustained.

This record of modest growth in a period of immense national urban expansion hurt both the pocketbooks and pride of the people. "Civis," writing in the *City Gazette* in 1824, drew a portrait that would be familiar to a generation of ante-bellum residents: "Charleston and neck present at this moment, a most gloomy and desponding picture; where scenes of industry, activity and growing prosperity were of late so apparent; where once reigned wealth and happiness, nothing now is to be found, but indolence, apathy, poverty and misery." In 1835 another wrote with irritation that "the South alone, and Carolina and Charleston in particular, appear to be standing still, slumbering in a sleepy hollow, or 'going ahead' in such small movements as scarcely to be perceptible." The changes were so slight during the next decade that one resident asserted that "but for two conflagrations which swept off many of her old houses" the city even looked the same. The 'fifties proved generally no better. When war came in 1861, the economic memory of most Charlestonians revolved around stagnation and hard times.

The "capital of the South" did not submit tamely to this "premature decay." In the decades before the Civil War business leaders experimented with manufacturing, merchants sought markets in the Ohio Valley, and local officials tried to improve commercial contacts with Europe and the Caribbean. In fact, for a period Charleston's railroad to Augusta was the longest such enterprise in the world. Yet these projects were only partially successful, for the economic tides of the time were running away from the Carolina entrepot. Cotton moved westward, up-country agriculture languished, and the mountains shut off the transappalachian trade. By the 1850's it was no longer possible to hide the decline. "I was disappointed," a British traveler wrote candidly, "by the general appearance of this capital of the South. On the whole, it has a somewhat poverty-struck look."

Richmond was the only state capital among Dixie's major cities. It was also the only major industrial one. Located on the James River at the head of navigation, it had centered its early hopes on trade. But gradually manufacturing and political affairs became the more important interests. Factories and ware-houses crowded along the river bank, their dull brick shells at once ugly and impressive. Farther back from the water stood the Capitol building, "an imposing Grecian edifice, standing alone, and firmly placed on open and elevated ground, in the center of town." Generous private mansions downtown attested to its wealth, but Richmond seemed less Southern than the coastal towns, and reminded visitors of Northern and British cities. "It is a metropolis," Olmsted wrote, "and, of course, the tide of modern life elsewhere reaches it, stirs it, and here and there possess it."

The strong manufacturing emphasis fortified this impression. As the nation's tobacco center, it stored and processed immense quantities every year. Its Tredegar Iron Company was renowned not only because of its success, but because it employed black labor, which permitted local enthusiasts to proclaim that it was possible to have slavery and industry too. And just beyond the city's edge were extensive coal fields, ready to feed Richmond's furnaces as well as to provide fuel for New York, Baltimore, and Newark. Olmsted first saw the town "through a cloud of bituminous smoke," and recalled "the sensation produced by a similar *coup d'oeil* of Edinburg." Commerce still played an important role in the life of the Virginia capital, but townspeople and visitors alike preferred to think of it as the manufacturing heart of Dixie.

Yet Richmond shared many of Charleston's problems. As the focus of Southern life moved westward, Virginia, too, suffered. The Old Dominion increasingly felt its economic and political power and its national prestige slipping away. "My pride has been humbled by her decline," one "patriot" confessed in 1828, "and I could weep for her fallen greatness." The fears were worse, however, than the facts. The city continued to grow even during depressions, though the pace was not dramatic. From some twelve thousand residents in 1820, the population increased four thousand in the next decade and reached twenty thousand by 1840. Local boosters usually included the suburbs in their estimates, thus adding considerably to the official figures. In 1839 the newspapers claimed 26,000 for the metropolitan area, leading a friendly neighbor to write that "she is going ahead with accumulating velocity," which he thought especially remarkable because until recently "she was in that lethargic condition so characteristic of Southern cities in the same period." On the eve of the Civil War the population had jumped to nearly thirty-eight thousand.

On the northeast corner of the South stood Baltimore and Washington—the former a thriving port and commercial center whose phenomenal rise after its incorporation in 1782 had threatened Philadelphia and concerned New York; the other growing steadily if not spectacularly as the national capital.

Both were essentially Southern in population and institutions. Indeed, in 1860, the Maryland port's 212,000 people made it the largest in Dixie and the country's fourth city; and Washington's 61,000 thrust it ahead of the older cities of the South Atlantic states.

On the upper periphery of the South were two other large urban centers, Louisville and St. Louis. Just across the river from each lay free territory, areas connected with the city in every important way but one—the institution of slavery. Indeed, in settlement and growth the two places were Western not Southern. It was only after the emergence of slavery as a divisive issue that the perspective changed. And, ironically, the shift took place at the very time when slavery itself was virtually disappearing from both towns. Yet in 1860 each had some Negro slaves, and as a Louisville editor put it, their "prejudices, interests and feelings" were "extremely Southern."

Louisville grew up at the Falls of the Ohio, the spot where the water strikes irregular shoals that force a break in transportation. The city early provided the facilities for moving goods and people around the hazard. From its founding in 1778 until the opening of the Louisville and Portland Canal in 1830, nearly all the riverborne commerce of the West passed through its hands. Even after the canal broke the initial monopoly, the town's strategic position permitted a generous prosperity.

Louisville's early interest was trade. In fact, in 1836 Gabriel Collins's *Directory* observed that the town depended "almost entirely upon . . . commerce." "No other city perhaps in the world," he continued, "with such a large commercial business, has a population so small, or employs as little capital in other occupations." This mercantile concentration later proved to be a liability, however, for when the panic of 1837 struck the Kentucky entrepot it did real damage. The census figures which had recorded constant gains in 1820 and 1830 suddenly dropped by five thousand.

Yet soon the old pace was renewed. By 1850 the population had reached over forty thousand, and ten years later it increased to nearly seventy thousand. "It has grown withall at a Western rapidity," Olmstead noted, having "great business, both as an entrepot and as itself, a manufacturing producer." Though "without the whirr of Cincinnati" or the charm of New Orleans, Louisville represented "a good specimen of a brisk and well-furnished city."

St. Louis was both a northern and western outpost of the ante-bellum South. Born in 1764 of French fur-trading activity, it was situated just below the confluence of the Mississippi and Missouri. Set aside the great waterways of the central continent, it early thrived on an almost imperial commerce. The coming of the steamboat greatly enhanced its growth and importance. Nearly every hour, the *Missouri Republican* observed in 1855, "some gallant steamer" plows "the waves of the Mississippi, bringing from the North, as far as St. Paul—from the West, beyond the Yellow Stone—from the South, almost to the Gulf, and from the Ohio to the very confluence of the Allegheny and Monongahela, the products of the richest and most improved country in the world." On the levee "the genius, enterprise and diversified interests of the nation" were represented. "The sugars of the South lay mingled with the cereals of the North, and the manufactures of civilization contrasted with the peltries of the Indian."

Nor was this merely parochial enthusiasm. *De Bow's Review* was at least as buoyant, claiming that "St. Louis is destined to become commercially more than Venice ever *was*—and in manufactures what *Lowell* is!" Local boosters never tired of chanting the statistics of metropolitan growth. Population increased from ten thousand in 1820 to seventy-eight thousand in 1850, and then jumped to over one hundred sixty thousand ten years later. Steamboat arrivals nearly doubled between 1840 and 1860, while the value of real estate increased more than tenfold in the same period. Nothing, it seemed, could halt the town's inevitable rise. "If vegetation should fail; if sunshine and rain should withhold their accustomed offices; . . . if our mighty rivers . . . should cease to flow," wrote one editor, "then will St. Louis be arrested in her upward march to greatness,—but not 'till then."

III

Southern cities would have grown even more rapidly if the Negro population had kept pace with the white. But the proportion of colored residents declined, and by 1860 most of the

major towns were actually losing blacks, both slave and free.
In each case the experience was the same. The number of slaves
mounted as the city became larger, often increasing faster than
whites. At some point, however, the ratio shifted. Negro populations leveled off as the others continued to rise; soon a gradual
reduction set in. Every Dixie metropolis went through at least
the first two phases of this cycle by 1860, and most had completed all three.

Travelers did not notice this attrition in the number of
urban blacks. Arriving by ship or train, they first saw town life
at the dock or station where colored porters, stevedores, and
draymen handled baggage and freight. At the hotels, boarding
houses, or fashionable homes they saw slaves as waiters, cham-
bermaids, and general domestics. A trip to the market place
would find Negro vendors, hawkers, and maintenance men.
Even a casual stroll on the street during the day or early evening
was likely to exaggerate the size of the black population, for
bondsmen could be seen running errands, driving wagons, and
doing much of the unskilled outdoor work. These contacts,
coupled with an intense interest in the South's system, obscured
for most visitors the proportionate decline of Negro residents
in the cities.

"The vast proportion of blacks in the street soon struck me,"
an Englishman wrote about New Orleans. "I should think they
were five to one of the white population." In fact, the ratio in
the Crescent City at that time was nearly the reverse. Likewise,
Fredrika Bremer, visiting Charleston in 1850 when whites outnumbered colored, could assert that "Negroes swarm the streets.
Two-thirds of the people one sees in town are negroes." Still
another contended in 1857 that "Richmond was at this time
literally swarming with negroes."

Yet the facts ran the other way. In Charleston, for example,
though initially both groups increased together, the proportion
of blacks substantially declined in the two ante-bellum decades.
In 1820 the total black population exceeded 58 per cent. But
in 1840 the relationship began to change. On the eve of the war
less than half the Charlestonians were Negroes, and only
slightly more than a third were slaves.

The same pattern emerged in New Orleans, except that the
number of free colored was always much higher. In 1805 more
than half the city's residents were Negroes, the bulk of them

slaves. The immense growth of the next fifteen years did not alter the proportions between the races significantly, though free blacks nearly equaled slaves. The 1830's, however, brought an almost revolutionary increase in population and an important change in the racial complexion of the city. Now over half of the hundred thousand or so inhabitants were white, though the blacks still numbered almost forty-three thousand.

New Orleans's expansion slowed but did not stop during the following twenty years. But colored residents declined both proportionately and absolutely. Indeed, in 1860, only one in every seven inhabitants was Negro. This trend, of course, ran sharply against the tendency in rural Louisiana, where the slave population rose markedly each year.

In Richmond the decline of bondsmen was relative not absolute by 1860. The decisive decade had been the 'thirties. Until then the blacks had a slight edge over the whites. In the next ten years the ratio changed slightly, then the gap soon widened. At the end of the period Richmond's slaves and free colored comprised less than 40 per cent of the city's population. And the increase in slaves in the last decade was modest—less than 2000—representing a reduction in the rate of growth and presaging a future reduction.

Mobile and Savannah enjoyed their greatest growth later than the larger places, hence the comparative decline of their Negro population did not appear as early. Nonetheless the story was the same. In 1830 the races were almost evenly divided in the Alabama port. By the 1860 census the percentage of blacks had fallen to just over a quarter of the total. Slaves still outnumbered free Negroes nearly ten to one, and while both continued to increase slowly, they lagged far behind the white advance.

In Savannah over half the population was colored in 1830. Within ten years, however, supremacy in the city shifted, the whites having a slight majority. But by 1860 the familiar difference appeared. The Negro population had dropped below 40 per cent, and the number of slaves to approximately a third.

The northeastern cities had a lower proportion of slaves in 1820 than other places, but they, too, conformed to the experience elsewhere. Baltimore's slave population was reduced by half in four decades, while Washington dropped slightly during the whole period. In both towns, however, the free Negro residents rose continuously but at greatly reduced rates in the

1850's. The combined black population, moreover, comprised a much smaller percentage of the total than before.

Dixie's northwestern cities revealed the pattern even more clearly. In St. Louis and Louisville the numerical distance between white and black was widest, and the Negro descent most precipitous. In both places colored people constituted nearly a quarter of the population in 1830. Yet within thirty years that proportion dipped to about 10 per cent in Louisville and to slightly over two per cent in St. Louis. Indeed, by 1860 there were more free blacks in St. Louis than slaves. And each year found fewer slaves in Louisville. These two towns, then, illustrate best the full cycle of slavery in the cities—early dynamic growth, stagnation, and finally decline.

The broad lines of this development could be conveniently traced in the decennial censuses of the federal government and in occasional local counts by municipalities. But in any given period slave populations varied considerably from year to year. The number of blacks might increase rapidly as masters brought coffles to town for sale, or be depleted as high prices elsewhere drew off urban Negroes. Some whites coming to the growing cities carried bondsmen with them, while others did not. In short, slave populations in the city were changing constantly. Rural statistics, on the other hand, show much more stability, with fewer variations and with steadier growth through the ante-bellum period.

IV

The fluctuations in the number of urban slaves, then, contrasted with rural patterns. Significantly, too, the distribution of bondsmen among city masters differed from the practice in the countryside. In towns, conditions seemed to foster a broad diffusion of ownership, with a large proportion of white families having at least a few Negroes. Indeed, for most of the period the percentage of slaveholders in most towns was higher than the surrounding areas. Of course, the number in each household was usually small, but the practice was widespread enough to give many a direct involvement in the "peculiar institution."

The 1820 census demonstrated the breadth of early urban slaveholding. In Charleston, of the 2100 "heads of families" listed, over three-quarters owned at least a single Negro. The Richmond figures reveal that about two-thirds of the households had blacks, while in Savannah and Mobile over one-half fell in this category. Even New Orleans, which had an extraordinary number of free colored in 1820, recorded owners as over a third of its white population. More remarkable, in Louisville over 50 per cent of whites held slaves. Clearly, in 1820 the city dwellers in Dixie had a substantial stake in slavery.

By 1840, however, the ratio of slaveholding to nonslaveholding began to change. To be sure, this did not happen in static cities like Charleston, where more than three-quarters of the white families still had colored bondsmen, nor in towns enjoying their first real expansion such as Mobile, where the proportion actually rose. But Richmond saw the percentage dip to about fifty; in New Orleans it fell below thirty. The most precipitous decline occurred in the border cities, Louisville showing fewer than a quarter of the family heads with slaves, while in St. Louis only one in seven owned any.

This tendency accelerated during the last two ante-bellum decades. A new system of scheduling by the federal census bureau in 1850 and 1860 makes comparison with early figures difficult, but local tax ledgers disclose a continuous decline in the incidence of slaveholding. Richmond's experience was typical. The city's personal property levy hit only a portion of white families, since it applied to just a handful of items. But it included slaves over twelve years old. In 1840 all but a small fraction of the residents paid on Negroes. In 1860 more than 60 per cent of the returns were without taxable slaves. In short, by the Civil War most inhabitants in the Virginia city had no direct financial investment in the system.

During the forty-year period, then, the extent of urban slaveholding can be traced in the census returns and tax ledgers. Until about 1840 the percentage of ownership was higher in the cities than in the countryside. In the 'forties, however, the trend changed, first slowly, then rapidly. Initially the proportion of masters declined as the total population of each community grew. Later the decrease could be measured in absolute terms. By the end of the period most of Dixie's metropolises were shedding slaves, and each year fewer of the residents had a monetary stake in the system.

V

The high incidence of slaveowning through most of the ante-
bellum decades meant that, by and large, individual holdings
would be modest. A few blacks was the normal unit, though
each locality had some masters with more than a score of
Negroes. This distribution again set off slavery in the cities
from the rural institution, where the plantation, large or small,
with its cluster of slaves around a white household, was more
characteristic. This pattern of ownership was present almost
from the beginning of each town, and it became more distinct
as communities grew and populations expanded.

Charleston, with the highest percentage of slaves, provides
a good illustration. The 1830 census listed 2873 "heads of
families"; 379 had no bondsmen; and 401 had at least ten. A few
had more extensive holdings, 87 owners with 20 or more and
19 with over 30. Yet the great majority of Charlestonians in
this year owned some slaves and the number usually was not
large. Three decades later there were fewer masters and fewer
slaves in the South Carolina metropolis; and the proportion of
those with big holdings dropped substantially.

New Orleans had the same experience. The number of large
slaveowners was never impressive, but even those few diminished as the decades passed. In 1830, 215 residents had over ten
blacks and 22 listed more than 20. On the eve of the Civil War
the city listed only 83 "heads of families" owning at least ten
Negroes and but 20 with better than a score. In short, substantial holdings had almost disappeared in Dixie's largest urban
center.

Though border-city statistics followed the same trend, the
Richmond picture was more complex. Over the forty-year
period the number of large units increased. Those of ten to
twenty rose from 14 to 47 and, more importantly, those of 20
and more jumped from 7 to 93. But this growth was almost exclusively in corporate ownership, representing a widespread use
of Negroes in manufacturing. Individual holdings, on the other
hand, showed the normal curve, with substantial holdings becoming scarcer as the decades passed.

Though the small unit characterized urban ownership, there
were some masters in every city with extensive holdings. Any

census of New Orleans, for example, would contain such listings as I. A. Blanc, 69, James Higgins, 155, J. M. Wilson, 45, Walter Campbell, 59, or Isaac Cubrer, 59. Charleston's tax list in 1860 included several entries, like J. W. Bennett, 77, Eliza Ball, 40, Abraham Wilson, 37, Jacob Barrett, 46, Mrs. M. A. Mathews, 36. A similar levy in Richmond in the same year furnishes further examples: R. A. Blackburn, 44, James J. Dorwin, 48, A. W. Taylor, 40, William Graener, 60, William H. Grant, 60.

Increasingly, the large urban slaveowners were business partnerships or corporations. Working the blacks in shops and factories, they could utilize many more than most individual masters; and some accumulated great numbers. For instance, on Charleston "Neck" two mills, Canonboro and Chrisolus, each had over 70 Negroes in 1840. The Louisville firms Crutchfield & Company and William A. Richardson Bagging Factory both possessed over 40 a decade later. And Factor's Press Company ranked among the largest of Mobile's slaveholders in 1860 with 95 Negroes.

The most spectacular figures, however, were always in industrial Richmond. On the eve of the Civil War, over 54 corporations owned at least ten slaves each. The Virginia Central Railroad held as many as 274, but several others had 75 or more. The possessions of many others, moreover, easily outstripped all but the most affluent individual masters. In New Orleans the incidence of corporate holding was never as high, yet firms like the New Orleans Canal and Banking Company, the Fireproof Cotton Press, and L. A. Garidal & Company could generally be found among the more substantial owners.

VI

Urban slavery increasingly contained an imbalance between male and female Negroes. As early as 1820 women had begun to outnumber men; by 1860 the difference was striking. In the later decades owners began to sell their younger males to planters, especially into the cane and cotton country. Left behind in the cities was a growing surplus of women. Hence, on the eve of the war almost every Southern town had a greatly distorted population distribution, with a glaring shortage of men.

Richmond alone seemed exempt from the trend, but conditions there were so special as almost to prove the rule. It was the place which most widely employed young male slaves in manufacturing, and it was the only city with a significant majority of Negro men. Indeed, the population figures reflect the increasing industrial utilization of this class. At the beginning of the period there was a slight excess of females; by 1860, 57 per cent of the town's slaves were male. No other urban center developed an economy that absorbed this kind of labor, hence other Southern cities saw women in the majority in Negro life.

The sex distribution among urban free colored also followed the same trend found in slave statistics. New Orleans, for example, had 1750 more females than males in this category in 1860, while Charleston developed a large imbalance, the census listing 2000 free Negro women and only 1200 men. Even Richmond, where the slave figures ran the other way, had a 10 per cent surplus of females in the free group on the eve of the war.

Smaller places displayed the same tendency. Savannah initially had more free colored men than women, but by 1840 the ratio changed. In Mobile a similar development left a disparity of more than 10 per cent by 1860. Nor did border cities break the pattern. In both Louisville and St. Louis the female margin was seldom less than in the others and usually greater. But the most compelling illustration of this peculiar urban tendency was Baltimore, which had the largest group of free Negroes in Dixie. There the female surplus was almost five thousand in an aggregate of over twenty-five thousand blacks.

In the cities, the colored women, both bond and free, easily outnumbered the men. In the white population, however, precisely the reverse was true. Nearly every Southern urban center had many more males than females, a disparity that was especially great in the periods of most rapid municipal growth. For instance, when Mobile enjoyed its first important expansion, it had twice as many men as women. As the pace of development slowed, however, a more normal distribution appeared.

New Orleans, too, showed the same imbalance in the era of its largest growth. In 1830 the census reported the division among whites at 7300 males and 4900 females. Ten years later the figures were 34,900 to 24,600. But as the city's expansion slackened during the next two decades, the numerical gap between the sexes closed substantially. St. Louis's experience brought similar distortions in the population structure, but the disparity was not so quickly reduced, remaining almost 10,000 out of more than 157,000 in 1860.

Less dynamic towns acquired more evenly proportioned white populations. Seldom did women exceed men, and often the difference was not great. Throughout the ante-bellum decades Charleston's statistics reveal no important discrepancy, and in 1860 male supremacy was barely sustained. In Richmond the sex differential among whites was never significant and was only about 5 per cent at the end of the period. At the same time Savannah's surplus of men was somewhat larger, yet it appeared to be declining.

VII

These shifting statistics suggest that in the cities slavery was never a static institution. In fact, nearly every critical aspect of the system changed constantly in the ante-bellum years. The Negro population, the number of slaveowners, the incidence and size of slaveholding, and the sex differentials all varied considerably in each decade. Furthermore, the towns themselves also changed, altering the conditions in which bondage functioned and forcing institutional adjustments to meet new situations. This flux was less conspicuous on the countryside. There the rural setting promoted a stability seldom found in towns. Indeed, a recent historian has asserted that by the 1830's "Slavery had crystallized; its form was fixed. In 1860 the peculiar institution was almost precisely what it had been thirty years before." Hence, he continues, it is possible "to examine it institutionally with only slight regard for chronology."

These generalizations were perhaps too sweeping even for slavery on the plantations, but they are clearly inappropriate for the cities. In fact, urban slavery developed through two distinct phases in the ante-bellum years. It is hard to find a single dividing point that would fit all places because of the variations in the speed and the extent of growth of Southern towns. Yet a rough watershed can be established between 1835 and 1845. Before that period slavery was an integral part of urban life. As the cities grew, so did slavery. But at some moment the system began to lose ground in the metropolis, and though still present it played an increasingly less important role. That "moment" usually came in the late 'thirties or early 'forties. But whether earlier or later its appearance was common in all Dixie's cities.

In the earlier period urban slavery resembled the plantation system. The incidence of ownership was high, the size of the holdings often substantial, and the presumption of permanence widespread. While slavery encountered difficulties in the city, no one predicted, much less advocated, its abandonment. And the statistical indices in 1820 and 1830 apparently pointed to further steady and substantial growth.

Yet within a decade or two there were many indications of change. The number of urban Negroes declined, fewer whites owned any, and the size of holdings dwindled. In addition, the sale of young bondsmen to the countryside produced an increasing surplus of female slaves remaining in the towns. New people meanwhile swelled Dixie's cities, which further reduced the importance of the blacks. Clearly the vitality was gone from the system in the urban centers, and each year witnessed a further waning. The transformation was never uniform, but every city experienced it.

No such development occurred in the rural South. "If anything," writes Kenneth Stampp in *The Peculiar Institution*, "the chains of bondage were strengthened, not weakened, in this ante-bellum period." It may be, as some contemporaries and historians have contended, that slavery contained a residual weakness and its vigor in 1860 was largely illusory. Yet, as a Virginian put it, it was "a fixed fact" in that year, and few indices suggested an early collapse. And certainly few Southerners were of a mind to overturn it themselves.

The contrast, then, between urban and rural slavery was marked. Whether the comparison be made of the proportion of slaves to the general population, the distribution of bondsmen among whites, the size of the holdings, or the sex ratio among the blacks, the statistical differences are striking. These figures, however, merely outline a deeper antithesis. Behind the census returns, tax ledgers, and official reports lies a sharper cleavage between ways of living. The city had created its own kind of world, with a pace, sophistication, and environment that separated it from rural modes. In the process it transformed Negro no less than white, slave no less than free man. Hence it is not surprising that slavery as an urban institution differed greatly from its rural counterpart, and that the city slave was often quite unlike his country brother.

PATTERNS OF MID-NINETEENTH-CENTURY URBANIZATION IN THE MIDDLE WEST

BAYRD STILL

Bayrd Still, head of the History Department at New York University, cites urbanization as an important component of the westward movement and traces the remarkably similar developmental patterns of five Great Lakes cities.

Until recently a persistent preoccupation with the agrarian aspects of the westward march of American settlement has to some extent obscured the fact that the prospect of future towns and cities as well as the promise of broad and fertile acres lured settlers to the "sunset regions." On many a frontier the town builder was as conspicuous as the farmer pioneer; the western city, through the efforts of its founders to extend its economic hinterland, actually facilitated the agrarian development of the West; and the opportunities attending city growth as well as those afforded by cheap farm lands contributed to the dynamic sense of economic abundance felt by Americans of the mid-nineteenth century. As early as 1845 one middle western editor identified this urban growth with the rapid development of the West when he wrote:

From Bayrd Still, "Patterns of Mid-Nineteenth Century Urbanization in the Middle West," *Mississippi Valley Historical Review*, XXVIII (September 1941), 187–206. Copyright 1941 by the Mississippi Valley Historical Association. Reprinted by permission of The Organization of American Historians.

The tide of emigration to the West seems to increase daily. . . . What an enterprising spirit characterizes the American people. . . . This . . . activity and enterprise . . . are the result of free institutions, which give an impetus to the human mind. In no other country have towns and villages sprung up so suddenly as in this. Everything seems to go ahead with railroad velocity. Well might Marryat remark that cities grow up here to more importance in ten years than they do in Europe in a century.

The growth of cities is admittedly a significant aspect of the history of the West. But any precise estimate of the bearing either of urbanization upon the expansion of the American frontier or of the westward movement of population upon city growth in the United States awaits a more adequate exposition of urban development in specific sections of the country than has as yet been set forth.

The migrants who poured into the Mississippi Valley in the middle of the nineteenth century built cities as well as cultivated farms. By the seventies, when the American people were first becoming conscious of the drift of population to the city, the Middle West showed a spectacular urban growth. It could then boast seven cities of more than a hundred thousand people, whereas thirty years before only New Orleans had achieved that size. To be sure, the total population of the ten major midwestern cities in 1870 still fell slightly short of the more than 1,800,000 city dwellers then living in New York, Philadelphia, and Boston; but in the rate of their growth the former were putting to shame the cities of the Atlantic coast. Among these mushroom metropolises of the West, the lake cities—Buffalo, Cleveland, Detroit, Chicago, and Milwaukee—rather than the valley cities—Pittsburgh, Cincinnati, Louisville, Nashville, and St. Louis—showed the greatest proportional increase in numbers. By 1870 the five lake cities had attained a combined population of more than sixteen times their total of 1840, although the population of the states in which they were located had barely tripled.*

* Comparative population of the Great Lakes cities:

	1820	1830	1840	1850	1860	1870
Buffalo	2,095	8,668	18,213	42,261	81,129	117,714
Cleveland	606	1,076	6,071	17,034	43,417	92,829
Detroit	1,422	2,222	9,102	21,019	45,619	79,577
Chicago			4,470	29,963	109,260	298,977
Milwaukee			1,712	20,061	45,246	71,440

Because of their rapid and parallel growth, a comparative analysis of these five lake cities provides a useful means of studying the nature of the emerging city in the Middle West. With striking similarity, they all limited themselves to those duties of the urban community which were common to eighteenth century cities. They all responded to the democratic movement by extending popular participation in municipal government and then by broadening the authority of the executive or administrative commission. Not only did they rely upon the individual to provide most of the services which are demanded today of the city itself but they also expected him to promote the city's growth—a promotion which in every case involved substituting the encouragement of manufacturing for an earlier emphasis on trade. And with equal uniformity they imitated the experience of one another in ordering the details of their municipal life. While it is never too wise to try to compress the variety of human behavior into patterns, the common responses of the five cities suggest the conclusion that these at least are qualities which may well be characteristic of mid-nineteenth century urbanization in the upper Middle West.

A comparative study of the charters under which the Great Lakes cities were governed between 1830 and 1870 discloses the imitation of form and limitation of function in which the powers of the urban community were at that time conceived. These charters were cut from an almost identical constitutional pattern, laid down in the spirit of eighteenth century America. Admittedly the creature of the legislative will of the state, each city nevertheless resorted frequently to the public meeting for the purpose of proposing charter changes and civic improvement. With the advance to city status the meagre functions of the village period—protection against fire, opening and repairing streets, regulating markets, licensing shows, and sinking public wells—were considerably expanded. These functions were enlarged by a uniform extension of regulatory powers, services, and guarantees—additions which were, however, more boldly granted than enforced if one judges from the charges of non-enforcement levied against the city administration by the Milwaukee press.

The first city charters of Buffalo (1832), Cleveland (1836), and Chicago (1837) were strikingly similar in form. The Chicago charter is almost an identical copy of the Buffalo document save for certain local references. In the more than thirty clauses enumerating the powers of the council, the wording of the Chicago charter is different from that of Buffalo in less than half a dozen instances. The Chicago charter added provisions with respect to street lamps and ferries, but lacked the provision for the assize of bread that is found in the Buffalo framework of government. Significantly, the contemporaneous government of Milwaukee, organized at virtually the same time (1836), was still confined to the restricted duties of a village. Ten years later, however, when it emerged as a city, its citizens sought, and the state legislature granted, an expansion of powers quite similar to those of its sister cities of the Great Lakes. The Chicago consolidation act of 1851 found an echo in a like measure for Milwaukee in 1852 and in a revision of Buffalo's charter in 1853. These charters elaborated rather than expanded the powers of the municipality in ways dictated by closer acquaintance with the problems of city government. Again the customary parallelism in form stands out both in the general pattern of the documents and in the many identical clauses, such as those setting up the fire department and compelling the removal of ill-smelling nuisances.

The advance from village to city brought an extension of municipal responsibilities, but only to an extent normally resulting, especially in America, from the crowding of people into small compass. These new powers were limited in general to the protection of life and property, although the results of each extension of authority were recognized as having a bearing on the promotion of trade and hence on the prosperity of the municipality. Concern for securing property against the chronic fire hazard of the western city made possible the enactment of building restrictions and encouraged the organization of fire-fighting facilities. Concern for health prompted the authorities to establish pesthouses, to quarantine immigrants coming through the lake ports, and to abate such nuisances as stagnant pools, foul-smelling substances, and slaughter houses—reforms stimulated not so much by aesthetic considerations as by the prevailing conviction that urban filth and the spread of cholera went hand in hand. While thus exhorting cleanliness, the authorities at the same time, perhaps paradoxically, laid restrictions on wasting water and prohibited bathing in the rivers from which the city water supply was drawn.

In the interests of urban order, the city councils were empowered to provide watchmen and police; to suppress disorderly houses; to impound animals running at large; to prevent immoderate driving, rolling hoops or playing ball in the streets, and the cluttering of sidewalks with snow, dirt, firewood, awnings, or cigar store Indians; to restrain "runners" for boats and stages; and to curtail city noises. Nor were these idle grants of authority. The Cleveland council, as one of its first acts, passed an ordinance on May 9, 1836, which provided that the streets were to be swept semi-monthly on Friday mornings by the owners or occupants of property; that horses should not be fastened so as to obstruct passage in the streets nor be driven on the sidewalks; and that the huge wooden replicas of boots, saddles, and kettles with which merchants advertised their wares were not to project over three feet into the street. In addition to providing for quarantine and hospitalization of the sick poor, the health ordinances of Milwaukee required that physicians report cases of contagious diseases and that records of burials show the cause of death lest criminal or dangerous causes be left unknown; decreed a fine of ten dollars for refusal to be vaccinated on the request of a physician employed by the city council; set up barriers to the immigration of the diseased, going so far as to empower constables to call upon the aid of bystanders in forcibly keeping immigrants from landing; and banned slaughter houses within the city limits. The Buffalo council prohibited interment within certain limits and ordered that graves be not less than five feet deep. Anti-noise ordinances in Buffalo and Milwaukee prevented the playing of musical instruments on docks or wharves on Sunday, and in Milwaukee the ringing of bells or loud outcries at public sales were forbidden.

In providing for markets and the regulation of traffic in necessary commodities, these western cities followed practices by which frontier and colonial communities had attempted to protect an often insufficient food supply, prevent monopolistic practices detrimental to the public health and security, avoid the competition of foreign vendors and hucksters, and at the same time force competition upon the licensed merchants. In 1849 Chicago had three markets for the retailing of perishable foods. Butchers were forced to hold stalls there until an act of 1851 permitted the establishment of meat shops outside the market.

City markets and strict market ordinances were justified as a means of supplying large cities with fresh and wholesome provisions, because leniency in this respect, it was felt, might encourage disease. Vendors of fresh meat, poultry, eggs, butter, lard, fruit, and vegetables were forced to sell their goods at the market during the market hours unless licensed to sell at some other place or in some other way. To guarantee the wholesomeness of the products, cleanliness of the stalls, and orderliness of the market, prohibitions were set up against pitching quoits, the presence of dogs, and the use of obscene and profane language in the vicinity of the market place. Purchasing goods at the markets for resale elsewhere or forestalling country producers for the purpose of buying their produce for resale was prohibited.

Similar regulations for supervising weights and measures affected the purchase of boards, brick, coal, firewood, casks, hay, flour, tobacco, potash, and salted provisions such as fish. According to a Cleveland ordinance of May 8, 1839, vendors of hay without a certificate of weight were subject to a fine of twenty-five dollars. In 1859 Milwaukee farmers opposed as an inequitable tax the weighing charge of five cents per load of wood and twenty-five cents per load of hay—a concession sold by the city to the highest bidder. The assize of bread, customary in the colonial city charter and in early charters in the West, was apparently abandoned in Chicago and for a while in Cleveland, though provided for elsewhere. In these young urban communities, commerce in such necessary commodities as food, fodder, and firewood was of sufficient public interest to warrant close regulation. Other pursuits related to the public welfare were also restricted. For instance, ordinances regulating the fees of hackmen and carters were not unusual. Chapter XIII of the Buffalo ordinances of 1855 stipulated that a hackman might be fined for refusing to carry a passenger or for going by other than the shortest route. Interest in attracting immigrants prompted a Milwaukee ordinance of May 3, 1849, which fixed a maximum charge of ten cents per article on the goods of immigrants and other passengers landed on the piers of the city.

These principal activities of the mid-nineteenth century city were laid down at the inception of cityhood and were based upon the regulations commonly existing during the colonial period. Later amendments elaborated these functions of mu-

nicipal government as specific problems arose, and occasionally
a measure was passed which suggested an expanding concept of
city government, as in the Chicago provision of 1851 with
respect to planting and preserving ornamental trees along the
streets and in the public grounds of the city. In general, however, the close of this middle period saw only a limited expansion
of urban responsibilities beyond those assumed with the grant of
the original charter. Nor did these differ in any marked way
from the eighteenth century pattern of powers granted the
government of New York City at the close of the colonial
period.

However, in defining the political authority underlying municipal management, these cities, developing in the current of
nineteenth century democracy, left eighteenth century limitations far behind. Here again is a striking uniformity of behavior
in the five lake cities. Each began its career as a city with a
property qualification, in addition to a residence requirement of
varying length, for at least one class of voters—whites, aliens,
or Negroes. Detroit in 1824 required its electors to be freemen
who had paid a city tax. Buffalo extended the suffrage to United
States citizens but required Negro voters to have a freehold
estate of $250 on which taxes had been actually rated and paid.
A tax qualification was prerequisite to voting in Cleveland in
1836, and Chicago in 1837 expected its voters to be householders
or to have paid a city tax of not less than three dollars within
the year. As late as 1846 Milwaukee exacted payment of a property tax or required highway or fire duty of male aliens who had
declared their intention of becoming citizens. At the outset of
cityhood in Chicago, Detroit, and Buffalo, only those owning a
freehold estate were eligible for the major elective posts; Milwaukee, having demanded a similar qualification of her village
trustees, abandoned this provision upon becoming a city in 1846.

Chicago took the lead in a democratic movement which
brought by the early fifties the abolition of property qualifications for suffrage and office holding. Milwaukeeans called a proposal to restrict the suffrage to United States citizens an "odious
and anti-republican" attempt to deprive "one-half of the citizens
of Milwaukee, who will be taxed for the support of the city
government, of their right to a voice in electing their officers or
making their laws." Like the framers of the state constitutions of
the middle period, these mid-western city dwellers believed in

representative government closely responsive to the popular will. A proposal to allow aldermen to hold their offices for three years was opposed in Milwaukee as "placing them beyond the reach of public opinion for a time almost equal to an age in older communities." Consequently, annually-elected councils were endowed with wide authority and the power of the executive office was greatly curtailed. In Buffalo the mayor was the creature of the council, and in the other cities little more than a figurehead. Chicagoans in 1840 openly resented the fact that their mayor was given a salary and pointed to Detroit and Buffalo where, they said, the mayors "in fact receive nothing." Adherence to the democratic principle of passing jobs around was the practice if not the provision. In Cleveland between 1836 and 1870 only five mayors succeeded themselves in office, and of the twelve available council positions the yearly average of councilmen who were reëlected was two. A study of the situation in Chicago and Milwaukee shows a similar rotation in office. In Detroit it became necessary to force men by threat or danger of fine to serve once they had been elected, although they were specifically exempted from holding the same office two years in succession. The municipal legislators served without salary, but this did not prevent many of them from amassing fortunes, especially when they held the office of street commissioner. To judge from an analysis of the trades and occupations of those who were councilmen in Cleveland and Milwaukee in the first twenty years of their cityhood, commission merchants, grocers, joiners, builders, masons, and attorneys took a predominantly active part in the government of these young western cities.

Charter changes both in the early fifties and after the financial crisis of 1857 brought some decrease in the amateur management of these governments and a consequent strengthening of the executive arm. In 1852 Milwaukee was provided with an appointed comptroller, soon made elective, to manage city finances. In 1858 the state legislature devised a bicameral council for the city in the hope of retarding hasty legislation. The mayor was granted the veto power in Chicago in 1851 and in Milwaukee in 1859, a negative that was strengthened in the latter city in 1861 and in the former in 1872 by requiring two-thirds rather than a majority of the elected councilmen to override it. The major development in all the Great Lakes cities at the close of the period under discussion was in the direction of establishing boards and commissions as a means of divorcing city management from amateur direction and political interference. This trend, realized in the late sixties and early seventies, was motivated, according to the Milwaukee *Sentinel*, by a feeling that it was inefficient and costly to commit the complicated problems of street improvements and urban services to elected councilmen. It would be better, said the editor, to trust the outlay of great sums of the people's money to "three capable, honest, experienced business men . . . with a moderate compensation for their services, than take the chances under the elective principle of having men of doubtful qualities . . . without compensation . . . under the constant imputation of petty frauds and speculations upon the ward funds." Vesting in the mayor the power of appointing the members of these boards and commissions is an index of the increased prestige of the executive and the decreasing influence of the legislative branch of city government at the opening of the seventies. The Great Lakes cities, growing to maturity in the environment of nineteenth century democracy, thus broadened the base of urban politics but narrowed the administration of municipal affairs.

These major cities of the Middle West did not "just grow." The promotional activities of the original speculator-founders were only the beginning of a long-time program in which newspaper editors, merchants, and citizens at large combined their efforts to attract settlers and business to a given city and away from its neighboring rivals. The promoters of the embryo village on the east side of the Milwaukee river expended nearly $100,000 laying out streets and effecting other improvements designed to attract the settler. By the exertion of political influence and the donation of land they secured the county courthouse for their growing community. Across the river, the promoters of the "west side" were spending similar sums upon improvements, filling the columns of the Milwaukee *Advertiser* with glowing reports of their city's promise, and, by employing a river boat to meet the lake steamers that touched Milwaukee harbor, preëmpting immigrants possibly destined for their rivals' village. Subsequently many a subterfuge was devised by Chicago and Milwaukee in an attempt to discredit the other in the eyes of European immigrants and eastern capitalists. Only the combination of geography and the railroad left Milwaukee a tired but still confident second in the race. "Forcing" immigrants was accomplished through the use of representatives and promotional advertising in eastern cities. For example, propaganda concerning deaths from cholera, or the absence of them, figured prominently in such campaigns.

The promotion of business in these cities followed a common pattern. A predominant concern for trade and commerce gave way in the middle sixties to the encouragement of manufacturing. Economic developments in Milwaukee and Cleveland substantiate this interpretation. The early interest in trade was reflected by the editor of the Milwaukee *Daily Sentinel and Gazette* in 1846: "It is . . . clearly to the interest of our merchants, millers, forwarders, and business men generally to unite upon some plan for extending and improving roads leading to Milwaukee." Even before this, popular contributions had subsidized a bridge that promised to facilitate the trade of neighboring farmers with the village merchants. Plank roads and railroads were heralded as a means of tapping the markets of the hinterland. Connections by rail with the Columbia River, with the Mississippi River (completed by 1857), and with the Minnesota country, and routes eastward by steam ferry across Lake Michigan and by the Detroit and Michigan railroad were only a few of the projects. They were supported by city funds, by loans of city credit, and by popular subscription—contributions often appealed for and given as a matter of civic duty. Clevelanders were equally convinced of the importance of roads and railways for prosperity. The editor of the Cleveland *Daily True Democrat* wrote in 1849: "Let us, like the wise Cincinnati merchants, spend liberally for these [plank] roads and do all to arouse our farmers and everybody to the importance of increasing our facilities for trade and travel and thus make Cleveland the center of a large region." By 1856 it was asserted in the Cleveland *Leader* that railroads were responsible for the city's growth. The establishment of Boards of Trade in Buffalo (1844), Detroit (1847), Cleveland and Chicago (1848), and Milwaukee (1849); the organization and promotional excursions of merchants; the contesting of disputed trade areas through the use of runners and drummers—these activities suggest the early emphasis on trade and commerce as the key to civic prosperity. In 1857, Milwaukee merchants were urged to compete for trade in Iowa and Minnesota where already Chicago, St. Louis, Dubuque, Galena, Cincinnati even, have their runners, posters, and advertisements scattered broadcast . . . offering tempting inducements to merchants to come and buy. . . . Now is the time for our merchants, manufacturers, and traders to . . . scatter their cards, handbills, circulars, and advertisements up and down the Mississippi. Let them dispatch some of their shrewdest clerks to La Crosse, Winona, Prescott, Hudson, St. Paul . . . and canvass thoroughly for orders.

By 1855, however, Cleveland editors were sounding a warning note. Business men were blinded, they said, "by the belief that commerce alone" would make the city great. The *Leader* asserted in 1856 that "no thinking man with capital will stop here when we have only commerce to sustain us. A manufacturing town gives a man full scope for his ambitions." That newspaper encouraged popular subscriptions to factory enterprises, urged the reduction of real estate prices as an inducement to capital, and agitated for the protection and consumption of home manufactures. An appeal to civic duty attended this promotion as it had the earlier agitation for railroad connections. By the late sixties when Cleveland had become a manufacturing center, earlier arguments used there were being echoed in Milwaukee. Vigorous newspaper agitation, together with the organization of the Milwaukee Manufacturers Association in January 1863, excited industrial ambitions. "Commerce alone can never give us a permanent prosperity," counselled a Milwaukee editor in 1866. By 1872, as a result, one-third to one-half of the working population of Milwaukee was engaged in manufacturing goods valued at $20,000,000. Stimulated by the economic developments of the Civil War period, pressed by the expansion of population into areas farther west of them, and in a sense taking a cue each from the economic experiences of the other, the lake cities had turned by 1870 from an almost exclusive interest in commerce to endorse sentiments to the effect that "a thousand dollars put into manufacturing does more to gather population than a million dollars put into trade."

A major source of the urban services of these young communities developed from the sense of individual responsibility which prompted thousands of city dwellers to invest their savings in the railroads and factories that were supposed to bring prosperity to the urban center. The mid-nineteenth century saw the Great Lakes cities in what might be called the "subscription period" of their municipal growth. Two to three days' work on the streets, for which money payments could be substituted, was expected of all able-bodied men. Street and sidewalk improvements as well as the eradication of nuisances were to be taken care of individually or charged against the property benefited. For protection against theft and riot Milwaukeeans had to rely upon occasional watchmen, volunteer firemen, and members of free military companies until a night watch and a police force were organized in 1852. As late as 1855 men carried weapons for their own protection, and an ordinance of that year compelled all citizens to aid the police when called upon to do so. In 1837 the Cleveland *Herald and Gazette* referred to the "Mutual Protecting Society," and in 1839 a number of the citizens "with commendable spirit formed themselves into companies for a city watch." In 1859 the merchants of Detroit, where as early as 1825 volunteer watchmen had been mobilized by passing around a subscription paper, subscribed to the support of a patrol for the business district, and the Milwaukee Board of Trade offered a bonus for additional protection in 1860. By the late fifties and early sixties police service was generally provided at city expense, and the management of the police by a commission was agitated or passed in Milwaukee (1864), Detroit (1865), and Cleveland (1866).

Fire protection came also in a major degree from individual contributions of time and money. In the middle thirties Clevelanders were fined when they refused to serve in the bucket line at fires. Local editors appealed to property owners to contribute their share of volunteer firemen and in 1840 congratulated Phoenix Company Number Four for having won the premiums offered annually by the insurance companies to stimulate competitive-minded fire fighters to efficiency and accomplishment. Milwaukeeans from all levels of society were members of the organized volunteer firemen, who met a portion of the costs of their own equipment and whose service exempted them from highway or militia duty. Donations, benefit concerts, and dinners raised $2,500 in 1851 to swell the funds by which the Ocean, Neptune, and Cataract companies of volunteer firemen carried on their work. Despite the pleas of property owners for more efficient service than unpaid volunteers could give, it was not until the appearance of the steam fire engine in the sixties that professional fire fighters were generally maintained from public funds.

Aside from a meagre and inadequate tax to support alms-houses and to furnish medical care for the sick poor, urban relief, too, was provided by individual donation. Invariably the cessation of navigation in the winter season brought demands from the unemployed of the city. Out of public meetings came plans for raising money and organizations for dispensing relief. Mayor D. A. J. Upham of Milwaukee expressed a general opinion in 1849 when he held that private enterprise was best equipped to meet the problem. The Cleveland *Daily True Democrat* said the poor could not be taken care of "unless individual activity and associated effort act." Women's organizations, such as the Martha Washington Society of Cleveland and the Ladies Benevolent Society of Milwaukee, were soon supplanted by more systematically managed relief groups, like the Milwaukee Provident Association and the Cleveland Relief Association. The Milwaukee group advertised its cause as a community responsibility, raised over $20,000 in the five years ending in 1867, and distributed fuel and provisions only after careful investigation of the needy. Private contributions were the chief means of support of the Chicago Relief and Aid Society, incorporated in 1857. Soup kitchens were also subsidized by private gifts and meal tickets were sold to those citizens who wished to offer them to the poor. The Milwaukee women who managed these enterprises trusted "to the benevolence of our citizens . . . for the food to be supplied."

To a large extent the cultural services of the city, beyond the provision for public schools, were the result of support by subscription. Forerunners of the public libraries of the seventies were the membership libraries of such organizations as the Young Men's Associations in Chicago and Milwaukee and the Reading Room Association in Cleveland. Imitating Chicago's example, and realizing that the lack of private libraries compelled "voluntary association," several Milwaukeeans organized to promote a library in 1847. In canvassing for funds and members they did not neglect to stress community obligation and the example of other cities. The promotional value of good libraries to the city was "a pretty safe index of the mental advancement . . . of a city." They also emphasized the "gallantry of the Association [which] admits even ladies to a full participation of the advantages of membership, with the exception, we think, of voting." Chartered in 1848, the Cleveland Library Association issued stock certificates and charged yearly dues.

Soliciting subscriptions in 1851 for a reading room, the editor of the Cleveland *Daily True Democrat* was convinced that "nothing . . . adds so much to the reputation of a city as a good Reading Room and Library."

Many other cultural activities were fostered by subscription. Local musicians and actors volunteered their services in aid of the fire department, orphan asylum, and other causes. The Milwaukee Musical Society when soliciting members in 1857 advised the public that its monthly dues of forty cents plus a two dollar initiation fee were "but a moderate tax to pay towards the support of an organization which ministers so largely to the enjoyment of our citizens and which reflects such credit upon our city." The founders of academies and colleges in asking for endowments also appealed to civic duty. By 1870 the beginning of public libraries and the agitation for parks—following New York's example with Central Park—were slight but indicative signs of the rôle that the urban government was ultimately to play in providing aesthetic satisfaction and social and cultural benefits to its citizens. A Cleveland editor went so far as to start a crusade in 1870 against city noises—"an evil rapidly becoming unendurable." He wrote: "While suppressing so rigorously all offences to the sight and smell, and punishing in general all disturbances of the peace, it would be only consistent to include in the proscription the still greater plague of noise." Yet he concluded a year later that the cure for city noises still lay in the field of individual responsibility: "We have not yet reached that point where the law will guard the nerves of the aged, the tender, and infirm from unnecessary torture." Such a concept of city function did not square with the "subscription period" of city growth.

These striking parallels in the institutional history of the five major cities of the Great Lakes are to be explained in part by the contemporaneous character of their growth, by the common sources from which their population sprang, and by the similarity of the economic forces influencing their behavior. In all five cities, the foreign born provided about half the population, with natives of Germany, Ireland, and Great Britain distributing themselves in nearly identical proportions, except in Milwaukee where European immigrants were more predominantly German. In the sectional origins of native Americans these cities were also similar. New York, Massachusetts, and Pennsylvania contributed most abundantly to each of the five cities save Chicago, which drew a large number from neighboring Michigan. The census of 1870 showed as well a remarkable uniformity in the percentages of people engaged in various occupational pursuits. But it was not simply a matter of similar social ingredients, for this municipal development of the Great Lakes area was apparently following a pattern or process not unusual to urban evolution elsewhere. As they grew to comparable size these cities were in many ways merely repeating the experience of the coastal cities half a century earlier. For example, after a generation of city growth the expanded powers of the lake cities in 1870, like those of the seaboard cities in 1800, represented a response more to the problems of size than to any changed philosophy of the functions of urban communities for which a difference in environment or personality might have been responsible. By 1870 each of these lake cities was a more conscious "municipal entity" than in its village period. Commercial regulations for the common good, cooperation through taxes and subscriptions for the promotion and improvement of the city, and the recognition of some of the social responsibilities presented by the interdependence of city life certainly had fostered a group consciousness—a group attitude, however, still very largely articulated by and pivoting around the individual. The "municipal consciousness," twentieth century pattern, was more than a generation in the future. Its full development awaited the flow of population, new economic needs, and changing social philosophy of the late nineteenth and early twentieth centuries.

In these urban centers of the Middle West in the mid-nineteenth century, the houses, to one traveller's surprise, were not "wigwamified," the dress and ornament not "wampumized." As Anthony Trollope said, the "general level of . . . material and intellectual well-being—of beef . . . and book learning" was "no doubt infinitely higher than in a European town." These cities sprang from beginnings closely associated in practice and attitude with the westward expansion of the American people. As they grew, their concern for popular management and their emphasis upon the intrinsic rôle of the individual in the promotion of the physical and cultural growth of the city reveal attitudes often observed by students of the agrarian frontier. At the same time, they showed a willing dependence upon eastern sources in the transmission of culture, a studied imitation of tested forms of municipal practice and urban service, and an expanding assumption of community responsibility. Such influences suggest that in the rise of the large city in the West, as elsewhere, one sees another—perhaps equally important if less explored—side of American social history in the nineteenth century.

IV

The Industrial City

———

During the period from the Civil War through the early years of the twentieth century, the American city reached maturity. While the urbanization of many advancing cities rested on industry and manufacturing, industrialization alone did not attract the multitudes that composed and contributed to the modern city. In addition, a complex concatenation of advances in communication, transportation, and technology nourished the industrial city.

In all sections of the country, concentrated population centers grew rapidly. The major cities established in the East before 1860—New York, Philadelphia, Baltimore, and Boston—continued their growth. But the most striking urban expansion occurred in the Midwest. Chicago, which in 1860 had little more than 100,000 people, passed a million by 1890 and had a population of over 2,185,000 in 1910. St. Louis, Cleveland, and Detroit also grew rapidly, but the expansion of many smaller cities had the most pronounced effect over the years. From 1880 to 1890, for example, Omaha's population increased more than 450 per cent, Kansas City, Missouri, more than doubled, Minneapolis expanded 350 per cent, Wichita rose from 5000 to 23,000, Duluth from 3300 to 33,000. During the same decade, in the South, Birmingham grew more than 850 per cent, and in the Far West, Denver tripled, Spokane jumped from 350 to 20,000 and Tacoma from 1100 to 36,000. On the aggregate, the number of dwellers in cities of 2500 or more rose from 19.8 per cent of the population in 1860 to 45.7 per cent in 1910.

Urbanization and its ramifications generated numerous responses. Economic opportunity brought multitudes of foreign and native rural migrants to the city. During times of prosperity problems of acculturation and adjustment were tempered by a relatively high standard of living. But the industrial depressions of the 1870's and 1890's brought poverty, destruction of trade unionism, massive violence, and urban disorder. Because of ethnic communication barriers, lack of interclass dialogue, and archaic governmental machinery, municipalities failed to adapt to increasing populations. Inadequate sewage systems and foul drinking water often resulted in unhealthy, stench-plagued central urban areas, particularly those inhabited by the poor.

Numerous politicians met the challenge creatively. The municipal boss, capitalizing on the amoral business ethics of the day, managed to expand urban facilities and provide a form of *de facto* public assistance to the poor in return for votes. In an era which sanctified the myths of rugged individualism and *laissez-faire*, urban bosses provided positive government, acting as precursors of the welfare state. Many of their innovations, particularly in welfare services, could not be officially institutionalized. Thus the bosses instituted costly devices, such as extensive political patronage and inflated city expenses, draining large sums from municipal treasuries but providing a necessary residue which trickled down to the urban poor.

The middle class viewed these developments with concern. Most reformers considered the elimination of violence, crime, and political corruption major objectives. But some, including adherents of the religious reform movement called the social gospel, believed that urban problems reflected underlying poverty of the industrial worker. Thus Protestant reformers established settlement houses and welfare agencies and even engaged in politics in order to uplift the worker and bring salvation to society by reforming the existing system. Catholic reformers established agencies primarily to dispense urban charity, to Americanize Catholic immigrants, and to support and influence the conservative American Federation of Labor. German Jews who had immigrated in the mid-nineteenth century also carried out a Jewish variation of the social gospel. Often aghast at the manner of their orthodox brethren newly arrived from East Europe, the German Jews soon replaced repugnance with social reformism and welfare agencies.

While the social gospel hoped to redeem the poor, the worker also attempted to overcome the social and economic impact of the industrial city. Through the Knights of Labor he hoped to unify the working class to realistically confront concentrated capitalism with labor solidarity. The Knights failed as a viable countervailing power, but what they could not do for the many, the American Federation of Labor accomplished more successfully for the few. By ignoring pleas of the unskilled immigrant worker and organizing only the highly skilled whose market advantages permitted victories over capital, the AFL added a measure of strength and dignity to an elite portion of the urban work force.

Just as the social gospel and labor movements emanated from the city, so also did much of the progressive movement. On the local level, progressives assaulted the corruption of immigrant-oriented political bosses. This manifestation of middle-class hostility to the immigrant worker extended, particularly in the Far West, to the labor movement as well. However, in time, coalitions between progressives, immigrants, and labor arose which directed a mutual hostility against the industrial monopolist on the state, and then on the federal, level.

Another dimension of urban self-consciousness can be found in the "city beautiful movement." The Chicago World's Fair of 1893 stimulated urban planning, most spectacularly on the Chicago shoreline. Architectural influences of the fair included urban plazas, domed buildings, occasional towers, a revival of classical motifs, and parks in the inner cities. The use of structural steel permitted proliferation of skyscrapers which altered the urban skyline, but the architectural innovation of the time that affected most urban dwellers, the class of industrial workers, was the tenement house. It provided for the most economical vertical stacking of humans by removing to the periphery light, air, heat, and bathroom facilities.

While society derived mixed benefits from urban changes, the modern city with its transportation system, abundant entertainment, and widened employment opportunities continued to attract rural dwellers who sought a better life. By the twentieth century, the city had clearly become the new frontier in American society.

THE EMERGENCE OF
INDUSTRIAL CITIES

BLAKE MCKELVEY

Blake McKelvey, City Historian of Rochester, New York, relates industrial development and urban growth in post-Civil War America.

So many ambitious towns sprang up in the early days on each frontier that many were threatened with atrophy when the railroads enabled a few to stake out broad hinterlands at the expense of their neighbors. Only through industrial enterprise could most cities hope to prosper. Some enjoyed special opportunities as a result of the timely discovery of mineral resources nearby or at points easily reached by cheap water transport. A few achieved industrial leadership through the exploitation of local water power or by the invention of machinery to process regional products more efficiently. Others escaped a way-station fate because a steady flow of immigrants spurred residents to develop new industries based in part on cheap labor and to produce for a national market. Still others prospered through the manufacture of patented or specialty articles. Several combined these tactics, and all labored to produce a marketable surplus.

The rise or decline of an individual town was of major concern only to its promoters and its more settled residents; others could and did move elsewhere without loss. But the widespread survival of many threatened communities by means of industrial enterprise was of primary significance. A few such towns became the prototypes of the industrial city and endowed it with special characteristics. Several others pressed the advantages their manufacturing activities brought and did so with such vigor that they achieved metropolitan status; a few of these, notably Minneapolis, acquired regional hegemony. Moreover the emphasis they gave to industry forced their commercial rivals also to accord it increased attention. To promote these efforts, the business leaders of most communities reorganized old boards of trade or established new associations. By the turn of the century the industrial output of American cities had so outstripped that of any foreign country that the character of international trade was transformed, and with it the services performed by the great ports.

The industrialization of America is a separate story, but the impetus given to that development by the rise of the city cannot be overlooked. The impetus given to industrialism by the rapid discovery and exploitation of the country's natural resources is more fully documented and understood, and so also is the effect of the great influx of immigrant workmen in this period. Here, however, we are interested in the converse side of these historic movements—the contributions that new sources of energy and raw materials, new supplies of labor and industrial skills, new machines and techniques of production made to urban growth.

Because of their glamour, the successive gold rushes have long had a place in American history, yet their product never compared in value with that of the silver and copper mines and appeared insignificant when measured against the output of the iron and coal fields. Similar contrasts marked their respective towns. Gold-mining towns such as Virginia City were more pretentious than those based on silver and copper, but their permanence depended on the discovery nearby of "baser" metals. Not even the iron- and copper-mining camps became major cities (Butte, Montana, was a possible exception). Only where abundant supplies of coal or other fuels were found was manufacturing encouraged and urban growth maintained.

Even in the coal fields, few mining towns became major cities. In the hard-coal region of Pennsylvania, where the ore deposits extended over several counties, numerous settlements or "patches" sprang up about many colliery shafts, creating a density of as much as 1300 persons per square mile without achieving the integration essential for urban status. By 1900 only Scranton and Wilkes-Barre had exceeded 100,000 and 50,000 respectively, and this chiefly because they were not as exclusively occupied with mining as, for example, neighboring Hazleton, which barely numbered 25,000 a decade later. In fact Scranton, at the turn of the century, had more industrial workers than either miners or tradesmen.

Generally a nearby commercial or industrial city supplied the marketing, banking, and other urban services for mining districts, thus strengthening its claim to regional leadership. Sometimes a mining town developed a new industry to convert the products of neighboring collieries, as in the coke district around Uniontown and Brownville, only to see its control absorbed in time by a regional capital, in this case Pittsburgh. Most mining communities, victims of absentee ownership and constricted by their specialty, failed to develop the internal leadership necessary to attract competing transport arteries or to tap new sources of credit.

Other fuel strikes brought dubious benefits to communities at their sites, but presented great opportunities to the commercial marts that acquired control. The oil towns of northwestern Pennsylvania, which displayed great vitality during the seventies, were soon checked as monopoly control over refining and marketing siphoned the profits of the industry into the hands of Rockefeller and his colleagues in Cleveland and other processing centers. Natural gas brought a sudden boom to several communities, notably Findlay and Toledo, Ohio, but their fortunes ebbed with the arrival of outside control. Toledo, already an important railroad hub and advantageously situated for lake trade, remained primarily a regional market until civic leaders, reasserting the town's rights to its power resources, enabled industry finally to pull ahead of commerce and boost the city into the 100,000 bracket by the close of the period.

Some cities prospered as processors of regional farm products. Minneapolis, a small neighbor of St. Paul in the seventies, captured leadership in the wheat belt of the Northwest during the eighties by developing mills able to produce a better flour from the spring wheat of that area than St. Louis or other rivals could mill from winter wheat. Kansas City won its independence from St. Louis and Chicago by building up its meat-packing industry. Milwaukee ventured with less success into each of these fields but achieved its greatest triumph in the brewing industry, likewise based on products of the area. Memphis competed with many other places in lumber milling but excelled in the production of cotton-seed oil. Each of these and several like them strengthened their positions by developing accessory industries and by extending urban economic services to a hinterland which they constantly endeavored to expand. All attained metropolitan status chiefly because of their manufacturing services.

Many cities, even when overshadowed by near neighbors, prospered through the employment of cheap immigrant labor. The shoe industry, in which the introduction of machinery after the mid-century tended to supersede old craft skills, lent itself to this use. Lynn and Haverhill had developed a reputation for shoes in earlier decades, and after the Civil War Cincinnati and Rochester, among others, began to specialize in this field. New York and Philadelphia, because of their large markets and abundant supply of newcomers, became shoe producers, although not as important as the older New England centers, where the earlier craftsmen supervised a new work force of immigrants.

But cheap labor, even when supplied from abroad, did not long remain content in America, and the shoe industry produced some of the most determined union-organizing drives of these decades. Unfortunately, from the viewpoint of the cities involved, when union demands mounted in one town, many firms (except those engaged in quality production) sought new sites, such as Milwaukee, Chicago, or Manchester, New Hampshire, where the organizers had not yet penetrated. The migration of shoe companies, facilitated by the practice of leasing rather than purchasing the machinery, presented a constant threat to cities in this field. It also provided an extreme example of the industrial mobility that contributed to both the diffusion and the fluidity of America's urban development.

The textile industry, too, displayed an intense interest in cheap labor, but the range of its migrations was limited. Originally established at water-power sites in New England, where textiles nurtured several of the country's first factory towns, notably Lowell and Manchester, this industry quickly replaced its early native-born labor from the first influx of Irish and other immigrant groups, thus speeding the urbanization as well as the cosmopolitan transformation of the Yankee homeland. During the post-Civil War expansion, when steam began to supplement water power, Fall River pulled into the lead among textile centers because of its easy access to water-borne coal and its cheap immigrant labor, including that of women and children. Some textile towns added other specialties; Chicopee developed tool shops and began to produce bicycles; Holyoke became a paper city; Lowell ventured into woolens, carpets, knitted products, and other enterprises. Successive waves of new immigrants—Polish, French Canadian, and Portuguese—enabled management to fight off many union demands; yet pressure from the workers and the restraints of labor legislation in America's second most urbanized commonwealth presented Massachusetts textile firms with an increasing disadvantage in competition with the new cotton mills of the South.

The development of the textile industry in the South had a substantial economic basis. The slow spread of cotton factories in North and South Carolina and Georgia during post-Civil War years uncovered a new supply of cheap labor in the poor whites of the Piedmont area and began in the eighties to attract northern capital, some of it from the New England firms themselves. Advances in technology—the Northrop automatic loom and the ring spindle, which eliminated the skilled mule spinners who had formed the backbone of textile unions in the North—enabled the southern mills to employ unskilled labor and to defeat the first effort at organization around 1900. Since many northern firms hesitated to make the fresh investments that new machinery required, New England textile cities saw the greater part of the expanding market after 1890 pass by default to new towns in the South.

A major reason for the embarrassment of some of the New England towns was the defection of their absentee entrepreneurs and the failure to replace their talents from among the immigrant workers. On the other hand, some cities prospered because of the enterprise and skills that waves of newcomers brought. British and Dutch glassmakers strengthened the economy of Pittsburgh and Toledo and gave economic vitality to Corning, New York, La Salle, Illinois, and many other towns. German brewers helped to build up Cincinnati, St. Louis, Ro-

chester, Chicago, and especially Milwaukee; despite some opposition from local temperance forces, they ultimately won
acceptance and influence in each place. Skilled mechanics and
technicians from England, Germany, and elsewhere received a
more immediate welcome and financial support in developing
enterprises ranging in one town from buttons to optical instruments; the classic example of immigrant enterprise, however,
was the clothing industry, and many cities fattened upon it.

When the ready-to-wear clothing trade appeared at mid-
century its most enterprising leaders were German Jews. Many
who had gained a footing as tailors or peddlers or retail merchants now expanded their operations by employing some of
their more recently arrived fellow countrymen. Several of these
firms, which sprang up in the more populous centers and engaged the talents of vigorous salesmen, installed the newly invented sewing machines, employing women and girls to operate
them. As cutting machines were perfected and the specialization
of tasks increased, some of the shops blossomed into factories.
Others, particularly in New York and Chicago, where the
largest influx of a new wave of Eastern European Jews occurred, developed a contract system that enabled the recent
comers to work under men of their own group and in neighborhood lofts where they could speak their native tongue.

This activity spread widely and unobtrusively, helping to
sustain sizable colonies of Eastern Jews in Boston and Baltimore,
in Cleveland, Cincinnati, Rochester, and a dozen smaller places.
Every member of the family lent a hand, but it soon became
evident that only the contract bosses were prospering. Again
a union movement developed and brought long years of bitter
strife, with both the owners and the organizers seeking to gain
an advantage by playing one city against another in regional
lockouts and boycotts. Nevertheless the industry, responding to
the rapid urban growth, continued to expand, and the companies, closely dependent on their labor supply, could not migrate freely. Wages remained low, and the wide use of sweat-
shops helped to foster living standards that were among the
worst in America—so wretched, in fact, that the public conscience was pricked. Soon local, state, and federal investigations
began to study the problem. New pressure for governmental
supervision developed, and a resurgence of union effort occurred
among the workers as the period closed.

If the classic example of immigrant enterprise was the clothing industry, that of the native was the commercial bank, though foreign-born bankers increased in number after the seventies. Each new settlement boasted one or more of these institutions, which quickly multiplied as the towns grew. By 1880, 6532 banks with national, state, or private charters—one to every 2000 urban residents—served a variety of functions, among them the promotion of city growth. Although the accumulation and use of private savings was still a minor feature, as was investment banking, the facility these establishments brought to commercial transactions, and the concentration they effected of fluid capital in the sixteen cities designated as redemption centers under the National Banking Act of 1863-64, strengthened the leading marts within their respective regions and tied their economy to the great central reserve capital in New York.

It was not the banks, however, but enterprising men who determined the direction of a city's industrial development. Sometimes an influx of newcomers with special skills transformed a town's activity. Thus at Rochester after the midcentury, when flour milling and canalling had passed their apogee, a host of immigrant craftsmen created the clothing, shoe, nursery, brewing, and woodworking industries that gave it a new burst of growth, placing it in the 100,000 bracket by 1885. The lack of convenient coal, iron, and other natural resources had threatened to blight the "Flower City's" manufacturing prospects, but the new industries depended less on raw materials than on human skills and on the excellence of their products. Such varied and specialized instruments were designed and built that they again transformed Rochester, within three decades, into a center of technical industry. A young bank clerk, George Eastman, discovered that the photographic laboratory he set up in his mother's kitchen held more fascination than a teller's cage, and the city soon shared his rewards.

Enterprise in abundance characterized most cities throughout these decades. Growth itself created a rich market, not only for food and apparel and building materials but also for a variety of new articles that promised urban convenience. Ingenious men perfected the telephone, the elevator, the trolley car, the bicycle, and the automobile—to name only a few that contributed to the ease and speed of communications in cities, thus increasing the momentum of their growth. Energetic promoters extended the use of these products widely through the towns of America and at the same time greatly benefited those where the factories were located.

The widespread technological advance frequently prompted independent inventors to work on similar problems at the same time. Occasionally a city assembled so many skilled craftsmen in a particular industry that it generated innovations and attracted experts from distant places. The Edison shops at Harrison, New Jersey, the Brush Electric Company at Cleveland, and the Thomson-Houston works at Lynn drew proficient electrical workers to these centers; Eastman attracted to Rochester rival photographic and optical companies eager to share its concentration of specialized skills. Although many manufacturers, impelled to acquire patent rights that might obstruct the development of their products, hastened to absorb competitors, the formation of new firms almost in the shadow of the expanding companies often continued unabated. Some of the new concerns developed subsidiary articles which they produced for the major distributors—speed shutters for cameras in Rochester, lamp stems for incandescent globes at Harrison—thus contributing to the integration of major community industries while retaining the enterprise many restless but talented craftsmen desired.

The upsurge of inventiveness flooded the patent office with applications as the 120,000 registered before 1870 mounted by 1910 to well over a million. Promoters who helped to develop the new mechanical devices generally enlisted support from local capitalists. The limited-dividend corporation, freely available under the general laws of most states, proved especially attractive, and such incorporations, almost nonexistent in manufacturing in 1860, numbered over 40,000 at the close of the century. Although they comprised barely a tenth of all establishments, they produced 60 per cent of the value, and almost completely dominated the metal and technical branches. The flexibility of these economic "persons"—their capacity for expansion or consolidation, for a shift in leadership or a change in product—fitted them admirably for growing cities faced with problems of economic integration.

The most rapid increase among giant corporations occurred at the turn of the century, as they mushroomed from twelve in 1896, each valued at $10 million or more, to fifty that exceeded

$50 million by 1903. Even after the move for consolidation began and strong, often monopolistic groups took hold, a rapidly expanding market and more effective sales promotion frequently enabled the trust to keep all its affiliated plants in operation, at least for a time. Sometimes a new factory site was selected, as in the case of the General Electric Company, a consolidation of Edison and rival concerns, but the new beginning it made at Schenectady in 1886 could not absorb all the work in process at Harrison, Lynn, and Cleveland, among other places. Several of the old centers prospered, while Schenectady became an industrial city of high quality.

Numerous towns, though not the majority, enjoyed similar benefits. The typewriter brought life to Ilion, New York, and new vigor to Syracuse; telephone factories clustered for a time at Boston and Chicago, but soon spread out; the cash register placed Dayton on the industrial map. A score of cities manufactured elevators, and many more contributed to the production of trolley cars and their equipment. Bicycle companies sprang up in a host of towns during the early nineties, but shortly after 1899, when the American Bicycle Company absorbed forty-eight of them, production was centered in ten plants at Springfield, Massachusetts, and Hartford, Connecticut, each of which suffered a severe blow when the trust collapsed a few seasons later. Several former cycle factories had meanwhile shifted to the manufacture of automobiles, in which Detroit quickly took the lead. Its surplus of capital from an expiring lumber trade, together with an overabundance of skilled marine-engine mechanics, welcomed the new industry.

So many cities suffered from the migration of old companies and other effects of consolidation that the antitrust forces won general approval. The long battle for the regulation of railroads had spread antimonopoly doctrines, nurturing a strong faith in competition, and prepared the way for the speedy adoption of the Sherman Anti-Trust Act in 1890. Yet its vague provisions left many issues undecided. In the courts, where the rising trusts had much more effective representation than in the legislatures, the legal curbs atrophied and almost disappeared. Protests against government interference with "free enterprise," on which the welfare, particularly of industrial cities, seemed to depend, enlisted support from most business groups and discouraged efforts to halt consolidations. Only the more flagrant invasions of local community interests aroused effective action, such as the Standard Oil Company's stranglehold over the fortunes of Toledo and other Ohio towns in the early nineties, or the Trans-Missouri Freight Association's attempt to control the traffic of the Southwest a few years later. Champions of the efficiency of large-scale enterprise multiplied, and in 1889 New Jersey provided a corporate form for the holding companies that widely superseded the old trusts.

In most cities new firms quickly replaced those absorbed or otherwise lost, and many small market towns grew into promising industrial centers. The number reporting at least 10,000 factory workers increased from thirty to fifty-four during the last two decades of the century; those listing 5000 or more rose from forty-five to eighty-one. After 1900 many factories migrated to the suburbs, and this presented the parent city with new problems of economic integration. All growing towns felt an increasing need for local leadership.

Boards of trade and chambers of commerce sprang up in city after city as rallying points for their businessmen. Only a few of the thirty or more such organizations formed before the Civil War had survived, notably those of Chicago, Buffalo, Pittsburgh, and New York. Now the extension of the telegraph and the laying of the Atlantic cable in 1866 opened new possibilities for long-distance trade negotiations and stimulated the formation of organizations to conduct local exchanges and disseminate trade information. Most of the new crop of business clubs were, like their predecessors, chiefly concerned with commerce, but in 1869 the Milwaukee Chamber of Commerce raised a fund of $860 "to promote the city's industrial growth." Its list of the town's advantages for trade and industry, published in 1871 and widely circulated, heralded a new, more industrial approach. A few years later, the same body initiated an industrial exposition patterned after the Centennial in Philadelphia. Its building, erected at a cost of $300,000 and opened in 1881, supplied facilities for annual exhibitions during the next two decades and inspired businessmen in St. Louis, Chicago, and Minneapolis to similar efforts.

The most forthright move in this direction occurred at Philadelphia in 1894, when the city council organized a Commercial Museum and provided it with a building and equipment to display local industrial products and to promote foreign trade. San Francisco, St. Louis, and Boston established similar museums. Not to be outdone, an Association for the Advancement of Milwaukee urged real-estate men to grant free sites or free rent to new industrial ventures and collected subscriptions from capitalists to back them. The association, which also proposed tax concessions, boasted after two years that its efforts had attracted a score of new industries to the city, helping it to reach fifteenth place by 1900.

Some of the post-Civil War boards of trade declined after a few seasons, but new organizations generally appeared in response to urgent business needs. Several midwestern towns formed promotional bodies similar to Milwaukee's. In 1892 the Cleveland Board of Trade created a committee for the promotion of industry, which led in turn to the reorganization of the board as a Chamber of Commerce a year later, when a full-time secretary was engaged to handle such activities and to develop new civic and welfare functions. Other chambers, too, were seeking competent secretaries, and in 1913 as their activities became standardized the newly established Harvard Business School organized a course for them.

The effort to provide free sites or other subsidies for new industries lost favor in some chambers after concerns of questionable merit accepted such benefits only to move on when a higher bid arrived. But the promotional value of numerous trade conventions, industrial exhibitions, and publications that featured local advantages gained wide acceptance among the several hundred boards and chambers of the early 1900's. If the annual reports often sounded a bit boastful, even to local observers, such growing industrial cities as Milwaukee, Cleveland, Pittsburgh, Detroit, Buffalo, Columbus, and Rochester—not to mention several of the newer towns of the West—all gladly supported active groups.

Although the basic philosophy of most of these chambers involved unfaltering support for "free enterprise," especially after events in the nineties sharpened the issue, some of their committees did try to establish voluntary standards of production and fair dealing. Their resolutions generally opposed state and federal regulations, but many were quick to appeal to the I. C. C. or to an appropriate state authority when a long-haul railroad rate schedule or some other monopoly practice seemed prejudicial to the locality. Their concern for the city's welfare often aligned them against freebooting utility combines and high-handed industrial giants. Leadership in the continuing attack on trusts and corporate monopolies generally came from other sources, but the chambers were exponents of community business interests.

Most growing towns had, of course, developed a sense of the community's interest long before organizations to promote it emerged. An informal leadership, which later sociologists would call the power structure, generally directed important aspects of the development of each city. The promoters of town sites and urban subdivisions, who frequently joined the merchants to support and direct the expansive projects of the commercial centers, seldom gave effective leadership to the industrial cities. There the initiative more frequently came from ambitious craftsmen, often men with inventive talents, whose struggle to produce and market new products transformed them into captains of industry. They were the most alert developers of each town's external economy. Newcomers from abroad, and others from small towns nearby, rose in this fashion to positions of influence.

Many industrial cities developed specialties based on the skills of their workers or the inventive talents of their technicians. On the other hand the mining towns and some others largely dependent on one industry frequently lost control to absentee owners who opposed the development of independent enterprise. The widespread reaction to, or fear of, that fate strengthened the antimonopoly forces of the commercial centers, plagued by railroad pools, and hastened the triumph of the progressive movement.

The most important contribution of the industrial cities was the mounting output of their factories. Statistics show that the value added by manufacturing doubled between 1859 and 1879 and more than doubled again in the prosperous eighties, and yet again, despite two depressions, by 1909. The value added by manufacturing increased tenfold in the half-century, almost trebling the increased value of farm products. Moreover the portion of the national income derived from manufacturing mounted from 16.6 to 20.8 per cent during the last three decades, while that derived from agriculture held steady and the contributions of both trade and transportation declined.

In this period, at least, industry rather than commerce was the chief source of urban growth. Over nine-tenths of the industrial production occurred in urban factories, and as their output increased a surplus for export developed in some fields. Shipments abroad of manufactured foodstuffs and of finished industrial products mounted steadily after 1876 until, by 1898, even the latter exceeded comparable imports. As American factories progressively crowded European products out of the domestic consumer trade, the American farm was relieved of the burden of balancing foreign payments. The export of foodstuffs, both raw and manufactured, declined after the turn of the century, but the exports of other manufactured products more than took up the slack, maintaining a sufficiently favorable balance of trade to liquidate some of the foreign investments. Thus urban industrial growth freed the national economy not only from dependence on European factories, but also from reliance on foreign banks for new capital. That, however, was only a minor aspect of the industrial city's accomplishment, for the value added to its products exceeded the total value of all imports almost seven to one by 1899, as contrasted with a ratio of five to two, four decades earlier. As foreign trade diminished in relative importance, domestic trade mounted, and the industrial worker produced material goods in sufficient volume to raise the standards of consumption throughout the country.

URBANIZATION, MIGRATION, AND SOCIAL MOBILITY IN LATE-NINETEENTH-CENTURY AMERICA

STEPHAN THERNSTROM

Stephan Thernstrom, Associate Professor of History at Brandeis University, examines various kinds of mobility and contends that urbanization stimulated transiency and lessened economic opportunity for "the common people of America."

The United States, it has been said, was born in the country and has moved to the city. It was during the half-century between the Civil War and World War I that the move was made. In 1860, less than a quarter of the American population lived in a city or town; by 1890, the figure had reached a third; by 1910, nearly half. By more sophisticated measures than the mere count of heads, the center of gravity of the society had obviously tilted cityward well before the last date.

If to speak of "the rise of the city" in those years is a textbook cliché, the impact of this great social transformation upon the common people of America has never been sufficiently explored. This essay is intended as a small contribution toward that task. It sketches the process by which ordinary men and women were drawn to the burgeoning cities of post-Civil War America, assesses what little we know about how they were integrated into the urban class structure, and suggests how these matters affected the viability of the political system.

I

The urbanization of late nineteenth-century America took place at a dizzying pace. Chicago, for instance, doubled its population every decade but one between 1850 and 1890, growing from 30,000 to over a million in little more than a generation. And it was not merely the conspicuous metropolitan giants but the Akrons, the Duluths, the Tacomas that were bursting at the seams; no less than 101 American communities grew by 100 percent or more in the 1880s.

Why did Americans flock into these all too often unlovely places? There were some who were not pulled to the city but rather pushed out of their previous habitats and dropped there, more or less by accident. But the overriding fact is that the cities could draw on an enormous reservoir of people who were dissatisfied with their present lot and eager to seize the new opportunities offered by the metropolis.

Who were these people? It is conventional to distinguish two broad types of migrants to the American city: the immigrant from another culture, and the farm lad who moved from a rural to an urban setting within the culture. It is also conventional in historical accounts to overlook the latter type and to focus on the more exotic of the migrants, those who had to undergo the arduous process of becoming Americanized.

This is regrettable. To be sure, immigration from abroad was extremely important in the building of America's cities down to World War I. But the most important source of population for the burgeoning cities was not the fields of Ireland and Austria, but those of Vermont and Iowa. The prime cause of population growth in nineteenth-century America, and the main source of urban growth, was simply the high fertility of natives living outside the city.

We tend to neglect internal migration from country to city, partly because the immigrants from abroad seem exotic and thus conspicuous, partly because of the unfortunate legacy left by Frederick Jackson Turner's frontier theory, one element of which was the notion that the open frontier served as a safety valve for urban discontent. When there were hard times in the city, according to Turner, the American worker didn't join a union or vote Socialist; he moved West and grabbed some of that free land. This theory has been subjected to the rather devastating criticism that by 1860 it took something like $1,000 capital to purchase sufficient transportation, seed, equipment, livestock, and food (to live on until the first crop) to make a go of it; that it took even more than $1,000 later in the century; and that it was precisely the unemployed workmen who were least likely to have that kind of money at their command. It is estimated that for every industrial worker who became a farmer, twenty farm boys became urban dwellers. There was an urban safety valve for rural discontent, and an extremely important one. The dominant form of population movement was precisely the opposite of that described by Turner.

Since scholarly attention has been focused upon immigrants from abroad, upon Oscar Handlin's "Uprooted," it will be useful to review what is known about their movement to the American city and then to ask how much the same generalizations might hold for native Americans uprooted from the countryside and plunged into the city.

Immigration is as old as America, but a seismic shift in the character of European immigration to these shores occurred in the nineteenth century, as a consequence of the commercial transformation of traditional European agriculture and the consequent displacement of millions of peasants. Compared to earlier newcomers, these were people who were closer to the land and more tradition-bound, and they generally had fewer resources to bring with them than their predecessors. One shouldn't overwork this; a substantial fraction of the German and Scandinavian immigrants had enough capital to get to the West to pick up land. But some of the Germans and Scandinavians, and most men of other nationalities, had just enough cash to make it to the New World and were stuck for a time at least where they landed—New York, Boston, or wherever. They swelled the population appreciably and the relief rolls dramatically, particularly in the pre-Civil War years, when they entered cities which were basically commercial and had little use for men whose only skill in many cases was that they knew how to dig. Eventually, however, the stimulus of this vast pool of cheap labor and the demands of the growing city itself opened up a good many unskilled jobs—in the construction of roads, houses, and commercial buildings, and in the manufacturing that began to spring up in the cities.

That they were driven off the land in the Old World, that they arrived without resources, immobilized by their poverty, and that they often suffered a great deal before they secured stable employment is true enough. But these harsh facts may lead us to overlook other aspects which were extremely significant.

One is that immigration was a *selective* process. However powerful the pressures to leave, in no case did everyone in a community pull up stakes. This observation may be uncomfortably reminiscent of the popular opinion on this point: that it was the best of the Old World stock that came to the New— the most intelligent, enterprising, courageous. But this should not lead us to neglect the point altogether. The traits that led some men to leave and allowed them to survive the harrowing journey to the port, the trip itself, and the perils of the New World, could be described in somewhat different terms: substitute cunning for intelligence, for example, or ruthlessness for courage. Still, whatever the emphasis, the fact remains: as weighed in the scales of the marketplace, those who came—however driven by cruel circumstance—were better adapted to American life than those who remained in the village or died on the way.

The other main point about the immigrants, and especially those who suffered the most extreme hardships—the Irish in the 1840s and 1850s, the French Canadians in the 1870s, the Italians and various East Europeans after 1880—is that they appraised their new situations with standards developed in peasant society. Lowell was terrible, with its cramped stinking tenements, and factory workers labored from dawn till dark for what seems a mere pittance. Children were forced to work at a brutally early age; the factories and dwellings were deathtraps. But Lowell was a damn sight better than County Cork, and men who knew from bitter experience what County Cork was like could not view their life in Lowell with quite the same simple revulsion as the middle-class reformers who judged Lowell by altogether different standards. It is not so much the objectively horrible character of a situation that goads men to action as it is a nagging discrepancy between what *is* and what is *expected*. And what one expects is determined by one's reference group—

which can be a class, an ethnic or religious subculture, or some other entity which defines people's horizon of expectation. Immigration provided an ever renewed stream of men who entered the American economy to fill its least attractive and least well rewarded positions, men who happen to have brought with them very low horizons of expectation fixed in peasant Europe.

That those Americans with greatest reason to feel outrageously exploited judged their situation against the dismally low standards of the decaying European village is an important clue to the stunted growth of the labor movement and the failure of American Socialism. Working in the same direction was what might be called the Tower of Babel factor. A firm sense of class solidarity was extremely difficult to develop in communities where people literally didn't speak each other's language. Even in cases where groups of immigrant workers had unusually high expectations and previous familiarity with advanced forms of collective action—such as the English artisans who led the Massachusetts textile strikes in the 1870s—they found it hard to keep the other troops in line; a clever Italian-speaking or Polish-speaking foreman could easily exploit national differences for his own ends, and if necessary there were always the most recent immigrants of all (and the Negroes) to serve as scabs to replace the dissenters en masse.

A somewhat similar analysis applies to the migrants who left the Kansas farms for Chicago. They were linguistically and culturally set apart from many of their fellow workers; they too had low horizons of expectation fixed in the countryside and brought to the city. The latter point is often missed because of the peculiar American reverence for an idealized agrarian way of life. As we have become a nation of city dwellers, we have come more and more to believe that it is virtuous and beautiful to slave for fourteen hours a day with manure on your boots. Recently that sturdy small farmer from Johnson City, Texas, remarked that "it does not make sense on this great continent which God has blessed to have more than 70 percent of our people crammed into one percent of the land." A national "keep them down on the farm" campaign is therefore in the offing. But it is damnably hard to keep them down on the farm after they've seen New York (or even Indianapolis), and it was just as hard a century ago, for the very good reason that the work is brutal, the profits are often miserably low, and the isolation is psychologically murderous. Virtuous this life may be, especially to people who don't have to live it, but enjoyable it is not—not, at least, to a very substantial fraction of our ever shrinking farm population.

This applies particularly to young men and women growing up on a farm. Their parents had a certain stake in staying where they were, even if it was a rut. And the eldest son, who would inherit the place eventually, was sometimes tempted by that. But the others left in droves, to tend machines, to dig and haul and hammer—or in the case of the girls, to sell underwear in Marshall Field's, to mind someone else's kitchen, or in some instances to follow in the footsteps of Sister Carrie.

There were some large differences between native-born migrants to the cities and immigrants from another land, to be sure. But the familiar argument that native workmen "stood on the shoulders" of the immigrant and were subjected to less severe exploitation is somewhat misleading. The advantages enjoyed by many American-born laborers stemmed more from their urban experience than their birth, and they did not generally accrue to freshly arrived native migrants to the city. The latter were little better off than their immigrant counterparts, but then they were spiritually prepared to endure a great deal of privation and discomfort because even the bottom of the urban heap was a step up from the farms they had left behind. The two groups were one in this respect, and perceptive employers recognized the fact. In 1875, the Superintendent of one of Andrew Carnegie's steel mills summed up his experience this way: "We must steer clear as far as we can of Englishmen, who are great sticklers for high wages, small production and strikes. My experience has shown that Germans and Irish, Swedes and what I denominate 'Buckwheats'—young American country boys, judiciously mixed, make the most honest and tractable force you can find."

II

The move to the city, therefore, was an advance of a kind for the typical migrant. Were there further opportunities for advancement there, or did he then find himself crushed by circumstance and reduced to the ranks of the permanent proletariat? Did his children, whose expectations were presumably higher, discover correspondingly greater opportunities open to them? Remarkably little serious research has been devoted to these issues. Historians who see American history as a success story have been content to assume, without benefit of data, that the American dream of mobility was true, apparently on the principle that popular ideology is a sure guide to social reality. Dissenting scholars have been more inclined to the view that class barriers were relatively impassable, an assumption based upon generalized skepticism about American mythology rather than upon careful empirical study. Some recent work, however, provides the basis for a tentative reappraisal of the problem.

We know most about mobility into the more rarified reaches of the social order regarding such elite groups as millionaires, railroad presidents, directors of large corporations, or persons listed in the *Dictionary of American Biography*. What is most impressive about the literature on the American elite is that, in spite of many variations in the way in which the elite is defined, the results of these studies are much the same. It is clear that growing up in rags is not in the least conducive to the attainment of later riches, and that it was no more so a century ago than it is today. There have been spectacular instances of mobility from low down on the social scale to the very top—Andrew Carnegie, for instance. But colorful examples cannot sustain broad generalizations about social phenomena, however often they are impressed into service toward that end. Systematic investigation reveals that even in the days of Andrew Carnegie, there was little room at the top, except for those who started very close to it.

Furthermore, this seems to have been the case throughout most of American history, despite many dramatic alterations in the character of the economy. It seems perfectly plausible to assume, as many historians have on the basis of impressionistic evidence, that the precipitous growth of heavy industry in the latter half of the nineteenth century opened the doors to men with very different talents from the educated merchants who constituted the elite of the preindustrial age; that unlettered, horny-handed types like Thomas Alva Edison and Henry Ford, crude inventors and tinkerers, then came into their own; that the connection between parental wealth and status and the son's career was loosened, so that members of the business elite typically had lower social origins and less education, and were often of immigrant stock. Plausible, yes, but true, no. It helped to go to Harvard in Thomas Jefferson's America, and it seems to have helped just about as much in William McKinley's America. There were the Edisons and Fords, who rose spectacularly from low origins, but there were always a few such. Cases like these were about as exceptional in the late nineteenth century as they were earlier. The image of the great inventor springing from common soil, unspoiled by book-larnin', is a red herring. It is doubtful, to say the least, that the less you know, the more likely you are to build a better mousetrap. And in any event it was not the great inventor who raked in the money, in most cases—Henry Ford never invented anything—but rather the organizer and manipulator, whose talents seem to have been highly valued through all periods of American history.

These conclusions are interesting, but an important caution is in order. It by no means follows that if there was very little room at the top, there was little room anywhere else. It is absurd to judge the openness or lack of openness of an entire social system solely by the extent of recruitment from below into the highest positions of all. One can imagine a society in which all members of the tiny elite are democratically recruited from below, and yet where the social structure as a whole is extremely rigid with that small exception. Conversely, one can imagine a society with a hereditary ruling group at the very top, a group completely closed to aspiring men of talent but lowly birth, and yet with an enormous amount of movement back and forth below that pinnacle. Late nineteenth-century America could have approximated this latter model, with lineage, parental wealth, and education as decisive assets in the race for the very peak, as the business elite studies suggest, and yet with great fluidity at the lower and middle levels of the class structure.

Was this in fact the case? The evidence available today is regrettably scanty, but here are the broad outlines of an answer, insofar as we can generalize from a handful of studies. At the lower and middle ranges of the class structure there was impressive mobility, though often of an unexpected and rather ambiguous kind. I will distinguish three types of mobility: geographical, occupational, and property, and say a little about the extent and significance of each.

First is geographical mobility, physical movement from place to place, which is tied up in an interesting way with movement through the social scale. Americans have long been thought a restless, footloose people, and it has been assumed that the man on the move has been the man on the make; he knows that this little town doesn't provide a grand enough stage for him to display his talents, and so he goes off to the big city to win fame and fortune, or to the open frontier to do likewise. When you examine actual behavior instead of popular beliefs, however, you discover that things are more complicated than that.

It proves to be true that Americans are indeed a footloose people. In my work on Newburyport, a small industrial city, I attempted to find out what fraction of the families present in the community in the initial year of my study—1850—were still living there in the closing year, 1880, one short generation. Less than a fifth of them, it turned out—and this not in a community on the moving frontier, like Merle Curti's Trempealeau County, where you would expect a very high turnover. There the true pioneer types, who liked to clear the land, became nervous when there was another family within a half day's ride of them and sold out to the second wave of settlers (often immigrants who knew better than to try to tame the wilderness without previous experience at it). But to find roughly the same volatility in a city forty miles north of Boston suggests that the whole society was in motion.

The statistics bear out the legend that Americans are a restless people. What of the assertion that movement and success go hand in hand, that physical mobility and upward social mobility are positively correlated? Here the legend seems more questionable. It seems likely that some who pulled up stakes and went elsewhere for a new start did improve their positions; they found better land, or discovered that they possessed talents which were much more highly valued in the big city than in the place they came from. What ever would have happened to Theodore Dreiser in small-town Indiana had there been no Chicago for him to flee to?

But the point to underline, for it is less commonly understood, is that much of this remarkable population turnover was of quite a different kind. As you trace the flow of immigrants into and then out of the cities, you begin to see that a great many of those who departed did so in circumstances which make it exceedingly hard to believe that they were moving on to bigger and better things elsewhere. There is no way to be certain about this, no feasible method of tracing individuals once they disappear from the universe of the community under consideration. These questions can be explored for contemporary America by administering questionnaires to people and collecting life histories which display migration patterns, but dead men tell no tales and fill out no questionnaires, so that part of the past is irrevocably lost. But some plausible inferences can be drawn about the nature of this turnover from the fact that so many ordinary working people on the move owned no property, had no savings accounts, had acquired no special skills, and were most likely to leave when they were unemployed. They were, in short, people who had made the least successful economic adjustment to the community and who were no longer able to hang on there. At the lower reaches of the social order, getting out of town did not ordinarily mean a step up the ladder somewhere else; there is no reason to assume that in their new destinations migrant laborers found anything but more of the same. When middle-class families, who already had a niche in the world, moved on, it was often in response to greater opportunities elsewhere; for ordinary working people physical movement meant something very different.

That is a less rosy picture than the one usually painted, but I think it is more accurate. And we should notice one very important implication of this argument: namely, that the people who were least successful and who had the greatest grievances are precisely those who never stayed put very long in any one place. Students of labor economics and trade union history have long been aware of the fact that there are certain occupations which are inordinately difficult to organize simply because they have incessant job turnover. When only 5 percent or 1 percent of the men working at a particular job in a given city at the start of the year are still employed twelve months later, as is the case with some occupations in the economic underworld today (short-order cooks or menial hospital workers, for instance), how do you build a stable organization and conduct a successful strike?

An analogous consideration applies not merely to certain selected occupations but to a large fraction of the late nineteenth-century urban working class as a whole. The Marxist model of the conditions which promote proletarian consciousness presumes not only permanency of membership in this class— the absence of upward mobility—but also, I suggest, some continuity of class membership *in one setting* so that workers come to know each other and to develop bonds of solidarity and common opposition to the ruling group above them. This would seem to entail a stable labor force in a single factory; at a minimum it assumes considerable stability in a community. One reason that a permanent proletariat along the lines envisaged by Marx did not develop in the course of American industrialization is perhaps that few Americans have *stayed* in one place, one workplace, or even one city long enough to discover a sense of common identity and common grievance. This may be a vital clue to the divergent political development of America and Western Europe in the industrial age, to the striking weakness of socialism here, as compared to Europe—though we can't be sure because we don't definitely know that the European working-class population was less volatile. I suspect that it was, to some degree, and that America was distinctive in this respect, but this is a question of glaring importance which no one has yet taken the trouble to investigate.

When I first stumbled upon this phenomenon in sifting through manuscript census schedules for nineteenth-century Newburyport, I was very doubtful that the findings could be generalized to apply to the big cities of the period. It seemed reasonable to assume that the laborers who drifted out of Newburyport so quickly after their arrival must have settled down somewhere else, and to think that a great metropolis would have offered a more inviting haven than a small city, where anonymity was impossible and where middle-class institutions of social control intruded into one's daily life with some frequency, as compared to a classic big-city lower-class ghetto, where the down-and-out could perhaps huddle together for protective warmth and be left to their own devices—for instance, those Irish wards of New York where the police made no attempt to enforce law and order until late in the century. Here if anywhere one should be able to find a continuous lower-class population, a permanent proletariat, and I began my Boston research with great curiosity about this point.

If Boston is any example, in no American city was there a sizable lower class with great continuity of membership. You can identify some more or less continuously lower-class areas, but the crucial point is that *the same people do not stay in them.* If you take a sample of unskilled and semiskilled laborers in Boston in 1880 and look for them in 1890, you are not much more likely to find them still in the city than was the case in Newburyport.

The bottom layer of the social order in the nineteenth-century American city was thus a group of families who appear to have been permanent transients, buffeted about from place to place, never quite able to sink roots. We know very little about these people, and it is difficult to know how we can learn much about them. You get only occasional glimpses into the part of this iceberg that appears above the surface, in the person of the tramp, who first is perceived as a problem for America in the 1870s and reappears in hard times after that—in the 1890s and in the great depression most notably. But what has been said here at least suggests the significance of the phenomenon.

So much for geographical mobility. What can be said about the people who come to the city and remain there under our microscope so that we can discern what happened to them? I have already anticipated my general line of argument here in my discussion of migration out of the city—which amounted to the claim that the city was a kind of Darwinian jungle in which the fittest survived and the others drifted on to try another place. Those who did stay in the city and make their way there did, in general, succeed in advancing themselves economically and socially. There was very impressive mobility, though not always of the kind we might expect.

In approaching this matter, we must make a distinction which is obscured by applying labels like "open" or "fluid" to entire whole social structures. There are, after all, two sets of escalators in any community; one set goes down. To describe a society as enormously fluid implies that there are lots of people moving down while lots of others are moving up to take their place. This would obviously be a socially explosive situation, for all those men descending against their will would arrive at the bottom, not with low horizons of expectation set in some peasant village, but with expectations established when they were at one of the comfortable top floors of the structure.

Downward mobility is by no means an unknown phenomenon in American history. There have been socially displaced groups, especially if you take into account rather subtle shifts in the relative status of such groups as professionals. But the chief generalization to make is that Americans who started their working life in a middle-class job strongly tended to end up in the middle class; sons reared in middle-class families also attained middle-class occupations in the great majority of cases. Relatively few men born into the middle class fell from there; a good many born into the working class either escaped from it altogether or advanced themselves significantly within the class. There is a well-established tradition of writing about the skilled workman, associated with such names as the Hammonds, the Lynds, Lloyd Warner, and Norman Ware, which holds the contrary, to be sure. This tradition still has its defenders, who argue that with industrialization "class lines assumed a new and forbidding rigidity" and that "machines made obsolete many of the skilled trades of the antebellum years, drawing the once self-respecting handicraftsmen into the drudgery and monotony of factory life, where they were called upon to perform only one step in the minutely divided and automatic processes of mass production." Rapid technological change doubtless did displace some skilled artisans, doubtless produced some downward mobility into semiskilled positions. But defenders of this view have built their case upon little more than scattered complaints by labor leaders, and have not conducted systematic research to verify these complaints.

Careful statistical analysis provides a very different perspective on the matter. Two points stand out. One is that as certain traditional skilled callings became obsolete, there was an enormous expansion of *other* skilled trades, and, since many of the craftsmen under pressure from technological change had rather generalized skills, they moved rapidly into these new positions and thus retained their place in the labor aristocracy. Second, it is quite mistaken to assume that the sons of the threatened artisan were commonly driven down into the ranks of the factory operatives; they typically found a place either in the expanding skilled trades or in the even more rapidly expanding white-collar occupations.

As for workers on the lower rungs of the occupational ladder, the unskilled and semiskilled, they had rarely drifted down from a higher beginning point. Characteristically, they were newcomers to the urban world. A substantial minority of them appear to have been able to advance themselves a notch or two occupationally, especially among the second generation; a good many of their sons became clerks, salesmen, and other petty white-collar functionaries. And the first generation, which had less success occupationally, was commonly experiencing mobility of another kind—property mobility. Despite a pathetically low (but generally rising) wage level, despite heavy unemployment rates, many were able to accumulate significant property holdings and to establish themselves as members of the stable working class, as opposed to the drifting lower class.

It may seem paradoxical to suggest that so many Americans were rising in the world and so few falling; where did the room at the top come from? The paradox is readily resolved. For one thing, our attention has been fastened upon individuals who remained physically situated in one place in which their careers could be traced; an indeterminate but substantial fraction of the population was floating and presumably unsuccessful. By no means everyone at the bottom was upwardly mobile; the point is rather that those who were not were largely invisible. Furthermore, the occupational structure itself was changing in a manner that created disproportionately more positions in the middle and upper ranges, despite the common nineteenth-century belief that industrialization was homogenizing the work force and reducing all manual employees to identical robots. The homogenizing and degrading tendencies that caught the eye of Marx and others were more than offset, it appears, by developments which made for both a more differentiated and a more top-heavy occupational structure. Third, there were important sources of social mobility that could be attained without changing one's occupation, most notably the property mobility that was stimulated by the increases in real wages that occurred in this period. Finally, there was the so-called "demographic vacuum" created by the differential fertility of the social classes, best illustrated in the gloomy late nineteenth-century estimate that in two hundred years 1,000 Harvard graduates would have only 50 living descendants while 1,000 Italians would have 100,000. The calculation is dubious, but the example nicely clarifies the point that high-status groups failed to reproduce themselves, thus opening up vacancies which had necessarily to be filled by new men from below.

For all the brutality and rapacity which marked the American scene in the years in which the new urban industrial order came into being, what stands out most is the relative absence of collective working-class protest aimed at reshaping capitalist society. The foregoing, while hardly a full explanation, should help to make this more comprehensible. The American working class was drawn into the new society by a process that encouraged accommodation and rendered disciplined protest difficult. Within the urban industrial orbit, most of its members found modest but significant opportunities to feel that they and their children were edging their way upwards. Those who did not find such opportunities were tossed helplessly about from city to city, from state to state, alienated but invisible and impotent.

URBANISM
AND THE CHURCH

Harvey Wish, Professor of History at Western Reserve University, analyzes the effect of nineteenth-century urbanization upon American religious thought and church institutions.

I

The growth of the metropolis, with all that it implied in secularism and anti-traditionalism, gave the churches the greatest challenge in their history. Yet the foreign visitor was impressed by all the external signs of the majestic victory of religion in America between Appomattox and Sarajevo. Never had the urban churches, enriched by the captains of industry, been so crowded; if the modern Gothic buildings with their expensive organs did not outshine the art of the medieval cathedrals, it was not for lack of money; and never before had theological schools, Sunday schools, missions, and church charities attained such dimensions and prosperity in this country. Church attendance figures soared in geometrical ratio, despite the secular world of Charles Darwin, Robert Ingersoll, and Jacques Loeb.

The shift of immigration sources in this era from Northwestern Europe, where Protestants predominated, to South-

From Harvey Wish, *Society and Thought in Modern America*, 2nd ed. (New York: David McKay Company, Inc., 1962), pp. 148–173. Copyright © 1952, 1962 by David McKay Company, Inc. Reprinted by permission of David McKay Company, Inc.

eastern Europe, with its huge Catholic and Jewish elements, gave the metropolis a large non-Protestant quality.

Catholics and Protestants, Jews and Gentiles, believers and atheists rubbed shoulders in an intimacy foreign to rural society. If the Utopian religious cultists of the mid-century had been unable to shield their followers from error through isolated settlements, how could each urban church retain its unique doctrinal differences when denominational intermarriages daily reflected biological rather than religious promptings? *Interdenominationalism* of the Y.M.C.A. type was inevitable under these circumstances.

In the rootless industrial city, workingmen built their dingy homes around their workplaces and factories. They had little leisure left for church affairs. Low wages, sickness, and joblessness were apt to be more real than the fires of hell and the bliss of eternal salvation. Drink, gambling, and prostitution flourished in this environment. To the perplexed, socialism seemed a more convincing panacea than did personal regeneration. To aid in this difficult task of garnering souls, both Protestant and Catholic churches invoked the social gospel, which meant that the social order was to be transformed into a kingdom of righteousness on earth based upon the social teachings of Jesus. To vie with the attractions of gregarious city life as well as to solve the social evils, there arose, especially after 1890, the "institutional church," handsomely outfitted with welfare services, game and club rooms, and classes for the foreign-born.

The urban intellectuals, even more than the workmen, led the trek away from the church. This generation debated over and over again the problem of reconciling modern science with religion and failed to resolve its secret doubts, even while reaffirming the unity of both. Before the Civil War German theological schools fostered "scientific criticism" of the Bible. David Friedrich Strauss of Tübingen shocked the orthodox world in 1835 with his naturalistic "higher criticism" of the Bible and of Christ, in his *Life of Jesus*. Revelation, miracles, and the supernatural suffered their most severe attacks since the time of Voltaire. Protestantism, leaning heavily on the doctrine that the Bible was literally inspired and the sole authority for religion, staggered under the attacks of the "higher critics" upon the origin and development of Christian sacred writings. Scholars, armed with vast linguistic knowledge, challenged the accuracy and authorship of various biblical texts, and anthropologists like Edward Tylor and James Frazer in Britain undermined the assumptions of orthodoxy through the new science of "comparative religion." Frazer's monumental work, *The Golden Bough* (1890), a critical collection of religious and superstitious practices and beliefs, stimulated the reader's impression that Christianity consisted of myths analogous to those of primitive religions.

To the Bible literalists, science was definitely at war with religion. Sir Charles Lyell, the geologist, had already disturbed the Bible literalists by showing that the earth was far older than the mere six thousand years or so suggested by clerical calculations of the date of creation. He had pointed out that any analysis of geological processes proved that the earth had a far greater antiquity than the year 4004 B.C. But the greatest blow to the literalists came from Darwin's *Origin of Species* (1859) and *Descent of Man* (1871). Darwin's theory of natural selection gave the *coup de grâce* in many minds to the idea that man was literally created in the physical image of God. Evolution implied that man was an imperfect product that had developed from some humble amoeba. There seemed cold comfort in the impersonal God whom the deterministic scientists had resurrected from the eighteenth century Deists. This concept of God might please secularists, but it offered no attraction whatever to those who believed in the efficacy of prayer and miracles to correct the inequities of life.

Darwin needed all the help of American philosophers like John Fiske and scientists like Asa Gray to reconcile the idea of divine purpose in the universe with the blind determinism implied in his idea that chance biological variations are selected for survival by the impersonal agency of the environment. Even Darwin, who was too optimistic to believe that "this magnificent world," as he put it, could be the product of blind chance, doubted that God was interested in deciding upon what species were to survive. Many of the organic variations were too useless, he felt, to be the result of special design and merely reflected a struggle for existence. To him the philosophic problem of chance versus design was insoluble. Such reasoning may have led William James and the pragmatists to decide that the search for absolute certainties was futile and that it was enough to know how ideas "worked" in concrete situations.

The impact of evolutionary thought on religion led theologians to make several kinds of intellectual adjustments. Among liberal Protestants, Darwinism and the "higher criticism" were the parents of Modernism which looked upon religious truths as evolutionary, adapting themselves to changing conditions, rather than acting as eternally fixed dogmas. Modernism stimulated the growth of liberal Christianity beyond the confines of Unitarianism and Emersonian transcendentalism. Progressive Protestant theologians, interested in solving the urban problems of labor and poverty, were attracted to a "social gospel" based on evolutionary ideas, particularly as implied in the doctrine of the immanence of God in human society. According to the leading exponents of the social gospel, the evolutionists had proved that God was part of a changing cosmic process and that His divine plan was unfolded in the progress of man upward to an ever higher stage. From this idea, it was easy to reach the conclusion that God's design involved the early emergence of a kingdom of righteousness on earth no less than in heaven. Unlike the millennialist, who simply waited for the Second Coming, the social gospeler believed that the kingdom would come through the intelligent planning of religious men.

Catholicism escaped much of the revolutionary impact of secularism, for it had never shared the biblical literalism of orthodox Protestantism, but rested instead upon the teachings of church tradition, spiritual revelations, and miracles. Heresies like Modernism, schisms, and intellectual deviations could be felled at a blow by the spiritual weapons of the Vatican, ranging from doctrinal encyclicals to excommunications. Catholics contended that science, rightly construed, could not possibly challenge religious dogmas. The *Catholic Encyclopedia* held that the human soul, being of a spiritual nature, could not have evolved from that of the brute; and that a distinction must be made between "the theory of evolution as based on theistic principles and as based on a materialistic and atheistic foundation." To the author of the *Encyclopedia* article Darwin's theory of natural selection was open to scientific criticism as well.

Among the liberal Protestants who clung to economic conservatism rather than the social gospel were a number of fashionable preachers of the Gilded Age who minimized the labor problem but exalted the new science. The best-known of these is Henry Ward Beecher, minister of the well-to-do Plymouth

Church in Brooklyn. This remarkable brother of the immortal Harriet had steadily lost whatever he may have once had of the prewar tradition of social dissent. During the Panic of 1873, he refused to admit that there was any basic social maladjustment in the existence of millions of unemployed and the breadlines that taxed the resources of urban churches everywhere. However, he was outspoken in his denunciation of unions, strikes, and labor violence. A *New York Times* reporter in 1877 noted these defiant words of the Great Preacher:

The trade union, originated under the European system, destroys liberty . . . I do not say that a dollar a day is enough to support . . . a man and five children if a man would insist on smoking and drinking beer. . . . But the man who cannot live on bread and water is not fit to live.

His biographer, Paxton Hibben, relates that thirty police and a corps of secret service men guarded Beecher during this harangue. While Plymouth Church applauded, critical journalists caricatured him and his $20,000-a-year salary.

This son of strict old Lyman Beecher moved ever farther from the historic Calvinism and ideals of his Congregationalist background. While he clung to the language of the supernatural, his theology became increasingly "liberal" and "humanistic" in the crudest sense, betraying the most flagrant philosophical inconsistencies. His optimistic sermons made "love" their cardinal point, but he did not extend its application to the laboring man. He reassured his wealthy congregation that the Bible must not be taken too literally in its strictures upon the rich man's entering heaven. He could eulogize the militant agnostic, Colonel Robert Ingersoll (whose economic views coincided with his own) and, at the same time, tell his listeners that he could not accept predestination or Hell. Following closely in the footsteps of several prominent Anglican churchmen who, in 1877, had repudiated the traditional concept of Hell, Beecher was able to create a new sensation in the American pulpit—there were many of these "shockers" in his technique—by saying that he could not believe that God could be so malign as to destroy men in the fires of Hell like insects over a fire. In 1882, he publicly explained his convenient pragmatic theology to the Congregational Association:

I gradually formed a theology by practise—by trying it on, and the things that really did God's work in the hearts of men I set down as good theology, and the things that did not, *whether they were true or not, they were not true to me.*

He converted innumerable followers to an early acceptance of evolution and to his Spencerian version of "liberal religion." Religion to him was an adventure in personal well-being—limited to the middle class in its material benefits—and it was simple for Beecher to raise evolution to the status of a spiritual revelation, "God's thought in the evolution of matter." These ideas appeared in his exuberant book, *Evolution and Religion* (1885). He took issue with the "bigoted theologists, ignorant pietists, jealous churchmen," and unintelligent men who ridiculed Lyell's geology and Darwin's biology.

In an age of middle-class complacency, Beecher made a dogma of self-congratulation; at a time when severe social dislocations had been let loose by industrialism and crowded cities, he diverted the Christian doctrine of social responsibility into the irresponsibility of Spencerian laissez faire and the uncritical acceptance of the inevitability of social progress. Science was in effect equated with God and became a popular religion despite its lack of ethical content.

II

Rural Protestants and their orthodox allies in the cities rebelled against the "modernist" liberals and their faith in science as a guide to spiritual values. In many congregations liberals and conservatives quarreled, being too often held together only by their mutual stake in church property. By the twentieth century the conservatives had organized themselves into "fundamentalist" sects wherever it was necessary. In 1910, these religious authoritarians issued a booklet assailing Modernism, *The Fundamentals; a Testimony to the Truth,* which contained an uncompromising statement of fundamentalist views as against heresy. This pamphlet stressed five points of doctrine: the virgin birth of Christ, the resurrection, the imminent Second Coming, the atonement for man's sins by Christ's sacrifice, and the inerrancy of the Bible. As for the Catholic Church, its rejection

of Modernism was thorough; papal encyclicals emphatically denounced this as a flagrant heresy to be avoided by the faithful.

Not a few urban intellectuals and working-class radicals espoused a far more anti-traditional viewpoint than Modernism.
This was the agnosticism of Robert Ingersoll and his followers.
In England, Thomas Henry Huxley, an English biologist whose
militant championship of evolution on the public platform won
him the title, "Darwin's bulldog," attacked dogmatic theology
in the name of "agnosticism." He defined this as a scientific attitude of suspended judgment in which the individual finds a lack
of evidence to affirm the existence of God or a life after death.
In effect this meant a denial of the historic mission of the
Church and a reversion to Voltaire in its militant anti-clericalism.

The amazing popularity of Robert Green Ingersoll (1833-
99), dubbed "the great agnostic," suggests the increased toler-
ance of his generation to an irreligious position hitherto un-
forgivable in a major public figure. In antebellum times, it is
true, radical reformers like Robert Dale Owen and Frances
Wright had organized the "Free Enquirers" to oppose organized religion as well as to promote sweeping plans of social
reconstruction. A sprinkling of "freethinkers" had always in-
filtrated American radical thought in previous generations.

However, Ingersoll, like Voltaire, had no intention of assault-
ing the bastions of economic orthodoxy, for he was the friend
and legal counsel of the mighty in business and industry. He
broke with the Congregationalism of his minister-father in
which he had been reared. Gifted with a flair for spread-eagle
oratory, and buttressed by an impressive Civil War record, he
became a politician and a wealthy lawyer with a long list of
legal victories won before impressionable jurors. Not the least
of his laurels was his masterly and successful defense of the
defendants in the "Star Route" scandals involving large-scale
fraud against the government in the compensation of mail contractors. So orthodox were the views of Ingersoll in politics and
economics that he might possibly have reached the highest office
had his irreligious views not been a barrier to his "availability."
He could bury vital economic issues beneath the most contagious emotional appeals of the "bloody shirt" variety, keeping
green the memories of Civil War sectional hates. Best remembered as a service to his party was his nomination of James G.
Blaine in 1876 as the Republican presidential candidate. His

flattering characterization of the shifty Blaine as the Plumed Knight caught the imagination of his generation.

Influenced by Darwin, Huxley, and the "higher criticism" movement against the Bible's infallibility, he expounded his agnosticism before huge crowds for thirty years, attracting the young lawyer, Clarence Darrow, among many other liberals, to his position. His forceful oratory as well as his heterodox ideas drew audiences for such lecture topics as "Some Mistake of Moses" and "Why I Am an Agnostic." In the latter speech he defined the agnostic, "He gives up the hope of ascertaining first or final causes, of comprehending the supernatural, or of conceiving of an infinite personality." To him the world was without beginning and would be without end; religion and morals were in large part the product of soil, climate, and circumstance. He declared that Shakespeare was preferable to the prophets from a literary point of view and that Darwin and Humboldt were superior to the author of Genesis as scientists. Constantly he attacked organized religion. "With sword and flame, it destroyed the brave and thoughtful men who told the truth. It was the enemy of investigation and reason. Faith and fiction were in partnership." Unlike the agnostics and atheists among the working-class socialists, he avoided any criticism of the churches for conservative economic tenets.

III

The cityward movement challenged the evangelical exhorters who discarded formal theology for a simple emotional appeal to the uprooted semi-literate masses. Foremost among those to retain the soul-saving tradition of the camp meeting, though in a more dignified form, was Dwight L. Moody, once a Boston shoe salesman, but active in city missionary work and Sunday school teaching since the 1850's. He served as secretary of the Chicago Y.M.C.A. and during the Civil War became an active missionary on the field for the United States Christian Commission. Never ordained as a minister and lacking all but rudimentary book learning, he proved nevertheless one of the most effective preachers of all time. To the agnostics and Modernists who found inconsistencies in the Bible, he replied emphatically, "The Bible was not made to understand!"

In 1870, he met Ira David Sankey, a minor revenue clerk who desired above everything to use his powerful dramatic voice in winning souls. Moody and Sankey toured the British Isles as well as the United States and aroused the revivalist spirit wherever they went. The *New York Times* declared in 1876, "A new hope has lifted up hundreds of human beings; a new consolation has come to the sorrowful; and a better principle has entered the sordid life of the day through the labors of these plain men." Moody seemed to be a new John Wesley, eager to inspire religious excitement without the extremes of hysteria or the "jerks." Women often credited their conversion to the effect of a hymn sung by Sankey such as "Hold the Fort," "Watching and Waiting," and "Ninety and Nine." Moody recalled he had heard "Rock of Ages" once a day for six years.

These evangelists avoided the pressing economic questions of the day. Wall Street, like the East Side slums, had souls to save and the advantages of the world to come appeared far too great for quarrels over temporary advantages in this one. The wealthy as well as the poor contributed heavily to Moody's insistent fund-raising campaigns in behalf of his large chain of educational institutions. In 1889, he had built a citadel of evangelical training in the (Moody) Bible Institute for Home and Foreign Missions in Chicago. At his birthplace and residence, Northfield, Massachusetts, he introduced annual conferences of church workers and students. A master of publicity—his critics called him the Barnum of religion—he scattered tons of religious tracts wherever he went. When he died in 1899 the statistically-minded estimated that he had carried his gospel messages fully a million miles, addressed 100,000,000 people, and prayed directly with 750,000 sinners. Admirers insisted that he had reduced the population of Hell by a million souls.

Moody's earnest words, spoken in rapid conversational style while he used only the simplest of gestures, deeply affected his listeners and drew masses back to the "Old Time Religion." Sankey sat at the organ, always facing the congregation and eagerly watching their expressions. He played the beloved gospel hymns and sang impressively like a basso profundo of the opera.

In the early twentieth century, evangelism had its most sensational champion in Billy Sunday, a professional baseball player from Iowa. Although, like Moody, he came to evangelical work through the Y.M.C.A., there was almost none of Moody's dignity in his pulpit manner, despite the fact that he was actually ordained a Presbyterian minister in 1903. In his Philadelphia pulpit Billy Sunday wound up like a baseball pitcher and exhorted the audience "to put it over the plate for Jesus." But he, too, like Moody, ignored the basic economic and social abuses of his day except for his heated campaign against the saloon. To the fundamentalist, Sabbath-breaking and drink were the chief social problems of the times.

IV

The Young Men's Christian Association, which had provided such militants as Moody, Sunday, and Anthony Comstock, had been founded in England in 1844 by George Williams and had been sponsored by men of at least four different Protestant denominations. It was an interdenominational laymen's movement to convert youth, particularly those spiritually adrift in the cities, to religion. The movement took root in America in 1851 with the founding of the Boston chapter and grew into vast national and international dimensions. The Y.M.C.A. did much to promote the religious revival of 1857-58, which penetrated into the financial districts as well as the homes of the humble, and it organized charities for the poor and nursing aid for the sick.

Beginning in 1868, "active" members were expected to be members in good standing of evangelical churches, while others might join as "associate" members, providing they were of good moral character. Each branch centered around the personality of a vigorous secretary. The New York "Y" introduced physical education, thereby giving an important impetus to the adoption of German calisthenics in the public schools of the nation. To rally the youth for religion and to reconcile class and race, the "Y" steadily expanded its Sunday school program to absorb a variety of social activities, such as reading rooms, clubs and classes of all types, as well as gymnastics. During the Civil War the various Y.M.C.A. groups united to form the United States Christian Commission to furnish to the soldiers wholesome books and tracts, both religious and secular. Such services were expanded to include recreation in the Spanish-American War and World War I.

Another such English institution transplanted to New York in 1858 was the Young Women's Christian Association. This, too, had urban as well as religious roots. Originally, women were attracted to the idea of a large prayer group for their sex. Too often they had been frowned upon or discriminated against in the conduct of missionary and evangelical work. The founders, such as Emma Robarts in England, cited their aim in the biblical thought that "thy sons and thy daughters shall prophesy." Their purpose was "to labor for the temporal, moral, and religious welfare of young self-supporting women." In 1887, after William T. Stead had publicized the immorality among girls who earned a pittance in industry, the London Y.W.C.A. added a strong social program to this limited gospel movement. Out of this grew women's hostels, the Traveller's Aid Society, and the Park Mission.

After 1866, the American Y.W.C.A., like others elsewhere, modeled their organizational structure after the Y.M.C.A. Physical education, schooling in many liberal and applied subjects, and social and recreational activities were added to religious training. The American Y.W.C.A. pioneered with the cafeteria idea in its Kansas City branch. Its main purpose was to reduce food prices for working girls by eliminating as much of the service cost as possible. From Kansas City the cafeteria system moved eastward and became popular both in "Y" circles and outside by 1900. So successful was the Y.W.C.A. in this country that it was able to report in 1910 a total membership of close to a quarter of a million spread over 196 city associations. Many hundreds were enrolled in mission study classes. Troubled immigrant women frequently turned to the "Y" for advice and assistance.

Since the battle for church survival in a secular age depended upon the success of youth programs, Protestants experimented with other institutions besides the two "Y" movements. The leading Methodist denominations forged their instrument in the Epworth League, originating in 1872 in Philadelphia from a group organized by the Reverend T. B. Neely of the Fifty-first

Street Methodist Episcopal Church. The most remarkably successful of the religious youth groups was the Young People's Society of Christian Endeavor. In February, 1881, the Reverend Francis E. Clark founded the first chapter at his Williston Congregational Church in Portland, Maine. By 1911, the Society had become an interdenominational movement of nearly 2,700,-000 American members while over 1,200,000 more belonged to Canadian and overseas chapters—a grand total of nearly four million young men and women. The Christian Endeavor pledge required each member to promise to apply religion through some concrete service, however small, to society. Their motto was "For Christ and the Church" and their activities embraced missions, charities, and social programs. Among the Christian Endeavor principles was this social-economic platform:

Christian endeavor stands for Peace and Good Will among men, and is opposed to all unjust war and unjust industrial strife, as contrary to the principles of the Prince of Peace. "Arbitration and Conciliation" are two of its watchwords for the twentieth century, and an International Christian Brotherhood and a universal language for intercommunication two of its ideals.

V

In a sense the efforts of Protestants to retain their urban membership may be considered as a militant counter-reformation against secularism and indifference. The leaders of this movement originated in industrial England and were the soldiers of the Salvation Army. This movement, like so many others of this period, was interdenominational and therefore tended to minimize dogmatic differences among Protestants in order to achieve the experience of Christian conversion.

The first general and founder of the Salvation Army was William Booth, who had been reared within the Church of England and had joined a band of Wesleyan Methodists as a youthful evangelist. In 1850 he became a minister and thereafter embarked as an independent evangelist in London, bringing his remarkable wife, Catherine, to his aid. He labored for the souls of slum dwellers, drunkards, and the human debris of

London. His audiences filled huge tents, theaters, and open fields. "The Christian Mission is the Salvation Army," he once said and this name became fixed in the reorganization of 1880. General Booth invoked "councils of war," moved his evangelists in "corps," and held meetings in "citadels." In seaports, evangelists called themselves "captains." Eventually, *The War Cry* became the official organ of the movement.

From the beginning the Salvation Army realized that hungry and homeless men must first be fed and sheltered before they were ready for a Christian life. Soup kitchens, shelters, and other social institutions quickly evolved. This strategy of combining social with spiritual services was stressed in Booth's book, *Darkest England and the Way Out*. The new and unusually prominent role of women as evangelists owed much to Catherine Booth, who was aware of the precedents set by the Quakers in this direction. By 1890, there were 5000 women officers in the Salvation Army, many wearing the distinctive bonnet fashioned by Catherine herself.

In 1880, the very year that the name Salvation Army was formally adopted, a branch was established in Pennsylvania under Commissioner George Railton and seven women workers from England. Younger members of the Booth family took charge of the American organization. One of the best known, Evangeline Cory Booth, daughter of the founder, held the leadership for thirty years after 1904 and then became the General of the Army. The Army's militant evangelical methods in the United States and elsewhere have been frankly explained by one of the Booths:

The Salvationist's vision of a rebellious world and of perishing souls seems to justify any and every device, however sharp, striking, or even vulgar for attracting, for compelling, the attention of the hardened and indifferent to whom his appeal is made. . . . The testimony meeting is described as a "free and easy" and the response of "Amen" as a "volley." Many Army services are punctuated from first to last with joyous exclamations, clapping of hands, laughter, or tears.

One of the best conversion methods had to do with the "mourner's bench," which is said to have been borrowed by William Booth from President Charles Finney of Oberlin, the noted evangelist. This was a row of seats in front of the speaker's platform at which sinners knelt in token of repentance. This version of the "anxious seat" added a keen dramatic interest to the services. Street marches by the "Hallelujah lasses," their familiar guitars, tambourines, and brass instruments, and lively or sentimental tunes from the Salvation Army Song Books were part of their appeal to prospective converts. Many of these songs were secular in origin but were sung with specially adapted salvationist words. By 1900, the Salvation Army had grown in this country to 700 corps of 20,000 privates commanded by 3000 officers. At this time, too, they were conducting an average of 11,000 weekly meetings with an attendance of over two million people.

After 1890, William Booth's plan for a large-scale welfare program began to unfold. The American branch of the Army helped the derelicts through numerous soup kitchens, old clothes depots, cheap hotels, and homes for alcoholics. Destitute families were housed in special shelters, permitted to buy necessities at cheap food stores, given employment, or aided generously through a loan service. Mothers were sent to maternity homes and cared for through public nursing agencies; unmarried mothers and prostitutes were aided through rescue homes. A special prison-gate bureau helped newly released prisoners to start fresh lives. The salvage of human derelicts was a mighty industry with the Army.

This vast program might be stigmatized as consisting of "palliatives" instead of social reform, but to the destitute it meant immediate sympathetic aid until such time as the nation and the municipalities were ready to shoulder the burden in a more scientific way. For the churches, it meant vast recruits of members, and for society, it led to the physical as well as spiritual rehabilitation of a submerged class that normally had no outlets but drink and unbridled sensualism.

In 1896, General Ballington Booth and his wife led a group of secessionists out of the Salvation Army to form an exclusively American movement with a more democratic internal structure, the Volunteers of America. They continued the military paraphernalia on a lesser scale, but avoided direct competition with the churches. In their evangelical work they stressed conversion among convicts and alcoholics. Their Volunteer Prison League enrolled thousands of convicts who pledged themselves to a disciplined Christian life. Ex-convicts were assisted to find secure niches in society where the stigma of their past might not force them back into criminal acts.

VI

The long dreary depression eras of 1873 and 1893 and the violent nation-wide strikes associated with them led many thoughtful clergymen to revise their exclusive emphasis on otherworldliness. Besides, the rapid growth of Marxist socialism among laborers during the 1880's and afterwards alarmed churchmen in both Europe and America. Radical clubs ridiculed the clergyman's promises of salvation as "pie in the sky" and in Marxian terms assailed religion as an opiate for the people to divert attention from the class struggle. After 1890, many Protestants and Catholics devoted serious attention to formulating a "social gospel," which taught that the principles of Christianity were broad enough to support a just social order of a cooperative nature. For them, the traditional kingdom of heaven could not be allowed to obscure the hope of a kingdom of righteousness on earth.

Socially-minded critics attacked the orthodox who were only concerned with the problem of personal redemption without realizing that society, too, must be redeemed from its economic abuses. They were dissatisfied with the limited ascetic program of the churches—temperance, Sabbatarianism, Comstockian morality, and persistent campaigns to halt smoking and card-playing. Within the traditional church doctrine of stewardship, churchmen insisted that all wealth is held and administered for the common good. Catholics recurred to the pre-capitalistic Christian society of the medieval guild community with its subordination to the common good—in theory at least—of profits and competitive conflict. Social gospelers also found theological sanctions in the doctrine that God was immanent in human society—a formula that tended to blur the usually sharp distinctions between secular and religious interests.

England directly influenced the social gospel movement and its institutions, for her urban-industrial problems resembled those of the United States in an accentuated form. Within the

Church of England a group of clerics and laymen, led by Frederick D. Maurice, took up where Chartism had left off in 1848 to rebel against laissez-faire capitalism and to demand that the economic order conform to Christian ethics within a co-operative system. Best-known of these "Christian Socialists" to American readers was the clergyman-novelist Charles Kingsley, who wrote *Alton Locke* (1850) and *Yeast* (1851) to picture working-class conditions. In England, too, there was the esthetic and individualistic Socialism of William Morris and John Ruskin. These men seldom went beyond plans or experiments for a producer's or consumer's cooperative, but they influenced the gradualist tradition of the Fabian Socialists and the British Labour Party. From England, too, came the settlement movement, which was originated by an Anglican vicar, Samuel A. Barnett, as an experiment in London slum rehabilitation. Barnett founded Toynbee Hall in 1884 to provide university-trained "residents" in a poor district of the East End. Essentially, all these activities were merely middle-class efforts to direct the economic salvation of the working classes. Some groups of the Christian Socialists were even cool to secular trade-union movements and none favored the revolutionary Marxist or anarchist panaceas for the ills of the world.

Much more influential upon the later Christian Socialist movement was Washington Gladden, outspoken pastor of the First Congregational Church in Columbus, Ohio. He insisted that now that slavery had been abolished, the emancipation of labor came next and the social problem was therefore primary. Active in various municipal and social reforms, he expressed his conviction that the laborer's real wages had declined during 1860-86 and were still falling. He was one of the early clerical figures to give the weight of church support to trade unions and the right to strike; his wrath fell upon the abuses of unregulated economic competition. Adam Smith and classical economics, he charged, had come to replace the Bible. His numerous books, such as *Applied Christianity* (1886), popularized the social gospel. In 1891 appeared his challenging exposition of religious Modernism in *Who Wrote the Bible?*

While Gladden offered little in the way of concrete reforms, the developing English movement of Christian Socialism crossed the Atlantic and gave a program to many American social gospelers. One of these American leaders of Christian Socialism was an Episcopal clergyman of Boston, William D. P. Bliss, who named his organization the Church of the Carpenter and even joined the Knights of Labor. Like other radical clergymen, he had been attracted at first by Edward Bellamy's Utopian Socialist book *Looking Backward, 2000-1887* (1888), in which the leading character awakens in the midst of a socialist society that plans almost every phase of daily life. However, the secular nature of Bellamy's Nationalist movement led Bliss and other churchmen to turn away and organize in 1889 the Society of Christian Socialists in Boston, editing *The Dawn,* and attacking plutocracy and economic planlessness in favor of a gradualist program of regulations and control of capital.

The greatest name and influence in American Social Christianity was undoubtedly Walter Rauschenbusch, a Baptist clergyman of Rochester, New York, the son of German liberal Forty-eighters. As a young idealistic pastor in New York City's slums, he had seen poverty at first hand; as a result, his religion was imbued with a strong social quality. He had read sympathetically Henry George's single-tax doctrines, Tolstoy's idealistic essays on personal redemption, and John Spargo's socialist writings. He emerged a Christian Socialist, devoted to the goal of a socialist state based on biblical principles.

To Marxians, however, his rejection of the principles of the class struggle as a cardinal tenet of socialism put him outside the pale of "scientific socialism." Rauschenbusch denounced the jungle philosophy of unregulated competition and proposed a social order in which the profit motive would be replaced by a cooperative ideal. In *Christianizing the Social Order* (1912), written at the height of the Bull Moose movement, he predicted gloomily, "An ever increasing number of people are henceforth to live in a land owned by an ever decreasing number." It was time to turn away from mammonism and corporate control of government and time for all society to experience the exalted sense of personal regeneration that the convert knew.

In his published Yale lectures of 1917, *A Theology for the Social Gospel,* Rauschenbusch formulated the doctrinal basis of Social Christianity. Most popular of all was *The Social Principles of Jesus* (1917). These titles alone suggest the consistent emphasis that he put upon his central tenets of a kingdom of righteousness on earth. Under his leadership Christian Socialists organized the Brotherhood of the Kingdom. More important

than this is the fact that, for an entire generation at least, innumerable idealistic young clergymen were profoundly influenced by the social teachings of Rauschenbusch.

No man in the entire Social Christian movement enjoyed so
vast an audience as the Reverend Charles Monroe Sheldon of
Topeka, Kansas, whose mass appeal as a novelist may justly be
compared with that of Harriet Beecher Stowe. A prolific writer
of idealistic sketches for denominational papers, this Congregationalist minister knew poverty and unemployment from close
observation. In 1896, he published *In His Steps: What Would
Jesus Do?* This began with a story related to a congregation by
an unemployed youth whose wife had died in a New York
tenement. The young man challenged the congregation by asking what Jesus would do if He were a member of this church.
After the youth died the aroused pastor asked his congregation
to live for a year exactly as they thought Jesus would, regardless of consequences. Thereafter a wholesale transformation
took place as members gave up narrow or harmful activities to
promote better housing for the poor, mission work, and temperance. So sensational was the success here and abroad of *In His
Steps* that the book sold over 100,000 copies in a year and
quickly passed the million mark and the story was shown on
the motion picture screen in 1936.

The climax of the social gospel movement came in 1908 after
Unitarians, Episcopalians, Methodists, Baptists, and Congrega-
tionalists had already formed welfare organizations and adopted
social principles going beyond the older restricted notions of
charity. In May, 1908, the Methodist Episcopal Church issued
its famous "Social Creed," which included these principles: industrial conciliation and arbitration; elimination of factory
hazards to life and health; the abolition of child labor; protection
of women in industry; abolition of the sweat shop; the "gradual
and reasonable reduction of the hours of labor to the lowest
practical point, with work for all"; and the acquisition of "that
degree of leisure for all which is the condition of the highest
human life." They advocated a holiday of one day in seven,
"a living wage in every industry," and particularly "the highest
wage that each industry can afford, and for the most equitable
division of the products in industry that can ultimately be devised."

This ambitious program was implemented that same year by

the formation of the most important interdenominational group in the history of Protestantism: The Federal Council of the Churches of Christ in America, eventually representing twenty-seven national denominations, including both races, and dealing with practically every problem of human welfare. This organization took over as its own the Social Creed of the Methodists and set up local and state councils to assist it in dealing with national and international questions including evangelical programs, reform of marriage laws, philanthropy, and social legislation. "The Council holds it a Christian duty to make the influence of Christ effective in all human relations," reads a recent semi-official statement; "it draws Christian representatives of management, labor, and agriculture together to consider what light is shed upon their problems by their common Christian commitment." Thus in the twentieth century centrifugal tendencies of Protestantism had been partially checked through such interdenominational forms as the F.C.C.C.A. More and more churches took up the "labor question," investigated strikes sympathetically, or offered their services as labor mediators. The "institutional" church grew after 1890 to include a wide variety of welfare, educational, and recreational activities. Such urban churches often added employment bureaus, charitable relief agencies, kindergartens, gymnasiums, libraries, clubs, dispensaries, soup kitchens, hospitals, and home economics classes. A "Christian sociology" pervaded their philosophy.

VII

With the urban emphasis upon interdenominationalism and the social gospel, the birth of new sects became an increasing rarity. One of the most important of the few urban sects that were organized in this period was the Christian Science Church. Appealing to the middle class primarily, it did not take an active role in the social gospel movement. Its emphasis on mental healing, suggesting certain of the therapeutic values of psychoanalysis, seemed well-adapted to uprooted urban culture in which mental adjustments often took physical forms baffling to the techniques of ordinary medicine. This "Church of Christ,

Scientist" was chartered in 1879 in Boston by a unique figure in American church history, Mary Baker Eddy, already a woman of fifty-eight.

Mrs. Eddy was born in 1821 on a farm in New Hampshire of a long line of Congregational ancestors. She was largely self-educated, though she had an unmistakably keen native intelligence. Her personal life was not happy, for her first husband died, she divorced her second, and the third, Asa Eddy, whom she loved dearly, died a few years after their marriage. Throughout her early life she had suffered from sudden pains in her spine and chronic invalidism and she had tried the current healing panaceas, including mesmerism and spiritualism. She consulted Phineas P. Quimby of Portland, Maine, regarding her health and thought that she had secured some relief. Quimby used no medicines, but relied upon manipulation and mental suggestion. When he died in 1866, Mrs. Eddy turned to other hopes of cure and became immersed in the idea of the healing mission of Jesus. She had long been interested in the mental factors in illness and hoped to convince the churches to take up her emphasis on faith healing. When this hope failed to materialize, she developed her own church to carry out the principles she had discovered.

In 1875, she published *Science and Health*, which in various revised forms became the textbook of the Christian Science movement. She developed the idea that Jesus came upon earth not only to redeem man from sin, but also from disease. Men must discover "the Christ in us." In one of her most-quoted passages, she said,

> There is no life, truth, intelligence, nor substance in matter. All is infinite Mind and its infinite manifestations, for God is All-in-All. Spirit is immortal Truth; matter is mortal error. . . . Spirit is God, and man is His image and likeness. Therefore man is not material; he is spiritual.

This, in a highly condensed form, gave the essence of her teachings. By living the life of a genuine Christian, one might hope to overcome error and unreality, which includes sickness and sin. These cheerful ideas of mind-cure were especially attractive to the optimistic psychology of many Americans. To spread the faith, Mrs. Eddy founded monthly, weekly, and daily newspapers. By 1890, her *Christian Science Journal* ad-

vertised the presence of 250 healers, 20 churches, and 90 societies. The phenomenon of a woman at the head of a large
church was not new in New England, for Mother Ann Lee had
founded Shaker colonies there a century before.

In 1906 a two-million-dollar addition to the Mother Church
at Boston was completed. At that time the Boston organization
was estimated to have over 40,000 members, and there were at
least 25,000 more elsewhere. Two years later the *Christian
Science Monitor* appeared; it offered lectures on the faith together with an unusually high level of journalism in which the
sections on foreign affairs ranked with the best in the country.
It avoided any emphasis on vice or crime and sought to keep
a neutral position between capital and labor. In 1910, the eighty-
nine-year-old woman who had obviously built up a powerful
organization died. Within a few years, her church won many
converts in England, Germany, and elsewhere.

VIII

The American Roman Catholic Church was overwhelmingly
recruited from immigrants who found their livelihood in the
cities and thus it became predominantly an urban church. Despite the poverty of the newcomers, the hierarchy was able to
build parochial schools, churches, colleges, hospitals, and mon-
astic institutions. In addition, the church had to support its own
extensive program of charities. Besides the unique Catholic problem of adjusting millions of incoming Irishmen, Bavarians,
Italians, Poles, Czechs, Austrians, and others to the American
environment, there were also the same problems faced by
Protestants: secularism, Marxist socialism, and urban indifference.

In this era the leadership of Cardinal Gibbons was often decisive in Catholic affairs. Without demanding any special status
for the large American Catholic population within the Roman
Church, he urged the Vatican that the Church must not be
stigmatized by Americans as an alien institution. Instead, bishops
should be chosen who were in accord with American ideas of
democracy. When in 1891 certain nationalistic German Catho-

lics sought a special status for their nationality, the Cardinal successfully fought this "Cahenslyism" as a threat to the homogeneity of American Catholicism. On that occasion a Peter Cahensly had presented a church memorial recommending that each nationality be given its churches, priests, and proportion of bishops according to their respective numbers. Although it had been the practice of the hierarchy to provide each foreign language group with a priest who could speak its language, the Cardinal denounced any effort to segregate each group on a rigid nationality basis.

Next to the Cardinal in influence was the very able archbishop of St. Paul, John Ireland. At one time President Roosevelt even intervened indirectly to help the archbishop get a cardinal's hat—an odd activity for a Protestant! Like Cardinal Gibbons, Archbishop Ireland favored an American policy for the church in this country with special emphasis upon an enthusiastic acceptance of political democracy. However, he tended to minimize the great economic problems of the time except to advocate temperance and conservative trade unionism. In 1903, he publicly declared, "I have no fear of great fortunes in the hands of individuals, nor of vast aggregations of capital in the hands of corporations." His friendships with James J. Hill, railroad magnate, and with President McKinley exposed him to the shafts of progressives. Yet he often expressed strong sympathies for organized labor, even remarking on one occasion, "Until their material condition is improved it is futile to speak to them of spiritual life and duties."

Many Catholic priests and laymen did support radical causes. A particularly significant case was that of Father Edward McGlynn who made ardent speeches in behalf of Henry George and the single tax doctrines. In 1886, the attention of the entire nation was arrested by the news that he had been suspended by his superiors from his priestly duties. When he refused a summons to Rome to defend his opinons, he was excommunicated. However, the decree was revoked by the end of 1892 and he resumed his duties. Father McGlynns' victory encouraged other Catholics to espouse radical labor reforms. The attitude of the American hierarchy may perhaps be inferred from a significant letter in the Baltimore Cathedral Archives. On July 21, 1894, at the height of the disorders of the Pullman Strike, Archbishop Ireland wrote to Cardinal Gibbons:

The Church must be kept before the American people as the great prop of social order and law—all the more so that Catholics are numerous in strikes and riots. Socialistic ideas have gone into our people and into many of our priests. We have been siding with labor in its grievances: The unthinking ones transgress the golden mean, and rush into war against property.

For Catholics everywhere who hoped for a vigorous program of social action to meet the problems of poverty and materialism, a ready-made creed appeared in the famous papal encyclical, *Rerum Novarum*, issued by Leo XIII in 1891. Pope Leo had been an able social reformer while still a young priest; and some years before issuing the encyclical he had directed that social problems be made a part of the training curriculum for priests. An erudite philosopher with a special interest in the teachings of St. Thomas Aquinas, Pope Leo revived Thomism and there-by gave a new vitality to Catholic philosophy in the ensuing decades. The encyclical condemned laissez-faire in industry as unchristian, declared that labor was not a commodity to be bought and sold on the market, upheld the right to organize unions, and asserted the principle of the living wage based upon the needs of the family. Class collaboration, instead of class con-flict, was the keynote of the encyclical: "Capital cannot do without labor nor labor without capital." *Rerum Novarum* made slow progress as far as adoption in this country is con-cerned, but there were many militant Catholic advocates of its ideas.

The American Catholic who devoted his life most effectively and brilliantly to the application of the principles of *Rerum Novarum* was a priestly professor of social economics at Catho-lic University, Father John A. Ryan. Born of Irish parents in 1869 in a village near St. Paul, he had learned his Populist ideas from rebels like Ignatius Donnelly and from the anti-landlord sentiments of *The Irish World* to which his family had long subscribed. Professor Richard T. Ely of the University of Wisconsin, who may have influenced him, wrote an introduction to Ryan's doctoral dissertation, which appeared in 1906 as *A Living Wage*. This book attracted wide interest and almost certainly left an impression on the thinking of innumerable social reformers.

Father Ryan asserted the principle that no employer had any

right to take interest on his investment until all his employees had received a living wage. This he estimated at $600 a year as a minimum subsistence for a family. He later wrote that this book was the first in English to advocate a legally established compulsory minimum wage sufficient for the decent maintenance of the worker's family. Unlike certain other Catholic critics of the economic order, this priest-economist refused to escape to the Middle Ages for a just social order. He believed that Americans had definitely broken with European tradition and would seek their solution in terms of their own experience. "The laborer's right to a living wage," he declared, "is like all other moral rights, based on his intrinsic worth as a person, and on the sacredness of those needs that are essential to the reasonable development of personality." Charity was good, but no substitute for justice. His wage ideas were developed more maturely in *Distributive Justice* (1917), which carried the subtitle, *The Right and Wrong of Our Present Distribution of Wealth*. Throughout his life he combined his scholarly interests with active social work.

The monolithic structure of the Roman Catholic Church made it relatively simple to escape schisms and to deal with heresies and secularist doctrines arising out of the new age of science. In 1864, Pope Pius IX issued the *Syllabus of Errors* to denounce freethinkers, agnostics, materialists, anticlericals, freemasons, and doctrinal liberals. The papal encyclical *Pascendi* (1907) issued by Pope Pius X condemned Modernism as a union of faith with a false philosophy. Inevitably, the cities made some inroads upon orthodoxy, but these were far more than offset by steady accretions of strictly orthodox immigrant groups.

Unlike conservative Protestant churches, the Catholic hierarchy met the new science unencumbered by any inflexible belief in the literal truth of the Bible; and while very slow to accept Darwinism they were not compelled to stake the validity of doctrine upon the truth or falsehood of evolution. On the other hand, Protestantism, traditionally consecrated to "justification by faith alone," had moved over—except for a fundamentalist wing—to a humanitarian program ever more devoted to "good works" as a way of salvation. Critics of social Christianity wondered whether churchmen were competent to solve the complex economic problems of contemporary society or were even well-advised to attempt it. Well-to-do congregations resented clerical meddling in the employer's problems; but the fashionable liberal Christianity of Henry Ward Beecher could only end in altogether estranging the working classes from religion.

BOSS COX'S CINCINNATI:
A STUDY IN
URBANIZATION AND POLITICS,
1880–1914

ZANE L. MILLER

Zane L. Miller, of the history faculty at the University of Cincinnati, analyzes the role of George B. Cox in the political and social fabric of Cincinnati and argues that the municipal boss provided positive government which eased the process of urbanization.

Many observers of the turn-of-the-century urban scene have depicted bossism as one of the great unmitigated evils of the American city, as a tyrannical, authoritarian, relentlessly efficient and virtually invulnerable political system. Between 1904 and 1912, for example, George B. Cox was castigated by writers in four national magazines. Gustav Karger called him the "Proprietor of Cincinnati." Lincoln Steffens declared that "Cox's System" was "one great graft," "the most perfect thing of the kind in this country." Frank Parker Stockbridge claimed that "The Biggest Boss of Them All" had an organization "more compact and closely knit than any of the political machines which have dominated New York, Philadelphia, Chicago, St.

From Zane L. Miller, "Boss Cox's Cincinnati: A Study in Urbanization and Politics, 1880–1914," *Journal of American History*, LIV (March 1968), 823–838. Copyright © 1968 by the Organization of American Historians. Reprinted by permission of The Organization of American Historians.

Louis or San Francisco." And George Kibbe Turner concluded
that in the 1890s "the man from Dead Man's Corner . . . seated
himself over the city of Cincinnati. For twenty years he remained there—a figure like no other in the United States, or
in the world." Yet these knowledgable and sensitive journalists
obscured as much as they revealed about the nature of Queen
City politics in the Progressive era. A new kind of city had
developed, and "the boss" comprised only a fraction of its novel
political system.

Paradoxically, Cox and his machine were produced by, fed on,
and ultimately helped dispel the spectacular disorder which en-
gulfed Cincinnati in the late-nineteenth century and threatened
the very survival of the democratic political process. In these
years, increasing industrialization, technological innovations in
communication and transportation—especially the coming of
rapid transit—and continued foreign and domestic migration had
reversed the physical pattern of the mid-century walking city
and transformed Cincinnati into a physically enlarged, divided,
and potentially explosive metropolis.

Old citizens were shocked as familiar landmarks and neighborhoods vanished. By 1900, railroads and warehouses had
monopolized the Ohio River bottoms. The financial and retail
districts had moved up into the Basin around Fountain Square,
the focus of the street railway system; new club, theater, and
tenderloin districts had developed; and industries had plunged
up Mill Creek Valley, converting Mohawk-Brighton into "the
undisputed industrial bee-hive of the Great Queen City of the
West," surrounding once fashionable Dayton Street, creating a
new community called Ivorydale, and reaching out to the
villages of Norwood and Oakley in search of cheap land, ready
access to railroads, and less congested and more cheerful surroundings.

The Over-the-Rhine entertainment section along Vine Street
became tawdry with commercialism. It now had, complained
one habitué, "all the tarnished tinsel of a Bohemianism with the
trimmings of a gutter and the morals of a sewer"—a repulsive
contrast, he felt, to "the old-time concert and music halls . . .
where one could take wife, sister, or sweetheart and feel secure
. . . that not one obnoxious word would profane their ears."

The fashionable residential districts which had flanked the
center of the walking city began to disintegrate. One family

after another fled the East End for the hills around the Basin,
leaving only a small coterie led by the Charles P. Tafts to stave
off the advance of factories and slums. The elite West End
seemed to disappear overnight. It "did not go down imperceptibly," recalled one old resident. "It went to ruin almost as if a
bombshell sent it to destruction."

The Hilltops, at mid-century the private preserve of cemeteries, colleges, and a handful of wealthy families, became the
prime residential district in the new city. The crush to get in
generated new tensions. In 1899 one observer acidly remarked:
"when rapid transit came the Hebrews . . . flocked to" Walnut
Hills

until it was known by the name of New Jerusalem. Avondale was
then heralded as the suburb of deliverance, but again rapid transit
brought the wealthy Hebrews . . . in numbers greater than the flock
of crows that every morning and evening darkens her skies, until
now it has been facetiously said that the congregation has assembled
in force and . . . when Avondale is roofed over the synagogue will
be complete.

The diffusion of wealthy families, the reduction in casual
social and business contacts, and the construction of new communities made ardent joiners of the Hilltops elite. Each neighborhood had an improvement association, and between 1880 and
1905 five new businessmen's organizations devoted to boosting
the city's lethargic economy had appeared. In the same period
six social clubs opened downtown facilities, and three country
clubs were started. By 1913, moreover, there were twenty-two
exclusive clubs and patriotic societies and innumerable women's
groups. These developments helped counteract the disruptive
effects of the "country movement," as one visitor labeled it,
which was "so general that church-going became an affair of
some difficulty" and "society itself . . . more or less disinte-
grated."

But not all those moving out were affluent. Liberated by rapid
transit, skilled and semiskilled workers and moderately prosperous professional and white-collar men with life savings, the
courage to take out a mortgage, an equity in a building and
loan association, or a willingness to rent a flat in a double or
triple decker, also fled the Basin. They took refuge in a no-
man's-land between the center of the city and the Hilltops

frontier which was similar to an era dubbed the Zone of Emergence by Boston social workers.

Zone residents formed what the Cincinnati *Post* referred to as "the so-called middle class . . . , the class that makes any city . . . what it is . . . [,] the class that takes in the great body of people between wealth and poverty" and builds up "many organizations, societies, associations, fraternities and clubs that bring together people who are striving upward, trying to uplift themselves, and hence human society."

They, too, found life in the new city a novel experience. A retired leather factory porter who moved into the Zone lamented:

When I lived down on Richmond in a little house we cooked the corn beef and cabbage in the house and ate in there, and when we wanted to go to the toilet we went out into the yard, now I live in a fine house, I am made to eat . . . out in the yard, and when I want to go to the toilet I have to go into the house.

Graham R. Taylor had noted that since most Zone residents commuted they suffered a severe "dislocation of the normal routine of factory and home": they had to adjust to "the need for travel and its curtailment of leisure and income . . . ," to eating lunches away from home, to doing without "customary city facilities," and to knowing the feeling of "isolation from their fellows." Price Hill—like the rest of the Zone a heavily Catholic area—felt itself conspicuously cut off. In the 1890s the editor of the *Catholic-Telegraph*, denouncing the traction company as the "octopus," joined the Price Hill Improvement Association in begging both city and traction company officials to bring the area "within range of the civilized world" and suggested secession as a means of dramatizing to the "people east of Millcreek" that a new public school, "granted by the unbounded munificence of the City of Cincinnati," did not amount to a redemption of the city's annexation pledges.

The exodus, however, did not depopulate the Basin. Instead, a great residential Circle formed around the central business district. It filled with newcomers and those who lacked the means to get out—rural whites and Negroes from the South, Germans, Irish, Greeks, Italians, and Jews from eastern Europe. Working at the poorest paying jobs available, they were jammed into the most congested quarters. The Circle led all other areas of the city in arrests, mortality, and disease.

Although the pressure to escape was enormous, the barriers were formidable. Ignorant of the ways of the city, as an Associated Charities report put it, Circle dwellers had to be "shown how to buy, how to cook, how to make the home attractive, how to find employment." Many, "utterly friendless and discouraged," succumbed to "the damnable absence of want or desire" and grew "indifferent . . . to their own elevation." Plagued by "physical bankruptcy," they found it difficult to find and hold jobs, let alone form and maintain the kind of organizations which enabled Zone residents to shield themselves from economic disaster, legal pitfalls, social isolation, and apathy.

The immediate impact of the emergence of the new city pushed Cincinnati to the brink of anarchy. In March 1884, the *Enquirer* complained that the police had failed to choke off a crime wave although, in the last year alone, there had been twelve arrests for malicious shooting, twenty-nine for malicious cutting, forty-seven for cutting with intent to wound, 284 for shooting with intent to kill, ninety-two for murder and manslaughter, and 948 for carrying a concealed weapon. The total number of arrests came to 56,784. The city's population was 250,000. Later that same month, a lynch mob descended on the county jail. While police and militia fought off the mob, gangs looted stores and shops on the fringe of the downtown district. In three days of riot the courthouse was burned to the ground, fifty-four people were killed, and an estimated 200 people wounded.

During the fall elections, violence erupted in the lower wards; two policemen and one Negro were killed. Congressman Benjamin Butterworth remarked that he had "never witnessed anywhere such coarse brutality and such riotous demonstrations. . . ." Cincinnati, he concluded, "seems . . . doomed to perdition."

Less than two years later the city faced another major crisis. On May 1, 1886, Cincinnati workers joined in nationwide demonstrations for the eight-hour day. These were followed by a series of strikes. The militia was called out, and for two weeks the city resembled an armed camp. Only the show of force and, perhaps, the memory of the courthouse catastrophe prevented another riot.

Yet labor remained restive, and a rash of strikes followed. By 1892, the paternalistic system which had dominated the breweries was smashed. And in 1894, Judge William Howard Taft

spent the hot days of June and July "trying to say nothing to
reporters" and "issuing injunctions" in an effort to control and
prevent the railroad strike from leading to mass violence.

The Sunday-closing question was another explosive issue. The
Post, the *Catholic-Telegraph,* a Committee of Five Hundred,
and many Protestant clergymen all leveled scathing attacks on
the continental Sabbath. "Sunday in Cincinnati," asserted one
Methodist minister, "is a high carnival of drunkenness, base
sensuality, reeking debauchery and bloody, often fatal crime."
Other spokesmen tied the open Sunday to anarchism, atheism,
corrupt politicians, a decadent daily press, indifferent public
officials, and the ruthless exploitation of labor. "The modern
Puritan," insisted Charles P. Taft, "intends to rise up and oppose
to the uttermost this kind of Sunday."

When, in 1889, the mayor announced his intention to enforce
the Sunday-closing law for saloons, the city almost faced another riot. Some 1,000 saloonkeepers vowed to ignore the new
policy. When a cadre of police and firemen marched over the
Rhine to close Kissell's saloon, an unruly crowd gathered,
epithets were hurled, but no violence occurred. Kissell's was
closed; the "era of the back door," with "front doors locked
and curtains up, but back doors widened," had opened.

These spectacular outbreaks plus other pressures overwhelmed
city hall. Indeed, scarcely a residental area, economic interest,
or social or occupational group was left unscathed by the multi-
dimensional disorder. As the physical area of the city expanded,
officials were besieged by demands for the extension, improvement, and inauguration of public services of all kinds and for
lower taxes. Simultaneously, the relative decline of the city
heightened the urgency of the agitation. Municipal institutions
and agencies, established to meet the needs of the walking city,
became overburdened, outmoded, and dilapidated.

The new city, with old ways shattered, provided a fertile
breeding ground for turmoil and discontent and, as it turned
out, for innovation and creative reconstruction. Initially, however, this unprecedented change accompanied by unprecedented
demands for government action produced only the hope of reform. In 1885, on the eve of the repudiation of a Democratic
administration, William Howard Taft predicted that "the clouds
are beginning to break over this Sodom of ours and the sun of
decency is beginning to dispel the moral miasma that has rested

on us now for so many years. It's the beginning of an era of reform."

Yet for almost a decade no party could put together a decisive ruling majority. The city's political processes seemed frozen by a paralyzing factionalism. The division of the city into residential districts which roughly coincided with socioeconomic lines made it difficult for the wealthy and well-educated to keep in contact with and control ward politics. As a result, extreme factionalism developed which could, apparently, be surmounted only by appealing to a host of neighborhood leaders and by constructing alliances which crossed party lines.

According to close observers, the chief products of this system were the use of money in city conventions and the rise of what Charles P. Taft called the "bummer," a "queer creature" who "evolves somehow from the slums. . . ." In youth "a bootblack, a newsboy or a general loafer," he matured into "an Arab" who needed only "a good standing with a saloon that has a fine layout during the day." A "hustler at the polls and conventions," the bummer was in such demand that he could accept money from competing candidates, thus lengthening the convention and contributing to interfactional dealing. After studying the influence of the "bummer," Taft gloomily concluded that the "day of pure politics can never be . . . until a riot, a plague or flood kills off all the ward bummers."

By 1897, however, and without divine intervention, all this had changed. In January of that year, three months before the city election, the *Post* gravely announced its intention to describe "impassionately and without bias the means employed" in Cincinnati's "superior and unrecorded government." It was controlled by "the boss, whose power is absolute"—George B. Cox.

The *Post's* analysis closely paralleled those made after the turn of the century. It dissected the patronage system, outlined the sources of financial support, and noted the attempted appeasement of the city's various special groups—the soldiers, the Germans, the Republican clubs, the Reform Jews, the legal and medical professions, the socially prominent Hilltops businessmen, and certain cooperative Democrats. It excitedly reported the effectiveness of the organization's intelligence system, the way the "plugger" and the "knocker" wore "beaten paths to the office of the boss to urge the appointment of this man, the discharge of that [,] or to report some feature of misconduct or expression. . . ." The paper noted that Cox was always available for consultation with any citizen regardless of station or status and that he had been little more than one of several important factional leaders until, in 1886, Governor Joseph B. Foraker selected him to serve as chief adviser on patronage and political affairs in Hamilton County.

Foraker made a shrewd choice; Cox had grown up with the new city and received a liberal education in its ways. The son of British immigrants, he was born in 1853 and reared in the Eighteenth Ward, a district which by the 1880s contained fashionable as well as slum housing, factories, and its share of saloons and brothels. His father died when Cox was eight. Successively, Cox worked as a bootblack, newsboy, lookout for a gambling joint, grocery deliveryman, bartender, and tobacco salesman. His school principal, who later became superintendent of schools, claimed that Cox was frequently in boyish trouble in classes, exhibited an "undisguised love for his mother," and "never lied . . . bore malice, sulked, whined or moped." Cox had also been exposed to religion. Although not a churchgoer, as an adult he had, according to one journalist, "dormant powerful sentiments, which rest on foundations of the firmest faith."

In the mid-1870s Cox acquired a saloon in his home neighborhood. He entered politics and served on the city council from 1878 until 1885 when, after joining forces with the Republican reform mayoralty candidate, he ran unsuccessfully for county clerk. He tried for the same post in 1888, failed, and never again stood for public office.

At that time, moving away politically from the Circle, Cox worked with George Moerlein, perhaps the strongest of the GOP professionals in the Zone. In 1890, he and Moerlein quarreled over patronage; and in the city convention of 1891, Cox was able, with the support of the Blaine Club, a kind of political settlement house that he had helped to establish, to defeat Moerlein's candidate for police judge and nominate his own man. Moerlein men now became Cox men. So, too, did Charles P. Taft and the *Times-Star*, which had been one of the last, the most influential, and the most outspoken of Cox's critics in the Hilltops Republican ranks. It accepted Cox, the paper announced, to secure a "New Order" for Cincinnati. And the president of the gas company, sensing the political drift, confided to his diary that he had "concluded [an] arrangement with Geo.

B. Cox for services at $3500 per year quarterly to last for three years." In the spring election of 1894 the Republicans carried the city with a plurality of over 6,500 votes, the first decisive municipal election in a decade. In 1897, Cox was the honest broker in a coalition composed of Circle and Zone Negroes, Zone politicians, the gas and traction companies, and Hilltops Republican reformers.

Election returns after 1885 disclose a clear pattern. The GOP won five successive contests by uniting powerful Hilltops support with enough strength in the Zone to overcome the Democratic grip on the Circle. Until 1894 the margins of victory were perilously thin. The substantial triumph of that year merely marked the completion of the alliance which pitted a united periphery against the center of the city.

The heart of the Republican "New Order" coalition, and the critical factor in the election of 1894, was its appeal to voters in the Hilltops fringe who demanded order and reform. To satisfy the Hilltops, Cox and his associates eliminated the bummer, provided brief and decorous conventions, enfranchised Negroes by suppressing violence at the polls, reduced the rapid turnover in office, and cut down the incidence of petty graft and corporation raiding.

Moreover, the "machine" heeded the advice of its reform allies from the Hilltops. Cox accepted the secret ballot, voter registration, and a series of state laws which, though retaining the mayor-council form of government with ward representation, were designed to give the city a stable and more centralized government. The administrations which he indorsed started to build a professional police force, expanded and reequipped the fire department, pushed throught a $6,000,000 water-works program, renovated municipal institutions, supported the growth of the University of Cincinnati, launched extensive street-paving and sewer-constructing projects, and tried to reduce the smoke problem and expand the city's park acreage. They also opened the door to housing regulation, suppressed the Sunday saloon, flagrant public gambling, and disorderly brothels (the city was never really closed), began to bring order into the chaotic public-utilities field by favoring privately owned, publicly regulated monopolies under progressive management, and succeeded in keeping the tax rate low. The Republican regime, in short, brought positive government to Cincinnati.

While this program also won votes in the Zone, it was not the

sole basis for the party's popularity there. Many of the lieu-
tenants and captains closest to Cox were Zone residents. They
composed a colorful group known variously as "the gang," "the
sports," or the "bonifaces"—a clique which met nightly Over-
the-Rhine either at Schubert and Pels, where each had a special
beer mug with his name gilded on it, or at the round table in
Wielert's beer garden. Three of them owned or operated combination saloons, gambling joints, and dance halls; one was
prominent in German charitable associations and the author of
several textbooks used in the elementary schools; another served
twenty consecutive terms as president of the Hamilton County
League of Building Associations; and one was a former catcher
for the Cincinnati Redlegs.

Their tastes, behavior, and attitudes were conveniently sum-
marized in the biographical sketches of ward leaders and city
officials in the 1901 *Police and Municipal Guide*. All were characterized as friendly, well-known, "All Around Good-Fellows"
who liked a story, belonged to several social and fraternal
groups, gave generously to charity, and treated the poor and
sick with special kindness. They were all among the most ardent
supporters on any project to boost the city.

Cox is pictured in the *Guide* as an adherent to the code of the
Zone who had risen to the top. He was a *bon vivant* who enjoyed good cigars and good jokes, a man of wealth whose recently completed Clifton mansion was luxuriously decorated
and adorned with expensive works of art, a man of impressive
but quiet and private charity. Above all, he was true to his word,
loyal to his friends, yet quick to reprimand and replace those
who betrayed his trust by misusing public office.

Cox and his top civil servants—surrounded by a motley crowd
of newspaper reporters, former boxers and ball players, vaude-
ville and burlesque performers, and other Vine Street characters
—provided an attractive model for men awed by the glamour,
wealth, and power which was so visible yet so elusive in the new
city. Cox's opponents in the Zone seldom attacked him or this
inside group directly. Even in the heat of the 1897 campaign,
the *Volksfreund*, the German Catholic Democratic daily, carefully described Cox as an "amiable man" who had to be "ad-
mired" for his "success" and, either ignoring or unaware of the
process of negotiation and mediation by which he ruled, criticized him only for his illiberality in imposing "dictatorial meth-

ods" on the GOP. Indeed, most Zone residents, like those of
the Hilltops, found it difficult to object to a government which
seemed humane, efficient, and progressive.

Yet it would be a mistake to overestimate the strength of the
"New Order" Republican coalition. Its victories from 1885 to
1894 were won by perilously close pluralities. The organization,
moreover, failed to carry a referendum for the sale of the city-
owned Southern Railroad in 1896 and lost the municipal contest
in 1897 to a reform fusion ticket, and the fall elections of 1897,
1898, and 1899 to the Democrats. In all these reversals, crucial
defections occurred in both the Hilltops and the Zone. Skittish
voters grew indignant over alleged corruption, outraged by inaction on the traction and gas questions, piqued by the rising
cost of new city projects, annoyed by the slow expansion of the
educational program, or uneasy over the partial sacrifice of
democracy to efficiency within the Republican organization.

Thereafter, however, the Republicans rallied and won three
of the next four city elections by unprecedented margins. The
strategy and tactics remained essentially the same. Although not
wholly averse to raising national issues, Cox's group gave local
affairs the most emphasis. The organization was occasionally
purged of its less savory elements. Cox and his Zone advisors
continued to consult with their Hilltops allies on nominations.
The party promised and, in fact, tried to deliver order and reform. Without abolishing ward representation in the city council, it strengthened the mayor and streamlined the administration.
The party also broadened and deepened its program as civic
associations, women's clubs, social workers, social gospellers,
and spokesmen for the new unionism—all novel forces in urban
politics—expanded and elaborated their demands.

But voting patterns underwent a fundamental and, for the
GOP, an ultimately disastrous change. By 1903 the Republicans
dominated the entire city, carrying not only the Zone and Hilltops but also the center. The Circle was now the invincible
bulwark of Cox's power.

There were several factors involved in the conversion of
Circle Democrats to Republicanism. First, Cox had extensive
personal contacts with them which dated back to his unsuccessful races for county clerk in the 1880s. Second, the Democrats
had been unable to put down factionalism. By the late 1890s
there were two reform elements in the party, both of which

belabored the regulars from the center of the city as tainted with corruption, too cozy with Cox, and perhaps worst of all, as a discredit and burden to the party because they wore the charred shirt of the courthouse riot.

In the wake of the fusionist victory of 1897, Mike Mullen, the leader of a riverfront Democratic ward, explained why he would henceforth work with the Republican party.

I have worked hard [for the Democratic party] have suffered much and have won for it many victories. Yet all the while there was a certain element . . . that looked on me with distrust. . . . [L]eaders of the Fusionist Party did not think enough of me to let me look after the voting in my own ward, but sent down a lot of people to watch the count. That decided me.

He was later joined by Colonel Bob O'Brien who, like Mullen, specialized in Christmas turkey, soupline, and family-service politics. These Democrats led their constituents into the Republican fold.

It was this alliance with the Circle which ultimately destroyed Cox. Anti-machine spokesmen were convinced that they had to educate the city before they could redeem it. They felt, too, that politics was a potent educational tool. But campaigns had to be spectacular in order to engage the voters' attention and participation. As A. Julius Freiberg notes, the "psychology" of the electorate was such that years of "speaking, writing, explaining, even begging and imploring" had been "to no purpose." The "reformer and his fellow students may sit about the table and evolve high principles for action, but the people . . . will not be fed by those principles unless there is a dramatic setting, and the favorite dramatic setting is the killing of a dragon." And all the people "love the dramatic; not merely the poor, but the rich, and the middle class as well." All that was needed was a situation which would enable the right man to "bring to book the boss himself."

Reformers hammered relentlessly at the theme that Cox was not a good boss; he was the head of a "syndicate" which included the worst products of slum life. In "that part of the city where vice and infamy hold high revel," went one version of the charge, "the boss-made ticket finds its most numerous supporters. Every dive keeper, every creature who fattens upon the wages of sin . . . , all the elements at war with society have

enlisted." Men "who claim to be respectable," the chief "bene-
ficiaries of this unholy alliance . . . , go down into the gutter
and accept office from hands that are reeking with the filth of
the slums." Worse still, this "alliance of the hosts of iniquity
with the greed of special privilege and ambition for power and
place" plays so successfully "upon the prejudices and . . . superstition of the many that wrong is often espoused by those who
in the end are the victims of the wrong."

The reformers also impugned Cox's personal integrity. Democratic County Prosecutor Henry T. Hunt secured evidence
that Cox had perjured himself in 1906 when he said he had not
received a cent of some $250,000 of interest on public funds
which Republican county treasurers had been paid by bankers.
In the spring of 1911, Hunt and the grand jury indicted Cox and
123 others during a broad investigation of politics, corruption,
and vice.

Finally, Hunt, stressing the issue of moral indignation, ran for
mayor in the fall of 1911 on a Democratic reform ticket. Using
the moral rhetoric of the muckraker, Hunt and his associates
tied bossism, the chaos, poverty, and vice of the slums, and
the malefactors of great wealth together and pictured them as
a threat to the welfare of the whole city. Once again the Hilltops and Zone voted for order and reform. Hunt's progressive
coalition swept the periphery, lost only in the Circle wards, and
won the election.

By that time, however, Cox was no longer boss. President
Taft and Charles P. Taft had wanted Cox to step aside as early
as 1905, but they found him indispensable. After the grand jury
revelations, however, they were able to convince the "bonifaces" that Cox was a liability. With the organization against
him, Cox retired. For a time, he insisted that his two chief
assistants, August Herrmann and Rudolph Hynicka, should
also quit, apparently convinced that they, like himself, could no
longer command the confidence of the periphery. Charles P.
Taft's *Times-Star* agreed. The two men, backed by the Blaine
Club, merely resigned their official party positions but refused
to get out of politics entirely.

What, then, was Cox's role in politics and government in the
new city? He helped create and manage a voluntary political-
action organization which bridged the racial and cultural chasms
between the Circle, Zone, and Hilltops. He and his allies were

able to bring positive and moderate reform government to Cincinnati and to mitigate the conflict and disorder which accompanied the emergence of the new city. With the crisis atmosphere muted, ardent reformers could develop more sophisticated programs and agitate, educate, and organize without arousing the kind of divisive, emotional, and hysterical response which had immobilized municipal statesmen in the 1880s. In the process, while battering at the boss, the slums, and the special-privilege syndicate, they shattered the bonds of confidence which linked the Zone "bonifaces" and the moderate reformers of the Hilltops to Cox's organization. Cox, it seems, said more than he realized when, in 1892, he remarked that a boss was "not necessarily a public enemy."

PULLMAN: TOWN PLANNING
AND SOCIAL CONTROL
IN THE GILDED AGE

STANLEY BUDER

Stanley Buder, Associate Professor of Urban History and Co-ordinator of the Metropolitan Studies Center at the Illinois Institute of Technology, discusses the model town of Pullman —an experiment in urban planning—and its relationship to the model tenement and garden city movements.

After the Civil War, American cities experienced an era of un-controlled growth. By the 1870s thin lines of homes for the wealthy and comfortable were springing up in a few desirable areas—New York's Fifth Avenue and Chicago's Prairie Avenue—while around them lay the residences of the poor. Mansion and slum had become part of the American skyline. Their contrasting presence illustrated the promise and price of industrialization and urbanization. The Reverend Joseph Strong described the city of the Gilded Age: "Here . . . is the congestion of wealth severest. Dives and Lazarus are brought face to face, here in sharp contrast are the ennui of surfeit, and the desperation of the poor."

Epidemics, fires, and social disturbances originating among the poor raced contagiously to menace all citizens and frighten

From Stanley Buder, "The Model Town of Pullman: Town Planning and Social Control in the Gilded Age," *Journal of the American Institute of Planners*, 33, No. 1 (January 1967), 2–10. Copyright 1967 by the *Journal of the American Institute of Planners*. Reprinted by permission of the editor of the *Journal of the American Institute of Planners*.

municipal government. Overcrowded and ramshackle buildings
casually dispersed with industry; their streets, alive with ill-
kempt and sometimes alien people, soon became a matter for
concern. The harmful effects of such a physical environment
both on the individual and his community were the subject for
Sunday sermons and newspaper editorials. Sanitary regulations
were tightened and housing ordinances passed to restrain more
obvious abuses. Urban reformers wanted to go even further
and build decent and inexpensive housing for the working class.

Started early in the 1870s, the Model Tenement Movement
assumed that American workers could afford adequate housing
provided that site selection, design, and all phases of construction
were thoroughly planned in advance. Rents would be charged
returning seven percent on investment but would still be reasonable for tenants. Aesthetic considerations, though not wholly
ignored, were underplayed as luxuries which added to costs. The
Movement's goal was to improve the city by ending slums,
focusing on decent housing as the key to urban problems.

In 1880 George M. Pullman, a Chicago industrialist, took
these ideas and placed them in the different and more dramatic
setting of a model town. As a businessman, he abhorred the
waste resulting from employees' dissipating their time and health
and moving pointlessly from job to job. He thought these
"costly vices" were caused by urban circumstances which "compelled [workers] to live in crowded and unhealthy tenements,
in miserable streets, and subject to all the temptations and snares
of a great city." Pullman purchased a factory site eight miles
south of Chicago and erected a model town to house his workers. He wished to demonstrate that American industry could
plan and construct a community which would develop middle
class values in its citizens.

By perfecting and promoting the sleeping car, Pullman had
revolutionized rail travel and built a prosperous company. Asked
the secret of his success, he usually referred to the "Pullman
system": an eagerness for innovation, an emphasis upon quality
and a firm faith that large-scale operations, properly managed,
led to efficiency. The model town was to embody the "Pullman
system" and show its validity for community as well as business.
Solving the company's labor problems, the town would be its
"showplace" and influence others to leave the city's chaos for
the planned order of an industrial suburb.

To execute his plan, Pullman hired the young eastern architect, S. S. Beman, and landscape designer Nathan F. Barrett. Their unprecedented assignment, hailed by a Boston paper as a "professional dream come true," was to lay out, design, and supervise the construction of a factory and town where "everything fits." The aesthetic and the functional were to be equally emphasized and harmoniously related. All social, commercial, and industrial needs were to be anticipated and planned within the town.

Construction began in 1880, and the town was nearly complete four years later. All buildings were of brick made at the site. Where possible, such parts as doors, frames, and sashes were prefabricated. Careful consideration reduced costs through techniques of mass production then rare in the construction industry but already common in railroad car manufacturing. The town's remarkable growth on a previously empty prairie prompted an observer to suggest that the builders were aided by Aladdin's genii of the lamp. But what really attracted world attention was a community "made of whole cloth." Hundreds of thousands came to visit and sometimes study the model town of Pullman, Illinois. By 1888, the *London Times* stated that "no place in the United States has attracted more attention or has been more closely watched."

The town's physical plan was simple and indicative of the more progressive ideas of the time. Industrial structures were carefully grouped to expedite car building and segregated from residences by broad boulevards and ornamental walls. Their interiors were light and airy so as to improve morale and health, and consequently production. The shops' attractive, eclectic architecture was enhanced by surrounding greenery and an artificial lake. One impressed visitor described the effect as an "industrial park."

Residences and most public buildings were on a grid plan. As London's *Pall Mall Gazette* pointed out, "one would expect . . . [this] American utopia should be regularly laid out, with streets appointed and set forth very commodious and handsome." The plan's regularity was intentionally relieved by a market square, several parks, and a winding drive intended for Sunday outings. Tree-lined, paved streets and well seeded lawns were conscientiously maintained by the company. Public buildings grouped about a picturesque railroad station presented a handsome face to visitors, and those just riding by. However, placement of the school next to ungraded tracks was a mistake which later received critical notice.

George Pullman wanted public facilities centralized in large buildings. This, he thought, would add order and convenience to the plan, while enhancing the town's appearance. All retail stores were located in the Arcade and Market Hall. The former also contained a library and a theatre considered for a time the finest west of the Hudson, while the latter housed a gymnasium and meeting rooms. Only one large and handsome church was erected to serve the community's various denominations, but the congregations preferred to go their own ways in improvised accommodations. Consequently, Pullman's church stood vacant for several years.

Residences varied widely in type and cost. A few detached houses could be rented, usually by shopkeepers, professionals, and company officers, for as much as $65 a month; skilled workers often occupied row houses averaging $17, and unskilled laborers could choose from two or three room apartments ranging in cost from $5 to $11 in large three-story "block tenements." Despite Beman's varying of detail, there was a noticeable monotony of appearance which became particularly pronounced when winter stripped Pullman of its brilliant foliage. A common complaint was that the homes appeared "machine made," while the block tenements were occasionally dismissed as "barracks." The residences, however, were solidly constructed, competently designed, and contained indoor toilets and gas lights. Space was left behind tenements for children to play and clothes to be dried. As late as 1893, in a period of rapidly changing standards, inspectors from the U.S. Labor Commission found the tenement facilities still far superior to the usual housing for workers. Interestingly, though, they complained "that there are no arrangements to prevent the promiscuous mingling of occupants upon landings, stairways and corridors."

Insisting on beauty and order, Pullman refused sale to residents in order to preserve his plan. Agents conducted community affairs as an aspect of the company's business. Adult classes, educational societies, and athletic teams were encouraged, while bar and brothel were proscribed. Residents were expected to have proper manners, morals, and appearance. Behavior within the apartment was tightly regulated by company rules and by a lease which either party could void by ten days notice. To protect against undesirable outside influences, the company owned a "cordon sanitaire" of several thousand acres surrounding Pullman. The town's plan was clearly intended for social ends, and George Pullman in the role of landlord governed the community in order to direct its development. Ends beneficial were to be carefully nurtured, those baneful rigidly excluded.

There was little opportunity for political expression on town matters, and the only community election was for the school board. The town's supporters made no effort to conceal this because they viewed the absence of local rule as a virtue rather than a vice. The community newspaper in an editorial in 1890, two years after Lord Bryce's *American Commonwealth* called attention to the "conspicuous failure" of city governments, quoted with approval the statement of President Andrew White of Cornell University that "under our theory that a city is a political body, a crowd of illiterate peasants freshly raked in from Irish bogs, or Bohemian mines, or Italian robber-nests, may exercise virtual control. How such men govern we know too well." To George Pullman, municipal problems by and large were not proper questions for political consideration, but rather, as they concerned property and money, should be handled by a businessman trained in the rational ways of the market. In Pullman it was the executive, not the "boss," who made decisions. If detractors lamented the exclusion of the "town meeting," defenders rejoiced in the absence of the "political machine."

Until 1894, Pullman's model town was generally considered a success. Visitors found a picturesque village seated in a rural setting. All seemed ordered and arranged for attractiveness as well as convenience. A short distance from Chicago but far removed from "urban vices," the community contained cultural and recreational facilities usually found only in large cities where often they were reserved for the wealthy. Many praised Pullman as a "city on a hill," a "model in the present, and a pattern for the future."

Some compared the controlled propriety of Pullman with the neighboring town of Kensington, known as "bumtown." "Leave the . . . well cleaned streets of [Pullman], with its neat and convenient houses, and walk . . . along the . . . . streets of Kensington with its open sewers, its piles of decaying vegetation, its pools of stagnant water, its ill-ventilated and tumble-down tenements, its scores of liquor shops and houses of doubtful character." Ignored was the fact that the commercial vice of Kensington prospered from a Pullman clientele. Workers sought services there which were prohibited in their own town. The "disorder" of Kensington was as much the result of Pullman's plan as its own lack of one.

Reporters interviewing residents found men and women eager to tell of Pullman's superiority to their former homes in the city slums. A few, however, missed the vitality and variety of their old neighborhoods, but they were dismissed as incorrigibles warped by their earlier environment. A serious criticism increasingly heard was that the company's restrictive policies and high expectations intruded both during working hours and after. A company official confided to one reporter that frequently families moved to Pullman who "lacked a decent concern with appearance." In the evening they would be seen lounging on their doorsteps. The husband was in his shirtsleeves, smoking a pipe, while his untidy wife darned, and half-dressed children played about them. They were soon made aware that they were expected to appear in public properly attired and that the park, not their stoops, was the place for relaxation. Nor was sloth tolerated in the homes. When it was discovered that families "accustomed to filth and squalor" would not necessarily mend their ways because of superior housing, company inspectors visited to threaten fines unless proper care was taken. In many ways the people of Pullman were made to feel that they were part of the public display.

The ubiquitousness of this attention gave inhabitants an uncomfortable feeling of surveillance, and they carefully guarded their actions. The *Cleveland Post* in March, 1885, quoted a resident of Pullman who called the town an "exaggeration of the store-order system," and said that "the company owns everything and it exercises a surveillance over the movement and habits of the people in a way to lead one to suppose that it has a proprietary interest in [their] souls and bodies." A few months later the *New York Sun* observed, "The people of Pullman are not happy and grumble at their situation. . . . They say that all this perfection costs too much in money and imposes upon them an intolerable constraint. . . . They secretly rebel because the Pullman company [sic] continues its watch and authority over them after working hours. They declare they are bound hand and foot by a philanthropic monopoly." The model town was the company's showplace and residents were expected to act accordingly. One minister described Pullman as a town "girdled by red tape."

It was impossible to visit without constant reminder that this was a company town. A newspaperman, not necessarily in criticism, noted that:

A stranger arriving at Pullman puts up at a hotel managed by one of Mr. Pullman's employees, visits a theatre where all the attendants are in Mr. Pullman's service, drinks his water and uses his gas works supply, hires one of his outfits from the manager of Mr. Pullman's livery stable, visits a school in which the children of Mr. Pullman's employees are taught by other employees, gets a bill charged at Mr. Pullman's bank, is unable to make a purchase of any kind save from some tenant of Mr. Pullman's, and at night is guarded by a fire department every member of which from the chief down is in Mr. Pullman's service.

The Presidential Strike Commission of 1894 found the workers of Pullman to be of "comparatively excellent character and skill, but without local attachment or any interested responsibility in the town." A resident observed that "the people of Pullman are like the Chinese in America. They come here thinking to make what money they [can]." For most of the town's population, Pullman was primarily a place to work rather than to live. As long as employment was steady in the shops no major trouble erupted in the community. But it was only natural that irritations incurred in either factory or home would be nurtured against the company which managed both. Many of the workers moved from the town to buy or rent elsewhere. Asked why he had bought his own home an ex-resident answered laconically that he felt a greater freedom in his own place: "I own this little patch of ground and the house and that is how it comes that I live outside Pullman."

Richard Ely, then a young economist, visited the model town in October, 1894. He thought the town "systematically [constructed] upon scientific principles." To Ely, Pullman illustrated and proved "both the advantages of enterprise on a large scale and the benefits of a unified and intelligent municipal administration." Confident that "science" provided the means for a rational ordering of life, the town offered Ely a gratifying example of how planning and industrial power could be woven together to provide a beneficial environment. After the first few days, however, his enthusiasm waned as he realized the total absence of self-government. In consequence, he observed, the resident had "everything done for him, nothing by him." This caused a lack of commitment, while impossibility of home ownership prevented many from putting down roots. Ely's "unavoidable conclusion" was that the "idea of Pullman is un-American. . . . It is benevolent, well-wishing feudalism which desires the happiness of the people, but in such a way as shall please the authorities."

Mark Twain's coauthor of the *Gilded Age*, Charles Dudley Warner, admitted Pullman was a "gilded cage" and an example of "paternalism," but thought "it . . . worth some sacrifice to teach people that it is better for them morally and pecuniarily to live cleanly and under educational influences that increase their self-respect." Until the famous Pullman strike, doubtlessly more people agreed with Warner than Ely. What could be more American than a town dedicated to improving workers? Its "physical perfection" alone was taken as visible proof that planning worked.

A severe depression which began in 1893 created misery in the shops and homes of Pullman. To attract business, the company cut car construction prices and slashed wages but held rents constant. Dissatisfied with working conditions and wages, and with no clearly defined manner of expressing or resolving industrial or community grievance, the men walked out in May of 1894. Then Eugene Debs' American Railway Union called a sympathetic boycott of all lines running Pullman cars. This disrupted transportation from Ohio to California, while violence in and around Chicago brought intervention by U.S. troops. Ironically, the model town intended as a solution to industrial and urban problems had become identified with the century's worst labor disturbance.

Both during and after the strike Pullman was attacked as a dressed-up company town whose parks and gardens concealed exploitative rents and widespread oppression. A Chicago newspaper which formerly was an enthusiastic supporter now reviled

it: "Apparently to reach the high administrative ideal aimed at,
. . . there is nothing needed but the knout, a liberal supply of
shackles, and cheap transit to Siberia." Another paper called
Pullman a "white slave quarter." Blame was usually laid to
George Pullman's "tyrannical" and "grasping" nature.

Completely overlooked was a basic flaw in his plan. He
erected his community because of a conviction that workers
could afford superior homes when built with the economies of
mass production. This went beyond the Model Tenement
Movement's intention to erect decent housing renting for less
than $10 a month. Pullman's residents were expected to pay for
the town's beauty and order with rents fixed to return six percent on the company's investment. The company never made its
expected profit, but rents averaged $14 which was high for
workers during good times and unbearable during slack periods.
Particularly hard hit were the skilled workers living in the more
expensive row houses and who were leaders of the strike.
According to a federal commission which investigated the
trouble: "If we exclude the aesthetic and sanitary features of
Pullman the rents there are from 20 to 25 percent higher than
rents in Chicago."

But the "aesthetic and sanitary features" were what made
Pullman a model town. Fifty years after his visit to the town,
Ely wrote in his Autobiography: "In ways of material comforts
and beautiful surroundings Pullman probably offered to the
majority of its residents quite as much as they were in a position
to enjoy, and in many cases, even more." A price on parks and
paved streets seemed exorbitant when families wanted necessities. In the final analysis, the model town was probably on too
grand a scale for the workers of the day to afford unassisted.

George Pullman refused to abandon his community despite
heavy attack. After his death in 1897, however, the company
readily complied with a court order requiring the town's sale
on the grounds that its charter did not permit ownership of
residential land. In 1899, Chicago assumed municipal functions
and the plan was ended. Parks were used for industry, while the
shops' appearance became neglected. Many row houses were
purchased by residents, but tenements and public buildings went
to investors and speculators. Buildings were remodeled to suit
individual tastes. Paint concealed brick, and shutters and porches
were added to Beman's design. Small stores sprang up around

the town, eventually to drive the Arcade merchants from business. In 1908, home owners organized to restore Pullman's "original quality." However, at least as a community it continued to decline. Observers in 1915 and 1926 noted that the row houses, despite some cutting up, were usually well maintained by the owners, but that conditions in the tenements were unpleasant. Public areas were relatively unattended to, and the planned splendor of Pullman rapidly disappeared.

Chicago expanded to Pullman's border by 1910, transforming it from a suburban town to an urban neighborhood. The middle class fled to more desirable areas of the city. Conversion of car construction from wood to steel in 1907 brought a new type of worker to the shops, one less skilled and often a recent arrival from eastern and southern Europe. Losing its prominence, the former model town was chiefly remembered by the historian for a tragic strike rather than as a novel experiment in town building. At present, only Beman's original buildings remain to distinguish Pullman from its surroundings.

Close-ended and self-contained, the Pullman plan is clearly of little practical interest. Ignoring its surroundings, the plan provided no direction for growth or flexibility for change. In many ways it was little more than a blueprint for instant town building according to the normative values of the times. As an early experiment in what the twentieth century would call social engineering, the town of Pullman was a disappointment. Yet the model town's significance to the American planning tradition is considerable.

Its contemporaries variously interpreted the Pullman experience. To businessmen it demonstrated the danger of assuming responsibility for a community's welfare. When U. S. Steel built nearby Gary, the company for this reason sold homes to workers. Urban reformers, however, thought Pullman's mistake was imposing his will upon a community. Jane Addams, Richard Ely, and Graham Taylor praised everything about the town but its social context. Planning, they believed, could only work in a democratic setting of self-government where professional planners rather than a businessman would decide what was in the interests of the community.

The model town bears relationship to three important planning movements. It went well beyond the Model Tenement

Movement in housing standards and in providing community facilities. Its theme that municipal beauty and efficiency were complementary and should be made paramount through advance planning was the basis of the City Beautiful Movement, while the success of Daniel Burnham and other advocates of this movement in selling their programs to city businessmen rested in part upon an emphasis on planning as an instrument of social control and industrial economy.

Burnham's Chicago plan, however, assumed that cities would continue to expand indefinitely; Pullman believed that planned industrial towns offered an alternative to urban growth. Part of his model town's charm and appeal rested on the sight of industry located in a community whose scale suggested the familiar and manageable size of the New England small town. It also seemed somehow more reasonable and natural to contemporaries that workers were being trained in the old ethics of industry and frugality amidst a background of flowers and greenery. Without question, Pullman was eager to show that industrialization, which he and others considered a beneficial development, was not necessarily married to urbanization, which he thought disruptive to health and morals. Though his experiment failed, it was the forerunner of the later Garden City Movement and other efforts to resettle men and industry in planned communities away from the cities.

Historians have only recently realized that the nineteenth-century businessman was not always an enemy of reform, and they are now making more sophisticated exploration of the relations between the two. The model town of Pullman, with its use of an industrial system for purposes of social experimentation, suggests that modern America's search for control and order through city and regional planning may have been derived in part from the early activity of the business community in its quest for industrial efficiency.

The problem of "develop[ing] standards of order and beauty which amount to something more than the foisting of one man's tastes and self-interests on another," still remains unsolved. George Pullman's intentions were honorable and his mistakes honest. His model town can no longer be dismissed as a mere exercise in paternalism, but must be considered a milestone in the development of an American planning tradition.

ITALIANS IN URBAN AMERICA: A STUDY IN ETHNIC ADJUSTMENT

HUMBERT S. NELLI

Humbert S. Nelli, of the Department of History of the University of Kentucky, describes the acculturation of Italian immigrants in industrial Chicago.

Nearly four million Italians entered the United States between 1890 and 1920, the period of large-scale Italian immigration to this country. Contemporaries expressed deep concern about the influx of this alien horde, composed, many claimed, of criminals, paupers, ignorant peasants and illegal contract laborers, all congregated in closely packed colonies where they perpetuated old world traits and compounded urban problems.

Scholars and laymen alike still too often ignore or fail to recognize values and contributions of the immigrant community and its institutions. Because it served as a staging area where new arrivals remained until they absorbed new ideas and habits which made possible their adjustment to the alien environment, the ethnic community fulfilled a vitally important function both to the newcomer and to the receiving society. It bridged the gap between rural (old world) traditions and the new urban world, and acquainted each immigrant group, from the Irish and Ger-

From Humbert S. Nelli, "Italians in Urban America: A Study in Ethnic Adjustment," *International Migration Review*, New Series, I (Summer 1967), 38–55. Copyright 1967 by the Center for Migration Studies. Reprinted by permission of the Center for Migration Studies.

mans of the 1840s and the Italians and Slavs of the 1890s, to the Puerto Ricans and Negroes of the 1960s, with American urban ideas and values. Another point generally overlooked is the fact that not every member of a particular group reacted in the same way to the colony, its available institutions, or the outside environment.

The Immigrant Community

The pattern of Italian settlement in cities east of the Mississippi and north of the Ohio began with the founding of the immigrant community by Northern Italians, who tended to predominate until the 1880s; after that time, southerners and Sicilians formed the bulk of the new arrivals. The original enclave started in or near the city's central portion—that is, the business area—and was characterized by the movement of economically successful newcomers out of the settlement and into the American community. New arrivals from overseas swarmed into the colony, filling vacancies and creating or aggravating overcrowded, rapidly deteriorating neighborhoods.

In general, settlement in Chicago typified the Italian experience in urban America. Northern Italians, most of them from Genoa, formed the early colony in the years after 1850. Whether from the North, in the first three decades of immigration, or from the South and Sicily after the 1880s, newcomers tended to settle along the same streets and in the same tenement houses according to town or province of origin, probably seeking familiar faces, names and dialects. They lived together and, if possible, worked together. This early concentration broke down as immigrants met and mingled with newcomers from other towns and provinces in the homeland and with non-Italians who lived and worked in close proximity. In the process, they began to think and talk of themselves as Italians, a considerable expansion of provincial horizons.

Not only did they live and work with Italians from throughout the Kingdom as well as with Irishmen, Poles, Germans, Scandinavians and others; they often went to church with these "foreigners" and their children attended the same schools. In contrast to the homeland tradition of seeking a spouse from the same place of birth, they began to intermarry with outsiders. On occasion they married non-Italians. More often they took mates from elsewhere in Italy. Both choices represented a shift from old world attitudes, although of varying significance.

Continuing the pattern set by their predecessors, Southern Italians and Sicilians who obtained the financial means moved away from the colony. Commenting on the later group, a long-time (German-born) resident of the lower north side noted in 1928 that "the good Italians have moved up north and out west, and it is only the rough class that remains along Division Street." If migration from the ethnic settlement—a sign of economic mobility and an indication of desires for better housing and living conditions—did not take place in the first generation, it generally did in the second or third. Nevertheless, the continued presence of numbers of Italians in neighborhoods led contemporaries to the erroneous conclusion (not corrected by present-day scholars) that Italians, their children and their grandchildren after them, remained on the same streets and in the same tenements from the time they arrived in the city until they died, and that compact, unchanging settlements grouped according to place of immigrant origin. While this description might have fitted the first phase of settlement, new relationships quickly formed both with other Italians and with members of different nationality groups. A major cause of this constant regrouping and expanding of relationships was the fact that the composition of Italian colonies (as well as of other ethnic groups) was in constant flux, with at least half the community residents changing their place of dwelling each year.

It is also a mistake to assume that certain districts were inhabited exclusively or even predominantly by Italians. Chicago, like other urban areas, had few solidly Italian blocks and even fewer Italian neighborhoods. Between 1890 and 1920, only limited sections of certain Chicago streets contained a 60% or higher concentration of Italian immigrants and their children. The population density of Italians in the city's so-called "little Italies" seldom reached 50%. Throughout this period the near west side community in the vicinity of Hull House made up the largest and most heavily concentrated Italian group in the city. According to the City Homes Association *Report* of 1901 this west side "Italian district" extended from Polk Street to Twelfth Street and Halsted to Canal. Here, while first and second genera-

tion Italians constituted 50-70% of the population in portions
the size of blocks or slightly more, they comprised approximately *one third* of the area's total population. By 1920 the
major Italian community was located west of Halsted, where
similar concentrations could be found. This mixing of nationalities made inevitable innumerable contacts among members of
different immigrant groups.

Italians (and most recent immigrants) appeared to move out-
ward from the urban core more slowly and reluctantly than had
Irish, Germans and other older groups. The obvious reason was
the fact that the "old" elements arrived in Chicago, and in other
northern cities, considerably earlier than did the bulk of Italians,
Russians, Jews, Poles, Lithuanians and Greeks. The earlier arrivals, therefore, had the opportunity, as sociologist Richard
Ford has pointed out, of profiting economically and socially in
cities that had not developed rigid political, social or financial
patterns. "The process of acculturation," noted Ford, "has been
going on considerably longer for the Swedish, German and
Irish immigrants than the Italians and Russians." While accurate,
this explanation ignores a positive factor, that of extensive
amounts of residential mobility among Italians and other late
arrivals. In the early years of settlement, Southern Italians and
Sicilians generally moved either from one building or block
within a colony to another in the same community, or from one
community to another; by the 1920s, however, there was a
noticeable and significant movement toward the outlying areas
of the city. Italian districts began to decline perceptibly during
the 1920s because of World War I and the immigration laws
of 1921 and 1924, which shut off sources of new immigration.
The cumulative effect, as noted by sociologist Harvey W. Zor-
baugh in the late 1920s, was that "few Italians are coming to
America. . . . The community without any influx from the old
country is fast becoming Americanized." While the pace of this
dispersion decelerated because of depression in the 1930s and
housing shortages in the 1940s, it has again accelerated since the
1950s. The old near north side community in Chicago no longer
exists, for example, Negroes and Puerto Ricans having replaced
Italians.

At the turn of the century, living conditions in urban areas
of the various cities in which Italians (and generally other
"new" groups) lived were typically unhealthy, unpleasant and

socially demoralizing. Many Americans expressed sincere concern over the situation and believed the problems could be alleviated or even solved by encouraging immigrants to move to rural surroundings where greater opportunities surely awaited them. Contrary to popular belief, many Italians had entered agriculture and could be found in farming operations throughout the country. Nevertheless, the Italian and American governments, individual states and private agencies (such as local Italian-American chambers of commerce) supported the establishment of agricultural colonies for Italian immigrants, especially in Texas, Arkansas, Mississippi, Louisiana and Alabama. Despite auspicious beginnings and official support, most such ventures came to nothing. An Italian visitor to an early farming settlement in the American South gave some reasons for the failures:

The colony lives in poorly constructed houses, made of wood, without the most elementary precautions against the weather: frequently, . . . the dwellings are really tents, where members of the colony sleep together without distinction as to age and sex. . . . Hygiene is unknown. . . . Our people are eternally deeply in debt, . . . and the current agricultural contracts, for sharecropping or renting, are not to the advantage of the Italians.

Another and more important factor contributed to immigrant distaste for farming settlements: most Italians simply did not travel to America with hopes or intentions of farming. Like the majority of immigrants, "old" as well as "new," they arrived seeking economic opportunities. In the last decades of the nineteenth century and the early ones of the twentieth, prospects of financial gain existed in commercial and industrial centers of the North and East. In 1919 Robert Foerster, the leading historian of Italian emigration, discussed this fact:

A century ago, manufacturing lagged because free land was an alternative to employment. Today . . . industry is a vociferous alternative which tempts away from the farm even the long-established whites and Negroes, and may in the future tempt away the American-born children of the cultivating Italians.

New arrivals faced the basic problem, then, not of finding agricultural jobs or of escaping from the urban "trap," but rather of settling into their new way of life. The cultural problem of adjusting to new living patterns, the result of moving to an urban environment, constituted a key factor responsible for immigrant difficulties in urban America. Contemporaries failed to recognize that adjustment would have been necessary had the villagers migrated to a European city rather than across the Atlantic. Americans of rural background who moved to urban areas faced many of the same problems.

Significantly, Americans and Italians who encouraged or supported agricultural ventures did so at least in part because of the conviction that foreigners would become Americanized more rapidly and completely in a rural setting than they would in a city. Probably the opposite was true. As the experience of Dutch and German agricultural colonies in Pennsylvania and the Middle West made clear, assimilation slowed or halted in rural environments where contacts with outside agencies and individuals were extremely limited. In sparsely populated areas, an ethnic community is forced in upon itself, or can maintain a desired isolation. In cities, on the other hand, contacts of one type or another were (and are) virtually impossible to prevent.

The American *urban environment* had a profound effect upon newcomers of Sicilian or Southern Italian background. In Southern Italy and Sicily (and in Eastern Europe as well) *family* formed the center of life. Needs were handled on that basis, and problems were viewed from the standpoint of the individual or the extended family. E. C. Banfield described a Southern Italian society dominated by amoral familism. Many immigration scholars and students of Italian history accept this description. If it is accurate, then the existence of community and group consciousness among Italians and Sicilians in the United States was not a transplantation from the old country, but a development of the new world. In the homeland, Banfield found peasants and gentry alike unable to act "for any end transcending the immediate, material interest of the nuclear family." In the United States (specifically, Chicago), one leader of a Sicilian-Southern Italian community described his neighborhood as having "unusual unity and strength," and continued,

Perhaps nowhere else in the city is there to be found a neighborhood where as many people know each other as they do in our district. We have to a very great extent the same kind of warmth, friendliness and intimacy in our community life that was to be found in the small towns of Sicily from whence our parents came.

It is ironic that this community life, which developed in response to the American environment, was assumed to be a carryover of old world habits.

Italo-American Institutions: Community Adjustments

In the United States, individual newcomers could not always deal with financial and social problems; nor did the extended family connection always provide dependable help. People who would not have considered the possibility of co-operation or even of contact with emigrants from other homeland towns and provinces found themselves forced to deal with urban difficulties as members of a group. In the process, Italians modified familiar institutions (like the Church), established some with which they had previously had very little contact (such as the press and mutual benefit societies), and organized agencies which did not exist in the home country (like the immigrant bank). Thus while some immigrant institutions had counterparts in the old world, Italians either came in contact with them for the first time in America, or recast them in new molds. Because the city prevented isolation, neither the community nor its institutions were fully Italian in character; nor were they American. They served an interim group, the immigrant generation with its old world traditions and new world surroundings. Community institutions more closely resembled those established by other immigrant groups in the United States than they did those in Italy. The mutual benefit society, for example, could be found among Poles, Ukrainians, Lithuanians, and Jews, among others. Non-Italian newcomers also established newspapers and depended upon services provided by immigrant bankers and labor bosses.

Immigrant bankers flourished in every part of the country where newcomers from Southern and Eastern Europe had gathered in any considerable numbers. The principal financial transaction of these bankers consisted of receiving deposits and sending money abroad. Most also served as steamship ticket agents, and often conducted some other business as well. Hence some "banks" were located in grocery stores, saloons, or other natural gathering places. The typical banker operated with a minimal accumulation of capital, had no legal responsibility, and, for the most part, acted freely outside legal controls. Because of the conditions under which they functioned, many bankers went out of business, some because they had practiced inefficient business methods, others because they had absconded with customers' savings.

The period of the 1890s formed the heyday of the Italian banker and the labor agent (or padrone), but conditions began to change shortly after the turn of the century. By the Italian Emigration Law of 1901, the Bank of Naples became officially designated as the financial institution entrusted with transmission of savings from all parts of the world, including the United States. The Bank therefore exerted a strong influence in forcing immigrant bankers to improve services for their clients, modify rates of exchange and lower charges for transmission of money. In addition, after 1900 various states which contained large immigrant populations enacted legislation more strictly controlling immigrant banking operations. In Massachusetts, New Jersey and New York, these laws had considerable success. In Illinois, on the other hand, rural American bankers effectively opposed regulations which might have limited their own free and easy activities.

Unlike immigrant bankers, the Church existed for newcomers before they left Italy; yet it, too, had undergone changes in the world. In comparison with their homeland institution, Italians found the Roman Catholic Church in America to be a cold and almost puritanical organization, controlled and operated, even in Italian neighborhoods, by the Irish. By 1900 Italians appeared to be so dissatisfied with the "American Church" that many clergy believed the problem posed a serious threat to the Church's future in the United States. Protestants and socialists alike saw in Catholicism's difficulties an ideal foundation for proselytizing. Some immigrants turned to Protestantism because it seemed to be one road to Americanization. Nevertheless, despite costly and prodigious efforts by non-Catholic churches, relatively few Italians were converted: socialists also found their hopes meagerly fulfilled. The tendency of many newcomers simply to turn away from all religious activity constituted a greater menace to the Church than either Protestantism or socialism. Undoubtedly what Father Joseph Schuyler calls "the stress of disorganization," the impact of migration and the influence of the American environment, distracted many immigrants from traditional organizations like the Church. Other newcomers, generally of a liberal persuasion, found distasteful the Church's opposition to Italian unification and its identification with anti-liberal and anti-national forces in Europe.

Appearances to the contrary, most immigrants remained nominally or actually loyal to the Church, but in their own way. Reflecting the situation in the home country, religion for most Italians in the United States made up an accepted part of life and did not indicate a central aspect of national loyalty (as it tended to be for Irish- and Polish-Americans, for example). It required neither extreme fervor nor public proclamation. Critics who "saw" an irreligious attitude in immigrant superstition and idolatry ignored the fact that image-worship, especially of the Virgin, and anthropomorphic views of nature and religion made Catholicism comprehensible to the unlettered mind. In the same way, critics could consider Italians' addiction to festivals, processions and feasts as a perversion of religion, although to participants they formed an integral part of it. In America immigrants celebrated these functions not only in an effort to re-establish those elements of religion which had strongly appealed to them in Italy, but also to counteract Irish influences in their new churches. Thus what seemed to Americans to be a falling-away from religion was at least in part a modification of old world habits to new world conditions. Prior to 1921, however, the Catholic Church did not occupy the position of prestige among Italian-Americans that it has since assumed, particularly since 1945.

Many immigrants sought to solve life's urban complexities by joining mutual benefit groups. These were not, however, "transplanted" institutions carried by Southern Italians and Sicilians to the United States. In Sicily and Southern Italy, where strong family ties ensured aid in times of need, group life featured recreational activities in a few social clubs (*circolo sociale*), most of which had small memberships and limited community importance. The mutual benefit society, although known in Italy, existed almost exclusively among middle classes, and especially among artisans, in the northern and central parts of the Kingdom. In the United States, mutual benefit organizations satisfied needs which immigrants could not or would not

secure elsewhere. These included sickness and death benefits
and medical care. Societies also offered companionship, recreation, a feeling of strength through numbers, and a sense of identity in the new environment.

It is difficult to determine both membership figures and the
number of societies in existence, because of the basis of group
organization—in many cases, town or province of birth and
neighborhood (even street or building) of residence—and the
fact that some societies formed with goals other than mutual aid
or recreation. Some existed to satisfy political, religious or military functions. Through necessity, small units which had organized on a town or provincial basis consolidated into, or were
absorbed by, larger organizations encompassing all Italians regardless of place of birth or residence. In all these respects the
Italian experience with societies paralleled that of other nationalities. Thus the merging of small groups into the Sons of Italy
had its counterpart in the establishment, for example, of the
Polish National Alliance.

The function and value of the "colonial" press (as those in
Italy and many in the immigrant community referred to it)
were temporary, specialized in nature, and vital only so long as
a sufficiently large group needed its services. Its major significance lay in easing the first critical years of immigrant adjustment to America. Articles about events in Italy and in towns
and provinces of origin, news of other immigrant communities,
reports of societies and listings of collections for needy newcomers, all helped Italian-Americans to develop and nurture a
sense of belonging within their new surroundings. Information
about local and national American events, emphasis on the values
of education and participation in politics, and advice regarding
behavior and modes of expression acceptable to Americans all
constituted attempts to lessen adjustment problems for readers.
The press served as a crutch for immigrants having difficulties
in adapting to their new surroundings, or those unable to break
away from homeland traditions. To many of the second generation and a number of more independent newcomers, colonial
journals offered little of interest or value; hence readership
reached its height during the first two decades of the twentieth
century, the time of arrival of great masses of immigrants des-
perately in need of services which foreign-language newspapers
could provide. During this period also, Italian-language tabloids

employed technological advances pioneered by American papers in order to attract attention and hold readership. Immigrant periodicals in the United States bore a stronger resemblance to the popular American press than to homeland journals. Thus they offered headlines, brief articles, special features, simple language and profuse illustrations. Editors who valued literary excellence over sensational news, pictures and frequent protestations of loyalty to Italy generally lasted but a short time. Like churches and societies, newspapers neither reached nor influenced the entire immigrant community.

Identification with the colony, and use of its facilities and institutions, comprised not only a growth away from homeland outlooks but also, for many newcomers, a vital step in assimilation. It is important to note, however, that Italians exhibited a variety of responses to urban America. Some ignored all community institutions and never expanded their loyalties or interests from the district of origin; even the Italian Kingdom lay outside their comprehension. Others made full use of some or all existing community institutions and enlarged personal horizons to include Italy, a nation which did not exist for them before their emigration from it. A third group preferred to make limited use of press, societies and churches as intermediaries through which to learn American customs and ideas. Often these first generation arrivals came as children or young adults and absorbed or consciously adopted American habits and speech in the outside community, from politics as well as in schools, settlement houses and streets.

From politics Italians gained patronage jobs and neighborhood conveniences like bath houses as well as a voice in the operation of city government. In the early years of settlement, this influence extended only to occasional machine support for Italian candidates for precinct or ward positions, in exchange for delivering the vote for Irish politicians (who generally controlled Italian and other "new" immigrant wards). It grew over the passage of time to the control of Italian wards and victories in city-wide elections.

Social workers reached and influenced many through classes in English, courses in sewing, handicrafts and other activities for women, the support of Italian theater groups, summer camps for children, and the sponsorship of political and social clubs for men. Along with public schools, social workers and settlement houses offered alternate channels of contact with the American community to those provided by American political bosses, Italian "prominenti," bankers and padroni. Some reformers sought to establish and support free employment agencies for immigrants and to destroy the padrone labor system, while others worked to procure the passage of child labor laws and strict observance of compulsory education legislation.

Italian immigrants gained notoriety (and the wrath of social workers) because their children were seldom permitted to obtain adequate schooling. While complaining that their own lack of education kept them from getting better jobs, parents sent their offspring out to work in order to supplement family income. Although in time most Italians complied with minimum requirements of compulsory education laws, they secured jobs for their children after school hours. When Italian children reached the legal withdrawal age of fourteen, they were "to an alarmingly high degree" withdrawn from school and put to work.

Despite dire predictions that Italians were caught in a "cycle of poverty," by 1900 they had begun progressing from unskilled labor into commercial, trade and professional classes, including printing, bricklaying, carpentering, import and export, banking, law and medicine. Notwithstanding complaints of reformers and laments of immigrant workers, financial success at this time did not absolutely require an education; ambition and cunning could, and did, overcome illiteracy. Crime, one means of economic advancement independent of education, social background or political connections, provided for all classes of Italians opportunities for quick and substantial monetary gain and sometimes for social and political advancement as well. Within the colony bankers and padroni, blackhanders and other lawbreakers all realized small but important profits by swindling or terrorizing compatriots. The "syndicate," a business operation reaping vast profits from the American community, offered almost limitless opportunities for promotion within its hierarchy. Thus for some, crime offered means of advancement within the ethnic community and for others, opportunities outside it.

By the same process that many Americans believed Italians to be naturally criminal, contemporaries assumed that certain nationalities were predisposed to particular occupations because of inborn traits or old world influences. The Irish, for example, were "natural politicians," although a comparison of Irish experiences in other parts of the world would have challenged this belief. Irish immigrants and their children did not achieve political successes in London, Liverpool or other urban centers in England and Scotland (to which Irish immigration was "more numerous though less celebrated" than to American cities) comparable to their achievements in New York, Chicago and other cities in the United States. Opportunities for political success were simply not present for Irish immigrants in England or Scotland, and Irish pre-eminence in American political life, like the later prominence of Italians in crime and Jews in the clothing industry, was due primarily to availability of opportunity rather than to inborn characteristics or old world habits.

Conclusion

The *process of adjustment* began for individual immigrants on their arrival in the United States. The community and its institutions admirably fulfilled their functions for a succession of newcomers. Immigrant districts were responsible not for perpetuating old world traits and patterns, but for providing vital first steps in introducing newcomers into the mainstream of American life. A residue remained when the composition of an immigrant area changed, but the bulk of an earlier group eventually moved out of the central city rather than live among residents new to urban life. This cycle operated when Poles, Jews or Italians moved into neighborhoods that had previously been inhabited by Swedes, Germans or Irish. Due to the effects of the depression and World War II, this process temporarily broke down, but is once again functioning. The newest arrivals who have driven Italians and Poles from their central city colonies are, of course, Negroes and Puerto Ricans. Many of the same bitter complaints against Italians sixty years ago are now being levelled against these newest inhabitants—filth, crime, social demoralization and hopeless degradation—among others—and with good reason. They have only begun their adjustment to urban America.

V

The Modern Metropolis

———

Urban population agglomeration and simultaneous diffusion from the central cores greatly accelerated in the twentieth century. Thus the metropolitan area superseded the city as suburbs enveloped commercial and industrial centers. In turn, the geographic cohesiveness of the metropolitan area succumbed to megalopolis, particularly in the Northeast, where the suburbs of major cities overlapped each other and transcended state boundaries.

In the 1960's urban areas in the South and West, especially in Florida, California, and Texas, grew more rapidly than those in other regions. Small and medium-sized cities such as Santa Barbara, Tampa, Orlando, Houston, Phoenix, Tucson, and Atlanta gained rapidly. Nevertheless, the flight from the centers of the largest cities to suburbs, and beyond to smaller cities, remained the most obvious demographic change over a long period of time.

Urban diffusion resulted from many interrelated forces and innovations. In the late nineteenth and early twentieth centuries hostility to immigrants and the desire to escape urban problems quickened the pace of migration from city to suburb. The trolley and inter-city railroad, and by the 1920's the automobile, facilitated urban dispersal by providing low-cost transportation. The automobile considerably increased the distance that predominantly white, middle-class Protestants put between themselves and the Catholic and Jewish immigrants of the central city. Urban sprawl followed transportation routes and reflected a lack of comprehensive city planning. Those who stayed in the twentieth-century city felt the impact of urban pressure but secured some advantages from city life.

The high living standard of an industrial center had its costs. Municipal bankruptcy and economic disaster of the Great Depression balanced full employment and relatively high wages during periods of prosperity. A general pollution affecting the city as a whole superseded the more confined stench of the nineteenth-century slum. The automobile provided an even slower means of transportation through many urban districts than did the horsecar in the already congested post-Civil War city. By mid-twentieth century, racial strife, the concomitant of institutionalized white racism in American society, and poverty overshadowed pre-World War II industrial violence and inter-ethnic hostilities. Seasonal riots that threatened urban society in the 1960's juxtaposed the black poor against supporters of the status quo. Though the industrial worker became the vanguard of white racism in Northern cities, the official labor movement did little to educate him, for unlike its radicalism during the Depression decade, the AFL-CIO had become rich and complacent.

In the 1960's, municipal revenues could not begin to cope with the enormity of these urban problems. Compounding fiscal weakness, the complexity of megalopolis transcended city boundaries. Like the municipal governments of the late nineteenth century that were immobilized before the advent of boss rule, the urban political order of the 1960's became archaic. Chicago and its suburbs, for example, had over 1100 separate and overlapping independent governmental administrations, while the 1400 governments in the New York City metropolitan area covered portions of three states, with each individual municipality duplicating such services as fire protection, water, and sanitation. This lack of coordination and planning wasted resources and reproduced municipal services at the cost of neglecting the urban poor, who would benefit most by an investment of such misused funds.

While urban problems clearly existed, the city remained not only the cosmopolitan center of intellectual and cultural excitement, but continued to have potential for human betterment. Its vigor could be seen in a multifaceted black renaissance. Like other ethnic groups in the past, black Americans, by the mid-twentieth century, began taking control of their own destiny. In government, intellectual currents, education, and business, blacks strove not merely for success, but for independence. A black elite, lionized by business, municipal and federal government, moved on the edge of the American establishment as a result of summer uprisings of the black poor. However, many black students and youths rejected the material advantages of upper-middle-class status. Instead of escape from the ghetto, they chose involvement in the total black community. To achieve this they established their own local action organizations and demanded an education relevant to their experience.

The federal government attempted to meet the needs of the city and its minorities by circumventing hostile, rural-dominated state legislatures which had refused to respond to urban concerns. Thus in the 1960's federal and municipal governments worked together to revitalize the cities. The U.S. Public Health Service, for instance, investigated pollution of Lake Michigan in conjunction with the Milwaukee Health Department; the Housing and Home Finance Agency jointly administered experimental projects with the city of Detroit. The federal government designed the Model Cities Program to supersede standard urban renewal, which had been little more than a rationalization for black removal. In contrast, among its many creative programs, Model Cities intended to keep neighborhoods intact by rehabilitating salvageable structures while replacing those thoroughly decayed. Congress, however, refused to allocate sufficient funds for an effective program in the 1960's, and when interests of local politicians conflicted with rational planning, the program was modified and the urban dweller sacrificed.

Also attempting to deal with urban problems, a 1962 presidential decree banned discrimination in housing built with federal aid. In addition, the federal government attempted to vocationally educate and find employment for the poor through projects such as Job Corps, Concentrated Employment Program, and Neighborhood Youth Corps, while Volunteers in Service to America (VISTA) and Project Head Start creatively challenged techniques traditionally used in dealing with urban poverty.

These attempts at reform presupposed that the American people would make a massive urban investment. However, their political spokesmen gave international and military alternatives priority over the domestic needs of the city; at the same time they frustrated community participation programs, a major thrust of the war on poverty. By the end of the décade, the decision makers had neither supplied the unprecedented funds nor permitted the local creativity needed to rebuild the cities. Urban reform slowed, and while the public called for greater police efficiency and lower taxes, the cities festered.

MEGALOPOLIS:
THE MAIN STREET
OF THE NATION

JEAN GOTTMANN

A renowned urban geographer now at Oxford University, Jean Gottmann examines Megalopolis—the urban complex that stretches from southern New Hampshire to northern Virginia and from the Atlantic coast to the Appalachian foothills.

The Northeastern seaboard of the United States is today the site of a remarkable development—an almost continuous stretch of urban and suburban areas from southern New Hampshire to northern Virginia and from the Atlantic shore to the Appalachian foothills. The processes of urbanization, rooted deep in the American past, have worked steadily here, endowing the region with unique ways of life and land use. No other section of the United States has such a large concentration of population, with such a high average density, spread over such a large area. And no other section has a comparable role within the nation or a comparable importance in the world. Here has been developed a kind of supremacy, in politics, in economics, and possibly even in cultural activities, seldom before attained by an area of this size.

A Very Special Region: Megalopolis

This region has indeed a "personality" of its own, which for some three centuries past has been changing and evolving, constantly creating new problems for its inhabitants and exerting a deep influence on the general organization of society. The modern trends in its development and its present degree of crowding provide both examples and warnings for other less urbanized areas in America and abroad and call for a profound revision of many old concepts, such as the usually accepted distinctions between city and country. As a result new meanings must be given to some old terms, and some news terms must be created.

Great, then, is the importance and significance of this section of the United States and of the processes now at work within it. And yet it is difficult to single this area out from surrounding areas, for its limits cut across established historical divisions, such as New England and the Middle Atlantic states, and across political entities, since it includes some states entirely and others only partially. A special name is needed, therefore, to identify this special geographical area.

This particular type of region is new, but it is the result of age-old processes, such as the growth of cities, the division of labor within a civilized society, the development of world resources. The name applied to it should, therefore, be new as a place name but old as a symbol of the long tradition of human aspirations and endeavor underlying the situations and problems now found here. Hence the choice of the term *Megalopolis*, used in this study.

Some two thousand years before the first European settlers landed on the shores of the James River, Massachusetts Bay, and Manhattan Island, a group of ancient people, planning a new city-state in the Peloponnesus in Greece, called it *Megalopolis*, for they dreamed of a great future for it and hoped it would become the largest of the Greek cities. Their hopes did not materialize. Megalopolis still appears on modern maps of the Peloponnesus but it is just a small town nestling in a small river basin. Through the centuries the word *Megalopolis* has been used in many senses by various people, and it has even found its way into Webster's dictionary, which defines it as "a very large city." Its use, however, has not become so common that it could not be applied in a new sense, as a geographical place name for the unique cluster of metropolitan areas of the North-eastern seaboard of the United States. There, if anywhere in our times, the dream of those ancient Greeks has come true.

An Urbanized Area with a Nebulous Structure

As one follows the main highways or railroads between Boston and Washington, D. C., one hardly loses sight of built-up areas, tightly woven residential communities, or powerful concentrations of manufacturing plants. Flying this same route one discovers, on the other hand, that behind the ribbons of densely occupied land along the principal arteries of traffic, and in between the clusters of suburbs around the old urban centers, there still remain large areas covered with woods and brush alternating with some carefully cultivated patches of farmland. These green spaces, however, when inspected at closer range, appear stuffed with a loose but immense scattering of buildings, most of them residential but some of industrial character. That is, many of these sections that look rural actually function largely as suburbs in the orbit of some city's downtown. Even the farms, which occupy the larger tilled patches, are seldom worked by people whose only occupation and income are properly agricultural. And yet these farm areas produce large quantities of farm goods!

Thus the old distinctions between rural and urban do not apply here any more. Even a quick look at the vast area of Megalopolis reveals a revolution in land use. Most of the people living in the so-called rural areas, and still classified as "rural population" by recent censuses, have very little, if anything, to do with agriculture. In terms of their interests and work they are what used to be classified as "city folks," but their way of life and the landscapes around their residences do not fit the old meaning of urban.

In this area, then, we must abandon the idea of the city as a tightly settled and organized unit in which people, activities, and riches are crowded into a very small area clearly separated from its nonurban surroundings. Every city in this region spreads out far and wide around its original nucleus; it grows amidst an irregularly colloidal mixture of rural and suburban landscapes; it melts on broad fronts with other mixtures, of somewhat similar though different texture, belonging to the suburban neighborhoods of other cities. Such coalescence can be observed, for example, along the main lines of traffic that link New York City and Philadelphia. Here there are many communities that might be classified as belonging to more than one orbit. It is hard to say whether they are suburbs, or "satellites," of Philadelphia or New York, Newark, New Brunswick, or Trenton. The latter three cities themselves have been reduced to the role of suburbs of New York City in many respects, although Trenton belongs also to the orbit of Philadelphia.

The "standard metropolitan areas," [1] first used by the U.S. Bureau of the Census in 1950, have clarified this confused situation somewhat but not entirely. For example, the New York–Northeastern New Jersey standard metropolitan area cuts across political boundaries to reveal the relationships of this vast region to the core city of New York. And yet the mechanical application of the term "standard metropolitan area" has resulted in the establishment of separate areas for Trenton, which is closely tied to both Philadelphia and New York, and for Bridgeport, which is for many practical purposes part of the New York area. Similar problems can be found in other parts of Megalopolis.[2]

[1] The U.S. Bureau of the Census defined a standard metropolitan area as "a county or group of contiguous counties which contains at least one city of 50,000 inhabitants or more. In addition to the county, or counties, containing such a city, or cities, contiguous counties are included in a standard metropolitan area if according to certain criteria they are essentially metropolitan in character and socially and economically integrated with the central city." In New England, "towns and cities, rather than counties, are the units used in defining standard metropolitan areas."

[2] For the 1960 Census the term "standard metropolitan area" was changed to "standard metropolitan statistical area." The definition was modified and a somewhat different set of criteria used which resulted in breaking down several of the formerly recognized larger metropolitan areas into smaller such units. The results thus achieved may be more precise in some respects but in the case of Megalopolis they may cause some confusion. The New York–Northeastern New Jersey standard metropolitan area of 1950 has been replaced by four standard metropolitan statistical areas: one for New York in New York State and three in New Jersey, those of Paterson-Clifton-Passaic, Jersey City, and Newark. The stricter definition of metropolitan integration of adjoining counties now excludes Somerset and Middlesex counties, formerly classified as metropolitan. As a result the percentage of the population of New

Thus an almost continuous system of deeply interwoven urban and suburban areas, with a total population of about 37 million people in 1960, has been erected along the Northeastern Atlantic seaboard. It straddles state boundaries, stretches across wide estuaries and bays, and encompasses many regional differences. In fact, the landscapes of Megalopolis offer such variety that the average observer may well doubt the unity of the region. And it may seem to him that the main urban nuclei of the seaboard are little related to one another. Six of its great cities would be great individual metropolises in their own right if they were located elsewhere. This region indeed reminds one of Aristotle's saying that cities such as Babylon had "the compass of a nation rather than a city."

Megalopolis— Main Street and Crossroads of the Nation

There are many other large metropolitan areas and even clusters of them in various parts of the United States, but none of them is yet comparable to Megalopolis in size of population, density of population, or density of activities, be these expressed in terms of transportation, communications, banking operations, or political conferences. Megalopolis provides the whole of America with so many essential services, of the sort a community used to obtain in its "downtown" section, that it may well deserve the nickname of "Main Street of the nation." And for three centuries it has performed this role, though the trans-

---

Jersey residing in metropolitan areas fell from 89.9 in 1950 to 78.9 in 1960—a statistical trend surprising to those who know how much more metropolitan—or should we say Megalopolitan—the whole of New Jersey grew through the 1950's. To compensate for such an impression and for the separation between New York City and Northeastern New Jersey, a new term has been created and defined: "Standard Consolidated Areas," of which there were two (recognized for 1960) in the country: the New York–Northeastern New Jersey area (which included Somerset and Middlesex counties in New Jersey), and the Chicago–Northwestern Indiana area. The recognition of these broader areas was intended to stress "the special importance of even more inclusive metropolitan statistics" (see Executive Office of the President, Bureau of the Budget, *Standard Metropolitan Statistical Areas*, U.S. Government Printing Office, Washington, D.C., 1961). The metropolitan area of Philadelphia remained unchanged in both its Pennsylvania and New Jersey parts.

continental march of settlement has developed along east-west axes perpendicular to this section of the Atlantic seaboard.

In recent times Megalopolis has had concentrated within it more of the Main Street type of functions than ever, and it does not yet seem prepared to relinquish any of them. Witness, for example, the impact of the Federal government in Washington, D.C., as it tightens up over many aspects of national life; the continued crowding of financial and managerial operations into Manhattan; New York's dominance of the national market for mass communication media, which resists all attempts at erosion; and the pre-eminent influence of the universities and cultural centers of Megalopolis on American thinking and policy-making. Megalopolis is also the country's chief façade toward the rest of the world. From it, as from the Main Street of a city, local people leave for distant travel, and to it arriving strangers come. For immigrants it has always served as the chief debarkation wharf. And just as passing visitors often see little of a city except a few blocks of its Main Street, so most foreign visitors see only a part of Megalopolis on their sojourns in the United States.

Just as a Main Street lives for and prospers because of the functions of the whole city, rather than because of any purely local advantages of its own, so is Megalopolis related to the whole United States and its rich resources. In general, Megalopolis itself was blessed only moderately by nature. It has no vast expanse of rich soils (there are some good soils but more poor ones), no special climatic advantages (its cyclonic climate is far from ideal), and no great mineral deposits (though there are some). In these respects it cannot compare with the generous natural potential of the Middle West or Texas or California. But it does excel in locational advantages—deep harbors of a drowned shoreline, on which its principal cities were early established, and a connecting-link relationship between the rich heart of the continent and the rest of the world. By hard work man has made the most of these locational resources, the most outstanding ones in an otherwise average natural endowment. As a result, early in its history Megalopolis became a dynamic hub of international relations, and it has maintained and constantly expanded that role to the present day. It is now the most active crossroads on earth, for people, ideas, and goods, extending its influence far beyond the national borders, and only as such a crossroads could it have achieved its present economic pre-eminence. . . .

Today it is essential that solutions be found to save this area from decay and to reassure the nation and the world about the kind of life modern urbanization trends presage for the future. Megalopolis has been built and often reshaped by its people. These people are now wealthier, better educated, and better endowed with technological means than ever. They ought to be able to find ways of avoiding decline of the area.

For the Better or for the Worse?

The preceding paragraph may seem to imply an unwarranted optimism about society's ability to control itself. True, history records a long list of brilliant civilizations that have sunk under the pressure of internal decay and external jealousy. We remember their names: Babylon, Corinth, Sparta, Athens, Rome, and many others. In the shadowy vistas of ancient times they vanished into the distance like shipwrecked ships loaded with ambition and precious cargo. Can such a fate be looming in the offing for Megalopolis? Modern urban sprawl is viewed by many as a threat to progress and general welfare. What is happening in Megalopolis today has been described as a pathological phenomenon, a sickness, a cancer. Such views are held by distinguished and respectable citizens of the area. One may well be alarmed by their invectives, all the more so as one does not have to go far away from Megalopolis to hear expressions of distrust and jealousy inspired by the amazing concentration of wealth and power in the great seaboard cities. Are people both in and out of this extraordinary region united in condemning it?

Urban growth in general has been discussed and condemned on moral grounds for a long time. Such debate is expectable and desirable, but on the whole history has shown the condemnation to be unjust, as can be seen by a brief review of some of the consequences of crowding.

Contrasts between rich and poor, for example, are especially striking in the crowded communities of cities. These may exist in rural areas too, but there they are diluted by scattering and veiled in greenery. The growth of urban pursuits (industries, trade, services) sharpens the contrasts by condensing them into a smaller area. Rich and poor live within short distances of one

another and mix together in the streets in a way that often
arouses righteous indignation. It seems brutally amoral to witness destitution neighboring on elegant sophistication, poverty
mixing with prosperity. And yet, alas, a growing city's environment can hardly escape offering such sights. For many centuries
there was an enormous difference between the advancement
possible in trade and industry on the one hand and in farming
on the other (though modern farm mechanization and subsidies
to agriculture have substantially increased the profit possibilities
of farming), and so to rise economically within the span of one
lifetime has traditionally been easier in cities than in rural areas.
The affluence of those who have so risen draws to the city large
groups of humbler people, who come there to profit by the
local abundance of money and the volume of spending and to
serve the wealthier. In contrast to the more conservative "open"
country, the "closed-in" city offers a more dynamic environment, socially and economically.

In cities, too, other vicious aspects of economic growth and
social life have always been more evident than in the country.
As urban development was accelerated by the Industrial Revolution, some of these vicious aspects became increasingly obvious.
Slums and mobs grew worse than ever, making the urban landscape ethically and aesthetically shocking to those who cared
about the people. From his sojourns in an industrializing western
Europe, and especially from Paris during the French Revolution,
Thomas Jefferson brought back impressions that reinforced his
normal Virginian opposition to great cities and the development of manufactures or large-scale commerce. As slums and
mobs became more general in European cities in the first half
of the nineteenth century there arose more awareness about the
classes of society and social injustice. There was more discussion
of these matters, and the early Socialist doctrines were largely
inspired by them. Then came the teachings of such philosophers
as Fourier and Proudhon in France and Engels and Karl Marx
in Germany, opposing great urban concentration as much as
great concentration of capital. Engels' writings on the slums
and working conditions in the then fast-developing British cities,
such as Manchester, are well known. Because urban conditions
of living and working were largely at the root of nineteenth-
century Socialist doctrines, Karl Marx stressed that his theories
applied much more to the industrialized countries of western
Europe, which had accumulated large amounts of capital, than

to the rural, little-urbanized countries to the east. Twentieth-century events have proved him wrong on this score, however, for communism has conquered the mainly rural countries, and the forms of socialism that developed in the more urban and capitalistic countries of the West have turned away from Marxism.

Crowding of population within a small area creates shortages of various resources, and most of the crowded people are bound to suffer in some ways because of the shortages. To alleviate them, to make crowding more bearable and the population happier, ways and means of constantly better distribution must be found. Otherwise no lasting growth can develop, and the whole enterprise will soon be doomed. From the struggle against such shortages have come some of mankind's most important advances. In the arid areas of the Middle East, for example, early civilization arose when people first congregated around the main springs and permanent rivers. As the settlement grew, the supply of both water and irrigable land became scarce. To insure survival of the people a proper distribution system had to be achieved, and rules and regulations had to be set up and accepted. Thus organized society, ruled by law, was born. Because authorities were needed to enforce law, political power arose, and people organized themselves to avoid more oppression than was necessary. Everywhere, the more crowded people have become in cities the more they have craved both security and freedom. Modern political life and its concepts of liberty, self-government, and democracy are the products of urban growth, the inheritance of cities in process of growth and development —places such as Jerusalem, Athens, Rome, Bruges, Florence, Paris, London, to mention only those that have been most studied by historians. And the same places, or similar urban centers, have contributed most of our scientific and technological developments, either because people there were struggling to solve pressing problems or because urban societies make possible a leisurely enough elite, some of whose members can devote themselves to disinterested research and a search for a better understanding of the universe.

Thus urban crowding and the slums and mobs characteristic of it may be considered growing pains in the endless process of civilization.

In the same way, the picture of Megalopolis is not as dark as the outspoken pessimists and frequent protests would seem to paint it. Crowded within its limits is an extremely distinguished population. It is, *on the average*, the richest, best educated, best housed, and best serviced group of similar size (i.e., in the 25-to-40-million-people range) in the world. The area is still a focus of attraction for successful or adventurous people from all over America and beyond. It is true that many of its sections have seen pretty rural landscapes replaced by ugly industrial agglomerations or drab and monstrous residential developments; it is true that in many parts of Megalopolis the air is not clean any more, the noise is disturbing day and night, the water is not as pure as one would wish, and transportation at times becomes a nightmare. Many of these problems reflect the revolutionary change that has taken place as cities have burst out of their narrow bounds to scatter over the "open" countryside. In some ways this suburban sprawl may have alleviated a crowding that had threatened to become unbearable, for residential densities of population per square mile have decreased. But new problems have arisen because of the new densities of activities and of traffic in the central cities and because the formerly rural areas or small towns have been unprepared to cope with the new demands made upon their resources. New programs are needed to conserve the natural beauty of the landscape and to assure the health, prosperity, and freedom of the people. In spite of these problems, however, available statistics demonstrate that in Megalopolis the population is on the average healthier, the consumption of goods higher, and the opportunity for advancement greater than in any other region of comparable extent.

Thus the type of urban growth experienced here generates many contrasts, paradoxes, and apparently contradictory trends. It calls for debate and naturally excites passionate opinions for and against it. Are its results for the better or for the worse? It is not for our generation to moralize on the matter, but to strive to make the outcome be for the better, whatever obstacles may be in the way. Megalopolis stands indeed at the threshold of a new way of life, and upon solution of its problems will rest civilization's ability to survive. In the search for such solutions there will be found no easy keys to success, no "gimmicks" or "open-sesames." Solutions must be thought out, ironed out, and constantly revised in the light of all the knowledge that can be acquired by all concerned.

AMERICAN POLITICAL
PARTIES AND THE RISE
OF THE CITY

*Stanford historian Carl Degler examines national politics in re-
lation to urban development and contends that the strength
of the party in power was dependent upon the allegiance of
the city voter.*

The ending of Reconstruction in 1877 deprived both Republican and Democratic parties of the issues that had sustained their
rivalry for half a century. As a result, in the presidential elections from 1876 to 1892, neither party won decisively; never
before nor since has popular political inertia been so noticeable.
More important, this indecision of the voters obscured the significant fact that the Republican party was popularly weak.
For despite the preponderance of Republican presidents during
these years, only James A. Garfield secured a popular plurality
and his was the smallest in history. The party's weak popular
base was even more evident in the congressional elections between 1874 and 1892 when the Democrats captured sizable
majorities in the House of Representatives in eight out of ten
Congresses. So serious was this popular weakness of the party
that Republican Presidents from Rutherford B. Hayes to Benjamin Harrison, as both Vincent P. De Santis and Stanley P.

From Carl N. Degler, "American Political Parties and the Rise of the City:
An Interpretation," *Journal of American History*, LI (June 1964), 41–59. Copyright 1964 by the Mississippi Valley Historical Association. Reprinted by permission of The Organization of American Historians.

Hirshson have shown, worked in a variety of ways to build up a stronger Republican party in the South, but with very limited success.

Thus in the opening years of the 1890s the Republicans as a national party were in obvious trouble. The elections of 1890 and 1892 were disastrous for them as the Democrats swept into firm control of the House of Representatives and into the White House as well. Despite the party's proud association with the winning of the War for the Union, the Republicans were no more popularly based than at their founding forty years earlier; the majority of the nation's voters remained stubbornly Democratic. Moreover, with each passing election the political value of that vaunted association depreciated further as memories grew dimmer. The party seemed destined to recapitulate the history of the Whigs by serving only as a convenient alternative to the Democrats.

At that point, though, a complete reversal in party prospects took place. In the congressional election of 1894 the Republicans clearly emerged as the majority party, leaving the Democrats to wander in the political wilderness for a generation. The transfer of seats in the election of 1894 from the Democratic to the Republican side of the House was the largest in history. The Republicans gained a majority of 132, whereas in twenty-four states not a single Democrat was elected and in six others only one Democrat was returned in each. Moreover, prominent Democrats like William L. Wilson of West Virginia, William McK. Springer of Illinois, and Richard L. Bland of Missouri—men associated with important Democratic doctrines like low tariffs and free silver—lost their places. This overwhelming Republican congressional victory in 1894 was confirmed two years later by what for the Republicans was to be their first decisive presidential victory without benefit of federal protection of Negro voting in the South. Measured against the margins of defeat in previous elections, William Jennings Bryan's defeat was crushing; he ran farther behind the winner than any candidate of a major party since Ulysses S. Grant trounced Horace Greeley.

Dramatic as the Republican victories for 1894 and 1896 undoubtedly were, their enduring significance lies in the continuance of the trend they began. For the next sixteen years the Republicans, without interruption, commanded the majorities in the House and elected the presidents. Thus in the middle of the 1890s the Republicans, for the first time, emerged as the majority party of the nation.

The question which arises is: why? At the outset one can reject the hypothesis of challenging new leadership, since the party enjoyed none in the 1890s. Furthermore, since the shift in votes took place when Grover Cleveland, an acknowledged conservative, was president, and continued when a radical Democrat, Bryan, was the party's candidate, the policies of the opposition party do not offer much help in explaining the change. The only place left to look is among the voters themselves. It is their attitudes that changed as the United States passed from an agricultural to an industrial economy.

In spite of all that has been written to emphasize that the 1890s was the period during which this agrarian to industrial transition occurred, there are valid reasons for placing this momentous shift in the preceding decade. It was, for example, during the 1880s that the production of manufactured goods surpassed farm goods in dollar value, and it was in this same decade that a majority of the nation's work force became engaged in non-agricultural rather than agricultural pursuits. Also during the 1880s railroad construction reached unprecedented heights, with more miles of track laid than in any other decade in American history. These were years of peak membership of the Knights of Labor, something over 700,000; the American Federation of Labor was formed, and the number of industrial strikes sharply increased. It was the decade of the frightening Haymarket riot in Chicago, which, in its nationwide notoriety, epitomized the arrival of the new world of the factory, the city, and the immigrant. In fact the number of immigrants who flooded into the country in that decade exceeded that of any other similar period in the century. Furthermore, those ten years were the seedtime of the city. According to a contemporary analysis of the census, the number of cities with 8,000 or more population jumped from 286 in 1880 to 443 in 1890. Many cities doubled in size in the ten years, and some, like Chicago, had been already large at the beginning of the decade. A few made spectacular records of rapid growth. Minneapolis jumped from 47,000 to 165,000; Omaha reached 140,000 in 1890, though ten years before its population had been no more than 31,000; Denver nearly tripled its population.

During that decade of transition neither the political parties nor the people were prepared by previous experience for the problems and nature of the new industrial, urban age. Hence the politics of the 1880s were sterile, uninteresting, and often trivial, as the parties and the voters rehashed stale issues and only reluctantly faced the new. Then, in the early 1890s, it would seem, the decision was made; the commitment of the voters hardened. The question then remains: why did the Republican party, which thus far had been sectionally based and numerically weak, rather than the popular Democratic party, emerge from this period of indecision as the dominant party of the nation?

A part of the answer seems to lie in the public image of the two parties. The Republican party was more suited to the needs and character of the new urban, industrial world that was beginning to dominate America. In those years the Republicans were the party of energy and change. They inherited from their antebellum beginnings as well as from the experience of Reconstruction a tradition which looked to the national authority first and to the states second. The party and its leaders had not hesitated to use the national power in behalf of economic growth by sponsoring such measures as the Homestead Act, land grants and loans to railroad construction companies, and protective tariffs. During the Civil War the Republicans demonstrated their willingness to use income and inheritance taxes, and fiat money when the nation's survival had seemed to require such novel measures. In the 1880s, it was Republican Senator Henry W. Blair who sought to employ the federal revenues and power in behalf of aid to the public schools. In each of the four times that the Blair education bill came before the Congress, Republican support always exceeded Democratic support.

This nationalistic tradition and these specific measures, of course, also added up to a national image of the party that would appeal to urban voters and immigrants. As the self-proclaimed party of prosperity and economic growth, the Republicans could expect to win support from those who manned the expanding factories and crowded into the tenements of the burgeoning cities. Certainly party spokesmen made appeals to the urban working class. In 1892, for example, President Harrison told the Congress: "I believe that the protective system, which has now for something more than thirty years continuously prevailed in our legislation, has been a mighty instrument for the development of our national wealth and a most powerful agency in protecting the homes of our workingmen from the invasion of want. I have felt a most solicitous interest to preserve to our working people rates of wages that would not only give daily bread, but supply a comfortable margin for those home attractions and family comforts and enjoyments without which life is neither hopeful nor sweet." Nor should such appeals be hastily brushed aside as empty rhetoric. Republican claims received substance, if not proof, from the steady rise in real wages during the last three decades of the century. Moreover, foreign observers, like Friedrich Engels, who certainly could not be accused of being partial to Republican propaganda, cited the tariff as one of the principal reasons why American workingmen were better off than European. In 1893 Engels wrote to his friend Friedrich A. Sorge that "through the protective tariff system and the steadily growing domestic market the workers must have been exposed to a prosperity no trace of which has been seen here in Europe for years now. . . ."

The Democratic party, to a greater extent than the Republican party, was more a congeries of state organizations than a national party. Certainly in the South and in a northern state like Illinois, there were many Democrats in the 1890s who were far from agreement with the national leadership. But even with these cautionary observations, of the two parties between 1880 and 1896, the Democrats undoubtedly presented the more conservative face to the electorate. The hallmark of the party under the dominance of Cleveland was economy, which in practice meant the paring down of government assistance to business, opposing veterans' pensions, hoarding the national resources, lowering the tariff, and, in general, stemming the Republican efforts to spur economic growth and to enhance the national power. Besides, the Democrats were ideologically unsuited to any ventures in the expansion of government activities. Still steeped in the Jeffersonian conception of the limited role of the federal government, the national Democrats were less likely than the Republicans to use federal powers in new ways to meet new problems. It was Cleveland, after all, who had vetoed a meager $10,000 relief appropriation for drought-stricken Texas farmers with the stern warning "though the people support the Government the Government should not support the people."

The election results of the 1880s suggest that the Republicans were even then receiving returns from their bid for working class support. Today it is axiomatic that the big cities of the country will vote Democratic, but in that period most of the large urban centers outside the South were more likely to be Republican than Democratic. It is true that cities like New York, Boston, and San Francisco were usually safely Democratic, but in the three presidential elections of the 1880s a majority of the nation's cities over 50,000 outside the South went Republican. In these three elections—even though in two of them Cleveland polled a larger vote than his Republican opponents—eastern and midwestern cities like Philadelphia, Chicago, Cleveland, Cincinnati, Buffalo, Providence, Milwaukee, Newark, Syracuse, Paterson, and Minneapolis invariably appeared in the Republican column. In the election of 1884, which was won by Democrats, the Republicans captured twenty of the thirty-three non-southern cities over 50,000. In 1888 the Republicans took twenty-six of the forty-four largest non-southern cities listed in the census of 1890.

Furthermore, many of these Republican cities contained substantial proportions of immigrants. The 1890 census showed thirty percent or more of the population of Chicago, Milwaukee, Paterson, Cleveland, Buffalo, Pittsburgh, Providence, and Rochester to be foreign-born. All of these cities voted consistently Republican in the three presidential elections of the 1880s.

But the tendency for Republicans to do better than Democrats in northern cities must not be exaggerated. The election of 1892, with its upsurge of Democratic strength in the cities, demonstrated that Republican popularity in the urban centers was neither so overwhelming nor so fixed that the popular Democracy might not reduce it. Clearly some other force, some other ingredient in the mixture, was operative. That additional factor appears to be the depression of 1893.

The depression of the 1890s was an earth-shaker. Not only did it last five years or more, but it was the first economic decline since the United States had made the transition to full-scale industrialism. As a consequence its effects were felt especially in the growing cities and among the working class. A recent historian of this depression has estimated that real earnings for the population dropped eighteen percent between 1892 and 1894. The single year of 1894 witnessed Coxey's army as well as other less well-known armies of unemployed workers on the march, widespread labor unrest, and the violence of the Pullman and Chicago railroad strikes. More workers went out on strike in that year than in any other in the century. The number was not equalled again until 1902.

Since it is true that the Republicans for all their belief in the national power would not have taken any stronger anti-depression measures than the incumbent Democrats, the election upset of 1894 might be considered as nothing more than a case of blind, rather than calculated, reprisal against the incumbents. Furthermore, it might be said that the Republicans had been chastised in much the same fashion in 1874 when they chanced to be in power at the beginning of the depression of 1873. The objection is not as telling as it appears. In the election of 1894 there was a third party, and if simple dissent were operating, the Populists should have benefited as much from it as the Republicans. But this they did not do. Although the total Populist vote in 1894 was higher than in 1892, not a single state that year, John D. Hicks has observed, could any longer be called predominantly Populist. Four western states, Kansas, Colorado, North Dakota, and Idaho, all of which had voted Populist in 1892, went Republican in 1894. In a real sense, then, the election was a victory for the Republican party and not simply a defeat for the Democrats.

If the terrible impact of the depression polarized the voting in a new way, thereby helping to explain the massive shift to the Republicans, the activities of the Democrats in 1896 could only confirm the urban voters in their belief that the Republican party was the more responsive political instrument. In their convention of 1896 the Democrats hardly noticed the cities; they had ears only for the cries of the farmers demanding currency reform. Many Populists, it is true, stood for something more than free silver, but the money issue was certainly accepted by Bryan and the vast majority of Democrats as the principal issue of the campaign. Free silver was at best uninteresting to the urban population and, at worst, anathema to them. The adoption of such a monetary policy would be inflationary and therefore contrary to the interests of all urban consumers, whether bankers, petty clerks, or factory workers. Mark Hanna, McKinley's campaign manager, sensed this defect in Bryan's appeal from the outset. Early in the campaign he said about Bryan: "He's talking silver all the time, and that's where we've got him."

And they did have him. The cities, where the industrial workers were concentrated, voted overwhelmingly Republican. Only twelve of the eighty-two cities with a population of 45,000 or more went for Bryan—and seven of the twelve were in the Democratic South while two others were located in silver-producing states. Seven of the seventeen cities in the states that Bryan carried gave a majority to McKinley; on the other hand, only three of the sixty-five cities in states going to McKinley provided a majority for Bryan. Bryan was hopeless in the industrial East; he did not carry a single county in all of New England, and only one in New York, and eleven rural counties in Pennsylvania. He even lost normally Democratic New York City.

Taken together, the elections of 1894 and 1896 mark the emergence of the Republican party as the party of the rising cities. Even a cataclysmic event like the Civil War, in which the Democrats were on the losing side, had not been able to dislodge the Democracy from its favored place in the voters' hearts. But the impact of an industrial-urban society with its new outlook and new electorate had done the trick. It is significant that several cities like San Francisco, Detroit, Indianapolis, Columbus, and St. Paul, which had been Democratic in the 1880s and early 1890s, voted Republican in 1896 and remained Republican well into the twentieth century. None of the large cities which had been Republican in the 1880s and early 1890s, on the other hand, changed party affiliation in 1896 or for decades thereafter. Another indication of the continuity between the elections of 1894 and 1896 is that the states which showed the greatest Republican congressional gains in 1894 also showed increased Republican strength in the presidential election two years later. There were twelve states, each of which gave the Republicans four or more new seats in 1894; of these, eight were among the states which in 1896 showed the greatest number of new counties going to the Republicans. Significantly, they were mainly industrial-urban states like Illinois, New Jersey, New York, Ohio, and Pennsylvania.

It is commonplace for textbooks to depict the Republican party of the late nineteenth century as the political arm of the Standard Oil Trust, but if the election returns are to be given any weight at all, that is not the way the voters saw the party in the 1890s. Not only was it the party of respectability, wealth, and the Union; it was also the party of progress, prosperity, and national authority. As such it could and did enlist the support of industrial workers and immigrants as well as merchants and millionaires. As one analyst of the 1896 New England vote saw it, the Democrats may have obtained their most consistent support among the poor and the immigrants of the cities, but the Republicans gained strength there, too, "just as they did in the silk-stocking wards. . . . They were able to place the blame for unemployment upon the Democrats and to propagate successfully a doctrine that the Republican party was the party of prosperity and the 'full dinner pail.' "

Ideologically, it is true, the Republican party in the 1890s had a long way to travel before it would translate its conception of the national power into an instrument for social amelioration. But it is suggestive that Robert M. La Follette in Wisconsin and Theodore Roosevelt in Washington, who are the best known of the early Progressives, were also Republicans. It is these men, and others like them in the party, who carried on the political revolution of 1894, which had first announced the Republican party as the majority party in the new America of cities and factories.

The significance of that political revolution is that the pattern of party allegiance then established continued for many years to come. To be sure, in 1912, because of a split in the Republican party, Woodrow Wilson was able to break the succession of Republican presidents. But it is also evident that the success of the Democrats in 1912 and 1916 should not be taken as a sign of a fundamental change in voter preferences. One reason for thinking so is that in 1916 Wilson was reelected by the very close margin of 600,000 popular and twenty-three electoral votes and in 1920 the Republicans swept back into the White House on a landslide. Another reason is provided by the Democratic losses in the House of Representatives after 1912. That year the Democrats achieved a margin of 160 seats over the Republicans, one of the largest in congressional history, but by the midterm elections the difference between the parties was down to 35; by 1916 it was less than 10. In 1918 the Democrats lost control of the House.

The most persuasive evidence for believing that the Republicans continued to be the majority party of the nation, despite the interruption of the Wilson administrations, is the history of elections during the 1920s. In 1920 Warren G. Harding received over 61 percent of the votes cast, a proportion of the total not achieved since the advent of universal manhood suffrage and only equalled once thereafter. Although other Republican presidential victories in the 1920s did not reach the proportions of the Harding landslide, they were all substantial. Furthermore, at no time between 1920 and 1928 was the Republican margin of strength in the House of Representatives endangered; it never went below twenty seats. In fact, near the end of the decade, Republican strength in the House was reaching out for a new high; in 1928 it was one hundred seats greater than the Democratic proportion. In the presidential election that year Herbert Hoover's majority over Alfred E. Smith was more than six million votes. In short, by the end of the 1920s the Republicans were as much the majority party of the nation as they had been in 1894 when the tide of history first turned in their favor.

Within four years, though, another political revolution had been consummated, this time returning the Democrats to the position of the majority party of the nation. In 1932 the Democrats elected their second president in forty-two years and captured the House of Representatives with a majority of unprecedented size, something like 190 seats. The true measure of the reversal of political patterns, though, did not come until 1934 and 1936. For with their overwhelming victories in those two elections, the Democrats showed that 1932 was not simply another 1912, when a large Democratic victory had been quickly eroded away in subsequent elections. Instead, in 1934 the Democrats reversed the patterns of the preceding fifty years; rather than losing seats in the House, as was customary in off-year elections, they actually added ten more to their swollen total. And then in 1936 they succeeded in reelecting Franklin D. Roosevelt by an overwhelming majority, with a proportion of votes that came very near topping Harding's landslide of 1920.

Because the Roosevelt revolution in politics coincided with the onset of the Great Depression, it is tempting to argue that it was economic adversity in 1932, much as it had been in 1894, which accounts for the shift in the voters' preferences. Certainly the impact of the depression had much to do with the long-range change; it undoubtedly accounts for the overwhelming character of the shift. But there is also much evidence to suggest that the shift which first became evident in 1932 was already in progress four years before. Beneath the surface of Hoover's victory the forces which would consummate the Roosevelt revolution were already in motion in 1928 in behalf of Alfred E. Smith.

The most obvious comment to be made about Smith's vote was its large size. Smith's 15 million votes were 6.5 million more than John W. Davis had polled in 1924, when La Follette's Progressive candidacy had drawn away some Democratic votes, and 5 million more than James M. Cox and Roosevelt had been able to capture in 1920. With this enormous gain, if by nothing else, Smith showed himself to be the most popular Democratic candidate since Bryan in 1896.

But important as Smith's ability to attract votes may have been, his contribution to the turn to the Democrats lay in something more than mere numbers. After all, Hoover increased the Republican vote by some five million over Coolidge's total in 1924 and Harding's in 1920. What was significant was that Smith's unique combination of politically effective personal attributes was attracting a new class of voters to the Democratic party. Many years after the election, Hoover pointed out that in 1928 the candidates of both major parties had risen from small beginnings to become figures of national prominence. But if this was true of the origins of Smith and Hoover, by 1928 the two men were poles apart. Unlike Hoover, or any previous presidential candidate of either party, Smith was both of lower class social background and a native of a big city. As is well known, his life and his career in politics were closely associated with New York City and the Tammany political machine. It is true that his four terms as governor of New York showed him to be progressive in thought and action as well as honest and courageous, but his loyalty to Tammany was both well known and unshakeable. Furthermore, Smith was a Roman Catholic and, though he had no intention of making his religion a political issue, many Protestants did. In fact, in 1927, an article that gained national prominence challenged him to show that his religion would not interfere with his proper execution of the duties of president. Although Smith's parents were native New Yorkers, his religion, his mother's Irish background and his close association with Irish-dominated Tammany Hall stamped him as a spokesman for the urban immigrants. In short, he was the first presidential candidate to exhibit the traits of a part of the population that had never before been represented by a candidate of a major party.

Smith's religion, which hurt him in the South and helped to

explain why Hoover was able to capture four southern states, undoubtedly assisted him in the North. Massachusetts and Rhode Island, both heavily Catholic in population, went Democratic in 1928 for the first time since the Civil War. In fact, while Hoover was taking 200 southern counties from the Democrats, Smith took 122 northern counties that had been consistently Republican. Moreover, of these 122 counties, 77 were predominantly Roman Catholic; most of these 77 counties remained in the Democratic column, it is worth emphasizing, in subsequent elections.

Since Roman Catholicism in America is an immigrant religion and its communicants are largely concentrated in the big cities, most of the new counties Smith gained were urban. Indeed, the striking thing about Smith's candidacy was that it attracted the big city vote away from the Republicans for the first time since the 1890s. In 1920 Harding had taken all of the twelve cities with a population over 500,000, but in 1928, among these twelve, New York, Cleveland, St. Louis, Milwaukee, and San Francisco went for Smith though their states did not. Moreover, Pittsburgh and Baltimore failed to give Smith a majority by fewer than 10,000 votes each. Of the twelve cities only Los Angeles was strongly for Hoover. If the votes of all twelve cities are added together, Smith secured 38,000 more votes than Hoover; in 1920 the Republicans had carried the same cities by 1,638,000 votes. In a broader sample, a recent student of the election has shown that in 1920 Harding carried all twenty-seven of the principal cities outside the South; in 1928, Smith captured eight, and made appreciable gains in the others. He ran behind Cox and Roosevelt in only three of the twenty-seven. Such a reversal was one sign that a socio-political revolution was under way.

Despite all that has been written about Smith's appeal to the voters of the big cities, the significant point, often overlooked, is that his appeal was not of equal force in all cities. For example, he ran badly in southern cities, the residents of which exhibited, when compared with other southerners, the weakest commitment to the historic party principles that had made the South a stronghold of the Democrats. In fact, Dallas and Houston in Texas, and Birmingham in Alabama went Republican in 1928. More important was Smith's strikingly uneven attraction for the cities of the North. His attractive power was considerably stronger in those cities in which immigrant stock predominated than in those in which it was in the minority. (Immigrant stock is defined here as foreign-born whites and native whites born of one or more foreign-born parents.) According to the census of 1930, the closest to the election of 1928, there were thirty-six cities with populations in excess of a quarter of a million. In nineteen of these cities, immigrants and children of immigrants constituted 50 percent or more of the population. In the presidential election of 1920, all of these nineteen cities voted Republican; in the election of 1924 all but one voted Republican. In the election of 1928, though, seven of them turned Democratic.

On the other hand, in the seventeen cities out of the thirty-six in which the native-born whites of native-born white parents constituted a majority of the population in 1930, only four went Democratic in 1928, and three of them were located in the traditionally Democratic South (Atlanta, New Orleans, and Memphis). The fourth was St. Louis. In fact, Democratic strength in these "native-white" cities actually declined in 1928, for in the 1920 and 1924 elections six of the seventeen had gone Democratic. All six of them, it should be noted, were in the Democratic South. Thus in the election of 1928 among the cities in which native whites constituted a majority, there was actually a loss in Democratic strength. In short, Smith's appeal to urban voters was not simply that he was of urban origin but that his Catholicism and Irish background stamped him as a champion of immigrants and children of immigrants. At the same time, those cities in which the immigrant stock was in the minority retained their allegiance to the Republican party—an allegiance which had been first clearly established in the 1890s for the big cities as a whole.

Yet it might be said that Smith failed, after all, to carry even a majority of the cities with a preponderance of immigrant stock. He won only seven of the nineteen cities of immigrant stock. Does not this fact call into serious question the assertion that there was a relationship between the social character of these cities and Democratic voting?

Closer analysis suggests not. As inspection of Table I makes evident, in every one of the cities with 50 percent or more immigrant stock, whether they were carried by Smith or not, the Democratic vote increased enormously in 1928 over 1920, when the Republican majorities had been very large. In fact, in none of the cities in which immigrant stock predominated was the Democratic increase less than 100 percent, and in many it was considerably higher. In these same cities, on the other hand, the Republican vote increased as much as 100 percent in only one of the nineteen cities and in only three did it go above 50 percent (Oakland, Pittsburgh, and Seattle). In several of the cities that Smith carried, the Republican vote actually fell from that of 1920.

If one examines the Democratic performance in those cities in which the native-white population predominated, the conclusion that there was a close association between the increase in Democratic votes and immigrant stock is further strengthened. In none of these cities was there much of an increase in either the total vote or in the vote for the Democratic candidate. (See Table II.) Only in Denver did the Democratic vote increase as much as 75 percent; in no city did it reach as high as 100 percent as it did in every one of the cities in Table I. In five the increase was less than 25 percent and in three there was actually a loss of Democratic votes. The median value is 26.0 percent.

The Republican vote in Table II provides a revealing contrast with the Democratic vote in Table I, for now it can be seen that the "native-white" cities produced no upsurge in voting for Republicans comparable to that in the cities of immigrant stock. Except for a marked—and what turned out to be temporary—upturn in Republican strength in the southern cities of Atlanta, Birmingham, Dallas, and Houston, the increase between 1920 and 1928 in none of these cities was as much as 100 percent. The median value is 53.2 percent.

From this examination of the variability in the response of the cities to Smith's candidacy it seems clear that Smith brought out the immigrant vote in unprecedented numbers. Some of these voters of immigrant stock had probably been voting Republican all along and now switched to the Democrats. But many more, it would seem, voted for the first time, for otherwise one cannot explain the enormous increase in Democratic votes in the short span of eight years without a commensurate decline in Republican votes. These same people, backed by even greater numbers, would come out in 1932 to vote for Franklin Roosevelt and consummate the Roosevelt Revolution in politics. But it was Smith, the Catholic and the recognized champion of the urban-based immigrant, who first made the Democratic party the party of the cities and the immigrant. This upsurge in immigrant voting in 1928 helps to explain, at least negatively, the apparent paradox of urban support for a Republican party in the 1920s that defended prohibition and pushed for restrictions on immigration. Prior to the galvanizing appearance of Smith on the political landscape, most urban immigrants just did not vote at all and many probably did not even think of themselves as part of the body politic. And to those who did vote, the Democratic party offered no candidates, other than Wilson, to lure them away from the party of national power, Theodore Roosevelt, and prosperity. Samuel Lubell has suggested, further, that the broadening educational opportunities of the 1920s also help to explain the upsurge in immigrant political participation in 1928.

Despite familiarity with the connection between the cities and the Democratic party today, that connection was not forged, as far as the nation was concerned, until 1928-1932. Indeed it is the conclusion of this paper that it was the political activity of urban voters which raised the Republican party to a position of dominance in American politics for a third of a century, just as it has been the cities which have been largely responsible for the Democratic party's leading place in the nation's political life for the most recent third of this century. For Franklin Roosevelt after the landslide of 1936 continued to receive the support of the vast majority of the 37 principal cities of over 250,000 population, carrying 32 of them in 1940 and 30 in 1944. Harry Truman in 1948 did about as well, even though the Dixiecrat candidate took three of the traditionally Democratic southern cities. Truman's score was 30 of the big cities against 4 for Thomas E. Dewey.

The real test of the Democratic power in the cities came in 1952 with the first campaign of Dwight D. Eisenhower, certainly the most popular Republican of the twentieth century. In that election and the next, Eisenhower made substantial inroads into the urban territory of the Democrats. In his first election, for example, he carried 21 of the 39 cities over 250,000 and in 1956 he did even better by taking 28 of them—almost as many as Franklin Roosevelt did in 1944.

But there are two good reasons for seeing this resurgence of Republican strength in the cities as temporary and nothing more than a reflection of the special appeal of Eisenhower rather than as a basic shift in popular party allegiance. The first reason is that Eisenhower was able to carry a majority of the House of Representatives for his party in only the first of his four congressional elections. Indeed, his own popular vote in 1956 was greater than that of 1952, but he proved unable, nonetheless, to do what every popular president since Zachary Taylor had been able to do: carry a majority of his party into the House of Representatives.

In this failure the cities played a part since many of them that voted for Eisenhower did not grant the same degree of support to the Republican congressional candidates. This tendency was most obvious in the southern cities, where he showed great strength. In 1952 he carried six of the eight southern cities and in 1956 he captured all but Atlanta. Yet in the congressional races in all of these cities, Democratic congressmen, because of the South's one-party system, were almost invariably returned. More important, the same tendency could be observed in cities outside the South. For example, in the Ninth Ohio District (Toledo) a Democratic congressman was returned in all four of Eisenhower's congressional elections, though the General personally carried the city in 1952 and 1956. Although Eisenhower won Cook County, Illinois in 1956, eight of the twelve congressional districts of the city of Chicago went Democratic. Newark and Denver, both of which supported Eisenhower in 1952 and 1956, sent only Democratic congressmen to Washington throughout the Eisenhower years. Eisenhower won Milwaukee in 1956, but the two congressmen elected from the city that year were Democrats.

The second reason for seeing Eisenhower's substantial victory as more personal than partisan is that in the election of 1960 John F. Kennedy, despite his close victory in the national popular vote, regained the cities for the Democrats. He carried 27 of the 39 cities, even though he did less well than Stevenson in 1952 among southern cities, capturing only New Orleans, San Antonio, and ever-faithful Atlanta. A large part of the explanation for Kennedy's failure to regain southern big city support commensurate with his general increase in urban backing is to be found, of course, in southern dislike of the Democratic party's stand on civil rights which began with Truman and which Kennedy went out of his way to support and advance. Nevertheless, the defection also calls attention to the quite different social character of southern, as compared with northern big cities.

There are very few Catholics or children of immigrants in southern cities, so that an Al Smith and a John F. Kennedy have no religious or social appeal there as they do in the North. That this difference was influential is suggested by the return to the Democratic fold in 1960 of San Antonio and New Orleans, the only two southern cities containing substantial numbers of Catholics and children of immigrants.

In short, as the congressional strength of the Democrats throughout the Eisenhower years had suggested, the election of 1960 showed that the Democrats still retained the long-term allegiance of the big city voters, whose support had first been evident thirty-two years before in another campaign by a Roman Catholic grandson of an Irish immigrant.

TABLE I

CITIES WITH FIFTY PERCENT OR MORE IMMIGRANT STOCK *

CITY	DEMOCRATIC VOTE IN NEAREST THOUSAND		PERCENT CHANGE	REPUBLICAN VOTE IN NEAREST THOUSAND		PERCENT CHANGE
	1920	1928		1920	1928	
Boston	68	205	202	108	99	− 7.7
Buffalo	40	126	215	100	145	45.0
Chicago	197	716	266	635	812	27.8
Cleveland	71	166	132	149	195	30.7
Detroit	52	157	201	221	265	19.9
Jersey City	63	153	143	102	100	− 1.9
Los Ángeles	56	210	275	178	514	189.0
Milwaukee	25	111	344	73	82	12.2
Minneapolis	143	396	178	519	561	8.1
Newark	41	118	188	116	169	45.6
New York	345	1,168	239	786	715	− 9.1
Oakland	21	61	190	73	119	63.2
Philadelphia	90	276	209	308	420	36.5
Pittsburgh	40	161	301	139	216	55.5
Providence	46	97	112	80	86	7.5
Rochester	29	74	156	74	100	35.2
St. Paul	21	57	171	40	53	32.5
San Francisco	33	97	195	96	96	0.0
Seattle	17	47	176	59	96	62.9

* Two cities in this list, Oakland and Seattle, counted 47.8 and 48.2 percent respectively of immigrant stock, but they have been included here rather than in Table II, because they also have less than 50 percent of native white population. Their proportions of native white population are 46.4 and 47.7 percent respectively. The missing proportions are accounted for by colored persons.

TABLE II

CITIES WITH LESS THAN FIFTY PERCENT
OF IMMIGRANT STOCK

CITIES	DEMOCRATIC VOTE IN NEAREST THOUSAND		PERCENT CHANGE	REPUBLICAN VOTE IN NEAREST THOUSAND		PERCENT CHANGE
	1920	1928		1920	1928	
Akron	28	32	14.3	44	79	79.5
Atlanta	9	7	— 22.5	3	6	100.0
Baltimore	87	126	44.8	126	135	7.3
Birmingham	25	17	— 32.0	7	18	157.0
Cincinnati	78	110	41.0	113	148	31.0
Columbus	48	47	— 2.3	60	92	53.2
Dallas	14	17	21.4	5	27	440.0
Denver	23	41	78.5	44	74	68.1
Houston	15	22	47.7	8	27	237.0
Indianapolis	61	73	19.7	80	110	37.4
Kansas City, Mo.	77	97	26.0	80	127	58.6
Louisville	56	64	14.3	68	98	44.3
Memphis	16	18	12.5	9	12	33.3
New Orleans	33	56	70.0	18	14	— 22.2
Portland, Ore.	28	45	60.5	45	76	68.8
St. Louis	106	176	66.0	163	162	— 0.68
Toledo	30	45	50.0	52	78	50.0

THE CITY IN THE
GREAT DEPRESSION

IRVING BERNSTEIN

Irving Bernstein, Associate Director of the Institute of Industrial Relations of the University of California at Los Angeles, describes the inability of municipal government to effectively cope with the social and economic crisis of the Great Depression.

The sheer magnitude of distress exposed the inadequacy of unorganized private relief at the outset of the depression. The family, the neighbor, the landlord, and the employer, even when they so wished, were incapable of grappling with unemployment relief on this scale. Hence the load shifted almost at once to the cities, to their private and public welfare agencies. *Fortune* posed the problem of the jobless urban worker: "What do you do?"

You are a carpenter. Your last cent is gone. They have cut off the gas. The kid is white and stupid looking. You have always earned your own way before but you can't get a job now for love or money. What do you do?

In some, but by no means all, cities you can get a meal at the Salvation Army or the Municipal Lodging House merely by waiting a few hours in a breadline. But that's no use now. So you go to the cop. He pulls out his directory and sends you to one of the listed charitable societies. The society takes your name and gives you

From Irving Bernstein, *The Lean Years: A History of the American Worker, 1920–1933* (Boston: Houghton Mifflin Company, 1960), pp. 291–302. Reprinted by permission of Houghton Mifflin Company.

emergency aid if you need it. It then asks you a list of questions about your age, your nationality, your religion, and your need. Your answers to these questions will determine to which of the charities specializing in Jews, Catholics, Protestants, abandoned babies, homeless boys, sickly children, pregnant women, disabled veterans, and the like you should be sent. You draw the Episcopal Family Relief Society. The Relief Society clears your name through the central agency to see that you are not receiving help elsewhere and sends around within the next few days to visit your family, prepare a budget, detail a nurse (if there is one), and eventually to allot you $2 to $8 a week, depending on the locality and the funds available. If its funds are exhausted it asks you to wait. Meanwhile you register for work. You wait anyway.

New York, of course, presented the biggest problem. On the other hand, it was the best equipped of the great cities to handle unemployment relief: it had many established welfare agencies run by competent social workers; it was highly organized in ethnic, religious, and economic groupings; many of its leading citizens and newspapers were conscious of a responsibility to the community; and its financial resources were unmatched. New York's prime weakness was its city government, headed by the Tammany dandy, Jimmy Walker. But Walker's peccadilloes were soon to be his undoing and there was as an outside resort a more competent and responsible administration in Albany.

In the first year of the depression the load fell almost entirely upon the established private agencies. The religious charities, especially the Catholic and Jewish agencies, sought to care for their own. The main program, however, was run by the Association for Improving the Condition of the Poor under William H. Matthews, a tireless and cheerful friend of the needy. AICP had pioneered with work relief during the depressions of 1914-15 and 1921-22 and so instituted a similar program in 1929-30. After arrangements with the city, AICP hired unemployed workers to make improvements in the public parks under the supervision of the regular staff. As of the year ending September 30, 1930, $200,000 had been spent in wages to employ 1564 men for varying periods. This outlay barely scratched the surface of the relief problem, and the AICP was without further resources.

Mounting unemployment and the anticipation of winter made a bigger program imperative. In August 1930, therefore, the Charity Organization Society drew up an emergency plan for work relief. The city estimated the number of men it could use on municipal projects, and nonprofit organizations—churches, settlements, educational institutions—indicated their work opportunities. The assumption was that the emergency would last six months. The program would be administered jointly by the AICP and COS though an Emergency Work Bureau headed by Matthews.

The central problem was money. In September, Seward Prosser of the Bankers Trust Company agreed to head an Emergency Employment Committee of financiers and industrialists to raise funds. When the Prosser Committee launched its drive on October 15, the announced goal was about $4 million—$150,000 a week to provide jobs for 10,000 men at the rate of $3 a day for a five-day week. It became clear almost at once that the sights were too low. On November 5, Prosser raised them to $6 million—$200,000 a week to provide 13,500 jobs for thirty weeks. New York, he declared, was experiencing "a community disaster" with some 300,000 jobless. Matthew Woll of the AFL protested the $3 wage rate. Early in December it was raised to $5 a day for a three-day week. By this time it was obvious that the funds would be insufficient. On December 4, for example, 158 men were in line at five o'clock in the morning at the Work Bureau and when the doors opened at eight the queue extended for two blocks. The Prosser Committee therefore lifted its goal once again, to $8 million. The campaign was a success: the Committee raised $8,520,000, mainly in large gifts. The Rockefellers contributed $1 million, Edward S. Harkness $500,000, and the Milbank Memorial Fund $250,000 from its capital resources.

The Emergency Work Bureau program was efficiently conducted. Each case was carefully screened to establish need and to avoid duplication. The program provided a substantial volume of employment for five months, from December 1930 to April 1931. In all, 37,531 persons received work relief, with a peak of 26,039 in January. Slightly over half were assigned to governmental projects—constructing roads, surfacing playgrounds, building fences and water fountains, clearing vacant lots, renovating hospitals, and so on. The remainder were employed in nonprofit institutions, chiefly in renovation and repair. A relatively small number of women who were family breadwinners were engaged, mainly in sewing rooms to produce garments for the needy. The administrative and operating expenses came to only $382,000, of which 56 per cent went in wages to people otherwise unemployed.

This program, however, gave relief to only a small fraction of the city's jobless. In the winter of 1930-31 it was necessary to improvise emergency feeding for thousands of New Yorkers who might otherwise have starved. The bread line, that most degrading and offensive form of relief, burgeoned all over the city. In January 1931 there were eighty-two lines serving 85,-ooo meals a day. Many—notably those run by the Salvation Army, the churches, and the missions—were designed to help the needy. Some, however, were set up by publicity seekers. Racketeers moved in on the philanthropic rich, setting up soup kitchens in swanky neighborhoods and pocketing a large part of the funds. Bowery bums never had it so good; they toured the bread lines, putting away ten or twelve meals a day. The respectably unemployed were either reluctant or refused to ask for food on the streets.

In the winter of 1930-31, the streets of Manhattan became a battleground in the struggle for survival. Beggars appeared in large numbers, asking, "Brother, can you spare a dime?" That absurd symbol of the depression, the apple, made its entrance. Threadbare jobless men stood on street corners peddling the fruit in frigid weather as the offices emptied. The apple became a minor issue of public policy. When the Bureau of the Census classified apple sellers as employed (with some reason), the enemies of the Hoover Administration joyfully trotted out their big guns. The President himself stubbornly argued that the peddlers demonstrated sound American enterprise in launching these ventures. Oregon and Washington growers had shrewdly devised a method of unloading their crop at high prices. "Many persons," Hoover later wrote, "left their jobs for the more profitable one of selling apples." The hit song of a 1931 Broadway musical, entitled "When Yuba Plays the Tuba Down in Cuba," developed this theme:

> *Any sap can sell an apple*
> *But this chap would rather grapple*
> *With his oompa, oompa, oompa.*
> *He prefers it to a boopa, doopa, doopa.*

The bread lines, the soup kitchens, the street beggars, and the apple sellers gave the City of New York a black eye. The world's richest city was losing its reputation—and not just in

America. In the spring of 1931, the natives of the Cameroons in West Africa sent over $3.77 for the relief of "the starving."

The inadequacies of the Prosser program, both as to size and duration, and public revulsion against the scenes on the streets made the city's intervention imperative. It began in a characteristically haphazard way. The police in the fall of 1930 made a count of the families in need. The city then "suggested" to its 125,000 employees that they donate 1 per cent of their earnings to a relief fund. The money was used by the police to purchase huge quantities of food which were doled out in the precincts especially at Thanksgiving and Christmas. More important was the emergency lunch program for school children established by the Board of Education and financed by teachers and school employees. Thousands of children were fed each day in the schools with hot balanced meals, cooked and served by women on relief. "Depression's children . . . are learning to look to the public-school system," Frances Warfield wrote, "not only for the three 'R's but for food, medical attention, and, if necessary, three 'C's: clothing, coal, and cash—just a little cash; enough, say, to fend off the landlord a while."

The big question was what would happen when the Prosser funds ran out in the spring of 1931. In the preceding November the Welfare Council created a coordinating committee of prominent citizens headed by Al Smith to plan a program. One of its first acts was to denounce the proliferation of bread lines and street begging. On January 6, 1931, Prosser warned the mayor that his committee was incapable of meeting the need and asked the city to appropriate $10 million for relief. Walker was noncommittal. At the end of the month Smith announced "a crisis" in relief. The mayor still did nothing. On February 27, a mass meeting staged by social workers at Town Hall demanded an appropriation of at least $10 million to be spent on work relief at the rate of $2 million a month. The city's Corporation Counsel, Arthur Hilly, responded that the charter forbade such an expenditure. By this time, the Prosser fund was virtually exhausted; there could be no further delay. On March 31, the state legislature passed an enabling act to allow the city to borrow for relief, and Governor Roosevelt promptly signed it. On April 10, a first installment of $2 million became available. The City of New York was now, willy-nilly, in the business of unemployment relief.

The program was administered by existing municipal departments, and the unemployed were registered in public buildings. To qualify, a needy person must have been a legal resident and voter for at least two years. No effort was made to avoid duplication. Men given work were considered city employees on part time and received the standard rate for common labor, $5.50 a day. At first they got three days a week (earnings of $71.50 a month), but it was soon cut to two ($44 a month). In the spring and summer of 1931, the program provided work relief for approximately 15,500 people at a cost of $1,250,000 per month. The program was riddled with inefficiency and political favoritism. Much of the work done was of no value. Some of the participants received help from other sources. The Seabury investigation revealed serious irregularities: employed persons accepting relief (one family had a weekly income of $115), the ignoring of the residence requirement, and preference for enrolled Democrats.

New York's relief programs provided a certain amount of wry humor. There was, for example, the story of the woman fired because of slack business whose final paycheck was short $1.52—"deducted for the unemployed." And there was the society matron with a big place in Westchester who let fourteen of her twenty-two servants go so that she could contribute their wages to the relief fund. Finally, there was the volunteer lady who feared that the amount given in relief by her agency was insufficient to support a family. "It's all right, my dear," she was told, "statistics prove that three people can live quite satisfactorily on fifteen dollars a week—without food, of course."

These jokes were not really very funny because it was not possible to laugh long at misery. The prospect of another winter of depression, as 1931 drew to its close, left New Yorkers grim. The number of jobless grew larger and hope dimmed for an early improvement. Private charity, even with the emergency help of leading financiers, was inadequate and exhausted. The city, reluctantly driven to action, had proved itself inept and corrupt.

But the New York relief program was masterfully organized in contrast with the chaos that ruled Chicago. That city entered the depression bankrupt—financially and morally. Its archaic tax structure had collapsed in the twenties. In order to meet day-to-day expenses, administrative units had been compelled to issue tax anticipation warrants that the banks accepted; by the time of the crash the combined obligations exceeded $125 million. Reassessment, undertaken in 1927, had not been completed by 1930. As a result, many property owners had not paid taxes for three years. In late 1929, the banks announced that they would accept no more warrants. Chicago was flat broke, heavily in debt and without credit. Policemen and firemen were discharged; schoolteachers received no salaries; the County Hospital and the public welfare stations had not paid their 1929 bills; mothers' pension checks were not sent out. The mayor, Big Bill Thompson, was incompetent and corrupt. His chief claim to fame was the political threat to punch King George V in the snoot. Organized crime, operating with the connivance of the Thompson regime, ruled Cook County as no American metropolis has been controlled before or since. The boss of Chicago was not the mayor but Al Capone. The city's leading citizens and newspapers were mainly without a sense of social responsibility.

Into this unsavory gumbo was poured the misery of mass unemployment. Joblessness was serious even before the crash and became acute thereafter. In the first year of the depression private charities on insignificant budgets struggled helplessly with the immense relief load. The schoolteachers, despite the fact that they were seldom paid, financed an emergency lunch program. As the winter of 1930-31 approached, outside help became indispensable. The city, obviously, was without resources. Hence in October 1930 Governor Louis L. Emmerson of Illinois established a Commission on Unemployment and Relief. "We are afraid, confidentially," he informed a top official of the Hoover Administration, "that the situation will be greater than we can cope with. . . ." The main function of his commission was to raise $5 million from private sources for relief in Chicago. The drive was barely successful. Direct relief absorbed $4 million. The remainder was set aside to expand a work-relief program that the United Charities had launched in the summer of 1930 on a $60,000 donation by an individual. About 8000 persons found employment in governmental and nonprofit agencies, none earning more than $50 a month.

Chicago, as the nation's transportation hub, had a severe transiency problem. Throngs of homeless men, joined by boys and women as the depression wore on, descended upon the city. In the fall of 1930, a shanty town appeared at the foot of Randolph Street. Its citizens called it Hooverville and its thoroughfares

Prosperity Road, Hard Times Avenue, and Easy Street. When food ran low, "Mayor" Donovan appointed a committee to visit the hotels for leavings. "There is not a garbage-dump in Chicago," Edmund Wilson observed, "which is not diligently haunted by the hungry." The relief agencies improvised means to deal with the flood of transients, putting them up in asylums, poorhouses, and veterans' homes, or, best of all, getting them out of town. The Oak Forest poorhouse in 1931 lodged them in the corridors and was compelled to turn away 19,000.

By the fall of 1931, Chicago was desperate. On October 15, according to the Illinois Department of Labor, 624,000 persons were out of work in the city. The private charities were incapable of handling the load and the municipality was incompetent to do anything. The only hope was outside aid—from the state or the federal government.

Philadelphia provided the most imaginative and effective of the municipal relief programs in the early years of the depression. The city had not spent public funds on relief since 1879, thereby making the burden of the private agencies notably heavy. Perhaps as a consequence community responsibility was highly developed. Both the University of Pennsylvania and Swarthmore College sponsored research programs on unemployment, and the entire press, and especially J. David Stern's *Record*, vigorously supported unemployment relief. Perhaps most important was the quality of leadership: two distinguished social workers, Jacob Billikopf, executive director of the Federation of Jewish Charities as well as impartial chairman in the New York men's clothing industry, and Karl de Schweinitz, secretary of the Community Council; a remarkable banker, Horatio Gates Lloyd, partner in Drexel & Company, the local branch of the House of Morgan; and to a lesser extent the Republican mayor, Harry A. Mackey.

Philadelphia's unemployment problem was unusually severe, the rate exceeding that in all major cities except Detroit and Cleveland. This was because several of its industries, especially in the textile trades, suffered sharp declines before the crash. By the fall of 1930, therefore, the need was acute. Billikopf and de Schweinitz sparked a mass meeting of leading citizens at the Bellevue-Stratford Hotel on November 7, 1930, which resulted in the creation of the Committee for Unemployment Relief. The social workers persuaded Lloyd to accept the chairmanship, a job to which he was to devote his full time at a salary of a dollar a year. De Schweinitz became the secretary. Drexel & Company made a whole floor of its building available as office space (the irony of relief for the jobless emanating from the nation's leading banking house aroused no comment). The Lloyd Committee raised almost $4 million at once in private donations and was responsible for the disbursement of over $14 million by the time of its demise in the summer of 1932.

The program was highly diversified. Between November 14, 1930, and July 15, 1931, direct relief was granted to 33,000 families through the facilities of nine established agencies. In early 1931, the Committee helped disburse, in addition to its own funds, $400,000 of city money for family relief. A large work-relief program was created in public and nonprofit agencies. A total of 15,515 heads of families found jobs on these projects, most of them at the rate of $4 a day. The Committee directed special attention to projects employing white-collar people: a study of the city's traffic problem by 650 unemployed men of various skills, a survey of colonial landmarks by jobless architects and draftsmen, Braille typesetting by unemployed typographers, concerts given by out-of-work musicians, and so on. The Baldwin Locomotive Works donated a building that was converted into a shelter for homeless men where 11,993 persons received lodging, supper, and breakfast between November 1930 and June 30, 1931. Mayor Mackey, disguised as a hobo, periodically visited the shelter to inspect its facilities. The Philadelphia Loan Fund was set up to aid families in straitened but not desperate circumstances. By May 1931 the Fund had issued loans either without interest or at very low rates to 563 families, ranging in amount from $18 to $175. Emergency school breakfasts, prepared and served by women on work relief, were given 10,000 children in private and parochial schools. A committee collected discarded clothing and arranged for its repair and distribution to the needy.

Despite its drive and ingenuity, the Lloyd Committee fought a losing battle. The number of jobless continuously outgrew its resources. Hence Billikopf, de Schweinitz, and even Lloyd became insistent champions of public relief. In late 1931, Philadelphia had 250,000 out of work. "We have unemployment in every third house," J. Prentice Murphy, executive director of the Philadelphia Children's Bureau, told the Senate Subcommittee on Manufactures. "It is almost like the visitation of death to the households of the Egyptians at the time of the escape of the Jews from Egypt."

Detroit suffered the most acute relief crisis of any major American city. Severe unemployment in the auto industry antedated the crash and mounted sharply afterward, giving the motor city the doubtful distinction of possessing the highest jobless rate in the nation. The Ford payroll slumped from 128,000 in March 1929 to 37,000 in August 1931. In contrast with a "normal" relief registration of 17,000, the city had 211,000 applications on hand in February 1931. By spring, they were coming in at the rate of 600 a day. On the basis of reduced demand for their services, the utilities estimated that 150,000 people moved out of Detroit in 1931. Civic responsibility was virtually nonexistent. Henry Ford's views on relief received wide publicity and set the tone. Senator Couzens' offer in late 1929 to donate $1 million for relief if other citizens would raise $9 million went begging. As late as January 1932, private groups had raised a mere $700,000, including $200,000 from Couzens. The press, excepting the Hearst paper, had little sympathy for the jobless. The bankers insisted upon a lowering of the relief standard to bare survival as a condition for loans to the city. The Department of Public Welfare at the outset of the depression was both inefficient and corrupt.

Detroit, as a consequence of these conditions, could do little more than mass-disaster relief. There was no time to distinguish the differential needs of families and no money for relatively costly work relief. In the municipal campaign of 1930, Frank Murphy won election as mayor on a platform of aid to the unemployed. A liberal Democrat, a devout Catholic, and a warm and sympathetic human being, Murphy's main preoccupation as mayor was the fulfillment of this pledge.

With a virtual absence of private resources, the city had no alternative but the assumption of public responsibility for relief. Murphy at once set about the reorganization of the Department of Public Welfare. He established the Mayor's Emergency Committee under the chairmanship of G. Hall Roosevelt to register the unemployed, help them find what little work was available, and screen out those in greatest need. He created a Homeless Men's Bureau, which by April 1931 was providing lodging or meals to over 10,000 persons. The load of the Department of Public Welfare mounted steadily from monthly expenditures of $116,000 in February 1929 to $1,582,000 in the same month of 1931. By April 1931 the Department was supporting 45,464 families. The standards, under banker pressure, were terribly low. In late 1931, Public Welfare gave two adults $3.60 a week for food with an added allowance for each child. The city was seldom able to provide for all of the needy. A study of 900 families dropped from the rolls in 1931 revealed that their average income per person from all sources was $1.56 a week.

When Mayor Murphy appeared before the Senate Manufactures Subcommittee on January 7, 1932, he admitted that Detroit was staggering under its relief burden. Tax income was declining and the city's capacity to borrow was narrowing. Though he was a strong advocate of local responsibility, Murphy reluctantly declared "that there ought to be Federal help, as at present the assistance we are able to render is inadequate. . . ."

New York, Chicago, Philadelphia, and Detroit attacked their relief problems in the early years of the depression with varying methods and uneven achievements. The thread that ran through all four experiences was the breakdown of private and municipal resources in face of the magnitude of the crisis. In this they were typical of all American cities. Many communities, particularly the smaller ones, did nothing at all. A survey of fifty-nine cities in New York State in the winter of 1930-31, for example, revealed that most were without definite programs, that few of their welfare commissioners felt competent to deal with the task, and that only a handful based relief upon actual need. Some towns substituted hokum for action. The "Grand Rapids Plan," put over by an advertising man, utilized the press and radio to sell "the basic soundness and greatness of the United States." Folks would not "think straight" until "panic" was removed from their minds. "A relaxed and determined mind is necessary to constructive thought." A full stomach, apparently, had no relationship to a happy mental state.

By the fall of 1931, municipal relief—private and public—was bankrupt in virtually every city of the United States. *Fortune* generalized the crisis in this fashion:

The theory was that private charitable organizations and semi-public welfare groups, established to care for the old and the sick and the indigent, were capable of caring for the casuals of a world-wide economic disaster. And the theory in application meant that social agencies manned for the service of a few hundred families, and city shelters set up to house and feed a handful of homeless men, were compelled by the brutal necessities of hunger to care for hundreds of thousands of families and whole armies of the displaced and the jobless. And to depend for their resources upon the contributions of communities no longer able to contribute, and upon the irresolution and vacillation of state Legislatures and municipal assemblies long since in the red on their annual budgets. The result was the picture now presented in city after city . . . heterogeneous groups of official and unofficial relief agencies struggling under the earnest and untrained leadership of the local men of affairs against an inertia of misery and suffering and want they are powerless to overcome.

THE URBANIZATION OF
NEGROES IN
THE UNITED STATES

REYNOLDS FARLEY

Reynolds Farley, of the Sociology Department at the University of Michigan, traces black migration to the city from the end of the Civil War to the 1960's.

The distribution of the Negro population with regard to urban or rural residence has followed a curious pattern in the United States. Negroes originally were brought to America in the seventeenth century to work in cities as laborers or house servants. During the latter part of that century and the next, the number of Negroes in the emerging cities grew as more workers were needed and European immigrants became difficult to obtain.

Agricultural prosperity during the eighteenth century opened a new economic niche for Negroes and many slaves entered the Southern colonies. After the Revolution, the invention of the cotton gin and the settling of the Gulf Coast states increased the need for slaves. In Northern cities the Negro population grew slowly, if at all, as European immigrants filled the need for unskilled labor. Southern cities contained some slaves and free Negroes, but by the time of the Civil War the Negro population was concentrated in rural southern areas. . . .

From Reynolds Farley, "The Urbanization of Negroes in the United States," *Journal of Social History*, I (Spring 1968), 241, 245, 247, 248–258. Copyright 1968 by the Regents of the University of California. Reprinted by permission of the editor of the *Journal of Social History*.

Urbanization of Negroes in the
Post-Civil War Period

For a long period subsequent to the Civil War, most Negroes remained in the South. During this period, the South failed to industrialize as rapidly as the North and the typical industry of Southerners—both Negro and white—was that of agriculture. From 1860 to 1900, the percentage of the nation's population in the South held steady at one-third, but the South's share of manufacturing output was not proportional. In 1860, 11 percent of the total value of products originated with southern manufactures. In 1870, this fell to 7 percent; in 1880, 7 percent; in 1890, 9 percent and in 1900, 11 percent. As a consequence, the South did not urbanize as rapidly in the later nineteenth century as did the other regions of the country. As recently as 1950, the majority of Southerners lived in rural areas; the Northeast became predominantly urban in the 1870's, and the North Central and Western regions during World War I. This slow growth of urban centers in the South meant that most Negroes lived in rural areas. The Census of 1890, the first to give a rural-urban breakdown of the Negro population, found 80 percent of all Negroes and 85 percent of the southern Negroes in rural areas (See Table IV).

In spite of the concentration of Negroes in rural areas for a lengthy span after the Civil War, there was a substantial movement of Negroes to cities immediately following the war. After emancipation, many Negroes left their farms of residence and flocked to cities, particularly those containing Union Army camps. For some, this freedom of movement was a certification of emancipation; others expected the Federal government to support them, on the assumption that the end of slavery meant they no longer would have to struggle for a living. Most southern towns, however, were severely devastated by the Civil War. Rail lines were destroyed and many of the factories found in southern cities were either wrecked or dependent upon the highly disrupted agricultural sector. The presence of unskilled and destitute Negroes in cities complicated attempts at reconstruction. The Freedman's Bureau tried to resettle Negoes in rural areas. Certain federally held lands in the South were turned over to the Bureau to be distributed to Negroes, but these tended to be marginal lands and apparently few Negroes benefited. In another effort to encourage Negroes to leave cities, the Freedman's Bureau arranged and acted as overseer in a contract labor system and paid transportation costs as well.

The efforts of the Freedman's Bureau may have been partly successful in resettling Negroes, but the Negro population of most southern cities jumped sharply following the Civil War. Such an increase was unprecedented and never duplicated. As noted in the previous section (see Table II), the proportion of Negroes fell until 1860. In contrast, the Civil War decade witnessed a very sizable increase in the proportion of Negroes in each of these cities.

Little change in the proportion of Negroes occurred in latter decades of the nineteenth century, which suggests that the urban Negro population grew about as rapidly as the urban white population. In most cities, Negroes filled the need for unskilled or semi-skilled labor and for house servants. In Memphis, many worked as stevedores; Negroes were employed in construction work in other cities. After Richmond industries resumed production, Negroes were employed at many jobs held by slaves prior to the war. In North Carolina cities many Negroes labored in tobacco factories. By 1890, there developed in many southern towns a small middle class Negro population. A few Negro doctors and lawyers and a large number of teachers were to be found in the larger cities. In some places, Negro banks and newspapers operated. And yet the Census of 1890 shows that practically all Negroes who held nonagricultural jobs worked as laborers, porters, or house servants. Contemporary descriptions of the Negro areas of southern cities indicate most Negroes lived at near-subsistence levels, often in dilapidated, unsanitary houses.

Outmigration of Negroes from the South

Although most Negroes remained in the South following the Civil War, outmigration trends did develop, which became more obvious and involved significant proportions of the Negro population in this century. Since 1850, the Census has included a question asking the respondent's state or country of birth. By comparing state of birth information and making appropriate allowances for mortality, it is possible to estimate the volume of outmigration from or inmigration to a region for decennial periods. Such estimates of net migration of Negroes are shown in Table III.

In the last ninety years, there has been a continual and generally increasing outflow of Negroes from the South and corresponding gains in the Negro population in other areas.

Immediately following the Civil War, outmigrants from the South were few in number. Some did move to the plains states, particularly Kansas, in the expectation of receiving free land. Beginning in the late 1880's a shift in the direction and an increase in the volume of Negro migration occurred—the movement was from the South to Northern cities. In fact, Negroes leaving the South since 1880 have consistently migrated to cities. In 1890, the first date for which the requisite data are available, three-fifths of all non-southern Negroes lived in towns and by 1910 this figure approached four-fifths.

Many reasons can be given for the outmigration of so many Negroes, reasons demographers typically categorize as push factors and pull factors. Among the most important push factors were the limited economic opportunities for Negroes in the South. Apparently the employment of Negroes in agriculture in either a wage, share crop, or tenancy basis was not satisfactory to either Negroes or white landowners. The depression of the 1890's and the gradual spread of the boll weevil from the Southwest across the cotton lands to the Southeast further exacerbated the economic status of Negroes and encouraged many to leave. The amount of land farmed by Negroes in the South apparently reached a peak in 1910 and has consistently declined since that date. Despite growth of the Negro population in the South, the number of Negro farmers has declined since 1920. As mechanization and modernization of agriculture occurred, the Negro farm population has continued to drop. From 1960 to 1965, the Negro farm population declined 41 percent while the white farm population fell 17 percent.

Another push factor was the abuse of Negroes in the South. Vann Woodward argues that southern states typically instituted or reinstated Jim Crow practices and laws toward the end of the nineteenth century. For some period during Reconstruction, Negroes participated in politics, utilized their civil rights, and assisted in the expansion of educational opportunities. Beginning with Mississippi in about 1875 and concluding with North Carolina in 1900 and Virginia in 1902, one state after another discovered some subterfuge to exclude Negroes from voting or political activities, to limit their civil rights and restrict their opportunities. As a consequence many Negroes left the South. Shortly after the turn of this century, New York, Philadelphia, and other northern cities apparently contained more than a few trained Negroes who had attempted to build careers in the South but found themselves limited by new Jim Crow laws. Some studies have claimed that rural areas in which attacks on Negroes, such as lynchings, were commonplace lost Negro population most rapidly.

The major pull factor responsible for migration was the promise of economic prosperity in the North. And yet this pull factor probably did not operate until the time of World War I. To be sure, Negroes had been used as strikebreakers by certain northern industries for a long period of time. Yet descriptions of Negro workers in the era before 1917 suggest there was little competition between white and Negro workers. Certain occupational niches, such as domestic service, pullman car porters, and some construction and slaughterhouse jobs provided employment for almost all Negroes; other jobs were typically closed to Negroes.

During the years from 1910 to 1914, an average of over 900,000 Europeans migrated to this country each year. In the following five years, the average fell to about 100,000 per year, due to World War I. In spite of this drop in immigration, the number of workers in manufacturing rose, as did the output of the manufacturing sector. One of the main sources of additional workers for northern industries was southern Negroes. Many firms sent labor recruiters to southern areas and paid the transportation costs of Negroes who would move to such cities as New York, Philadelphia, or Chicago. Thus from 1910 to 1920 over half a million Negroes left the South for northern cities.

The Immigration Laws of 1921 and 1924 effectively limited immigration from abroad and during the twenties the outmigration of Negroes from the South increased. The depression years dampened the outmigration streams, but World War II and the post-war prosperity witnessed a resumption of the movement of Negroes away from the South. During the forties Negro migrants to the West became numerous, apparently a response to military and industrial growth along the western seaboard.

One additional pull factor should be noted: At various times northern Negro newspapers undertook campaigns to encourage Negroes to migrate North. Perhaps the most outspoken of these campaigns was carried out by the *Chicago Defender*, a paper with a wide circulation in the South. The South was pictured as a land of oppression where the Negro had no access to jobs or schools and where he might be lynched without provocation. The North, on the other hand, was seen as a land of opportunity where jobs were available, schools open, and civil rights respected.

For more than sixty years, these push and pull factors have affected the distribution of the Negro population. Three major consequences may be noted.

First, the Negro population is now less concentrated in the South and more evenly distributed nationally. For the first 120 years of this nation's history, nine-tenths of all Negroes resided in the South. In the next fifty-year span the proportion in the South fell to slightly over one-half. The appropriate figures indicating these changes are shown in Table I.

Second, the Negro population has become a primarily urban population both within and outside the South. Table IV presents the percentages of the Negro population that were urban from 1890 to 1960, the only dates for which this information is available. From an early date Negroes in the North and West lived in cities. Urbanization of Negroes occurred more recently in the South, but there is no doubt that southern Negroes are becoming increasingly concentrated in cities.

Third, the racial composition of the large northern cities first, and later the large western cities, changed due to the immigration of Negroes. The proportion of Negroes in these cities climbed in the past and will continue to do so in the foreseeable future. Within southern cities there has been much less change in racial composition.

Figure I illustrates these changes. This figure refers to those urban places designed as central cities—non-suburban cities of 50,000 or more—in 1960. For cities in each region the proportion of Negroes is shown for each census date since 1900.

In recent years, many northern cities have lost large numbers of whites, but gained many Negroes as a consequence of both inmigration and high rates of natural increase. Because of these changes in such northern cities as Cleveland, Newark, and Gary, more than one-third of the population is nonwhite. In other cities, such as Philadelphia, St. Louis, and Detroit, more than one-fourth of the residents are nonwhite.

This pattern of loss of white population and gain in Negro population can readily be seen if figures showing net change in population by race for the period 1950 to 1960 are examined. Such figures are shown in Table V for the ten largest northern cities.

Prospects for the Future

The southern Negro population is still a large and growing population. Despite sixty years of outmigration the number of Negroes in the South has grown from about eight million at the turn of the century to eleven and one-quarter million in 1960. The loss through migration has failed to equal the gains due to natural increase and the fertility of southern Negro women seems to insure rapid future growth. In Table VI are shown rates of children ever born per 1,000 ever married women, indicating the high fertility of Negroes in general and southern Negroes in particular.

Within the South the rural Negro population will continue to decline. The rural farm population is sure to drop as aggregation occurs in agriculture.

The rural nonfarm Negro population may increase as it did from 1950 to 1960. As larger southern cities expand and smaller cities obtain industrial plants many Negroes can begin to work at nonfarm jobs while living in rural areas or small hamlets. As the cities of the South grow, the Negro urban population in this region will also increase as it has in the past.

Though there has been a long history of Negroes leaving the South, it is extremely difficult to predict the volume or direction of such migration in the future. If the outmigration rates of the 1950's persist into the 1960's, the number of outmigrants will be larger. One might argue that there are persistent social and economic systems which facilitate the migration of many Negroes away from the South to the cities of the North and West. However, increased economic opportunities in some regions of the South, such as Florida and Texas, may combine with decreasing economic opportunities in northern cities to diminish the outmigration of Negroes from the South.

TABLE I

NEGRO POPULATION, DISTRIBUTION BY REGION
1790–1964

	SOUTH	NORTHEAST	NORTHCENTRAL	WEST
1790	91.1%	8.9%		
1800	91.6	8.3	0.1	
1810	92.1	7.4	0.5	
1820	92.7	6.2	1.1	
1830	92.8	5.4	1.8	
1840	91.9	5.0	3.1	
1850	92.1	4.1	3.8	
1860	92.2	3.5	4.2	0.1
1870	90.6	3.7	5.6	0.1
1880	90.5	3.5	5.8	0.2
1890	90.3	3.6	5.7	0.4
1900	89.7	4.3	5.7	0.3
1910	89.0	4.9	5.6	0.5
1920	85.1	6.5	7.6	0.8
1930	78.8	9.6	10.6	1.0
1940	77.1	10.6	11.0	1.3
1950	68.0	13.4	14.8	3.8
1960	60.0	16.0	18.3	5.7
1964	54.4	18.1	19.4	8.1

TABLE II

PERCENTAGE OF POPULATION NEGRO, SELECTED SOUTHERN CITIES, 1840–1900

	ATLANTA	AUGUSTA	CHARLESTON	MEMPHIS	MOBILE
1840		46	55		35
1850	20	42	53	28	37
1860	20	32	42	17	29
1870	46	42	53	38	43
1880	44	46	55	44	42
1890	43	48	56	45	44
1900	40	47	57	49	44

	NASHVILLE	NEW ORLEANS	NORFOLK	RICHMOND	SAVAN-NAH
1840	36	42	43	47	47
1850	25	23	37	45	45
1860	23	14	30	38	38
1870	38	26	46	45	46
1880	38	27	46	44	51
1890	39	27	47	40	53
1900	37	27	43	38	52

TABLE III

NET MIGRATION OF NEGROES BY REGION, 1870–1960
(IN THOUSANDS)

	NORTHEAST	SOUTH	NORTHCENTRAL	WEST
1870–1880	26	− 68	42	
1880–1890	61	− 88	28	
1890–1900	136	− 185	49	
1900–1910	109	− 194	63	22
1910–1920	242	− 555	281	32
1920–1930	435	− 903	426	42
1930–1940	273	− 480	152	55
1940–1950	599	−1581	626	356
1950–1960*	541	−1458	560	347

* Figures for 1950–1960 were obtained from different source than those for earlier decades. The figures for the earlier decades refer to Negro population while those for 1950–1960 refer to nonwhite population.

TABLE IV

PERCENTAGE OF NEGRO POPULATION URBAN
1890–1960

	TOTAL USA	SOUTH	NORTH AND WEST
1890	19.8	15.3	61.5
1900	22.7	17.2	70.4
1910	27.4	21.2	77.5
1920	34.0	25.3	84.5
1930	43.7	31.7	88.1
1940	48.6	36.5	89.1
1950*	62.4	47.6	95.2
1960	73.2	58.4	95.2

* Beginning in 1950, a new definition for urban was used which included places of less than 2,500 if located in urban territory.

TABLE V

NET CHANGE IN POPULATION, 1950–1960
(IN THOUSANDS)

	WHITE	NONWHITE
New York	−1251	+366
Chicago	− 399	+328
Philadelphia	− 225	+156
Detroit	− 363	+183
Cleveland	− 142	+104
St. Louis	− 168	+ 62
Milwaukee	+ 61	+ 43
Boston	− 130	+ 26
Pittsburgh	− 91	+ 19
Buffalo	− 83	+ 36

TABLE VI

CHILDREN EVER BORN PER 1,000
EVER MARRIED WOMEN, 1960

	NEGROES IN SOUTH	NEGROES IN NORTH AND WEST	WHITES
Age			
20–24	2172	1840	1370
25–29	3082	2551	2171
30–34	3604	2715	2564
35–39	3639	2571	2625

FIGURE I

PERCENT OF CENTRAL CITIES' POPULATION NEGRO,
BY REGION, 1900–1960

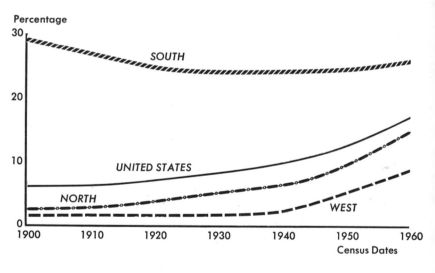

BLACK CHICAGO:
THE MAKING OF A
NEGRO GHETTO

ALLAN H. SPEAR

Allan H. Spear, Associate Professor of History at the University of Minnesota, analyzes the formation of a black ghetto as mainly the product of white racism.

Between 1890 and 1915, the Negro population of Chicago grew from less than fifteen thousand to over fifty thousand. Although this growth was overshadowed by the massive influx of Negroes during and after World War I, this was nevertheless a significant increase. By the eve of World War I, although Negroes were still a minor element in the city's population, they were far more conspicuous than they had been a generation earlier. The population increase was accompanied by the concentration of Negroes into ever more constricted sections of the city. In the late nineteenth century, while most Negroes lived in certain sections of the South Side, they lived interspersed among whites; there were few all-Negro blocks. By 1915, on the other hand, the physical ghetto had taken shape; a large, almost all-Negro enclave on the South Side, with a similar offshoot on the West Side, housed most of Chicago's Negroes.

Migration was the major factor in the growth of the Negro community, and most migrants were coming from outside of the state. Over 80 per cent of Chicago's Negro population in 1900 was born in states other than Illinois. The largest portion of these migrants originated in the border states and in the Upper South: Kentucky, and Missouri, in particular, had sent large groups of Negroes to Chicago. The states of the Deep South were, as yet, a secondary source of Chicago's Negro population; only 17 per cent had come from these states as opposed to 43 per cent from the Upper South. The states located directly south of Chicago supplied a larger segment of the population than the southeastern states, but there were sizable groups born in Virginia and Georgia.

From the beginning of Chicago's history, most Negroes had lived on the South Side. As early as 1850, 82 per cent of the Negro population lived in an area bounded by the Chicago River on the north, Sixteenth Street on the south, the South Branch of the river on the west, and Lake Michigan on the east. The famous South Side black belt was emerging—a narrow finger of land, wedged between the railroad yards and industrial plants just west of Wentworth Avenue and the fashionable homes east of Wabash Avenue. By 1900, the black belt stretched from the downtown business district as far south as Thirty-ninth Street. But there were also sizable Negro enclaves, usually of a few square blocks each, in several other sections of the city. The Thirteenth Ward Negro community stretched along West Lake Street from Ashland to Western. The Eighteenth Ward Negroes lived in the old immigrant neighborhood on the Near West Side near Hull House. On the Near North Side, Negroes had begun to settle in the Italian Seventeenth Ward. And on the South Side, beyond the black belt, communities of upper- and middle-class Negroes had emerged in Hyde Park, Wood- lawn, Englewood, and Morgan Park.

Despite this concentration of Negroes in enclaves, the Negro population of the city was still relatively well distributed in 1900. Nineteen of the city's thirty-five wards had a Negro population of at least .5 per cent of the total population of the ward and fourteen wards were at least 1 per cent Negro. Only two wards had a Negro population of more than 10 per cent. In 1898, just over a quarter of Chicago's Negroes lived in pre- cincts that were more than 50 per cent Negro, and over 30 per cent lived in precincts that were at least 95 per cent white. As late as 1910, Negroes were less highly segregated from native whites than were Italian immigrants.

The decade 1900 to 1910 saw several significant changes in the population pattern of Negroes in Chicago. The growth rate, which had far outpaced the white growth rate in the 1890's, declined from 111 per cent to 46 per cent, and the proportion of Negroes in the population increased from 1.9 per cent to only 2 per cent. Yet despite this stabilization, the Negro population was still composed largely of migrants. Over 77 per cent of Chicago's Negroes were born outside of Illinois. This represents only a slight drop from 1900 and was almost five times as great as the corresponding figure for white Chicagoans. Only three major Negro communities in the country—Los Angeles, Denver, and Oklahoma City, all young Western cities with highly mobile populations—had higher proportions of out-of-state migrants than Chicago. Even such burgeoning industrial centers as Detroit, Pittsburgh, and Cleveland had a lower percentage of Negroes born in other states.

The concentration of Negroes in enclaves was clearly increasing throughout this period. By 1910, over 30 per cent lived in predominantly Negro sections of the city and over 60 per cent in areas that were more than 20 per cent Negro. Whereas in 1900 nineteen of thirty-five wards had been over .5 per cent Negro, this figure was reduced to thirteen in 1910. Furthermore, the second and third wards, which included the heart of the black belt, were now 25 per cent Negro, while in 1900 only one ward had even approached that figure.

Negro residential patterns for 1910 can be seen most clearly through the use of census tract data. Of 431 census tracts in the city, Negroes could be found in all but ninety-four; eighty-eight were at least 1 per cent Negro. Four tracts were over 50 per cent Negro, but no tract was more than 61 per cent Negro. Despite greater concentration, therefore, there were still few all-Negro neighborhoods in Chicago.

The eight or nine neighborhoods that had been distinguishable as areas of Negro settlement in 1900 remained the core of the Chicago Negro community in 1910. The principal South Side black belt was slowly expanding to accommodate the growing population. Not only did Negroes push steadily southward, but the narrow strip of land that made up the black belt began to widen as Negroes moved into the comfortable neighborhood east of State Street. By the end of the decade, Negroes could be found as far east as Cottage Grove Avenue.

Statistical data, then, reveal several definite trends in the pattern of Negro population in Chicago in the early twentieth century. The growth rate between 1900 and 1910 had decreased from the previous decade, but was still 50 per cent greater than that of whites. Most of the population increase was the result of migration, particularly from the nearby border states. Negroes could be found throughout much of the city and the Negro neighborhoods were by no means exclusively black. But the concentration of Negroes in two enclaves on the South and West Sides was increasing. As the population grew, Negroes were not spreading throughout the city but were becoming confined to a clearly delineated area of Negro settlement.

The increasing physical separation of Chicago's Negroes was but one reflection of a growing pattern of segregation and discrimination in early twentieth-century Chicago. As the Negro community grew and opportunities for interracial conflict increased, so a pattern of discrimination and segregation became ever more pervasive. And perhaps the most critical aspect of interracial conflict came as the result of Negro attempts to secure adequate housing.

The South Side black belt could expand in only two directions in the early twentieth century—south and east. To the north lay the business district, which was moving south; in fact, commercial and light industrial concerns were pushing Negroes out of the area between Twelfth and Twenty-second Streets. West of Wentworth Avenue was a district of low-income immigrant homes, interspersed with railroad yards and light industry; the lack of adequate housing made this area undesirable for Negro expansion. East of State Street, on the other hand, was a neighborhood suitable for Negro residential requirements. This area, bounded by Twelfth and Thirty-ninth Streets, State Street and Lake Michigan, had, in the 1880's and early 1890's, included the most fashionable streets in the city— Prairie and Calumet Avenues. But by 1900, the wealthy residents were moving to the North Side, leaving behind them comfortable, if aging homes. South of Thirty-ninth Street was an even more desirable residential area—Kenwood and Hyde Park —and across Washington Park from the southern extremity of the black belt were the new and attractive communities of Woodlawn and Englewood. In these areas, between 1900 and 1915, the lines were drawn in the struggle for housing that would subsequently lead to full-scale racial war. If no major

battle was fought before 1915, there were at least several preliminary skirmishes that set the pattern for future, and more
serious, confrontations.

Negro expansion did not always mean conflict, nor did it
mean that a neighborhood would shortly become exclusively
black. In 1910, not more than a dozen blocks on the South Side
were entirely Negro, and in many mixed areas Negroes and
whites lived together harmoniously. But as Negroes became
more numerous east of State and south of Fifty-first, friction increased and white hostility grew. When a Negro family moved
into a previously all-white neighborhood, the neighbors frequently protested, tried to buy the property, and then, if unsuccessful, resorted to violence to drive out the interlopers. In
many cases, the residents organized to urge real estate agents and
property owners to sell and rent to whites only. The whites
often succeeded in keeping Negroes out, at least temporarily.
When their efforts failed, they gradually moved out, leaving the
neighborhood predominantly, although rarely exclusively,
Negro.

Such incidents occurred with only minor variations throughout the prewar period. In 1900, three Negro families brought
about "a nervous prostration epidemic" on Vernon Avenue.
Five years later, an attempt to oust Negroes from a Forrestville
Avenue building landed in court. In 1911, a committee of
Champlain Avenue residents dealt with a Negro family in the
neighborhood by the "judicious use of a wagon load of bricks";
the *Record-Herald* described the affair as "something as nearly
approaching the operations of the Ku Klux Klan as Chicago has
seen in many years." Englewood residents, two years later, did
not have to go quite so far; the objectionable party, this time a
white man with a Negro wife, agreed to sell his property to a
hastily organized "neighborhood improvement association." A
Negro who moved into a home on Forrestville Avenue in 1915,
on the other hand, termed an offer of this type "blackmail," but
after several days of intimidation, he too submitted and sold his
property.

Perhaps the most serious incident, and the one which provides
the most insight into the nature of the housing conflict, occurred
in Hyde Park—Chicago's most persistent racial trouble spot—in
1909. A separate town until 1892, Hyde Park was still an area
of pleasant, tree-shaded streets, large, comfortable homes, and a

vigorous cultural life centered on the campus of the new but thriving University of Chicago. Negroes were no strangers to the community: for many years a few families, mostly house servants and hotel employees who worked in the neighborhood, had clustered on Lake Avenue near Fifty-fifth Street, on the eastern edge of Hyde Park. Now this community began to expand and Negroes occupied homes in nearby white blocks.

White Hyde Parkers responded to the Negro "invasion" with a concerted drive to keep Negroes out of white areas. The Hyde Park Improvement Protective Club was organized in the autumn of 1908; headed by a prominent attorney, Francis Harper, it soon boasted 350 members, "including some of the wealthiest dwellers on the South Side." In the summer of 1909, the Club issued a manifesto: Negro residents of Hyde Park must confine themselves to the "so-called Districts," real estate agents must refuse to sell property in white blocks to Negroes, and landlords must hire only white janitors. To implement this policy, the Club appointed a committee to purchase property owned by Negroes in white blocks and to offer bonuses to Negro renters who would surrender their leases. Moreover, the Club threatened to blacklist any real estate firm that defied its edict. "The districts which are now white," said Harper, "must remain white. There will be no compromise."

Despite the efforts of the Negro residents of Hyde Park to counter the activities with indignation meetings and boycotts, the white campaign continued. The neighborhood newspaper supported the Improvement Club, and Harper maintained that he had "received hosts of letters commending the course of the organization." When the Club was unable to persuade a Negro family to move voluntarily, the neighbors used more direct tactics: vandals broke into a Negro home on Greenwood Avenue one night and broke all the windows; the family left the next day. In September, the Club announced a boycott of merchants who sold goods to Negroes living in white neighborhoods. It urged separate playgrounds and tennis courts for Negroes in Washington Park, and, in its annual report, advocated segregation of the public schools. "It is only a question of time," a Club spokesman predicted, "when there will be separate schools for Negroes throughout Illinois." The group operated more quietly after 1909, but it had achieved its major goal. The little Negro community on Lake Avenue dwindled in size and the rest of Hyde Park remained white for forty years.

The Hyde Park episode well illustrates the intensification of anti-Negro feeling in the early twentieth century. This feeling could even create strong sentiment among whites for a return to formalized segregation—separate schools and recreation facilities. Some white Chicagoans spoke of the necessity for a residential segregation ordinance. The incident also provided an early example of techniques that were to become increasingly important as whites continually tried to stem the tide of Negro residential "invasion": the neighborhood improvement association, the community newspaper, the boycott, and in the last resort, violence. Furthermore, the episode was significant because it occurred in a middle- and upper-class community, and its victims were middle- and upper-class Negroes attempting to find comfortable homes among people of their own economic status. The housing problem for Negroes was not restricted to the poor; even the affluent were blocked in their quest for a decent place to live.

The unwillingness of whites to tolerate Negroes as neighbors had far-reaching results. Because Negroes were so limited in their choice of housing, they were forced to pay higher rents in those buildings that were open to them. Real estate agents frequently converted buildings in marginal neighborhoods from white to Negro and demanded rents 10 to 15 per cent higher than they had previously received. Sophonisba Breckinridge of Hull House estimated that a Negro family "pays $12.50 for the same accommodations the Jew in the Ghetto received for $9 and the immigrant for $8." One realty company inserted two advertisements for the same apartment in a daily newspaper: one read, "seven rooms, $25"; the other, "seven rooms for colored people, $37.50." High rents often forced Negro families to take in lodgers. A 1912 survey of 1,775 South Side Negroes reported that 542, or 31 per cent, lived as lodgers in the homes of others.

Living conditions in much of the black belt closely resembled conditions in the West Side ghetto or in the Stockyards district. Although Negroes could find some decent homes on the fringes of the Negro section, the core of the black belt was a festering slum. Here was an area of one- and two-story frame houses (unlike the older Eastern cities Chicago had, as yet, few large tenements), usually dilapidated with boarded-up porches and rickety wooden walks. Most of the buildings contained two flats and, although less crowded than houses in the Jewish, Polish, and Bohemian slums, they were usually in worse repair. The 1912 survey revealed that in a four-block area in the black belt, only 26 per cent of the dwellings were in good repair—as compared to 71 per cent in a similar sampling in a Polish neighborhood, 57 per cent among Bohemians, and 54 per cent in the ethnically mixed Stockyards district. "Colored tenants," the survey reported, "found it impossible to persuade their landlords either to make the necessary repairs or to release them from their contracts; . . . it was so hard to find better places in which to live that they were forced to make the repairs themselves, which they could rarely afford to do, or to endure the conditions as best they might."

White real estate agents, insensitive to class differences among Negroes, made no attempt to uphold standards in middle-class Negro neighborhoods as they did in comparable white districts. They persistently rented flats in "respectable" Negro neighborhoods to members of the "sporting element," thus forcing middle-class Negroes to move continually in search of decent areas to live and rear families. As a result, neighborhood stability was at best temporary. The streets east of State, which had become the mecca of the Negro middle class of the 1890's, began to decline by 1905. A few years later the district was characterized by "men and women half clothed hanging out of a window," "rag-time piano playing . . . far into the night," and "shooting and cutting scrapes."

Municipal policy regarding vice further complicated the situation. City authorities, holding that the suppression of prostitution was impossible, tried to confine it to certain well-defined areas where it could be closely watched. The police frequently moved the vice district so as to keep it away from commercial and white residential areas. Invariably they located it in or near the black belt, often in Negro residential neighborhoods. The chief of police declared that so long as prostitutes confined their activities to the district between Wentworth and Wabash, they would not be apprehended. Neighborhood stability, then, was threatened not only by the influx of Negro "shadies," but by the presence of an officially sanctioned vice district catering primarily to whites.

Periodic attempts to clean up the red-light district received little support from Negro leaders who believed that such campaigns would merely drive the undesirables deeper into Negro residential neighborhoods. When legal prostitution was finally abolished in 1912, these fears were fully realized; vice in Chicago continued to be centered in the black belt. Fannie Barrier Williams, a prominent Negro civic leader, summed up the plight of the middle- and upper-class Negro: "The huddling together of the good and the bad, compelling the decent element of the colored people to witness the brazen display of vice of all kinds in front of their homes and in the faces of their children, are trying conditions under which to remain socially clean and respectable."

The pattern of Negro housing, then, was shaped by white hostility and indifference: limited in their choice of homes, Negroes were forced to pay higher rents for inferior dwellings and were frequently surrounded by prostitutes, panderers, and other undesirable elements. This, together with the poverty of the majority of Chicago Negroes, produced in the black belt the conditions of slum-living characteristic of American cities by the end of the nineteenth century.

The most striking feature of Negro housing, however, was not the existence of slum conditions, but the difficulty of escaping the slum. European immigrants needed only to prosper to be able to move to a more desirable neighborhood. Negroes, on the other hand, suffered from both economic deprivation and systematic racial discrimination. "The problem of the Chicago Negro," wrote Sophonisba Breckinridge,

is quite different from the white man and even that of the immigrants. With the Negro the housing dilemma was found to be an acute problem, not only among the poor, as in the case of the Polish, Jewish, or Italian immigrants, but also among the well-to-do. . . . Thus, even in the North, where the city administration does not recognize a "Ghetto" or "pale," the real estate agents who register and commercialize what they suppose to be a universal race prejudice are able to enforce one in practice.

The development of a physical ghetto in Chicago, then, was not the result chiefly of poverty; nor did Negroes cluster out of choice. The ghetto was primarily the product of white hostility. Attempts on the part of Negroes to seek housing in predominantly white sections of the city met with resistance from the residents and from real estate dealers. Some Negroes, in fact, who had formerly lived in white neighborhoods, were pushed back into the black districts. As the Chicago Negro population grew, Negroes had no alternative but to settle in well-delineated Negro areas. And with increasing pressure for Negro housing, property owners in the black belt found it profitable to force out white tenants and convert previously mixed blocks into all-Negro blocks. The geographical dimensions of Black Chicago in the early twentieth century underwent no dramatic shift similar, for instance, to Negro New York, where the center of Negro life moved to previously all-white Harlem in less than a decade. Negroes in Chicago were not establishing new communities. But to meet the needs of a growing population, in the face of mounting white resistance, Negro neighborhoods were becoming more exclusively Negro as they slowly expanded their boundaries.

TABLE I

NEGRO POPULATION OF CHICAGO
1850–1930

				PER CENT INCREASE	
DATE	TOTAL POPULATION	NEGRO POPULATION	PER CENT NEGRO	TOTAL POPULATION	NEGRO POPULATION
1850.....	29,963	323	1.1	....	
1860.....	109,260	955	0.9	265	196
1870.....	298,977	3,691	1.2	174	286
1880.....	503,185	6,480	1.1	68	75
1890.....	1,099,850	14,271	1.3	119	120
1900.....	1,698,575	30,150	1.9	54	111
1910.....	2,185,283	44,103	2.0	29	46
1920.....	2,701,705	109,458	4.1	24	148
1930.....	3,376,438	233,903	6.9	25	114

Source: *U.S. Census Reports,* 1850–1930.

PUERTO RICANS IN PERSPECTIVE: THE MEANING OF MIGRATION TO THE MAINLAND

JOSEPH P. FITZPATRICK

Fordham University sociologist Joseph P. Fitzpatrick examines the unique characteristics of Puerto Rican migration and studies the problems of assimilation in New York City.

It is now twenty years since the large scale migration of Puerto Ricans to the United States Mainland began to develop after World War II. In the year 1946 the net outmigration from Puerto Rico to the mainland was about 40,000. It reached a peak of almost 70,000 in 1953. It has fluctuated sharply from year to year but continues to be substantial. In the year 1966, the net outmigration was close to 29,000; in 1967, it was more than 26,000. The movement backward for permanent resettlement on the Island is considerable, but still does not compare with the movement to the Mainland. Clarence Senior is certainly correct when he insists that the migration of Puerto Ricans should be considered as part of the internal migration of American citizens. Nevertheless, Puerto Ricans come from a cultural background very different from that of the Mainland United States and,

From Joseph P. Fitzpatrick, "Puerto Ricans in Perspective: The Meaning of Migration to the Mainland," *International Migration Review*, New Series, II (Spring 1968), 7–19. Copyright 1967 by the Center for Migration Studies. Reprinted by permission of the Center for Migration Studies.

despite the benefits of citizenship, they face the problems of language difference, cultural difference and cultural adjustment which are the common experience of migrating people throughout the world. This large scale experience, therefore, has a universal meaning. This paper seeks to examine what it is particularly in the perspective of their experience in New York City.

This article will first examine the unique characteristics of the Puerto Rican migration; secondly, it will study the process of assimilation particularly in relation to the search for identity which presents a number of special problems to the Puerto Ricans. It will analyze one of the special problems of identity which consists in a shift from an emphasis on culture to an emphasis on power as the basis for the establishment of a strong Puerto Rican community. Finally it will seek to interpret the experience of the Puerto Ricans as part of the human effort and suffering inevitably involved in the continuing creative achievement of New York City. In the historical perspective of the past migrations to the City it is reasonable to be optimistic about the present one.

New Variations on an Old Theme

The Puerto Rican migration can be initially understood only by perceiving it as the continuation of the experience which New York City has always had with newcomers. It is not a new or unusual occurrence for New York City that Puerto Ricans should be coming in large numbers. Rather, it would be a new and unusual experience if the City did not have them, or millions of other strangers, in her midst. It is precisely the presence of the stranger that has given New York many of its unique characteristics. Furthermore, by coming into the City, the Puerto Ricans face an experience that is neither new nor unusual. They inherit the role of strangers and re-live that painful but exciting drama of adjustment, the source of suffering and challenge out of which the strangers have consistently emerged as a new and greater people.

There are new dimensions, however, to this migration as

there are new dimensions to the City's life. The Puerto Ricans
have come for the most part as the first great air-borne migration of people from abroad. They are decidedly newcomers of
the aviation age. A Puerto Rican can travel from San Juan to
New York in less time than it took a New Yorker to travel
from Coney Island to Times Square a century ago. They are
the first group to come in large numbers from a different cultural background, but who are, nevertheless, citizens of the
United States. They are the first group of newcomers who
bring with them a cultural practice of widespread intermingling
and intermarriage of people of different color. They are the
first group of predominantly Catholic migrants who have not
had a native clergy to accompany them. These and other characteristics make the migration of Puerto Ricans unique.

Finally they come to New York City when many characteristics of the City make their experience different. Change has
always been part of the City's life. But change today is more
mild than before and more extensive. Communication through
radio and television has created a context in which people are in
immediate, almost instantaneous contact; in which news in
all its visual detail is available in the home of a Puerto Rican migrant as soon as it happens. In a world of telephones, people in
Brooklyn and the Bronx can be neighbors more intimately than
people, separated by a city block, could have been neighbors a
century ago. The City is older and much of its real estate is de-
crepit and is being replaced on an enormous scale. The Puerto
Ricans come to New York when nearly a million and a half
Blacks are citizens of the City and the civil rights movement
and the movement for "Black Power" are at their height. They
come when automation is creating a new kind of economy, and
when jobs which once were the great channels of immigrant
advancement are being eliminated by the hundreds of thousands.
They come when the City and Federal Governments provide a
wide range of public services from public housing to welfare,
which did not exist a century ago. Thus the coming of the
Puerto Ricans is not just a repetition of the past, because the
past no longer exists; and no people quite like the Puerto Ricans
have ever come before. Therefore any interpretation of the
meaning of the migration must be related to these unique characteristics of the Puerto Rican people and the unique characteristics of New York City in the 1960's.

The Process of Assimilation:
The Problem of Identity

In the presence of the circumstances just mentioned, the Puerto Ricans face the process of becoming part of the life of New York City. Central to this process is the problem of identity: "Who are we," and the effort to answer this question largely determines the direction and dynamics of assimilation. The Puerto Ricans face a unique experience in their search for identity; they face some particular problems in relation to the three basic factors on which the identity of other groups was firmly anchored, namely: nationality, color, and religion.

In the first place, the Puerto Ricans have been struggling with a problem of identity on the Island itself. The question "who are we?" has been a critical one for many years. A confident sense of who they are and where they belong, a deep-rootedness in a culture and tradition of long standing which most immigrants had before they came, this sense of secure identity has been weakening on the Island, if indeed it ever existed. This can be seen in the rapid convergence of three developments.

a) *The Problem of Political Status.* Puerto Rico is neither independent nor is it a state. It is a Free Association State, a political status in which it enjoys a great deal of autonomy while still being part of the United States. For years, the problem of status has been a public debate around which the three major political parties are organized: the Popular Party which created the status of a Free Associated State continues to promote it as a permanent condition; the Statehood Party explicitly seeks to make Puerto Rico the fifty first state of the Union; the Independence Party seeks complete Independence. In July, 1967, a plebiscite was held to determine the preference of the electorate. The status of Free Associated State gained 60% of the votes; Statehood was second with 38%; Independence ran a poor third with 2%. Despite the vote, however, the problem of uncertainty remains. When asking themselves politically, "who are we?", large numbers of Puerto Ricans are not so sure.

b) *The Problem of Economic Development.* For the past twenty years, Puerto Rico has been passing through a period of rapid economic development. In fact, the movement, called "operation bootstrap," is considered the best example of the rapid economic development of an economically underdeveloped area in the world.

This development has had a massive impact on the traditional culture of the Island. The social and cultural adjustments to industrialization are evident everywhere, and the distress associated with them is deeply and widely felt. Almost ten years ago, the guiding spirit of economic development, Luis Muñoz Marín, began calling for a strong effort to preserve the traditional way of life. He wanted "operation serenity," as he called it, to be more parallel with "operation bootstrap." It is doubtful that "operation serenity" will be very effective in slowing down the cultural upheaval on the Island. From many points of view, Puerto Ricans have been culturally uprooted before they leave the Island.

c) *Changing Religious Conditions.* Since Puerto Rico became an American possession, the Island has relied increasingly on the religious care of priests, sisters and brothers from the Mainland. This has been an extremely generous effort, but it brought a decidedly Mainland style of Catholic life to the Island. In much of their religious life, Puerto Ricans have been conscious of dependence on a "foreign" clergy. They did not have that penetrating sense of Catholic identity which comes from a deeply rooted and untroubled folk attachment to Catholicism; there is nothing among Puerto Ricans, for example, comparable to Our Lady of Guadalupe among the Mexicans. Nor did many have a mature conscious loyalty to the Church as an organization. There was an ambiguity even in their religious experience. As a result, the sense of identity which was the basis around which ethnic loyalties crystallized in the lives of other immigrants, was weak in the Puerto Ricans before they came.

When they arrived in New York, the problem of identity became further complicated particularly around the problem of color. Puerto Ricans range from completely white to completely black with every mixture in between. They are certainly sensitive to color in Puerto Rico, but neither color consciousness nor prejudice nor discrimination focuses on color the way they do on the Mainland. Conscious of the disadvantage of color in the Mainland, they have used various devices to protect themselves against it, emphasizing that they were "Puerto Rican" and not American Negro; clinging to Spanish in the hope that language would protect them from identification as American Negroes. During the nineteen fifties when the civil rights movement was pressing strongly for integration, the movement created a dilemma for Puerto Ricans. They were integrated already, biologically and socially. A completely Puerto Rican school would be a completely integrated school. Consequently they were bewildered about their relationship to the civil rights movement. Literally, they did not know where they were at.

Secondly, the religious parish, more specifically the Catholic parish, which was the basis for the identity of earlier immigrant groups and the basis for the development of a strong immigrant community, has not fulfilled the same functions for Puerto Ricans. Early in the migration, the authorities of the New York Archdiocese adopted a policy of integrated parishes, that is Spanish speaking priests were added to existing parishes which had served and continued to serve older populations, and special services in Spanish were introduced into the parishes; but no separate churches devoted entirely to a Spanish speaking population were planned, and efforts were to be made to integrate the Spanish speaking with the older congregations. There are a number of serious reasons for this kind of policy. But it makes difficult, if not impossible, the establishment of a strong Puerto Rican community around a center of religious identification and practice. Wide dispersal in New York and the policy of integration in Public Housing projects also make it difficult for Puerto Ricans to form those tightly knit neighborhoods of older immigrant groups where immigrant communities were strong and supporting to their people in the process of adjustment, and which contributed psychologically to the sense of identity which gave many of the immigrants a sense of cultural and personal strength. The response of many Puerto Ricans to the Pentecostal and Evangelical sects, to the style of religious practice of the store front church, has been interpreted as one effort of Puerto Ricans to find the satisfaction and sense of belonging and identity which they have not achieved in the large, highly organized parishes of either the Catholic or Protestant faiths. The number of Puerto Ricans, however, who are seriously involved in the religious sects is very small. There is some speculation that the Island itself may be fulfilling the function which the immigrant community fulfilled for earlier immigrants. Travel back and forth to the Island is enormous; it consists mainly of Puerto Ricans moving in either direction to visit, to spend vacation, to escape problems, to seek financial or family help or to find work. In any event, they know that their home town on the Island is only three hours away. They have the sense of not being far removed, of always being able to return if life in New York proves too difficult.

From Community Based on Culture to Community Based on Power

It is clear from the foregoing that many of the factors which contributed to the strong sense of community and identity of earlier immigrant groups, will not be able to contribute in the same way to a sense of community and identity among Puerto Ricans. However, new developments have been taking place in recent years and a decided change has appeared in a shift from an emphasis on culture as the basis for community to an emphasis on power. This transition could best be expressed by a brief description of the experience of the Puerto Rican Community Development Project. This was a proposal, prepared by the Puerto Rican Forum and submitted to the Office of Economic Opportunity (the agency administering the Anti-Poverty Program) for a comprehensive, city-wide coordinating agency which would promote, integrate and supervise a system of projects designed to assist the Puerto Ricans in New York. The explicit philosophy of this proposal was presented in a lengthy chapter entitled "Rationale for a Culturally Based Project" which indicated the need to develop a project which would enable the Puerto Ricans to develop a strong sense of identity, and a strong sense of community. From this position of strength, they would be able to move more securely toward integration with the larger society of New York City. The proposal, in other words, reflected the theory of cultural pluralism, current until recently, which indicated that the preservation of traditional cultures was the best basis for a strong sense of community among immigrants. This proposal was turned down, particularly by city officials, who insisted, among other things, that they could not fund this kind of ethnic-based proposal; that it was administratively unsound; that it would duplicate what other programs were doing; that it was not practical enough—it emphasized an intangible thing like "sense of community" instead of getting down to the "nuts and bolts" of jobs. The proposal was funded sometime later when city officials expressed their confidence that it was in the hands of practical people instead of impractical intellectuals. It has since taken a decidedly political orientation and it illustrates the shift to an emphasis on power which has become the central issue in relation to Puerto Ricans and all other racial and ethnic minorities in the country.

The shift in emphasis from culture to power as the basis for community has resulted from a number of influences which have been growing stronger during the past fifteen years. One of the most important has been the influence of Saul Alinsky in community organizing. Alinsky, a very controversial figure, has always insisted that a sense of community strength is best developed around issues in which conflicts of interest are evident. He insists that the poor regularly suffer because they do not recognize that social institutions are organized and function for the protection of the interests of the people who control them, and at the expense of the interest of the poor. He first seeks to bring the poor to an awareness of their own interest which is involved, to make explicit the conflict of interest which is implicit, and to encourage the poor to marshall their strength, organize themselves to press for a change in the structure or function of the institutions in which they are at a disadvantage. Alinsky insists that the poor must bargain from a position of strength; that, if they can do this, they can participate as equals in a resolution of conflict, and an accommodation of interests in which they will have a decisive role to play in determining whose interests will be served and in what way. According to Alinsky, this growing self-awareness, definition of community needs, the marshalling of forces to promote community interests, and the maintaining of a strong position for the protection of community interests, all these contribute to an increase in the sense of community and of identity which enable the poor to lead a much more human existence. This is not the occasion for a detailed evaluation of Alinsky's theory or method. His influence had led people to recognize that community strength may lie, not in an emphasis on the preservation of a culture in a pluralistic society, but in the organizing of resources to promote a common interest.

In their book *Beyond the Melting Pot*, Nathan Glazer and Daniel Moynihan presented a theory of assimilation which, in its general lines, is somewhat similar to the theory of Alinsky. They indicated that, in the intermingling of people of many nationalities in a City like New York, the melting pot had never actually melted. In fact, they say, the ethnic group has not disappeared; it has become a new social form. Instead of people defining their interests around nationality background as they did when they first came to the United States, they now define their interests around race or religion. In brief, the ethnic groups have now become large scale interest groups. What the United States now faces, according to Glazer and Moynihan, is not the assimilation of people of different cultural backgrounds into one predominant culture, but rather the accommodation of conflicting interests in a politically unified society. A basic theme in this analysis of immigrant experience is the strategic use of political and economic power by the ethnic groups to promote their interests in a democratic society. The significant theme is not the achievement of identity by preserving traditional cultural forms; but by participating as an effective force in the important decisions of the larger society.

Meantime, from quite a different perspective, scholars began to call attention to the culture of the poor, not so much as a traditional form which they should preserve in a pluralistic society and from which they should move with security and strength toward assimilation into the larger society; but rather as the focus of interest of the poor around which they should marshall their political strength. Walter B. Miller, for example, insisted that the poor should not be looked upon as "deviant" from the dominant American way of life. It is important, Miller insisted, to view the behavior of the poor from within the context of their own lives. In this way, their culture, or style of life, can be seen as a positive thing, possessing its own strengths and values; it represents a creative response of the poor to cope with the kinds of challenges they must face. Social service policy, therefore, should not take the form of trying to impose the dominant culture upon the poor; but to enable them, within the context of their own strengths and values to identify their needs, marshall their own resources, and create their own response and adaptation to American life and experience. Miller is not saying that the poor should never become part of the dominant culture; neither is he saying what the traditional position of the cultural pluralists implied. Miller is saying that the culture of the poor whom he studied in the Roxbury Community in Boston was, within their disadvantaged situation, an understandable creative response to the pressures of the dominant society in which their interests were not being served. Their culture, in other words, was their effort to create a system in which they pursued their own interests in the framework of a dominant society in which they were at a disadvantage. Although Miller never spells it out, his position implies that the particular culture of the poor reflects a massive conflict of interest between the poor and the more affluent members of their society; if they can organize and bargain from a position of strength about the accommodation of their interests, the cultural differences may begin to disappear. In the extensive literature about "cultural deprivation," particularly around education and mental health, this same position is reflected.

The concept of the "culture of poverty" which Oscar Lewis first presented in *Five Families*, and which he sought to explore in *La Vida, a Puerto Rican Family in the Culture of Poverty in San Juan and New York*, also reflects this same position. Lewis never advocates the perpetuation of the culture of poverty; he sees it as a condition which is often destructive of the human personality. But he does recognize it not simply as behavior that is deviant from that of the dominant culture, but as a positive thing, a style of life with its own strengths and values, which represents a creative response of people who are marginal to a developing or developed industrial and commercial world; and who cannot find their way up the channels to advancement and the enjoyment of the privileges of an affluent society. Lewis is struck by the lack of organization in the lives of the people in the culture of poverty. In other words, according to Lewis, the culture of poverty develops among people who seek to pursue their interests in this style of life in the framework of a dominant society in which they are at a great disadvantage. Lewis seems to imply, without explicitly stating it, that if the poor were organized to participate as equals in the processes of the dominant society, the culture of poverty would disappear.

This type of thinking about culture has become quite common during the past ten years. What converted it into a significant political force was the shift among the Black Americans from an emphasis on civil rights and integration to an emphasis on Black Power. Explicit in the movement for Black Power is the insistence that Black people must find a positive strength and value in the color that gives them their identity; must define their interests as Black people; marshall their resources and bargain from a position of strength about the conditions of the society in which they expect to live. Central to the movement is the remarkable development of a sense of pride in their color among Black people. But also important has been the creation of a sense of community solidarity out of their effort to organize their strength for the promotion of their own interests; community identity and strength are not seen as something which emerged from the preservation of a cultural tradition, but from the political effort to press for a realization of their interests. This emphasis on power has expressed itself in many areas of the lives of Black Americans. As it has done so, it has created an impact on the lives of poor Puerto Ricans. The response of the Puerto Ricans has affected the problem of community and identity which is such an important issue in their lives.

In view of both the theory and the practice described above, it would seem that, if Puerto Ricans can organize around an effort to promote their political interests, the achievement of identity and community strength may advance despite the particular problems of identity which Puerto Ricans face on the Island or in New York. There is some indication that this may be taking place. In the first place the aggressiveness and success of the Black citizens in anti-poverty programs has resulted in a realization among Puerto Ricans that they must do likewise. As a result a great deal of aggressiveness is appearing in areas where many Puerto Ricans are located; indeed, so much aggressiveness has appeared in one area of the Bronx that it has provoked the intervention of City level authorities to try to maintain some balance between Black persons and Puerto Ricans on a Community Corporation. Furthermore, as indicated above, the Puerto Rican Community Development Project has been marked by the presence on its staff and Board, of politically interested and politically active people who see the need for political involvement if the Project is to remain strong. At the present time there is great open hostility between Puerto Ricans and Black citizens, particularly about control over public schools and anti-poverty programs.

At this moment, it is not possible to predict what effect the present developments will have on the adjustment of Puerto Ricans to the City of New York. It is possible that their militancy around their interests in anti-poverty programs, education, public welfare, housing, etc. may enable them to develop a sense of identity and a community solidarity which, thus far, they have found it difficult to achieve. If this does take place, it will support the validity of the new theories of the adjustment of migrants to a new and strange city. They will integrate from a position of strength, but the strength will rest not on the continuation of a traditional culture in the form of an immigrant community, but on the solidarity which results from organizing their efforts for the pursuit of group interests in the political arena.

The Perspective of the City's History

It is possible, however, at the present time to assess the development among the Puerto Ricans in the light of the history of previous migrations to the City. The present conflicts are distressing, not only to Puerto Ricans, but to all residents in the City. Nevertheless, difficult as the situation may be, it is very doubtful if it can compare with the distress of the City a century or more ago. New York has alway been a troubled city, sometimes a violent one, because the City has always insisted on accepting newcomers, on enabling them to become part of her own life. The pain of the newcomer as well as the pain of the older resident take on a great meaning when they are seen in the perspective of the creative achievement to which the City has been dedicated since its beginning. Achievement cannot be gained without a cost in effort and suffering, and the creation of what may be the greatest city man has built has certainly involved enormous costs. In a century and three quarters, it has absorbed millions of immigrants, from dozens of different cultural backgrounds as different as that of Iroquois Indians to Russian Emigres. To cope with this variety, to achieve a common life, to provide advancement, to create an economic, educational and political system which would enable the immigrants to develop themselves and participate actively in the City's life, is little less than a social miracle. The fact that it was attended by suffering is not a mystery; the mystery is that it was done at all.

In the perspective of that history, it is quite clear that the experience of the City is a continuing thing today. The actors change; the process appears to be the same. New York is again re-making itself, physically and socially. Together with millions of people, older and newer residents from a variety of backgrounds, the City now numbers an estimated 1,400,000 Black people among its citizens, making it the City with the largest Black population in the world; it numbers an estimated 700,000 Puerto Ricans, making it the largest Puerto Rican city in the world. The process continues of receiving newcomers, of enabling them to become part of the City's life. This time the creative effort is particularly difficult since it involves the integration of Black citizens into the life of the City. But the same process of upheaval, distress, and rapid change will be part of the life of the citizens today as it was of generations past.

At the center of this distress has been the political struggle to accommodate conflicting interests, to restrict corruption, to prevent the manipulation of the political system for purely partisan gains. It is clear from the analysis of Glazer and Moynihan that political conflict has been a means by which most earlier groups entered into active participation in the City's life. The fact that the process of increasing participation is now involving Blacks and Puerto Ricans in intense political conflict can reasonably be interpreted as a sign that, at last, they have arrived.

From this perspective of the City's history, the difficulties which Puerto Ricans must face are not signs of deterioration or decay; they may be recognized as part of the continued creative effort of the achievement of New York City. In this perspective they have a definite meaning. This point of view is strongly resisted by many New Yorkers as unrealistic and over-optimistic. They are convinced, many of them, that the City has reached a critical moment in its life, quite unlike anything that has happened before, that disorder and the fear of personal attack are signs of widespread social disorganization rather than the pains of creative growth. This conviction can easily be turned into an accusation against Blacks and Puerto Ricans as the responsible parties. But this conviction of decay is not new. It is found at every moment of the City's history, and the lamentations about the decline of the City are not nearly as serious today as they were in previous generations.

The resistance of many Puerto Ricans to the optimistic point of view takes a different form. They are generally appalled at the extent and intensity of suffering which they see their people facing in New York. Understandably, they attribute the problem not to the Puerto Rican people, but to the City. They project into a judgment on New York, the same judgment many of them make about the rapid industrialization of the Island. They see New York as the most evident example, not only of all that is right about an advanced technological age, but of all that is wrong with it also. It is impersonal, materialistic, secular, and it makes impossible that kind of personal relationships which characterize the culture of Puerto Rico. This point of view does not perceive the City in decay; but as too highly developed to permit the kind of human existence to which Puerto Ricans are adapted.

The objective of the present paper is not to attempt to prove or disprove any of the above positions. They all involve prophecy, and only history will prove which, if any of them, was right. The objective of this paper is simply to seek the meaning of the Puerto Rican migration, in the only sources from which the meaning of any migration to New York can be sought, that is, in the history of the migrations of the past. In this sense, the statement is not a matter of prophecy. It is clear that what many knowledgeable people considered to be signs of decay and deterioration were actually the pains of creative growth. In that perspective, as the experience of the past appears to be repeating itself, it is reasonable to interpret the distress of the Puerto Ricans as another period involving the pain of creative growth. In this perspective, the problem of identity, whether sought by an emphasis on their traditional culture or by an emphasis on political power, is simply part of the problem of becoming New Yorkers, of participating in the turbulent social process which has issued in the life of the world's greatest city.

WELFARE PROBLEMS OF
THE CITIES

ARTHUR J. NAPARSTEK
AND
GEORGE T. MARTIN, JR.

Contradictions in the present welfare system and major alternatives are examined in the following selection. Arthur J. Naparstek is Associate Director, and George T. Martin, Jr., Research Associate, at the Urban Development Institute of Purdue University.

In recent years, the plight of the American cities—particularly the inner city—has been labelled a "crisis." The rhetoric used to describe this crisis includes frequent references to anarchy, radical change, crime in the streets, and breakdowns in law and order. However, although it is true that violence has occurred with increasing frequency in the slums of many American cities, the conditions in the inner city have existed for a long time. The rhetoric of crisis is, principally, a response to the current problems in black-white relations, and not necessarily to significant urban problems. More specifically, this rhetoric is a result of a feeling of some members of the white majority that they are threatened by a black minority. The rhetoric of crisis was not propagated around critical urban problems such as air and water pollution, transportation, taxation and education. The term "crisis" reflects a fear of black violence.

The mood of crisis has elicited a series of rather hysterical responses in the nation's cities, including massive police and military actions, repressive laws, and the initiation of quickly-conceived crash programs in the areas of employment, housing and public welfare. Most of these programs have been aimed at cooling off the so-called crisis; many have been ineffective, if not irrelevant. Some of these programs, directed towards alleviating or even curing the problems, have actually created further frustrations.

The nation's present urban "crisis" can be more accurately described and treated as an endemic problem—a chronic disease. This is not simply a problem in semantics, for the manner in which the nation responds to the situation is based, in large measure, on how it is perceived and in what rhetoric it is expressed.

It is clear that there are serious difficulties structured into our urban society, including housing segregation and social discrimination leading to ghetto formation, and breakdowns in the educational system, the employment market and in political structures. Both as a cause and a result, the bitter facts of urban poverty underlie and pervade all these difficulties. As far as the general public is concerned, this poverty has only recently been "rediscovered."

One of the major problems confronting American urban centers, then, is poverty. For the black poor in the ghettos, of course, poverty is bred and nurtured by institutionalized racism. For both the black and the white poor, however, poverty leads to powerlessness. Poverty is not new to American cities—historically, it has been a chronic condition. In fact, even black poverty is not new to the American city. What is relatively new is violence on the part of the black poor, and society's resulting realization of the grim facts of urban poverty.

For the past six years, the nation has been committed to a struggle against this poverty. The current strategy is to develop more jobs and to train the poor to fill them. Efforts to increase the number of jobs and to improve the employability of potential workers have resulted in a bewildering array of programs. Federally-funded programs stemming from area redevelopment projects, from the Manpower Development and Training Act, from community work and training programs for public assistance recipients under the Social Security Act, from the Office of Economic Opportunity, and from the Department of Labor's education, training and human reclamation projects have all been initiated within the past six years. However, there is a serious question as to whether these employment and self-help programs are relevant to the majority of the nation's poor.

Data from the Bureau of the Census for the year 1963 show that, of a total of about 35 million people in the nation who live in poverty, almost one-half (15 million) are age 18 or younger, and over one-seventh (5.2 million) are age 65 or older. Also, of the some 7 million families who comprise the poverty group, over 1.5 million are headed by a female with at least one child age 18 or younger. Moreover, more than one-fourth of these poor families are headed by a fulltime worker. Thus, of those people who live in poverty, most are either too old or too young to work, and many others are already fully employed. As a consequence, government programs with an employment and training focus are irrelevant to the majority of the nation's poor.

Indeed, a careful analysis of the so-called war on poverty clearly reveals that the large bulk of the poor remain untouched by programs with this emphasis. One of the major difficulties is that self-help, bootstrap-type programs, while perhaps desirable in themselves, have been superimposed on a welfare system designed to deal with the economic and social problems of the 1930's and totally inadequate for contemporary needs.

As a matter of fact, the net effect of this unholy matrimony has been largely negative. In its discussion of public assistance, the *Report of the National Advisory Commission on Civil Disorders* indicated that the present welfare system contributes materially to the tensions and the social disorganization which have contributed to urban riots. Of the reasons which can be offered for this seeming paradox, two stand out: (1) the government programs do not basically reduce the powerlessness of their recipients, as they are most often controlled by the non-poor; (2) the programs have often raised aspiration levels without materially raising actual levels of living. It is this latter factor —the sense of relative deprivation—which may explain how many of the government programs created to remedy the nation's urban problems have actually helped to perpetuate them—by increasing the frustration and feeling of lack of hope among the urban poor.

For example, some of the employment programs have resulted in a process referred to as "creaming." In "creaming," only the most talented and skilled of the urban poor are recruited for programs, while the poor masses are left relatively untouched. Two consequences of this are significant: (1) actual and potential leadership in the ghettos is virtually eliminated; (2) the masses of the poor who are left unaffected by the program are even further frustrated.

Public Welfare and Poverty

The major thrust of the government's programs has been to deal with the symptoms of poverty, not with its causes. Programs have not been designed to alter significantly the social, political and economic systems which sustain poverty in the world's most affluent nation.

The nation's current public assistance system was a product of the New Deal. It was initiated in 1935 by the Committee on Economic Security and was intended to be residual in nature. In other words, it was assumed that the economic and social system was basically sound. Unemployment compensation would take care of any unemployment that rose out of temporary economic readjustments. Old-age assistance and aid-to-dependent-children would gradually be replaced by social security programs—primarily old age and survivors' insurance. Finally, locally-financed programs—known as general assistance programs—would cover those few not included in these programs. The public welfare programs remain residual in the 1960's, still unable to reduce national poverty on a systematic basis. At present, less than 10 million of the nation's some 35 million poor people receive any income maintenance payments under public assistance. In spite of this fact, the system is still overloaded.

Since 1935, the composition of the public assistance recipient groups has changed substantially. The Aid to Families with Dependent Children (A.F.D.C.) program is a prime example. In 1935, the typical recipient in the program was a white widow with one or two children; today, the typical recipient is a black woman with three or four children who, moreover, lives in a central city ghetto.

Among all the current national welfare programs, A.F.D.C. and A.F.D.C.-U.P. (Aid to Families with Dependent Children-with Unemployed Parents) clearly have the greatest impact upon family life in the central cities, and perhaps contribute to the chronically bad conditions there. States and local governments contribute an average of about 45 per cent of the cost of these programs. However, each state sets grant levels for its residents; consequently, monthly payments vary widely. The range is from $9.30 monthly for each A.F.D.C. recipient in Mississippi to $62.55 in New York. Not only are payments pitifully inadequate; they are often accompanied by degrading indignities of the means test and by unconscionable delays. It is not surprising that life on A.F.D.C. in the ghetto has been described as a treadmill to nowhere.

In his message to Congress on the welfare of children on February 8, 1967, President Lyndon Johnson pointed out that in 1966: (1) 12 million children in families living below the poverty line received no A.F.D.C. benefits (only 3.2 million children received any benefits in 1966), (2) 33 states do not even meet their own minimum standards for subsistence in their payments, (3) a number of states discourage parents from working by arbitrarily reducing welfare payments when parents earn their first dollar. This fact emphasizes the confiscatory nature of present regulations, and their negative effect upon the motivation to work of all family members, including adolescents.

It is clear that the present system excludes a great number of persons who are in need and provides only minimum assistance to those who are included. But perhaps the most serious indictment of the present system is that, for the relatively few poor who are reached, restrictions which encourage dependency and undermine self-respect are the rule. It is in this sense that current public assistance programs, particularly A.F.D.C., have contributed substantially to the sense of powerlessness felt by the urban poor.

Although public assistance laws are inadequate and punitive, administrative practices often are far worse. Broad discretion in doling out benefits is given to administrators—largely because there is little consensus at the legislative level concerning the programs' conceptual goals. State statutes are often vague, and the task of interpreting the law falls upon the welfare bureaucracies, so that political struggles are shifted from legislative to administrative arenas. Indeed, it has been asserted that the present climate of public welfare administration in the nation is based upon insidious, paranoid and primitive preoccupations stemming from the poor-law heritage of "keeping the town books clean."

Strategies for Change

Critics of the current public welfare system have advanced several strategies aimed at reform or elimination of the present program. These strategies focus on active protest against the welfare bureaucracies and on legal redress of grievances by recipients through the nation's courts. In addition, several alternative approaches to income maintenance have recently been much discussed.

The strategy of active protest centers upon the organization of welfare recipient groups across the nation. The general focus of these groups has been to demand from the present system the maximum it can legally give, and to confront the system with its own inequities. A more strategic goal of the welfare protest movement is the effective destruction of the present system and its replacement by a totally new approach to income maintenance, perhaps in the form of a guaranteed income. As some protesters plan it, the collapse of the system would come through overloading it; that is, efforts would be made to register the millions of people currently deemed eligible but not receiving assistance. The assumption is that an already overloaded public welfare bureaucracy can tolerate little addition to its rolls—that a breakdown would occur; any change would be for the better.

Such organization of welfare recipients into a protest movement serves the direct purpose of reducing the feeling—as well as the fact—of powerlessness. One recent study of A.F.D.C. mothers has shown that members of a welfare client organization were more likely to have feelings of mastery and control than non-members.

The strategy of legal change of the present system has focused upon the constitutional rights of the welfare recipient. Recent decisions by state courts have overturned such punitive public assistance regulations as the man-in-the-house rule and residency requirements. The decision overturning the man-in-the-house rule has been upheld by the Supreme Court; the residency requirement ruling is currently on its docket. Two types of legal action are required: one designed to achieve basic changes in the structure of social welfare laws (usually through the application of constitutional principles to the present laws), and the other designed to insure that present laws are implemented equitably at the administrative level.

Other approaches to change are being tentatively developed through experiments by such agencies as the Office of Economic Opportunity and by Model Cities. For example, the Model Cities program is considering the funding of local experiments with the family allowance scheme. This past summer the Office of Economic Opportunity awarded a community action program grant to the national coordinating organization of welfare rights groups "for a program to train welfare recipients on welfare rights, education and information."

Prominent among the possible alternatives to the nation's present income maintenance system which have been discussed in recent years are the negative income tax, the demogrant (a government grant of money to categories of individuals, either universal or partial), and a combination of basic reforms in both the public welfare and Social Security programs. All of these alternatives have been loosely referred to under the rubric of the "guaranteed income" when, in fact, only the universal demogrant would result in a guaranteed income for all citizens.

The negative income tax proposal, recently popularized by conservative economist Milton Friedman, has taken various forms, and has been presented for differing reasons. All the proposals, however, would use the nation's tax structure in some fashion. The basic idea is to define a minimum income for all citizens—perhaps adjusted regionally—and to supplement the income of those citizens which does not reach the minimum. Friedman would make the negative income tax replace all current income maintenance programs; the basic goal is to save money through the elimination of complicated administrative structures. Others would make the program an important supplement to current income maintenance programs.

The partial demogrant would allot funds to certain categories of the nation's population, such as children, regardless of their income. Some form of the children's or family allowance already exists in some 60 nations in the world, including almost all of the industrialized nations. All children of a specified age category receive a set allowance, paid to their parents. The universal demogrant, on the other hand, would allot funds to all persons. Each citizen would receive a specified amount of money. Utilization of the universal demogrant would probably be the best and most direct method of reducing the powerlessness of the poor. It could be used to redistribute the greatest amount of money to the poor with the fewest conditions attached. The great problem with this scheme is, of course, its very high initial cost, although taxes could recover the bulk of funds granted the non-poor.

Reforms in both the present public welfare and Social Security programs would be the least revolutionary of all the alternatives discussed. One important thrust of this approach is aimed at the creation of federal legislation which would be directed at establishing national minimum standards, uniform and applicable in all 50 states, for public assistance payments.

The public welfare system is only one example of an overworked and out-dated governmental system which attempts to serve the nation's cities. Although reform of public welfare is not a panacea for the urban "crisis," it is a prerequisite to the success of a wide range of programs. Programs to eliminate bad housing and racial discrimination and upgrade public education and improve city services have little chance of widespread success if the nation does not come to grips with the critical deficiencies of its public welfare system.

Indeed, the most pressing issue confronting American cities is the powerlessness of those who are poor. Only through the difficult task of restructuring the nation's economic system in such a way as to provide each citizen with an adequate and secure income can this problem be resolved. Although there are many fronts upon which to attack the urban "crisis," the problems of public welfare, poverty, and the powerlessness of the poor deserve priority in both policy and action.

SUMMARY, REPORT OF THE NATIONAL ADVISORY COMMISSION ON CIVIL DISORDERS

The report of this special presidential commission, headed by former governor Otto Kerner of Illinois, examines the 1967 ghetto insurrections and recommends programs to eliminate the underlying causes of urban unrest.

Introduction

The summer of 1967 again brought racial disorders to American cities, and with them shock, fear, and bewilderment to the Nation.

The worst came during a 2-week period in July, first in Newark and then in Detroit. Each set off a chain reaction in neighboring communities.

On July 28, 1967, the President of the United States established this Commission and directed us to answer three basic questions:

What happened?
Why did it happen?
What can be done to prevent it from happening again?

To respond to these questions, we have undertaken a broad range of studies and investigations. We have visited the riot

From *Report of the National Advisory Commission on Civil Disorders* (Washington, D.C.: Government Printing Office, 1968), pp. 1–13.

cities; we have heard many witnesses; we have sought the counsel of experts across the country.

This is our basic conclusion: Our Nation is moving toward two societies, one black, one white—separate and unequal.

Reaction to last summer's disorders has quickened the movement and deepened the division. Discrimination and segregation have long permeated much of American life; they now threaten the future of every American.

This deepening racial division is not inevitable. The movement apart can be reversed. Choice is still possible. Our principal task is to define that choice and to press for a national resolution.

To pursue our present course will involve the continuing polarization of the American community and, ultimately, the destruction of basic democratic values.

The alternative is not blind repression or capitulation to lawlessness. It is the realization of common opportunities for all within a single society.

This alternative will require a commitment to national action —compassionate, massive, and sustained, backed by the resources of the most powerful and the richest nation on this earth. From every American it will require new attitudes, new understanding, and, above all, new will.

The vital needs of the Nation must be met; hard choices must be made, and, if necessary, new taxes enacted.

Violence cannot build a better society. Disruption and disorder nourish repression, not justice. They strike at the freedom of every citizen. The community cannot—it will not—tolerate coercion and mob rule.

Violence and destruction must be ended—in the streets of the ghetto and in the lives of people.

Segregation and poverty have created in the racial ghetto a destructive environment totally unknown to most white Americans.

What white Americans have never fully understood—but what the Negro can never forget—is that white society is deeply implicated in the ghetto. White institutions created it, white institutions maintain it, and white society condones it.

It is time now to turn with all the purpose at our command to the major unfinished business of this Nation. It is time to adopt strategies for action that will produce quick and visible progress. It is time to make good the promises of American democracy to all citizens—urban and rural, white and black, Spanish-surname, American Indian, and every minority group.

Our recommendations embrace three basic principles:

■ To mount programs on a scale equal to the dimension of the problems;

■ To aim these programs for high impact in the immediate future in order to close the gap between promise and performance;

■ To undertake new initiatives and experiments that can change the system of failure and frustration that now dominates the ghetto and weakens our society.

These programs will require unprecedented levels of funding and performance, but they neither probe deeper nor demand more than the problems which called them forth. There can be no higher priority for national action and no higher claim on the Nation's conscience.

We issue this report now, 5 months before the date called for by the President. Much remains that can be learned. Continued study is essential.

As Commissioners we have worked together with a sense of the greatest urgency and have sought to compose whatever differences exist among us. Some differences remain. But the gravity of the problem and the pressing need for action are too clear to allow further delay in the issuance of this report.

I / What Happened?

Chapter 1.—Profiles of Disorder

The report contains profiles of a selection of the disorders that took place during the summer of 1967. These profiles are designed to indicate how the disorders happened, who participated in them, and how local officials, police forces, and the National Guard responded. Illustrative excerpts follow:

NEWARK

* * * It was decided to attempt to channel the energies of the people into a nonviolent protest. While Lofton promised the crowd that a full investigation would be made of the Smith incident, the other

Negro leaders began urging those on the scene to form a line of march toward the city hall.

Some persons joined the line of march. Others milled about in the narrow street. From the dark grounds of the housing project came a barrage of rocks. Some of them fell among the crowd. Others hit persons in the line of march. Many smashed the windows of the police station. The rock throwing, it was believed, was the work of youngsters; approximately 2,500 children lived in the housing project.

Almost at the same time, an old can was set afire in a parking lot. The line of march began to disintegrate. The police, their heads protected by World War I-type helmets, sallied forth to disperse the crowd. A fire engine, arriving on the scene, was pelted with rocks. As police drove people away from the station, they scattered in all directions.

A few minutes later a nearby liquor store was broken into. Some persons, seeing a caravan of cabs appear at city hall to protest Smith's arrest, interpreted this as evidence that the disturbance had been organized, and generated rumors to that effect.

However, only a few stores were looted. Within a short period of time, the disorder appeared to have run its course.

      *   *   *   *   *

* * * On Saturday, July 15, [Director of Police Dominick] Spina received a report of snipers in a housing project. When he arrived he saw approximately 100 National Guardsmen and police officers crouching behind vehicles, hiding in corners, and lying on the ground around the edge of the courtyard.

Since everything appeared quiet and it was broad daylight, Spina walked directly down the middle of the street. Nothing happened. As he came to the last building of the complex, he heard a shot. All around him the troopers jumped, believing themselves to be under sniper fire. A moment later a young Guardsman ran from behind a building.

The director of police went over and asked him if he had fired the shot. The soldier said "Yes," he had fired to scare a man away from a window; that his orders were to keep everyone away from windows.

Spina said he told the soldier: "Do you know what you just did? You have now created a state of hysteria. Every Guardsman up and down this street and every state policeman and every city policeman that is present thinks that somebody just fired a shot and that it is probably a sniper."

A short time later more "gunshots" were heard. Investigating,

Spina came upon a Puerto Rican sitting on a wall. In reply to a question as to whether he knew "where the firing is coming from?" the man said:

"That's no firing. That's fireworks. If you look up to the fourth floor, you will see the people who are throwing down these cherry bombs."

By this time four truckloads of National Guardsmen had arrived and troopers and policemen were again crouched everywhere looking for a sniper. The director of police remained at the scene for 3 hours, and the only shot fired was the one by the Guardsman.

Nevertheless, at 6 o'clock that evening two columns of National Guardsmen and State troopers were directing mass fire at the Hayes housing project in response to what they believed were snipers. * * *

DETROIT

* * * A spirit of carefree nihilism was taking hold. To riot and destroy appeared more and more to become ends in themselves. Late Sunday afternoon it appeared to one observer that the young people were "dancing amidst the flames."

A Negro plainclothes officer was standing at an intersection when a man threw a Molotov cocktail into a business establishment at the corner. In the heat of the afternoon, fanned by the 20 to 25 miles per hour winds of both Sunday and Monday, the fire reached the home next door within minutes. As residents uselessly sprayed the flames with garden hoses, the fire jumped from roof to roof of adjacent two- and three-story buildings. Within the hour the entire block was in flames. The ninth house in the burning row belonged to the arsonist who had thrown the Molotov cocktail. * * *

*   *   *   *   *

* * * Employed as a private guard, 55-year-old Julius L. Dorsey, a Negro, was standing in front of a market when accosted by two Negro men and a woman. They demanded he permit them to loot the market. He ignored their demands. They began to berate him. He asked a neighbor to call the police. As the argument grew more heated, Dorsey fired three shots from his pistol into the air.

The police radio reported: "Looters—they have rifles." A patrol car driven by a police officer and carrying three National Guardsmen arrived. As the looters fled, the law-enforcement personnel opened fire. When the firing ceased, one person lay dead.

He was Julius L. Dorsey.* * *

*   *   *   *   *

* * * As the riot alternately waxed and waned, one area of the ghetto remained insulated. On the northeast side the residents of

some 150 square blocks inhabited by 21,000 persons had, in 1966, banded together in the Positive Neighborhood Action Committee (PNAC). With professional help from the Institute of Urban Dynamics, they had organized block clubs and made plans for the improvement of the neighborhood.* * *

When the riot broke out, the residents, through the block clubs, were able to organize quickly. Youngsters, agreeing to stay in the neighborhood, participated in detouring traffic. While many persons reportedly sympathized with the idea of a rebellion against the "system" only two small fires were set—one in an empty building.

*   *   *   *   *

* * * According to Lieutenant General Throckmorton and Colonel Bolling, the city, at this time, was saturated with fear. The National Guardsmen were afraid, the citizens were afraid, and the police were afraid. Numerous persons, the majority of them Negroes, were being injured by gunshots of undetermined origin. The general and his staff felt that the major task of the troops was to reduce the fear and restore an air of normalcy.

In order to accomplish this, every effort was made to establish contact and rapport between the troops and the residents. The soldiers—20 percent of whom were Negro—began helping to clean up the streets, collect garbage, and trace persons who had disappeared in the confusion. Residents in the neighborhoods responded with soup and sandwiches for the troops. In areas where the National Guard tried to establish rapport with the citizens, there was a similar response.

NEW BRUNSWICK

* * * A short time later, elements of the crowd—an older and rougher one than the night before—appeared in front of the police station. The participants wanted to see the mayor.

Mayor [Patricia] Sheehan went out onto the steps of the station. Using a bull horn, she talked to the people and asked that she be given an opportunity to correct conditions. The crowd was boisterous. Some persons challenged the mayor. But, finally, the opinion, "She's new! Give her a chance!" prevailed.

A demand was issued by people in the crowd that all persons arrested the previous night be released. Told that this already had been done, the people were suspicious. They asked to be allowed to inspect the jail cells.

It was agreed to permit representatives of the people to look in the cells to satisfy themselves that everyone had been released.

The crowd dispersed. The New Brunswick riot had failed to materialize.

Chapter 2.—Patterns of Disorder

The "typical" riot did not take place. The disorders of 1967 were unusual, irregular, complex, and unpredictable social processes. Like most human events, they did not unfold in an orderly sequence. However, an analysis of our survey information leads to some conclusions about the riot process.

In general:

■ The civil disorders of 1967 involved Negroes acting against local symbols of white American society, authority, and property in Negro neighborhoods—rather than against white persons.

■ Of 164 disorders reported during the first nine months of 1967, eight (5 percent) were major in terms of violence and damage; 33 (20 percent) were serious but not major; 123 (75 percent) were minor and undoubtedly would not have received national attention as riots had the Nation not been sensitized by the more serious outbreaks.

■ In the 75 disorders studied by a Senate subcommittee, 83 deaths were reported. Eighty-two percent of the deaths and more than half the injuries occurred in Newark and Detroit. About 10 percent of the dead and 36 percent of the injured were public employees, primarily law officers and firemen. The overwhelming majority of the persons killed or injured in all the disorders were Negro civilians.

■ Initial damage estimates were greatly exaggerated. In Detroit, newspaper damage estimates at first ranged from $200 to $500 million; the highest recent estimate is $45 million. In Newark, early estimates ranged from $15 to $25 million. A month later damage was estimated at $10.2 million, 80 percent in inventory losses.

In the 24 disorders in 23 cities which we surveyed:

■ The final incident before the outbreak of disorder, and the initial violence itself, generally took place in the evening or at night at a place in which it was normal for many people to be on the streets.

■ Violence usually occurred almost immediately following the occurrence of the final precipitating incident, and then escalated rapidly. With but few exceptions, violence subsided during the day, and flared rapidly again at night. The night-day cycles continued through the early period of the major disorders.

■ Disorder generally began with rock and bottle throwing and window breaking. Once store windows were broken, looting usually followed.

■ Disorder did not erupt as a result of a single "triggering" or "precipitating" incident. Instead, it was generated out of an increasingly disturbed social atmosphere, in which typically a series of tension-heightening incidents over a period of weeks or months became linked in the minds of many in the Negro community with a reservoir of underlying grievances. At some point in the mounting tension, a further incident—in itself often routine or trivial—became the breaking point and the tension spilled over into violence.

■ "Prior" incidents, which increased tensions and ultimately led to violence, were police actions in almost half the cases; police actions were "final" incidents before the outbreak of violence in 12 of the 24 surveyed disorders.

■ No particular control tactic was successful in every situation. The varied effectiveness of control techniques emphasizes the need for advance training, planning, adequate intelligence systems, and knowledge of the ghetto community.

■ Negotiations between Negroes—including young militants as well as older Negro leaders—and white officials concerning "terms of peace" occurred during virtually all the disorders surveyed. In many cases, these negotiations involved discussion of underlying grievances as well as the handling of the disorder by control authorities.

■ The typical rioter was a teenager or young adult, a life-long resident of the city in which he rioted, a high school dropout; he was, nevertheless, somewhat better educated than his nonrioting Negro neighbor, and was usually underemployed or employed in a menial job. He was proud of his race, extremely hostile to both whites and middle-class Negroes and, although informed about politics, highly distrustful of the political system.

A Detroit survey revealed that approximately 11 percent of the total residents of two riot areas admitted participation in the rioting, 20 to 25 percent identified themselves as "bystanders," over 16 percent identified themselves as "counterrioters" who urged rioters to "cool it," and the remaining 48 to 53 percent said they were at home or elsewhere and did not participate. In a survey of Negro males between the ages of 15 and 35 residing in the disturbance area in Newark, about 45 percent identified themselves as rioters, and about 55 percent as "noninvolved."

■ Most rioters were young Negro males. Nearly 53 percent of arrestees were between 15 and 24 years of age; nearly 81 percent between 15 and 35.

■ In Detroit and Newark about 74 percent of the rioters were brought up in the North. In contrast, of the noninvolved, 36 percent in Detroit and 52 percent in Newark were brought up in the North.

■ What the rioters appeared to be seeking was fuller participation in the social order and the material benefits enjoyed by the majority of American citizens. Rather than rejecting the American system, they were anxious to obtain a place for themselves in it.

■ Numerous Negro counterrioters walked the streets urging rioters to "cool it." The typical counterrioter was better educated and had higher income than either the rioter or the noninvolved.

■ The proportion of Negroes in local government was substantially smaller than the Negro proportion of population. Only three of the 20 cities studied had more than one Negro legislator; none had ever had a Negro mayor or city manager. In only four cities did Negroes hold other important policy-making positions or serve as heads of municipal departments.

■ Although almost all cities had some sort of formal grievance mechanism for handling citizen complaints, this typically was regarded by Negroes as ineffective and was generally ignored.

■ Although specific grievances varied from city to city, at least 12 deeply held grievances can be identified and marked into three levels of relative intensity:

First level of intensity:
    1. Police practices.
    2. Unemployment and underemployment.
    3. Inadequate housing.

Second level of intensity:
    4. Inadequate education.
    5. Poor recreation facilities and programs.
    6. Ineffectiveness of the political structure and grievance mechanisms.

Third level of intensity:
    7. Disrespectful white attitudes.
    8. Discriminatory administration of justice.
    9. Inadequacy of Federal programs.
    10. Inadequacy of municipal services.
    11. Discriminatory consumer and credit practices.
    12. Inadequate welfare programs.

■ The results of a three-city survey of various Federal programs—manpower, education, housing, welfare and community action—indicate that, despite substantial expenditures, the number of persons assisted constituted only a fraction of those in need.

The background of disorder is often as complex and difficult to analyze as the disorder itself. But we find that certain general conclusions can be drawn:

■ Social and economic conditions in the riot cities constituted a clear pattern of severe disadvantage for Negroes compared with whites, whether the Negroes lived in the area where the riot took place or outside it. Negroes had completed fewer years of education and fewer had attended high school. Negroes were twice as likely to be unemployed and three times as likely to be in unskilled and service jobs. Negroes averaged 70 percent of the income earned by whites and were more than twice as likely to be living in poverty. Although housing cost Negroes relatively more, they had worse housing—three times as likely to be overcrowded and substandard. When compared to white suburbs, the relative disadvantage was even more pronounced.

A study of the aftermath of disorder leads to disturbing conclusions. We find that, despite the institution of some postriot programs:

■ Little basic change in the conditions underlying the outbreak of disorder has taken place. Actions to ameliorate Negro grievances have been limited and sporadic; with but few exceptions, they have not significantly reduced tensions.
■ In several cities, the principal official response has been to train and equip the police with more sophisticated weapons.
■ In several cities, increasing polarization is evident, with continuing breakdown of interracial communication, and growth of white segregationist or black separatist groups.

Chapter 3.—*Organized Activity*

The President directed the Commission to investigate "to what extent, if any, there has been planning or organization in any of the riots."

To carry out this part of the President's charge, the Commission established a special investigative staff supplementing the field teams that made the general examination of the riots in 23 cities. The unit examined data collected by Federal agencies and congressional committees, including thousands of documents supplied by the Federal Bureau of Investigation, gathered and evaluated information from local and state law enforcement agencies and officials, and conducted its own field investigation in selected cities.

On the basis of all the information collected, the Commission concludes that:

The urban disorders of the summer of 1967 were not caused by, nor were they the consequence of, any organized plan or "conspiracy."

Specifically, the Commission has found no evidence that all or any of the disorders or the incidents that led to them were planned or directed by any organization or group, international, national, or local.

Militant organizations, local and national, and individual agitators, who repeatedly forecast and called for violence, were active in the spring and summer of 1967. We believe that they sought to encourage violence, and that they helped to create an atmosphere that contributed to the outbreak of disorder.

We recognize that the continuation of disorders and the polarization of the races would provide fertile ground for organized exploitation in the future.

Investigations of organized activity are continuing at all levels of government, including committees of Congress. These investigations relate not only to the disorders of 1967 but also to the actions of groups and individuals, particularly in schools and colleges, during this last fall and winter. The Commission has cooperated in these investigations. They should continue.

II / Why Did It Happen?

Chapter 4.—The Basic Causes

In addressing the question "Why did it happen?" we shift our focus from the local to the national scene, from the particular events of the summer of 1967 to the factors within the society at large that created a mood of violence among many urban Negroes.

These factors are complex and interacting; they vary significantly in their effect from city to city and from year to year; and the consequences of one disorder, generating new grievances and new demands, become the causes of the next. Thus was created the "thicket of tension, conflicting evidence, and extreme opinions" cited by the President.

Despite these complexities, certain fundamental matters are clear. Of these, the most fundamental is the racial attitude and behavior of white Americans toward black Americans.

Race prejudice has shaped our history decisively; it now threatens to affect our future.

White racism is essentially responsible for the explosive mixture which has been accumulating in our cities since the end of World War II. Among the ingredients of this mixture are:

■ *Pervasive discrimination and segregation* in employment, education, and housing, which have resulted in the continuing exclusion of great numbers of Negroes from the benefits of economic progress.

■ *Black in-migration and white exodus,* which have produced the massive and growing concentrations of impoverished Negroes in our major cities, creating a growing crisis of deteriorating facilities and services and unmet human needs.

■ *The black ghettos,* where segregation and poverty converge on the young to destroy opportunity and enforce failure. Crime, drug addiction, dependency on welfare, and bitterness and resentment against society in general and white society in particular are the result.

At the same time, most whites and some Negroes outside the ghetto have prospered to a degree unparalleled in the history of civilization. Through television and other media, this affluence has been flaunted before the eyes of the Negro poor and the jobless ghetto youth.

Yet these facts alone cannot be said to have caused the disorders. Recently, other powerful ingredients have begun to catalyze the mixture:

■ *Frustrated hopes* are the residue of the unfulfilled expectations aroused by the great judicial and legislative victories of the civil rights movement and the dramatic struggle for equal rights in the South.

■ *A climate that tends toward approval and encouragement of violence* as a form of protest has been created by white terrorism directed against nonviolent protest; by the open defiance of law and Federal authority by state and local officials resisting desegregation; and by some protest groups engaging in civil disobedience who turn their backs on nonviolence, go beyond the constitutionally protected rights of petition and free assembly, and resort to violence to attempt to compel alteration of laws and policies with which they disagree.

■ *The frustrations of powerlessness* have led some Negroes to the conviction that there is no effective alternative to violence as a means of achieving redress of grievances, and of "moving the system." These frustrations are reflected in alienation and hostility toward the institutions of law and government and the white society which controls them, and in the reach toward racial consciousness and solidarity reflected in the slogan "Black Power."

■ *A new mood has* sprung up among Negroes, particularly among the young, in which self-esteem and enhanced racial pride are replacing apathy and submission to "the system."

■ *The police are not merely a "spark" factor.* To some Negroes police have come to symbolize white power, white racism, and white repression. And the fact is that many police do reflect and express these white attitudes. The atmosphere of hostility and cynicism is reinforced by a widespread belief among Negroes in the existence of police brutality and in a "double standard" of justice and protection—one for Negroes and one for whites.

*   *   *   *   *

To this point, we have attempted only to identify the prime components of the "explosive mixture." In the chapters that follow we seek to analyze them in the perspective of history. Their meaning, however, is clear:

In the summer of 1967, we have seen in our cities a chain reaction of racial violence. If we are heedless, none of us shall escape the consequences.

Chapter 5.—Rejection and Protest: An Historical Sketch

The causes of recent racial disorders are embedded in a tangle of issues and circumstances—social, economic, political, and psychological—which arise out of the historic pattern of Negro-white relations in America.

In this chapter we trace the pattern, identify the recurrent themes of Negro protest and, most importantly, provide a perspective on the protest activities of the present era.

We describe the Negro's experience in America and the development of slavery as an institution. We show his persistent striving for equality in the face of rigidly maintained social, economic, and educational barriers, and repeated mob violence. We portray the ebb and flow of the doctrinal tides—accommodation, separatism, and self-help—and their relationship to the current theme of Black Power. We conclude:

The Black Power advocates of today consciously feel that they are the most militant group in the Negro protest movement. Yet they have retreated from a direct confrontation with American society on the issue of integration and, by preaching separatism, unconsciously function as an accommodation to white racism. Much of their economic program, as well as their interest in Negro history, self-help, racial solidarity and separation, is reminiscent of Booker T. Washington. The rhetoric is different, but the ideas are remarkably similar.

Chapter 6.—*The Formation of the Racial Ghettos* [1]

Throughout the 20th century the Negro population of the United States has been moving steadily from rural areas to urban and from South to North and West. In 1910, 91 percent of the Nation's 9.8 million Negroes lived in the South and only 27 percent of American Negroes lived in cities of 2,500 persons or more. Between 1910 and 1966 the total Negro population more than doubled, reaching 21.5 million, and the number living in metropolitan areas rose more than fivefold (from 2.6 million to 14.8 million). The number outside the South rose elevenfold (from 885,000 to 9.7 million).

Negro migration from the South has resulted from the expectation of thousands of new and highly paid jobs for unskilled workers in the North and the shift to mechanized farming in the South. However, the Negro migration is small when compared to earlier waves of European immigrants. Even between 1960 and 1966, there were 1.8 million immigrants from abroad compared to the 613,000 Negroes who arrived in the North and West from the South.

As a result of the growing number of Negroes in urban areas, natural increase has replaced migration as the primary source of Negro population increase in the cities. Nevertheless, Negro migration from the South will continue unless economic conditions there change dramatically.

Basic data concerning Negro urbanization trends indicate that:

■ Almost all Negro population growth (98 percent from 1950 to

[1] The term "ghetto" as used in this Report refers to an area within a city characterized by poverty and acute social disorganization and inhabited by members of a racial or ethnic group under conditions of involuntary segregation.

1966) is occurring within metropolitan areas, primarily within central cities.[2]

■ The vast majority of white population growth (78 percent from 1960 to 1966) is occurring in suburban portions of metropolitan areas. Since 1960, white central-city population has declined by 1.3 million.

■ As a result, central cities are becoming more heavily Negro while the suburban fringes around them remain almost entirely white.

■ The 12 largest central cities now contain over two-thirds of the Negro population outside the South, and almost one-third of the Negro total in the United States.

Within the cities, Negroes have been excluded from white residential areas through discriminatory practices. Just as significant is the withdrawal of white families from, or their refusal to enter, neighborhoods where Negroes are moving or already residing. About 20 percent of the urban population of the United States changes residence every year. The refusal of whites to move into "changing" areas when vacancies occur means that most vacancies eventually are occupied by Negroes.

The result, according to a recent study, is that in 1960 the average segregation index for 207 of the largest U. S. cities was 86.2. In other words, to create an unsegregated population distribution, an average of over 86 percent of all Negroes would have to change their place of residence within the city.

Chapter 7.—Unemployment, Family Structure, and Social Disorganization

Although there have been gains in Negro income nationally, and a decline in the number of Negroes below the "poverty level," the condition of Negroes in the central city remains in a state of crisis. Between 2 and 2.5 million Negroes—16 to 20 percent of the total Negro population of all central cities—live in squalor and deprivation in ghetto neighborhoods.

Employment is a key problem. It not only controls the present for the Negro American but, in a most profound way, it is creating the future as well. Yet, despite continuing economic growth

[2] A "central city" is the largest city of a standard metropolitan statistical area, that is, a metropolitan area containing at least one city of 50,000 or more inhabitants.

and declining national unemployment rates, the unemployment rate for Negroes in 1967 was more than double that for whites.

Equally important is the undesirable nature of many jobs open to Negroes and other minorities. Negro men are more than three times as likely as white men to be in low-paying, unskilled, or service jobs. This concentration of male Negro employment at the lowest end of the occupational scale is the single most important cause of poverty among Negroes.

In one study of low-income neighborhoods, the "sub-employment rate," including both unemployment and underemployment, was about 33 percent, or 8.8 times greater than the overall unemployment rate for all U.S. workers.

Employment problems, aggravated by the constant arrival of new unemployed migrants, many of them from depressed rural areas, create persistent poverty in the ghetto. In 1966, about 11.9 percent of the Nation's whites and 40.6 percent of its nonwhites were below the poverty level defined by the Social Security Administration (in 1966, $3,335 per year for an urban family of four). Over 40 percent of the nonwhites below the poverty level live in the central cities.

Employment problems have drastic social impact in the ghetto. Men who are chronically unemployed or employed in the lowest status jobs are often unable or unwilling to remain with their families. The handicap imposed on children growing up without fathers in an atmosphere of deprivation is increased as mothers are forced to work to provide support.

The culture of poverty that results from unemployment and family breakup generates a system of ruthless, exploitative relationships within the ghetto. Prostitution, dope addiction, and crime create an environmental "jungle" characterized by personal insecurity and tension. Children growing up under such conditions are likely participants in civil disorder.

Chapter 8.—Conditions of Life in the Racial Ghetto

A striking difference in environment from that of white, middle-class Americans profoundly influences the lives of residents of the ghetto.

Crime rates, consistently higher than in other areas, create a pronounced sense of insecurity. For example, in one city one low-income Negro district had 35 times as many serious crimes against persons as a high-income white district. Unless drastic steps are taken, the crime problems in poverty areas are likely to continue to multiply as the growing youth and rapid urbanization of the population outstrip police resources.

Poor health and sanitation conditions in the ghetto result in higher mortality rates, a higher incidence of major diseases, and lower availability and utilization of medical services. The infant mortality rate for nonwhite babies under the age of 1 month is 58 percent higher than for whites; for 1 to 12 months it is almost three times as high. The level of sanitation in the ghetto is far below that in high-income areas. Garbage collection is often inadequate. Of an estimated 14,000 cases of rat bite in the United States in 1965, most were in ghetto neighborhoods.

Ghetto residents believe they are exploited by local merchants; and evidence substantiates some of these beliefs. A study conducted in one city by the Federal Trade Commission showed that higher prices were charged for goods sold in ghetto stores than in other areas.

Lack of knowledge regarding credit purchasing creates special pitfalls for the disadvantaged. In many states, garnishment practices compound these difficulties by allowing creditors to deprive individuals of their wages without hearing or trial.

Chapter 9.—Comparing the Immigrant and Negro Experience

In this chapter, we address ourselves to a fundamental question that many white Americans are asking: Why have so many Negroes, unlike the European immigrants, been unable to escape from the ghetto and from poverty?

We believe the following factors play a part:

■ *The maturing economy.*—When the European immigrants arrived, they gained an economic foothold by providing the unskilled labor needed by industry. Unlike the immigrant, the Negro migrant found little opportunity in the city. The economy, by then matured, had little use for the unskilled labor he had to offer.

■ *The disability of race.*—The structure of discrimination has stringently narrowed opportunities for the Negro and restricted his prospects. European immigrants suffered from discrimination, but never so pervasively.

■ *Entry into the political system.*—The immigrants usually settled in rapidly growing cities with powerful and expanding political machines, which traded economic advantages for political support. Ward-level grievance machinery, as well as personal representation, enabled the immigrant to make his voice heard and his power felt.

By the time the Negro arrived, these political machines were no longer so powerful or so well equipped to provide jobs or other favors, and in many cases were unwilling to share their remaining influence with Negroes.

■ *Cultural factors.*—Coming from societies with a low standard of living and at a time when job aspirations were low, the immigrants sensed little deprivation in being forced to take the less desirable and poorer paying jobs. Their large and cohesive families contributed to total income. Their vision of the future—one that led to a life outside of the ghetto—provided the incentive necessary to endure the present.

Although Negro men worked as hard as the immigrants, they were unable to support their families. The entrepreneurial opportunities had vanished. As a result of slavery and long periods of unemployment, the Negro family structure had become matriarchal; the males played a secondary and marginal family role—one which offered little compensation for their hard and unrewarding labor. Above all, segregation denied Negroes access to good jobs and the opportunity to leave the ghetto. For them, the future seemed to lead only to a dead end.

Today, whites tend to exaggerate how well and quickly they escaped from poverty. The fact is that immigrants who came from rural backgrounds, as many Negroes do, are only now, after three generations, finally beginning to move into the middle class.

By contrast, Negroes began concentrating in the city less than two generations ago, and under much less favorable conditions. Although some Negroes have escaped poverty, few have been able to escape the urban ghetto.

III / What Can Be Done?

Chapter 10.—*The Community Response*

Our investigation of the 1967 riot cities establishes that virtually every major episode of violence was foreshadowed by an accumulation of unresolved grievances and by widespread dissatisfaction among Negroes with the unwillingness or inability of local government to respond.

Overcoming these conditions is essential for community support of law enforcement and civil order. City governments need new and more vital channels of communication to the residents of the ghetto; they need to improve their capacity to respond effectively to community needs before they become community grievances; and they need to provide opportunity for meaningful involvement of ghetto residents in shaping policies and programs which affect the community.

The Commission recommends that local governments:

■ Develop Neighborhood Action Task Forces as joint community-government efforts through which more effective communication can be achieved, and the delivery of city services to ghetto residents improved.
■ Establish comprehensive grievance-response mechanisms in order to bring all public agencies under public scrutiny.
■ Bring the institutions of local government closer to the people they serve by establishing neighborhood outlets for local, state, and Federal administrative and public service agencies.
■ Expand opportunities for ghetto residents to participate in the formulation of public policy and the implementation of programs affecting them through improved political representation, creation of institutional channels for community action, expansion of legal services, and legislative hearings on ghetto problems.

In this effort, city governments will require State and Federal support.

The Commission recommends:

■ State and Federal financial assistance for mayors and city councils to support the research, consultants, staff, and other resources needed to respond effectively to Federal program initiatives.
■ State cooperation in providing municipalities with the jurisdictional tools needed to deal with their problems; a fuller measure of financial aid to urban areas; and the focusing of the interests of suburban communities on the physical, social, and cultural environment of the central city.

Chapter 11.—Police and the Community

The abrasive relationship between the police and minority communities has been a major—and explosive—source of grievance, tension, and disorder. The blame must be shared by the total society.

The police are faced with demands for increased protection and service in the ghetto. Yet the aggressive patrol practices thought necessary to meet these demands themselves create tension and hostility. The resulting grievances have been further aggravated by the lack of effective mechanisms for handling complaints against the police. Special programs for bettering police-community relations have been instituted, but these alone are not enough. Police administrators, with the guidance of public officials, and the support of the entire community, must take vigorous action to improve law enforcement and to decrease the potential for disorder.

The Commission recommends that city government and police authorities:

■ Review police operations in the ghetto to insure proper conduct by police officers, and eliminate abrasive practices.
■ Provide more adequate police protection to ghetto residents to eliminate their high sense of insecurity and the belief in the existence of a dual standard of law enforcement.
■ Establish fair and effective mechanisms for the redress of grievances against the police and other municipal employees.
■ Develop and adopt policy guidelines to assist officers in making critical decisions in areas where police conduct can create tension.
■ Develop and use innovative programs to insure widespread community support for law enforcement.
■ Recruit more Negroes into the regular police force, and review promotion policies to insure fair promotion for Negro officers.
■ Establish a "Community Service Officer" program to attract ghetto youths between the ages of 17 and 21 to police work. These junior officers would perform duties in ghetto neighborhoods, but would not have full police authority. The Federal Government should provide support equal to 90 percent of the costs of employing CSO's on the basis of one for every 10 regular officers.

Chapter 12.—Control of Disorder

Preserving civil peace is the first responsibility of government. Unless the rule of law prevails, our society will lack not only order but also the environment essential to social and economic progress.

The maintenance of civil order cannot be left to the police

alone. The police need guidance, as well as support, from mayors and other public officials. It is the responsibility of public officials to determine proper police policies, support adequate police standards for personnel and performance, and participate in planning for the control of disorders.

To maintain control of incidents which could lead to disorders, the Commission recommends that local officials:

■ Assign seasoned, well-trained policemen and supervisory officers to patrol ghetto areas, and to respond to disturbances.

■ Develop plans which will quickly muster maximum police manpower and highly qualified senior commanders at the outbreak of disorders.

■ Provide special training in the prevention of disorders, and prepare police for riot control and for operation in units, with adequate command and control and field communication for proper discipline and effectiveness.

■ Develop guidelines governing the use of control equipment and provide alternatives to the use of lethal weapons. Federal support for research in this area is needed.

■ Establish an intelligence system to provide police and other public officials with reliable information that may help to prevent the outbreak of a disorder and to institute effective control measures in the event a riot erupts.

■ Develop continuing contacts with ghetto residents to make use of the forces for order which exist within the community.

■ Establish machinery for neutralizing rumors and enabling Negro leaders and residents to obtain the facts. Create special rumor details to collect, evaluate, and dispel rumors that may lead to a civil disorder.

The Commission believes there is a grave danger that some communities may resort to the indiscriminate and excessive use of force. The harmful effects of over-reaction are incalculable. The Commission condemns moves to equip police departments with mass destruction weapons, such as automatic rifles, machine guns, and tanks. Weapons which are designed to destroy, not to control, have no place in densely populated urban communities.

The Commission recommends that the Federal Government share in the financing of programs for improvement of police forces, both in their normal law enforcement activities as well as in their response to civil disorders.

To assist government authorities in planning their response

to civil disorder, this report contains a Supplement on Control of Disorder. It deals with specific problems encountered during riot control operations, and includes:

■ Assessment of the present capabilities of police, National Guard and Army forces to control major riots, and recommendations for improvement.
■ Recommended means by which the control operations of those forces may be coordinated with the response of other agencies, such as fire departments, and with the community at large.
■ Recommendations for review and revision of Federal, state and local laws needed to provide the framework for control efforts and for the callup and interrelated action of public safety forces.

Chapter 13.—The Administration of Justice Under Emergency Conditions

In many of the cities which experienced disorders last summer, there were recurring breakdowns in the mechanisms for processing, prosecuting, and protecting arrested persons. These resulted mainly from long-standing structural deficiencies in criminal court systems, and from the failure of communities to anticipate and plan for the emergency demands of civil disorders.

In part, because of this, there were few successful prosecutions for serious crimes committed during the riots. In those cities where mass arrests occurred, many arrestees were deprived of basic legal rights.

The Commission recommends that the cities and states:

■ Undertake reform of the lower courts so as to improve the quality of justice rendered under normal conditions.
■ Plan comprehensive measures by which the criminal justice system may be supplemented during civil disorders so that its deliberative functions are protected, and the quality of justice is maintained.

Such emergency plans require broad community participation and dedicated leadership by the bench and bar. They should include:

■ Laws sufficient to deter and punish riot conduct.
■ Additional judges, bail and probation officers, and clerical staff.
■ Arrangements for volunteer lawyers to help prosecutors and to represent riot defendants at every stage of proceedings.

■ Policies to insure proper and individual bail, arraignment, pre-trial, trial, and sentencing proceedings.
■ Adequate emergency processing and detention facilities.

Chapter 14.—Damages: Repair and Compensation

The Commission recommends that the Federal Government:

■ Amend the Federal Disaster Act—which now applies only to natural disasters—to permit Federal emergency food and medical assistance to cities during major civil disorders, and provide long-term economic assistance afterwards.
■ With the cooperation of the states, create incentives for the private insurance industry to provide more adequate property insurance coverage in inner-city areas.

The Commission endorses the report of the National Advisory Panel on Insurance in Riot-Affected Areas: "Meeting the Insurance Crisis of our Cities."

Chapter 15.—The News Media and the Disorders

In his charge to the Commission, the President asked: "What effect do the mass media have on the riots?"

The Commission determined that the answer to the President's question did not lie solely in the performance of the press and broadcasters in reporting the riots. Our analysis had to consider also the overall treatment by the media of the Negro ghettos, community relations, racial attitudes, and poverty—day by day and month by month, year in and year out.

A wide range of interviews with Government officials, law enforcement authorities, media personnel and other citizens, including ghetto residents, as well as a quantitative analysis of riot coverage and a special conference with industry representatives, leads us to conclude that:

■ Despite instances of sensationalism, inaccuracy and distortion, newspapers, radio and television tried on the whole to give a balanced, factual account of the 1967 disorders.
■ Elements of the news media failed to portray accurately the scale and character of the violence that occurred last summer. The overall effect was, we believe, an exaggeration of both mood and event.
■ Important segments of the media failed to report adequately on

the causes and consequences of civil disorders and on the underlying problems of race relations. They have not communicated to the majority of their audience—which is white—a sense of the degradation, misery, and hopelessness of life in the ghetto.

These failings must be corrected, and the improvement must come from within the industry. Freedom of the press is not the issue. Any effort to impose governmental restrictions would be inconsistent with fundamental constitutional precepts.

We have seen evidence that the news media are becoming aware of and concerned about their performance in their field. As that concern grows, coverage will improve. But much more must be done, and it must be done soon.

The Commission recommends that the media:

■ Expand coverage of the Negro community and of race problems through permanent assignment of reporters familiar with urban and racial affairs, and through establishment of more and better links with the Negro community.

■ Integrate Negroes and Negro activities into all aspects of coverage and content, including newspaper articles and television programing. The news media must publish newspapers and produce programs that recognize the existence and activities of Negroes as a group within the community and as a part of the larger community.

■ Recruit more Negroes into journalism and broadcasting and promote those who are qualified to positions of significant responsibility. Recruitment should begin in high schools and continue through college; where necessary, aid for training should be provided.

■ Improve coordination with police in reporting riot news through advance planning, and cooperate with the police in the designation of police information officers, establishment of information centers, and development of mutually acceptable guidelines for riot reporting and the conduct of media personnel.

■ Accelerate efforts to insure accurate and responsible reporting of riot and racial news, through adoption by all news-gathering organizations of stringent internal staff guidelines.

■ Cooperate in the establishment of a privately organized and funded Institute of Urban Communications to train and educate journalists in urban affairs, recruit and train more Negro journalists, develop methods for improving police-press relations, review coverage of riots and racial issues, and support continuing research in the urban field.

Chapter 16.—The Future of the Cities

By 1985, the Negro population in central cities is expected to increase by 68 percent to approximately 20.3 million. Coupled with the continued exodus of white families to the suburbs, this growth will produce majority Negro populations in many of the Nation's largest cities.

The future of these cities, and of their burgeoning Negro populations, is grim. Most new employment opportunities are being created in suburbs and outlying areas. This trend will continue unless important changes in public policy are made.

In prospect, therefore, is further deterioration of already inadequate municipal tax bases in the face of increasing demands for public services, and continuing unemployment and poverty among urban Negro population:

Three choices are open to the Nation:

■ We can maintain present policies, continuing both the proportion of the Nation's resources now allocated to programs for the unemployed and the disadvantaged, and the inadequate and failing effort to achieve an integrated society.

■ We can adopt a policy of "enrichment" aimed at improving dramatically the quality of ghetto life while abandoning integration as a goal.

■ We can pursue integration by combining ghetto "enrichment" with policies which will encourage Negro movement out of central-city areas.

The first choice, continuance of present policies, has ominous consequences for our society. The share of the Nation's resources now allocated to programs for the disadvantaged is insufficient to arrest the deterioration of life in central-city ghettos. Under such conditions, a rising proportion of Negroes may come to see in the deprivation and segregation they experience, a justification for violent protest, or for extending support to now isolated extremists who advocate civil disruption. Large-scale and continuing violence could result, followed by white retaliation, and, ultimately, the separation of the two communities in a garrison state.

Even if violence does not occur, the consequences are unacceptable. Development of a racially integrated society, extraordinarily difficult today, will be virtually impossible when the present black central-city population of 12.1 million has grown to almost 21 million.

To continue present policies is to make permanent the division of our country into two societies: one, largely Negro and poor, located in the central cities; the other, predominantly white and affluent, located in the suburbs and in outlying areas.

The second choice, ghetto enrichment coupled with abandonment of integration, is also unacceptable. It is another way of choosing a permanently divided country. Moreover, equality cannot be achieved under conditions of nearly complete separation. In a country where the economy, and particularly the resources of employment, are predominantly white, a policy of separation can only relegate Negroes to a permanently inferior economic status.

We believe that the only possible choice for America is the third—a policy which combines ghetto enrichment with programs designed to encourage integration of substantial numbers of Negroes into the society outside the ghetto.

Enrichment must be an important adjunct to integration, for no matter how ambitious or energetic the program, few Negroes now living in central cities can be quickly integrated. In the meantime, large-scale improvement in the quality of ghetto life is essential.

But this can be no more than an interim strategy. Programs must be developed which will permit substantial Negro movement out of the ghettos. The primary goal must be a single society, in which every citizen will be free to live and work according to his capabilities and desires, not his color.

Chapter 17.—Recommendations for National Action

INTRODUCTION

No American—white or black—can escape the consequences of the continuing social and economic decay of our major cities.

Only a commitment to national action on an unprecedented scale can shape a future compatible with the historic ideals of American society.

The great productivity of our economy, and a Federal revenue system which is highly responsive to economic growth, can provide the resources.

The major need is to generate new will—the will to tax ourselves to the extent necessary to meet the vital needs of the Nation.

We have set forth goals and proposed strategies to reach those goals. We discuss and recommend programs not to commit each of us to specific parts of such programs, but to illustrate the type and dimension of action needed.

The major goal is the creation of a true union—a single society and a single American identity. Toward that goal, we propose the following objectives for national action:

■ Opening up opportunities to those who are restricted by racial segregation and discrimination, and eliminating all barriers to their choice of jobs, education, and housing.

■ Removing the frustration of powerlessness among the disadvantaged by providing the means for them to deal with the problems that affect their own lives and by increasing the capacity of our public and private institutions to respond to these problems.

■ Increasing communication across racial lines to destroy stereotypes, halt polarization, end distrust and hostility, and create common ground for efforts toward public order and social justice.

EMPLOYMENT

Pervasive unemployment and underemployment are the most persistent and serious grievances in minority areas. They are inextricably linked to the problem of civil disorder.

Despite growing Federal expenditures for manpower develop ment and training programs, and sustained general economic prosperity and increasing demands for skilled workers, about 2 million—white and nonwhite—are permanently unemployed. About 10 million are underemployed, of whom 6.5 million work full time for wages below the poverty line.

The 500,000 "hard-core" unemployed in the central cities who lack a basic education and are unable to hold a steady job are made up in large part of Negro males between the ages of 18 and 25. In the riot cities which we surveyed, Negroes were three times as likely as whites to hold unskilled jobs, which are often part time, seasonal, low paying and "dead end."

Negro males between the ages of 15 and 25 predominated among the rioters. More than 20 percent of the rioters were unemployed, and many who were employed held intermittent, low status, unskilled jobs which they regarded as below their education and ability.

The Commission recommends that the Federal Government:

■ Undertake joint efforts with cities and states to consolidate existing manpower programs to avoid fragmentation and duplication.
■ Take immediate action to create 2 million new jobs over the next 3 years—1 million in the public sector and 1 million in the private sector—to absorb the hard-core unemployed and materially reduce the level of underemployment for all workers, black and white. We propose 250,000 public sector and 300,000 private sector jobs in the first year.
■ Provide on-the-job training by both public and private employers with reimbursement to private employers for the extra costs of training the hard-core unemployed, by contract or by tax credits.
■ Provide tax and other incentives to investment in rural as well as urban poverty areas in order to offer to the rural poor an alternative to migration to urban centers.
■ Take new and vigorous action to remove artificial barriers to employment and promotion, including not only racial discrimination but, in certain cases, arrest records or lack of a high school diploma. Strengthen those agencies such as the Equal Employment Opportunity Commission, charged with eliminating discriminatory practices, and provide full support for Title VI of the 1964 Civil Rights Act allowing Federal grant-in-aid funds to be withheld from activities which discriminate on grounds of color or race.

The Commission commends the recent public commitment of the National Council of the Building and Construction Trakes Unions, AFL-CIO, to encourage and recruit Negro membership in apprenticeship programs. This commitment should be intensified and implemented.

EDUCATION

Education in a democratic society must equip children to develop their potential and to participate fully in American life. For the community at large, the schools have discharged this responsibility well. But for many minorities, and particularly for the children of the ghetto, the schools have failed to provide the educational experience which could overcome the effects of discrimination and deprivation.

This failure is one of the persistent sources of grievance and resentment within the Negro community. The hostility of Negro parents and students toward the school system is generating increased conflict and causing disruption within many city school districts. But the most dramatic evidence of the relationship between educational practices and civil disorders lies in the high incidence of riot participation by ghetto youth who have not completed high school.

The bleak record of public education for ghetto children is growing worse. In the critical skills—verbal and reading ability —Negro students are falling further behind whites with each year of school completed. The high unemployment and under-employment rate for Negro youth is evidence, in part, of the growing educational crisis.

We support integration as the priority education strategy; it is essential to the future of American society. In this last summer's disorders we have seen the consequences of racial isolation at all levels, and of attitudes toward race, on both sides, produced by three centuries of myth, ignorance, and bias. It is indispensable that opportunities for interaction between the races be expanded.

We recognize that the growing dominance of pupils from disadvantaged minorities in city school populations will not soon be reversed. No matter how great the effort toward desegregation, many children of the ghetto will not, within their school careers, attend integrated schools.

If existing disadvantages are not to be perpetuated, we must drastically improve the quality of ghetto education. Equality of results with all-white schools must be the goal.

To implement these strategies, the Commission recommends:

■ Sharply increased efforts to eliminate de facto segregation in our schools through substantial federal aid to school systems seeking to desegregate either within the system or in cooperation with neighboring school systems.

■ Elimination of racial discrimination in Northern as well as Southern schools by vigorous application of Title VI of the Civil Rights Act of 1964.

■ Extension of quality early childhood education to every disadvantaged child in the country.

■ Efforts to improve dramatically schools serving disadvantaged children through substantial federal funding of year-round quality compensatory education programs, improved teaching, and expanded experimentation and research.

■ Elimination of illiteracy through greater federal support for adult basic education.

■ Enlarged opportunities for parent and community participation in the public schools.

■ Reoriented vocational education emphasizing work-experience training and the involvement of business and industry.

■ Expanded opportunities for higher education through increased federal assistance to disadvantaged students.

■ Revision of state aid formulas to assure more per student aid to districts having a high proportion of disadvantaged school age children.

THE WELFARE SYSTEM

Our present system of public welfare is designed to save money instead of people, and tragically ends up doing neither. This system has two critical deficiencies:

First, it excludes large numbers of persons who are in great need, and who, if provided a decent level of support, might be able to become more productive and self-sufficient. No Federal funds are available for millions of unemployed and under-employed men and women who are needy but neither aged, handicapped nor the parents of minor children.

Second, for those included, the system provides assistance well below the minimum necessary for a decent level of exist-ence, and imposes restrictions that encourage continued de-pendency on welfare and undermine self-respect.

A welter of statutory requirements and administrative prac-tices and regulations operate to remind recipients that they are considered untrustworthy, promiscuous, and lazy. Residence requirements prevent assistance to people in need who are newly arrived in the state. Searches of recipients' homes violate privacy. Inadequate social services compound the problems.

The Commission recommends that the Federal Government, acting with state and local governments where necessary, reform the existing welfare system to:

■ Establish, for recipients in existing welfare categories, uniform national standards of assistance at least as high as the annual "pov-erty level" of income, now set by the Social Security Administration at $3,335 per year for an urban family of four.

■ Require that all states receiving Federal welfare contributions participate in the Aid to Families with Dependent Children-Unemployed Parents Program (AFDC–UP) that permits assistance to families with both father and mother in the home, thus aiding the family while it is still intact.

■ Bear a substantially greater portion of all welfare costs—at least 90 percent of total payments.

■ Increase incentives for seeking employment and job training, but remove restrictions recently enacted by the Congress that would compel mothers of young children to work.

■ Provide more adequate social services through neighborhood centers and family-planning program.

■ Remove the freeze placed by the 1967 welfare amendments on the percentage of children in a State that can be covered by Federal assistance.

■ Eliminate residence requirements.

As a long-range goal, the Commission recommends that the Federal Government seek to develop a national system of income supplementation based strictly on need with two broad and basic purposes:

■ To provide, for those who can work or who do work, any necessary supplements in such a way as to develop incentives for fuller employment.

■ To provide, for those who cannot work and for mothers who decide to remain with their children, a minimum standard of decent living, and to aid in saving children from the prison of poverty that has held their parents.

A broad system of supplementation would involve substantially greater Federal expenditures than anything now contemplated. The cost will range widely depending on the standard of need accepted as the "basic allowance" to individuals and families, and on the rate at which additional income above this level is taxed. Yet if the deepening cycle of poverty and dependence on welfare can be broken, if the children of the poor can be given the opportunity to scale the wall that now separates them from the rest of society, the return on this investment will be great indeed.

HOUSING

After more than three decades of fragmented and grossly underfunded Federal housing programs, nearly 6 million substandard housing units remain occupied in the United States.

The housing problem is particularly acute in the minority ghettos. Nearly two-thirds of all nonwhite families living in the central cities today live in neighborhoods marked by substandard housing and general urban blight. Two major factors are responsible:

First: Many ghetto residents simply cannot pay the rent necessary to support decent housing. In Detroit, for example, over 40 percent of the nonwhite-occupied units in 1960 required rent of over 35 percent of the tenants' income.

Second: Discrimination prevents access to many nonslum areas, particularly the suburbs, where good housing exists. In addition, by creating a "back pressure" in the racial ghettos, it makes it possible for landlords to break up apartments for denser occupancy, and keeps prices and rents of deteriorated ghetto housing higher than they would be in a truly free market.

To date, Federal programs have been able to do comparatively little to provide housing for the disadvantaged. In the 31-year history of subsidized Federal housing, only about 800,000 units have been constructed, with recent production averaging about 50,000 units a year. By comparison, over a period only 3 years longer, FHA insurance guarantees have made possible the construction of over 10 million middle and upper income units.

Two points are fundamental to the Commission's recommendations:

First: Federal housing programs must be given a new thrust aimed at overcoming the prevailing patterns of racial segregation. If this is not done, those programs will continue to concentrate the most impoverished and dependent segments of the population into the central-city ghettos where there is already a critical gap between the needs of the population and the public resources to deal with them.

Second: the private sector must be brought into the production and financing of low- and moderate-rental housing to supply the capabilities and capital necessary to meet the housing needs of the Nation.

The Commission recommends that the Federal Government:

■ Enact a comprehensive and enforceable Federal open-housing law to cover the sale or rental of all housing, including single-family homes.
■ Reorient Federal housing programs to place more low- and moderate-income housing outside of ghetto areas.
■ Bring within the reach of low- and moderate-income families within the next 5 years 6 million new and existing units of decent housing, beginning with 600,000 units in the next year.

To reach this goal we recommend:

■ Expansion and modification of the rent supplement program to permit use of supplements for existing housing, thus greatly increasing the reach of the program.

■ Expansion and modification of the below-market interest rate program to enlarge the interest subsidy to all sponsors, provide interest-free loans to nonprofit sponsors to cover preconstruction costs, and permit sale of projects to nonprofit corporations, co-operatives, or condominiums.

■ Creation of an ownership supplement program similar to present rent supplements, to make home ownership possible for low-income families.

■ Federal writedown of interest rates on loans to private builders constructing moderate-rent housing.

■ Expansion of the public housing program, with emphasis on small units on scattered sites, and leasing and "turnkey" programs.

■ Expansion of the Model Cities program.

■ Expansion and reorientation of the urban renewal program to give priority to projects directly assisting low-income households to obtain adequate housing.

Conclusion

One of the first witnesses to be invited to appear before this Commission was Dr. Kenneth B. Clark, a distinguished and perceptive scholar. Referring to the reports of earlier riot commissions, he said:

I read the report * * * of the 1919 riot in Chicago, and it is as if I were reading the report of the investigating committee on the Harlem riot of '35, the report of the investigating committee on the Harlem riot of '43, the report of the McCone Commission on the Watts riot.

I must again in candor say to you members of this Commission— it is a kind of Alice in Wonderland—with the same moving picture reshown over and over again, the same analysis, the same recommendations, and the same inaction.

These words come to our minds as we conclude this report.

We have provided an honest beginning. We have learned much. But we have uncovered no startling truths, no unique insights, no simple solutions. The destruction and the bitterness of racial disorder, the harsh polemics of black revolt and white repression have been seen and heard before in this country.

It is time now to end the destruction and the violence, not only in the streets of the ghetto but in the lives of people.

THE FRUSTRATIONS OF
URBAN PLANNING

LEWIS MUMFORD

Noted urbanologist Lewis Mumford critically discusses city problems, governmental approaches to metropolitan complexity, and various modes of urban planning.

Though it is a privilege to appear before this subcommittee to explore subjects of such vital importance as those you have under review, . . . it is not a privilege I sought. On the contrary, I have undertaken this task with great reluctance, since the conclusions I have come to as a student of urbanism, regionalism, and technology in the course of a half century of study do not lend themselves easily to a summary statement, still less to a series of pat recommendations.

What has brought me here, despite this reluctance, is merely a sense of duty as an American citizen, one who has actively promoted regional development and "urban renewal"—Heaven help me, I invented the word!—and yet is sufficiently detached from the responsibilities of office and the restrictive discipline of specialized research to be free to bring before you certain fundamental issues that as yet have scarcely been opened up, much less defined, discussed, and debated.

Do not, I beg, misread my occupational qualifications. By profession, I am a writer—not an architect, an engineer, or a

From "Statement of Lewis Mumford," in *Federal Role in Urban Affairs* (Hearings before the Subcommittee on Executive Reorganization of the Committee on Government Operations, United States Senate, April 21, 1967), Part 17, pp. 3595–3607.

city planner; and though I have been a professor of city and regional planning at the University of Pennsylvania I have no wish to appear before you as an urban specialist, an expert, an authority. But please do not read any false humility into this statement. All the colossal mistakes that have been made during the last quarter century in urban renewal, highway building, transportation, land use, and recreation, have been made by highly qualified experts and specialists—and as regards planning, I should blush to be found in their company.

While I have prudently reminded you of my limitations, I nevertheless have one genuine qualification, unfortunately still a rare one, that of a generalist, equally at home in many different areas of life and thought. My specialty is that of bringing the scattered specialisms together, to form an overall pattern that the specialist, precisely because of his overconcentration on one small section of existence, fatally overlooks or deliberately ignores. Emerson described his ideal of the American scholar as "man thinking"; and it is only insofar as I have been a scholar in this special sense, dedicated to seeing life steadily and seeing it whole, that I venture to appear before you.

I shall not waste time listing any other qualifications I may have; for what they are worth, you will find them in any "Who's Who" or biographical dictionary. But I must lay the ground for the constructive criticism I shall eventually make by briefly summarizing the experience that has led me to my present views.

While still at college—in fact, when only 18—I came under the influence of the Scots thinker, Prof. Patrick Geddes, who shares with Ebenezer Howard, Raymond Unwin, and our own Frederick Law Olmsted, Sr., the distinction not merely of reviving the art of town planning, but of awakening fresh interest in the nature and function of cities. Though there are now scores of books and college courses available on every aspect of urbanism, half a century ago you could almost count them on the fingers of one hand.

As a disciple of Geddes, I learned to study cities and regions at first hand, living in them, working in them, not least surveying every part of them on foot: not only my native city, New York, but many others, large and small—Philadelphia, Pittsburgh, Boston, London, Edinburgh, Honolulu, Berkeley, Geneva—not to speak of smaller places like Palo Alto, Middletown,

Hanover, and the Dutchess County hamlet of a dozen houses where I find the seclusion necessary for the writing of my books.

More than five-sevenths of my life has been spent in cities, mostly in great metropolises; and when in "The Culture of Cities," in 1938, I painted a picture of the prospective disintegration of megalopolis, my experience and my historic researches enabled me to anticipate by 30 years the conditions that you are now belatedly trying to cope with; for the formidable disorders I described in detail were already visible elsewhere, in London and Paris since the 18th century, and had become chronic in every congested urban center for the whole last century. No small part of this ugly urban barbarization has been due to sheer congestion: a diagnosis now confirmed by scientific experiments with rats—for, when they are placed in equally congested quarters, they exhibit the same symptoms of stress, alienation, hostility, sexual perversion, parental incompetence, and rabid violence that we now find in megalopolis.

My interest in cities brought me, as early as 1923, into close relations with a group of men whose human vision and practical judgment, had they been heeded in any large way, could have transformed American housing and planning. If their basic proposals had been carried further, we might have averted the grim conditions you now face.

In the early twenties this group incorporated itself into the Regional Planning Association of America, a small body, with never over 20 members, not to be confused with a quite different group, with a more conventional metropolitan approach, indeed a diametrically opposite one, the Regional Plan Association of New York. Such fresh, humanly significant ideas as came into planning and housing during the twenties and thirties was in no small measure the work of these two groups.

In urban planning, the two leaders of my own group were Clarence Stein and Henry Wright. They pioneered in the planning of a highly successful housing project for mixed-income families, Sunnyside Gardens, in Long Island City. And out of that experiment, with the help of a socially responsible realtor of considerable wealth, Alexander Bing, grew an even more important experiment, the proposed new town of Radburn, N.J. Though Radburn's career as a new town was abruptly cut short by the depression, it made a contribution in design that has had a worldwide influence.

Radburn was conceived originally as an experimental model under private enterprise for a series of new towns; and some of its principles were, in fact, partly embodied in the abortive Greenbelt towns, which unfortunately never became real towns, built by the Federal Government between 1935 and 1940. During the next 25 years Clarence Stein and I kept alive, almost singlehandedly, the fundamental ideas of the new towns movement.

We held that further increase of population in already congested centers should be met, not by intensifying the congestion in high-rise buildings, not by adding endless acres and square miles of suburbs, with ever-longer and more time-wasting journeys to work, but by building new planned communities on a better model; many sided, balanced, self-maintaining: in a word, to use your chairman's excellent term, "competent." We conceived that these communities, fully equipped for industry, business, social life, and culture, would be linked together with the central metropolis in a new kind of urban pattern. This pattern would permanently preserve the countryside for farming and recreation, and bring together the neighborhood, the city, and the metropolis in a new constellation, which we called the regional city.

Not merely was I an intellectual associate of Stein and Wright in these activities, but I was equally a close colleague of Benton MacKaye, another member of our group; he who is best known to you, perhaps, as the shrewd Yankee whose activities as forester, conservationist, and geotect led to his projecting the Appalachian Trail. Unlike most bold dreamers, he has lived to see his dream completely realized through the voluntary cooperation of local groups, without any Government aid whatever.

Like myself, MacKaye had served as researcher for the New York State Housing and Regional Planning Commission, of which Stein was chairman and Henry Wright planning adviser. The hearings and reports of that commission played a decisive part in the whole movement for government action, State and Federal, to build and subsidize adequate housing for the lower income groups; and so laid the foundation for the large-scale

Federal program that was begun during the depression and expanded after the Second World War.

The final report of Stein's commission, "A Regional Plan for the State of New York," was so farsighted and far reaching that, some 40 years later, it still served as the basis for a similar project by Governor Rockefeller's Office of Regional Development—though unfortunately he has not seen fit to follow it up.

In 1925 MacKaye and I edited the regional planning number of the Survey Graphic; the first time in which the ideas of regionalism and regional planning were set forth and treated as the essential key to anything fit to be called sound urban or metropolitan development. That number demonstrated the approaching strangulation of life in the great cities, dying because of that cancerous overgrowth and congestion which many highly esteemed experts, like Jane Jacobs and Charles Abrams, mistakenly confuse with economic dynamism and social vitality. But we also showed the importance of the electricity grid, the radio, and the motor highway in making possible a more balanced population pattern, distributed over a much wider area than the biggest metropolis, preserving the essential resources of the countryside, in a permanent green matrix, instead of wiping out every natural advantage by affluent suburban and slummy subsuburban expansion and sprawl.

One more point, and this biographic preface is done. Though MacKaye had laid down the main outlines for an effective regional approach to metropolitan problems, in his 1928 book, "The New Exploration"—a classic introduction now republished as a University of Illinois paperback—he added a new and important project in 1931—his plan for the townless highway. His article on this subject, which appeared in Harper's, was the very first one in which all the main elements of a new type of motor highway, which we now call the throughway or expressway, were put together. In the Appalachian Trail and the townless highway, this spiritual descendent of Thoreau effectually visualized the transportation backbone of a better environment and proved how much more practical he was than the "practical" specialists, who keep so closely to their familiar mole runs that they remain blind and baffled even when, by accident, they come above ground to the light.

Now, why, you must be asking yourself, have I used up your time in rehearsing these past efforts at planning? Not, certainly, to claim priority over those who are advancing many of these same ideas now, as if for the first time; such a claim would be too picayune for words. And certainly not to boast of our successes, though when the Tennessee Valley project was first put forward by President Roosevelt—whom, when Governor, we had chosen as chief speaker for our regional planning conference at the University of Virginia in 1931—we momentarily exulted in the thought that our 10 years of preparatory thinking and experimenting had not been in vain.

No; my reason for telling you these things is due to the realization that every advance we projected or even succeeded in establishing eventually came to grief; sometimes, like the regional plan for the State of New York, by stupid indifference and neglect; but even more, I regret to say, by being taken up on a national scale, with all the force, the authority, and the financial resources supplied by the Federal Government. In coming to life, our good ideas were done to death, caricatured or permanently disfigured by forces—technological, bureaucratic, financial, above all perhaps financial—that we had failed sufficiently to reckon with.

Certainly, no group worked harder than we did to establish governmental responsibility, State and Federal, for producing and subsidizing good housing for the lower income groups. But what was the result? Federal housing had hardly gotten underway before the financial bureaucratic process and the bulldozer mind had wiped out our new concepts for a better urban community, and produced those nightmares of urban anonymity and human desolation that dominate the skyline today—those high-rise housing developments in whose design only financial and mechanical calculations have played a part.

Everything that Jane Jacobs has said in condemnation of these sterile—indeed, humanly hostile—projects, is true. But, I hasten to add, they would not be any better if, on her pet formula, the designers had multiplied the number of streets and lined them with shops, and thus produced even more stifling and strangulating forms of congestion. The rapes, the robberies, the destructive delinquencies, the ever-threatening violence, for which she naively believes she has found a simple planning antidote, would still be there, since these are symptoms, not just of bad planning, or even of poverty, but of a radically deficient and depleted mode of life, a life from which both the most destitute slum-dwellers and the most affluent suburbanites equally, though in different ways, now suffer. There is no planning cure for this machine-centered existence which produces only psychotic stresses, meaningless "happenings," and murderous fantasies of revenge.

On the basis of this wholesale reversal of our good intentions I must ask you: Is there any reason to suppose that a massive effort by the Federal Government to wipe out the existing slums—however we may define them—will succeed any better than those we have been building on a large scale all over the country since 1947?

Is there any plausible reason for expecting any better results from wholesale Government intervention, under our present auspices, no matter how much money you are prepared to spend? If you embark on such a program without asking far more fundamental questions about the reasons for our past failures, and if you fail to set up more human goals than those which our expanding economy now pursues, you will be throwing public money down the drain. And worse: in the course of doing this, you will bring about even more villainous conditions than those which your are trying to correct; for you will wipe out on a greater scale than ever what is left of neighborly life, social cooperation, and human identity in our already depressed and congested urban areas. If you want to know the human reactions to this, read Studs Terkel's recent eye-opening book, "Division Street." Let me respectfully suggest unless we challenge the current money-oriented, computer-directed American way of life, all we can soberly expect is more and more of worse and worse.

Or take another failure: what happened to MacKaye's conception of the townless highway. When he put forth this proposal, he sought to apply to the motorway efficient transportation principles, like that of an independent right-of-way, with access only at reserved intervals, that had long been incorporated in the railroad line. He did not for a moment anticipate that, in the working out of this system, the extravagant Federal subsidies would incite the highway engineers to repeat all the dismal planning errors committed originally by the railroad engineers—such as invading the center of the city and pre-empting its most valuable urban land for eight-lane highways and parking lots and garages.

Unfortunately, the highway engineers took over every feature of MacKaye's plan except the most important one: that it should be "townless"; that is, that it should bypass every urban center, small or big. Indeed, with all the insolence of an overcoddled public authority, they have not merely become specialists in despoiling beautiful landscapes and violating land dedicated to national and local parks, but they actively welcome further urban congestion and blight as the best possible justification for still more highway and bridge and tunnel building. When the city does not create sufficient congestion, these authorities bring it about themselves, as the Port of New York Authority proposes with its 110-story buildings for the World Trade Center.

As a result, these incontinent erections and compulsive congestions are steadily breaking down variety and continuity in urban life, wiping out centers for human contacts, obstructing the social opportunities, and undermining further the intimate face-to-face cooperations that the city exists to promote.

There is no use in your voting huge sums for housing and so-called urban renewal while a large part of the funds you have allotted to highway building are still being misused for wholesale urban destruction.

I have only touched, necessarily in a sketchy way, on the dismaying results that followed from carrying out, through Federal agencies and Federal funds, some of the very policies that the regional planning association and its various active members not merely advocated but participated in. But what of our other contributions—those that were only half carried out, or not carried out at all?

There I have to expose another kind of failure, equally serious. In the 1930's the ideas of regional planning seemed about to bear promising fruit not only in the founding of the TVA, with its combination of electrification, improved soil management and farming, and general regional rehabilitation, but in the founding of the National Resources Planning Board, later called the National Resources Committee, which encouraged each State to prepare regional plans, based on more sufficient knowledge, for the better development of its own resources. From the beginning, unfortunately, compartmentalized habits of thinking kept regional planning entirely separate from urban planning—which is an absurdity. But if the planning boards had not been disbanded, the very necessities of economic and social life would eventually have brought them together.

Unfortunately, your predecessors in the Congress developed an almost pathological fear of planning, and hated the very word; though no great enterprise of any kind, as A.T. & T. or General Electric or DuPont would tell you, can be carried on without long-term planning of the most detailed sort, carefully coordinated, and constantly corrected in the light of new conditions and fresh appraisals—what is now, in the jargon of the computer specialists, called feedback.

The result of this rejection of planning was not, of course, that we have done away with planning: the result is rather that our country has been the victim of the worst kind of planning possible, that in which each governmental bureau or division, each industry or business, thinks only of its own needs and aims, and tries to seize, for its own narrow purposes, the largest share of the budget, the biggest staff, the greatest amount of power—or, in business, the greatest possible financial return. At the highway conference which I attended, held by the Connecticut General Life Insurance Co. in 1957, it turned out that the Federal head of housing and the Federal head of highway building had never met, still less exchanged views, until that occasion, though neither could possibly do his work intelligently without reference to the other.

If the surveys and inventories of resources undertaken by the regional planning boards in many States had been continued over the last quarter century, you would not only have an adequate local basis for highway planning, which has been done, so far, with callous indifference to local needs and with no effort to establish a better regional pattern, but you would likewise have a good notion—as you do not in the least have now—of where the new housing, the new neighborhoods, the new towns should be built. I fear that you may be taking for granted the notion that the foul and crowded slums of the past should be replaced by more orderly, more sanitary housing, at equally congested densities, on the same sites. That assumption needs critical reconsideration. It is far from obvious.

Had the State planning agencies supplied the necessary feedback they might have kept our successive housing authorities from making the errors about the location and density of housing that already have been made—or worse ones you may now be tempted to make on an even larger scale. If active regional planning boards had been created and maintained, our country would have produced a large corps of trained minds, architects, planners, geotects, regional surveyors, who would now be able to do the job without too much direction from Washington, because they would have accumulated an immense amount of detailed first hand knowledge of the basic natural and human resources. That knowledge cannot be derived solely from statistics, is not transferable to computers, and is not achievable by any crash programs for education.

May I suggest, then, that if you are not to do far more damage than good in establishing a new housing policy, you must first prepare to rebuild the effective organs for regional planning and regional government, on a State and interstate basis. This will also mean assembling, in the eight or 10 major regions of the country, the Federal agencies that will or should, at various points, participate in this program. The Regional Development Council of America, a group that after 1945 continued the older Regional Plan Association, proposed such a permanent decentralization of related Federal activities in 1950, but Mr. Stein could get no one in Washington to take this proposal seriously.

Surely it is time that there was a general realization of the fact that we must deliberately contrive a new urban pattern; one which will more effectively mobilize the immense resources of our great metropolises without accepting the intolerable congestion that has driven increasing numbers of people to seek—at whatever sacrifices of time and social opportunity—at least a temporary breathing space in less congested urban areas. The new form of the city must be conceived on a regional scale, not subordinated to a single dominant center, but as a network of cities of different forms and sizes, set in the midst of publicly protected open spaces permanently dedicated to agriculture and recreation. In such a regional scheme the great metropolises would be only "prima inter pares"—the first among equals.

This is the organic type of city that the technology of our time, the electric grid, the telephone, the radio, television, fast transportation, information storage and transmission, has made possible. A handful of planners, notably Christopher Tunnard, has seen the implications of this new scale in urban planning, but most of our planning authorities still remain, like a wornout scratched phonograph record, with the needle stuck in the old metropolitan groove. Many people, since the publication of Jean Gottmann's monumental survey, have tried to take comfort in the thought that the present disorder and disintegrating urban mass, which Gottmann has popularized as megalopolis, is in fact the modern form of the city, new, dynamic, and inevitable, whether we like it or not.

That is a slushy idea, worthy only of a Marshall McLuhan or a Timothy Leary. You might say of this sprawling megalopolitan nonentity, this "anticity," to use McLuhan's go-go terminology—that "the mess is the message." And the more massive the mess, the more muddled the message.

Now, I have had to explain to myself how it came that the ideas we put forward during the last half century often proved politically and financially acceptable, but only at the price of being sterilized, dehumanized, and degraded. The full explanation dawned on me only recently in the course of an analysis I have been making, in a book soon to be published, on the basic assumptions and goals that have governed all large-scale technology, since the pyramid age in Egypt some 5,000 years ago.

From the earliest stages of civilization on, as I read the evidence, the most striking advances in mass technology have been the outcome of centralized organizations, deliberately expanding power in every form—mechanical power, political power, military power, financial power, and not least the scientific power of accurate analysis and prediction—to achieve control, the key word is control, over both the natural environment and the human community. The astounding mechanical success of these high-powered technologies is due to their method of systematically breaking down ecological complexities by eliminating the recalcitrant human factor. I have called this ancient form of mechanized organization the "megamachine." Wherever it operates, it magnifies authoritarian power and minimizes or destroys human initiative, self-direction, and self-government.

Obviously I cannot, at this hearing, present a just appraisal of the many genuine goods produced by these power systems; nor can I offer a detailed explanation of their sinister countertendency to produce an unbalanced, deliberately wasteful, inherently destructive, and increasingly totalitarian economy, seemingly modern, but in fact based on ancient bureaucratic and military models. Even the book I have written only opens up the subject, and I have still to trace the story through the last four centuries.

Now, the main point to observe is that there is a deep-seated antagonism between a mechanistic, power-centered economy and the far older organic, life-centered economy; for a life economy seeks continuity, variety, orderly, and purposeful growth. Such an economy is cut to the human measure, and it respects the human scale so that every organism, every community, every human being, shall have the variety of goods and experiences necessary for the fulfillment of his own individual life course, from birth to death.

The mark of a life economy is a respect for organic limits, it seeks not the greatest possible quantity of any particular good, but the right quantity, of the right quality, at the right place, and the right time for the right purpose. Too much of any one thing is as fatal to living organisms as too little.

In contrast, a power economy is designed for the continuous and compulsory expansion of a limited number of uniform goods—those specially adapted to quantity production and remote control. Apart from enlarging the province of mechanization and automation, the chief goal of this system is to produce the greatest amount of power, prestige, or profit for the distant controllers of the megamachine. Though these modern systems produce a fantastic output of highly specialized products—motor cars, refrigerators, washing machines, rockets, nuclear bombs—they cannot, on their own terms, do justice to the far more complex and varied needs of human life, for these needs cannot be mechanized and automated, still less controlled and suppressed, without killing something essential to the life of the organism or to the self-respect of the human personality.

For the last century, we Americans have been systematically indoctrinated, with our own far from reluctant cooperation, in the virtues of mass production and have accepted, with unction, the plethora of goods offered, in which even those on public relief now participate. But we have been carefully trained to look only at the plus side of the equation, and to close our eyes to the appalling defects and failures that issue from the very success of the megamachine.

No sound public policy in housing and urban renewal can be formulated till we have reckoned with these liabilities. The over-production of motor cars has not only wrecked our once-efficient and well-balanced transportation system, and turned our big cities into hollow shells, exploding with violence; but it has polluted the air with lethal carbon monoxide, and even, through the use of lead in gasoline, dangerously poisoned our water and food. The chemical industry, in its undisciplined effort to sell a maximum amount of its products, has poisoned our soils and our foods with DDT, malathion, and other deadly compounds, while heedlessly befouling our water supply with detergents.

So, too, with the pharmaceutical industry, the rocket industry, the television industry, the pornography and narcotics industries. All have become immensely dynamic and profitable enterprises, automatically expanding, and by their compulsive expansion callously disregarding human health, safety, and welfare, while wiping out every trace of organic variety and human choice. As a result, the forces of life, if they break out at all, now must do so in the negative form of violence, crime, and psychotic disturbances. What we have unthinkingly accepted as brilliant technical progress has too often resulted in biological or social regression.

The point I am now making, I regret to say, challenges, not only some of the published views of your chairman, but possibly the views of the rest of this subcommittee. You accept, I take it, the current American faith in the necessity for an ever-expanding, machine-centered economy, as if this were one of the great laws of nature, or if not, then America's happiest contribution to human prosperity and freedom. I wish you were right.

But do you seriously believe that a housing industry based, as Senator Ribicoff has put it, on "the technology of megalopolis" will be any more regardful of human needs and human satisfactions, or any more eager to overcome the distortions and perversions of a power-obsessed, machine-driven, money-oriented economy? If so, you are ignoring the very factors that have mocked and ruined so many of our previous efforts at urban improvement. This expanding economy, for all its suffocating abundance of machine-made goods and gadgets, has resulted in a dismally contracted life, lived for the most part confined to a car or a television set; that is, a life so empty of vivid firsthand experiences that it might as well be lived in a space capsule, traveling from nowhere to nowhere at supersonic speeds.

Space capsules—yes, stationary space capsules—that is what most of our new buildings are, and our prefabricated foods taste increasingly like those supplied in tubes to astronauts; while in our urban planning schools I have encountered ominous designs for whole cities to be placed underground, or even underwater, so that their inhabitants may live and die without ever coming into contact with the living environment, that rich and varied environment which has been essential to the human race, for organic health, psychological stability, and cultural growth for at least 500,000 years. And in boasting of the fact that automation will soon be able to do away with all serious, humanly rewarding work, manual or mental, we are threatening to remove perhaps the most essential of all historic invention, work itself, and invention for preserving mental balance, and furthering the arts of life. These are all danger signals. Is it not time to give them heed?

Now, your chairman, in his able speech last January, attempted to bring together what seems to me, if I may speak frankly, two altogether incompatible, in fact downright antagonistic, proposals: On one hand for restoring neighborhoods as the basic human environment; on the other for applying to housing what he called, quite properly, the technology of megalopolis, what I would call the technology of the megamachine. Senator Ribicoff wisely recognized the need to respect the small unit, the neighborhood, the small town, in order to promote those qualities we associate, at least as an ideal, with the small town—meaning, I take it, a place where everyone has an identifiable face and is a recognizable and responsible person, not just a social security number, a draft card number, or a combination of digits on a computer.

As to neighborhoods, I am entirely on his side. I have not spent part of my life in a small country community, and another part in a planned neighborhood unit, Sunnyside Gardens, Long Island, without learning to appreciate these intimate small-town virtues. And I believe the greatest defect of the U.S. Constitution was its original failure, despite the example of the New England township and the town meeting, to make this democratic local unit the basic cell of our whole system of government. For democracy, in any active sense, begins and ends in communities small enough for their members to meet face to face. Without such units, capable of independent and automatic action, even the best contrived central governments, State and Federal, become party oriented, indifferent to criticism, resentful of correction, and in the end, all too often, highhanded and dictatorial.

But if your purpose is to do urban planning and renewal on the basis of neighborhoods and balanced urban communities, you would, I submit, be deceiving yourselves if you imagined that a vast contribution by the Federal Government—$50 billion over 10 years has been suggested—could possibly achieve the happy results you hope for. Such a massive expenditure succeeded, we all know, in producing the atom bomb; and it has been applied with equal success, more or less, in producing rockets, space satellites, supersonic jets, and similar instruments for the physical conquest of space and time, and large-scale physical destruction.

But note—this method can be applied only to those structures or machine assemblages that can be designed without the faintest regard for the human factor, and without any feedback from the human reaction. This patently leaves out the neighborhood and the city. Unless human needs and human interactions and human responses are the first consideration, the city, in any valid human sense, cannot be said to exist, for, as Sophocles long ago said, "The city is people."

Accordingly, I beg you to look a little more closely at what such a huge supply of capital, with such large prospective profits, would do. Not merely would it skyrocket already inflated land values so that a disproportionate amount would go to the property owner and real estate speculator; but even worse—it would invite great megamachines to invade the building industry. With $50 billion as bait, a new kind of aerospace industry would move in, with all its typical paraphernalia of scientific research and engineering design. At that moment your plans for creating humanly satisfactory neighborhoods would go up in smoke.

"General-space housing incorporated" will solve your housing problem, swiftly and efficiently, though not painlessly, by following their own typical method, derived from the ancient pyramid builders and now applied by many other corporations: General Motors, General Electric, General Foods, all the great "General" corporations. What is this method? *Eliminate the human factor! Enforce mechanical conformity and destroy choice.* With the aid of their systems analyzers and computers, these high-powered organizations would design housing units even more prisonlike in character, if that is possible, than those we now have, and as unfit for permanent human habitation.

Once started, such a scientifically ordered housing industry, commanding virtually unlimited capital at national expense, and providing, as in the Pentagon's favored industries, indecently large salaries and exorbitant profits for private investors, would be geared for further expansion. And it would achieve this expansion, not only by designing units, prefabricated for early obsolescence, but likewise by wiping out, as dangerous rivals, those parts of the remaining rural or urban environment that were built on a more human plan. In the name of urban renewal this method would complete the urban devastation and destruction that you now seek to repair. That is not a pretty prospect. But it is a realistic interpretation of what a $50 billion program, designed to use the existing power systems and feed an expanding economy, would probably do.

I have exhausted the time allotted to me, and have, I fear, more than exhausted your patience; though I have only nibbled at the edges of this difficult subject. So my final words must be brief, and, I regret, mostly words of negation and caution. Go slow. Experiment with small measures and small units. Whatever you do in extending and amplifying the policies followed in the past will almost surely meet the same embarrassment and the same dreadful failures.

Remember that you cannot overcome the metropolitan congestion of the last century, or the cataclysmic disintegration of urban life that has taken place during the last 30 years, by instituting a crash program. You are much more likely to produce more lethal congestion, more rapid disintegration, all ending in a greater social cataclysm. The time for action on a massive scale has not yet come. But the time for fresh thinking on this whole subject is long overdue.

BIBLIOGRAPHY

This bibliography does not pretend to be comprehensive, but merely indicates some of the more useful books and articles and suggests the richness and variety of American urban history. The literature of urban history covers a wide range of topics and is rapidly increasing in volume. The most ambitious study remains Lewis Mumford, *The City in History: Its Origins, Its Transformations, and Its Prospects* (1961). Charles N. Glaab and A. Theodore Brown, *A History of Urban America* (1967), is an interpretive, but challenging, study of American urbanization. More detailed are the volumes by Blake McKelvey: *The Urbanization of America, 1860–1915* (1963) and *The Emergence of Metropolitan America, 1915–1966* (1968). Less comprehensive, but nevertheless useful, are two books by Constance M. Green: *American Cities in the Growth of the Nation* (1957) and *The Rise of Urban America* (1965).

Several interpretive studies analyzing the role of the city in American history have appeared in article form. The best of these are: Albert B. Hart, "The Rise of American Cities," *Quarterly Journal of Economics*, IV (1890), 129–157; Lawrence V. Roth, "The Growth of American Cities," *Geographical Review*, V (1918), 384–398; N. S. B. Gras, "The Development of Metropolitan Economy in Europe and America," *American Historical Review*, XXVII (July 1922), 695–708; Charles A. Beard, "The City's Place in Civilization," *National Municipal Review*, XVII (Dec. 1928), 726–731; Arthur M. Schlesinger, "The City in American History," *Mississippi Valley Historical Review*, XXVII (June 1940), 43–66; W. Stull Holt, "Some Consequences of the Urban Movement in American History," *Pacific Historical Review*, XXII (Nov. 1953), 337–351; Blake McKelvey, "Urban Social and Economic Institutions in North America," *Recueils de la Société Jean Bodin*, VII (1955), 653–676; Bayrd Still, "The History of the City in American Life," *American Review*, II (1962), 20–34; and two essays by Richard C. Wade: "The City in History—Some American Perspectives," in Werner Z. Hirsch, ed., *Urban Life and Form* (1963), 59–79, and "Urbanization," in C. Vann Woodward, ed., *The Comparative Approach to American History* (1968), 187–205.

Basic for an understanding of the theoretical underpinnings of urban history are a variety of books and articles which elaborate methods of conceptualization and approaches to research. Among the most important of these studies are: Oscar Handlin and John Burchard, eds., *The Historian and the City* (1963); Philip M. Hauser and Leo F. Schnore, eds., *The Study of Urbanization* (1965); H. J. Dyos, ed., *The Study of Urban History* (1968); Robert E. Park, "The City: Suggestions for the Investigation of Human Behavior in the City Environment," *American Journal of Sociology*, XX (March 1915), 577–612; Louis Wirth, "Urbanism as a Way of Life," *ibid.*, XLIV (July 1938), 1–24; Hope Tisdale, "The Process of Urbanization," *Social Forces*, XX (March 1942), 311–316; William Diamond, "On the Dangers of an Urban Interpretation of History," in Eric F. Goldman, ed., *Historiography and Urbanization: Essays in American History in Honor of W. Stull Holt* (1941),

67–108; R. Richard Wohl, "Urbanism, Urbanity, and the Historian," *University of Kansas City Review*, XXII (Oct. 1955), 53–61; Eric E. Lampard, "The History of Cities in the Economically Advanced Areas," *Economic Development and Cultural Change*, III (Jan. 1955), 81–136; Eric E. Lampard, "American Historians and the Study of Urbanization," *American Historical Review*, LXVII (Oct. 1961), 49–61; Asa Briggs, "The Study of Cities," *Confluence*, VII (Summer 1958), 107–114; Charles N. Glaab, "The Historian and the American Urban Tradition," *Wisconsin Magazine of History*, XLVII (Autumn 1963), 12–25; Leo F. Schnore and Eric E. Lampard, "Social Science and the City: A Survey of Research Needs," in Leo F. Schnore and Henry Fagin, eds., *Urban Research and Policy Planning* (1967), 21–47; Roy Lubove, "The Urbanization Process: An Approach to Historical Research," *Journal of the American Institute of Planners*, XXXIII (Jan. 1967), 33–39; Sam Bass Warner, Jr., "If All the World Were Philadelphia: A Scaffolding for Urban History, 1774–1930," *American Historical Review*, LXXIV (Oct. 1968), 26–43; Richard L. Meier, *A Communications Theory of Urban Growth* (1962); and Allan R. Pred, *The Spatial Dynamics of U.S. Urban-Industrial Growth, 1800–1914* (1966).

A number of urban biographies—studies in the history of individual cities—provide useful perspectives on urbanism and urbanization. Particularly good are: Blake McKelvey, *Rochester* (4 vols., 1945–1961); Bessie L. Pierce, *A History of Chicago* (3 vols., 1937–1957); Constance M. Green, *Washington* (2 vols., 1962–1963); Bayrd Still, *Milwaukee: The History of a City* (rev. ed., 1965); Thomas J. Wertenbaker, *Norfolk: Historic Southern Port* (rev. ed., 1962); Gerald M. Capers, *The Biography of a River Town: Memphis, Its Heroic Age* (1939); Rollin G. Osterweis, *Three Centuries of New Haven, 1638–1938* (1953); Constance M. Green, *Holyoke, Massachusetts* (1939) and *History of Naugatuck, Connecticut* (1948); Vera Shlakman, *Economic History of a Factory Town: A Study of Chicopee, Massachusetts* (1935); Sam Bass Warner, Jr., *The Private City: Philadelphia in Three Periods of Its Growth* (1968); Edmund H. Chapman, *Cleveland: Village to Metropolis* (1965); Sidney Glazer, *Detroit: A Study in Urban Development* (1965); A. Theodore Brown, *Frontier Community: Kansas City to 1870* (1963); Marilyn M. Sibley, *The Port of Houston: A History* (1968); Lawrence L. Graves, *A History of Lubbock* (1962); Robert M. Fogelson, *The Fragmented Metropolis: Los Angeles, 1850–1930* (1967).

Two massively researched volumes by Carl Bridenbaugh cover the colonial period in depth: *Cities in the Wilderness: The First Century of Urban Life in America, 1625–1742* (1938) and *Cities in Revolt: Urban Life in America, 1743–1776* (1955). Also very useful on colonial urban life are: Darrett B. Rutman, *Winthrop's Boston: A Portrait of a Puritan Town, 1630–1649* (1965); Sumner C. Powell, *Puritan Village: The Formation of a New England Town* (1963); Bernard Bailyn, *The New England Merchants in the Seventeenth Century* (1955); William Haller, *The Puritan Frontier: Town-Planting in New England Colonial Development, 1630–1660* (1951); Thomas J. Condon, *New York Beginnings: The Commercial Origins of New Netherland* (1968); George W. Edwards and Arthur E. Peterson, *New York as an Eighteenth-Century Municipality* (1917); Frederick B. Tolles, *Meeting House and Counting House* (1948); Carl and Jessica Bridenbaugh, *Rebels and Gentlemen: Philadelphia in the Age of Franklin* (1942); Arthur L. Jensen, *The Maritime Commerce of Colonial Philadelphia* (1963); Curtis P. Nettels, "The Economic Relations of Boston, Philadelphia, and New York, 1680–1715," *Journal of Economic and*

Business History, III (1930–1931), 185–215; James T. Lemmon, "Urbanization and the Development of Eighteenth-Century Southeastern Pennsylvania and Adjacent Delaware," *William and Mary Quarterly*, XXIV (Oct. 1967), 501–542; Clarence P. Gould, "The Economic Causes of the Rise of Baltimore," in Leonard W. Labaree, ed., *Essays in Colonial History Presented to Charles McLean Andrews by His Students* (1931), 225–251; James H. Soltow, *The Economic Role of Williamsburg* (1965); Carl Bridenbaugh, *The Colonial Craftsman* (1950); Thomas J. Wertenbaker, *The Golden Age of Colonial Culture* (1942); Ernest S. Griffith, *History of American City Government: The Colonial Period* (1938).

The role of the city in the American Revolution is a topic which deserves much additional research. Only a few studies bear upon this subject: Arthur M. Schlesinger, *The Colonial Merchants and the American Revolution* (1918); Virginia D. Harrington, *The New York Merchant on the Eve of the Revolution* (1935); Leila Sellers, *Charleston Business on the Eve of the American Revolution* (1934); Richard Walsh, *Charleston's Sons of Liberty: A Study of the Artisans, 1763–1789* (1959); and Jackson Turner Main, *The Social Structure of Revolutionary America* (1965).

Urban historians have supplied a new perspective to the history of the American West. Several recent works have revealed the importance of the urban dimension of the frontier. The most significant study is Richard C. Wade, *The Urban Frontier: The Rise of Western Cities, 1790–1830* (1959). Some other useful books are: Lewis E. Atherton, *Main Street on the Middle Border* (1954); Kenneth Wheeler, *To Wear a City's Crown: The Beginnings of Urban Growth in Texas, 1836–1865* (1968); Duane Smith, *Rocky Mountain Mining Camps: The Urban Frontier* (1967); James B. Allen, *The Company Town in the American West* (1966); Glen C. Quiett, *They Built the West: An Epic of Rails and Cities* (1934); Robert Dykstra, *The Cattle Towns* (1968); and portions of Daniel J. Boorstin, *The Americans: The National Experience* (1965). Important material may also be found in several articles, including Francis P. Weisenburger, "The Urbanization of the Middle West: Town and Village in the Pioneer Period," *Indiana Magazine of History*, XLI (March 1954), 19–30; Bessie L. Pierce, "Changing Urban Patterns in the Mississippi Valley," *Journal of the Illinois Historical Society*, XLIII (Spring 1950), 46–57; and Oscar O. Winther, "The Rise of Metropolitan Los Angeles, 1870–1910," *Huntington Library Quarterly*, X (Aug. 1947), 391–405.

Urbanism in the Southern states has also received historical examination in recent years, most importantly in Richard C. Wade's pioneering study, *Slavery in the Cities: The South, 1800–1860* (1964). Other valuable works are: George C. Rogers, Jr., *Charleston in the Age of the Pinckneys* (1969); D. Clayton James, *Antebellum Natchez* (1968); Kenneth Coleman, *Confederate Athens* (1967); Gerald M. Capers, *Occupied City: New Orleans under the Federals, 1862–1865* (1965); and C. Vann Woodward, *The Origins of the New South, 1877–1913* (1951). Rupert B. Vance and Nicholas J. Demerath, eds., *The Urban South* (1954), applies social science techniques to the twentieth-century South.

Many urban historians have related urbanization to economic development and focused on the urban commercial rivalries which frequently spurred city growth. General studies in this vein include: George Rogers Taylor, *The Transportation Revolution, 1815–1860* (1951); Edward C. Kirkland, *Industry Comes of Age: Business, Labor, and Public Policy, 1860–1897* (1961); David T. Gilchrist, ed., *The Growth of the Seaport Cities, 1790–1825* (1967); and

George R. Taylor "American Urban Growth Preceding the Railway Age," *Journal of Economic History*, XXVII (Sept. 1967), 309–339. Some of the more useful specific studies are: James W. Livingood, *The Philadelphia-Baltimore Trade Rivalry* (1947); Julius Rubin, *Canal or Railroad: Imitation and Innovation in the Response to the Erie Canal in Philadelphia, Baltimore, and Boston* (1961); Robert G. Albion, *The Rise of the New York Port, 1815–1860* (1939); Edward C. Kirkland, *Men, Cities and Transportation: A Study in New England History, 1820–1900* (2 vols., 1948); Catherine E. Reiser, *Pittsburgh's Commercial Development, 1800–1850* (1951); Wyatt W. Belcher, *The Economic Rivalry Between St. Louis and Chicago, 1850–1880* (1947); Charles N. Glaab, *Kansas City and the Railroads* (1962); Merl E. Reed, *New Orleans and the Railroads* (1966). Significant articles on urban rivalries and promotion include: David M. Ellis, "Albany and Troy—Commercial Rivals," *New York History*, XXIV (Oct. 1943), 484–511; Blake McKelvey, "The Erie Canal: Mother of Cities," *New-York Historical Society Quarterly*, XXXV (Jan. 1951), 55–71; Harry N. Scheiber, "Urban Rivalry and Internal Improvements in the Old Northwest, 1820–1860," *Ohio History*, LXXI (Oct. 1962), 227–239; Herbert W. Rice, "Early Rivalry Among Wisconsin Cities for Railroads," *Wisconsin Magazine of History*, XXXV (Autumn 1951), 10–15; and Charles N. Glaab, "Historical Perspective on Urban Development Schemes," in Leo F. Schnore and Henry Fagin, eds., *Urban Research and Policy Planning* (1967), 197–219.

A number of studies have examined urban social problems and efforts at humanitarian reform. Representative works include: Robert H. Bremner, *From the Depths: The Discovery of Poverty in the United States* (1956); Raymond A. Mohl, "Urban Reform in Early New York, 1787–1831," *New-York Historical Society Quarterly*, LIV (Jan. 1970); Blanche D. Coll, "The Baltimore Society for the Prevention of Pauperism, 1820–1822," *American Historical Review*, LVI (Oct. 1955), 77–87; Douglas T. Miller, *Jacksonian Aristocracy: Class and Democracy in New York, 1830–1860* (1967); Charles Rosenberg, *The Cholera Years* (1962); Gordon Atkins, *Health, Housing, and Poverty in New York City, 1865–1898* (1947); Roy Lubove, *The Progressives and the Slums* (1963); James Ford, *et al.*, *Slums and Housing: With Special Reference to New York City* (2 vols., 1936); Edith Abbott, *The Tenements of Chicago, 1908–1935* (1936); Allen F. Davis, *Spearheads for Reform* (1967); Kenneth T. Jackson, *The Ku Klux Klan in the City, 1915–1930* (1967). Also very useful on social history and social mobility are: Arthur M. Schlesinger, *The Rise of the City, 1878–1898* (1933); Stephan Thernstrom, *Poverty and Progress: Social Mobility in a Nineteenth Century City* (1964); Richard J. Hopkins, "Occupational and Geographic Mobility in Atlanta, 1870–1896," *Journal of Southern History*, XXXIV (May 1968), 200–213.

The working class has always formed an important component in urban society. General works in labor history which have relevance for urban historians are: John R. Commons, *et al.*, eds., *Documentary History of American Industrial Society* (10 vols., 1910–1911); John R. Commons, *et al.*, *History of Labour in the United States* (4 vols., 1918–1935); and Philip S. Foner's Marxist-oriented *History of the Labor Movement in the United States* (4 vols., 1947–1967). More specific studies include: Walter Hugins, *Jacksonian Democracy and the Working Class* (1960); Edward Pessen, *Most Uncommon Jacksonians: The Radical Leaders of the Early Labor Movement* (1967); Norman J. Ware, *The Industrial Worker 1840–1860* (1924); Henry F. Bedford, *Socialism and the Workers in Massachusetts, 1886–1912* (1968); Melvyn Dubofsky, *When*

Workers Organize: New York City in the Progressive Era (1968); Barbara W. Newell, *Chicago and the Labor Movement* (1961); Louis B. and Richard S. Perry, *A History of the Los Angeles Labor Movement, 1911–1941* (1963).

Among a number of useful works on urban government and municipal services, the following are representative: Ernest S. Griffith, *The Modern Development of City Government* (1927); Nelson M. Blake, *Water for the Cities* (1956); John Duffy, *A History of Public Health in New York City, 1625–1866* (1968); John B. Blake, *Public Health in the Town of Boston, 1630–1822* (1959); Roger Lane, *Policing the City: Boston, 1822–1885* (1967); George W. Hilton and John F. Due, *The Electric Interurban Railways in America* (1960); George R. Taylor, "The Beginnings of Mass Transportation in Urban America," *Smithsonian Journal of History*, I (1966), No. 2, 35–50, No. 3, 31–54; Frederick M. Bender, "Gas Light, 1816–1860," *Pennsylvania History*, XXII (Oct. 1955), 359–373; and Richard Skolnik, "George Edwin Waring, Jr.: A Model for Reformers," *New-York Historical Society Quarterly*, LII (Oct. 1968), 354–378, which deals with a leading sanitationist of the late nineteenth century. Sam Bass Warner, Jr., *Streetcar Suburbs: The Process of Growth in Boston, 1870–1900* (1962), is a unique study which relates suburban growth to the expansion of municipal services.

Municipal bossism and political reform has been closely studied by historians. Some of the more important books include: Clifford W. Patton, *The Battle for Municipal Reform, 1875–1900* (1940); Alexander B. Callow, *The Tweed Ring* (1966); Seymour J. Mandelbaum, *Boss Tweed's New York* (1965); Zane L. Miller, *Boss Cox's Cincinnati* (1968); Walton Bean, *Boss Ruef's San Francisco* (1952); Lloyd Wendt and Herman Kogan, *Bosses in Lusty Chicago* (1943); Melvin Holli, *Reform in Detroit: Hazen S. Pingree and Urban Politics* (1969); Lyle Dorsett, *The Pendergast Machine* (1968); Arthur Mann, *Yankee Reformers in the Urban Age* (1954); James B. Crooks, *Politics and Progress: The Rise of Urban Progressivism in Baltimore, 1895–1911* (1968); William D. Miller, *Memphis During the Progressive Era, 1900–1917* (1957); Jack Tager, *The Intellectual as Urban Reformer: Brand Whitlock and the Progressive Movement* (1968); and Arthur Mann, *LaGuardia Comes to Power: 1933* (1965). Among the important articles on municipal corruption and reform, see especially: Eric McKitrick, "The Study of Corruption," *Political Science Quarterly*, LXXII (Dec. 1957), 502–514; Samuel P. Hays, "The Politics of Reform in Municipal Government in the Progressive Era," *Pacific Northwest Quarterly*, LV (Oct. 1964), 157–169; Elmer E. Cornwell, "Bosses, Machines, and Ethnic Groups," *Annals of the American Academy of Political and Social Science*, CCCLIII (May 1964), 27–39; Roy Lubove, "The Twentieth Century City: The Progressive as Municipal Reformer," *Mid-America*, XXXI (Oct. 1959), 195–209; J. Joseph Huthmacher, "Urban Liberalism and the Age of Reform," *Mississippi Valley Historical Review*, XLIX, (Sept. 1962), 231–241; and Mark D. Hirsch "Reflections on Urban History and Urban Reform, 1865–1915," in Donald Sheehan and Harold C. Syrett, eds., *Essays in American Historiography in Honor of Allan Nevins* (1960), 109–137.

On immigration and ethnic groups in the city, the most useful studies for the urban historian are: Robert Ernst, *Immigrant Life in New York City, 1825–1863* (1949); Donald B. Cole, *Immigrant City: Lawrence, Massachusetts, 1845–1921* (1963); Rowland T. Berthoff, *British Immigrants in Industrial America, 1790–1950* (1953); Earl F. Niehaus, *The Irish in New Orleans, 1800–1860* (1965); Gerd Korman, *Industrialization, Immigrants and Americanizers: The View from Milwaukee, 1866–1921* (1967); Moses Rischin, *The Promised City:*

New York's Jews, 1870–1914 (1962); Nathan Glazer and Daniel P. Moynihan, *Beyond the Melting Pot* (1963); Oscar Lewis, *La Vida: A Puerto Rican Family in the Culture of Poverty—San Juan and New York* (1965); and several books by Oscar Handlin: *The Uprooted* (1951), *Boston's Immigrants* (rev. ed., 1959), and *The Newcomers* (1959). Important articles are: Nathan Glazer, "The Integration of American Immigrants," *Law and Contemporary Problems*, XXI (Spring 1956), 256–269; Milton G. Gordon, "Assimilation in America: Theory and Reality," *Daedalus*, 90 (Spring 1961), 263–285; and a number of studies in recent issues of the *International Migration Review*.

Many recent historians have focused on the Negro in the city, tracing the formation of black ghettos and the expression of racial violence. The best works of this kind are: Leon F. Litwack, *North of Slavery: The Negro in the Free States, 1790–1860* (1961); Gilbert Osofsky, "The Enduring Ghetto," *Journal of American History*, LV (Sept. 1968), 243–255; W. E. B. DuBois, *The Philadelphia Negro* (1899); Seth M. Scheiner, *Negro Mecca: A History of the Negro in New York City, 1865–1920* (1965); Gilbert Osofsky, *Harlem: The Making of a Ghetto* (1966); Allan H. Spear, *Black Chicago: The Making of a Negro Ghetto, 1890–1920* (1967); Constance M. Green, *The Secret City: A History of Race Relations in the Nation's Capital* (1967); Arvah E. Strickland, *History of the Chicago Urban League* (1966); Elliott M. Rudwick, *Race Riot in East St. Louis, July 2, 1917* (1964); Robert Shogun and Tom Craig, *The Detroit Race Riot: A Study in Violence* (1964); A. I. Waskow, *From Race Riot to Sit-In: 1919 and the 1960's* (1966); Hubert G. Locke, *The Detroit Riot of 1967* (1969); John A. Williams, "The Long Hot Summers of Yesteryear," *History Teacher*, II (March 1968), 9–23.

The impact of urbanization on American religious groups is traced in: Arthur M. Schlesinger, "A Critical Period in American Religion, 1875–1900," *Proceedings of the Massachusetts Historical Society*, LXIV (June 1932), 523–547; Charles H. Hopkins, *The Rise of the Social Gospel in American Protestantism, 1865–1915* (1940); Henry F. May, *Protestant Churches and Industrial America* (1949); Aaron Abell, *The Urban Impact on American Protestantism* (1962); Aaron Abell, *American Catholicism and Social Action* (1960); David O'Brien, *American Catholics and Social Reform: The New Deal Years* (1968); Neil Betten, "Catholic Urban Reform: The Association of Catholic Trade Unionists," *Thought*, XLV (1970); and Robert D. Cross, ed., *The Church and the City* (1967).

Relevant material on city planning and urban architecture may be found in a variety of works. The most important study of city planning is John W. Reps, *The Making of Urban America: A History of City Planning in the United States* (1965). See also two other books by Reps: *Town Planning in Frontier America* (1968) and *Monumental Washington: The Planning and Development of the Capital Center* (1966). Other useful studies of planning and architecture are: Christopher Tunnard and Henry Hope Reed, *American Skyline* (1955); Wayne Andrews, *Architecture, Ambition, and Americans* (1955); John Burchard and Albert Bush-Brown, *The Architecture of America: A Social and Cultural History* (1961); Carl Bridenbaugh, *Peter Harrison, First American Architect* (1949); Anthony N. B. Garvan, *Architecture and Town Planning in Colonial Connecticut* (1951); Harold and James Kirker, *Bulfinch's Boston, 1787–1817* (1964); Albert Fein, ed., *Landscape into Cityscape: Frederick Law Olmsted's Plans for a Greater New York City* (1967); John Coolidge, *Mill and Mansion: A Study of Architecture and Society in Lowell, Massachusetts* (1942); William H. Wilson, *The City Beautiful Movement in Kansas*

City (1964); Stanley Buder, *Pullman: An Experiment in Industrial Order and Community Planning, 1880–1930* (1967); Lewis Mumford, *The Brown Decades* (1931); Carl W. Condit, *The Chicago School of Architecture* (1964); Roy Lubove, *Community Planning in the 1920's: The Contribution of the Regional Planning Association of America* (1965); and Paul A. Conkin, *Tomorrow a New World: The New Deal Community Program* (1959). Not to be over-looked are a number of articles from the *Journal of the American Institute of Planners* and the *Journal of the Society of Architectural Historians.*

Important for the study of urban history is an awareness of shifting American attitudes toward the city. The best study of this nature is Morton and Lucia White, *The Intellectual Versus the City* (1962). Also relevant are: Anselm Strauss, *Images of the American City* (1961); Kevin Lynch, *The Image of the City* (1960); George Dunlap, *The City in the American Novel, 1789–1900* (1934); Blanche H. Gelfant, *The American City Novel* (1954); Eugene Arden, "The Evil City in American Fiction," *New York History*, XXXV (July 1954), 259–279; Robert D. Cross, "The Changing Image of the City Among American Catholics," *Catholic Historical Review*, XLVIII (April 1962), 33–52; and Robert H. Walker, "The Poet and the Rise of the City," *Mississippi Valley Historical Review*, XLIX (June 1962), 85–99.

Accompanying the crisis of the modern metropolis has come a flood of writings which examine the urban condition, diagnose urban ills, and prescribe cures for America's urbanized society. Only a few representative studies may be mentioned here: Jean Gottmann, *Megalopolis: The Urbanized Northeastern Seaboard of the United States* (1961); George E. Mowry, *The Urban Nation, 1920–1960* (1965); Edgar M. Hoover and Raymond Vernon, *Anatomy of a Metropolis* (1959); Jane Jacobs, *The Death and Life of Great American Cities* (1961); Michael Harrington, *The Other America: Poverty in the United States* (1962); Robert A. Dahl, *Who Governs? Democracy and Power in an American City* (1961); Victor Gruen, *The Heart of Our Cities* (1964); Charles Abrams, *The City Is the Frontier* (1965); Leo F. Schnore, *The Urban Scene* (1965); Sam Bass Warner, ed., *Planning for a Nation of Cities* (1966); Jeanne R. Lowe, *Cities in a Race with Time: Progress and Poverty in America's Renewing Cities* (1967); H. Wentworth Eldredge, ed., *Taming Megalopolis* (2 vols., 1967); Hans Blumenfeld, *The Modern Metropolis* (1967); Lewis Mumford, *The Urban Prospect* (1968); William H. Whyte, *The Last Land-scape* (1968); Scott Greer, *et al.*, eds., *The New Urbanization* (1968); James Q. Wilson, ed., *The Metropolitan Enigma* (1968); Gerald D. Suttles, *The Social Order of the Slum: Ethnicity and Territory in the Inner City* (1968); Jane Jacobs, *The Economy of Cities* (1969). Also very useful are relevant government publications, including: *Report of the National Advisory Commission on Civil Disorders* (1968); *Federal Role in Urban Affairs* (Hearings Before the Subcommittee on Executive Reorganization of the Committee on Government Operations, United States Senate, 1966–1967); *Building the American City* (Report of the National Commission on Urban Problems, 1968).

Some useful documentary collections of urban materials are: Charles N. Glaab, ed., *The American City: A Documentary History* (1963); Wilson Smith, ed., *Cities of Our Past and Present* (1964); David Weimer, ed., *City and Country in America* (1962); Christopher Tunnard, ed., *The Modern American City* (1968); Bessie L. Pierce, ed., *As Others See Chicago* (1933); Bayrd Still, ed., *Mirror for Gotham* (1956).

Additional bibliography may be found in Charles N. Glaab, "The Historian

and the American City: A Bibliographic Survey," in Philip M. Hauser and
Leo F. Schnore, eds., *The Study of Urbanization* (1965) and Allen F. Davis,
"The American Historian vs. the City," *Social Studies*, LVI (March, April
1965), 91–96, 127–135. The *Urban History Newsletter,* published twice yearly
by the history department of the University of Wisconsin-Milwaukee, contains up-to-date bibliography in each issue.

INDEX

INDEX

immigration in, 93–103, 113–26, 164, 166, 169–70, 174
manufacture in, 91, 93, 96–97
merchants in, 92
in Middle-Western United States, 161–76
  amateur government, 168–69
  comparison to eighteenth-century cities, 163, 166–67, 175
  government functions, 163–67, 171–74
  manufacture, 163, 170–71
  patterns of urbanization, 163–76
  trade, 163, 170–71
  urban similarity, 163, 164, 167
population of, 91, 92, 96–97
sanitation in, 93–94, 164–66
slavery in, 140–60
  corporations, 155–56
  decline of, 141, 150–60
  imbalance of sexes, 156–58
  patterns of ownership, 153–56
  visibility of, 151, 157
social structure of, 93–94
in South, 140–60
trade-union movement in, 93, 103, 111–12
transportation and, 91–92, 127–39, 170
  canals, 128–38
  controversy over, 130–39
  private construction of, 131, 133, 134
  railroads, 129–38
  urban rivalry, 128
women in, 108–10
working class in, 95–112
  attitudes, 95, 104, 111
  immigrants, 101–3
  poverty, 105–6
  rural migrants, 100–101
  social mobility, 97–98
  wage scales, 98, 99, 103–4, 107–8
See also specific cities
Presidential Strike Commission of 1894, 253
Privatism, 32–34
Project Head Start, 273
Prosser Committee, 305–7
Prosser, Steward, 305–7
Protestantism in Industrial cities, 209–13, 217–19, 222–26
  See also Religion in Industrial cities
Proudhon, Pierre Joseph, 287
Public welfare, *see* Welfare programs
Puerto Rican Community Development Project, 341, 345
Puerto Rican Forum, 341

Puerto Rican immigrants, 335–48
  assimilation of, 336, 340
  automation and, 337
  characteristics of migration of, 336–37
  cultural background of, 235–39
  identity problems of, 338–40
  integrated parishes of, 340
  New York City and, 336–48
  numbers of, 335
  political power and, 341–46
  racial discrimination against, 339–40
Puerto Rico, 235, 338–39
  economic development of, 338–39
  industrialization of, 339, 348
  political status of, 338
  religious conditions, 339
Pullman, George, 248, 250–57
Pullman, Ill., 247–57
  absence of self-government in, 250, 254
  Chicago consolidation with, 255
  City Beautiful Movement and, 257
  commercial vice in, 252–53
  company control over, 251, 252
  criticism of, 250, 252, 255, 256–57
  depression of 1893 and, 254
  Garden City Movement and, 257
  Model Tenement Movement and, 256–57
  physical plan of, 249–50
  as planned city, 248–57
  Pullman strike and, 254–55
  rents in, 254–55
Pullman strike, 229, 291, 254–55

Quimly, Ian, 98
Quimly, Phineas P., 227
Quincy, Mass., 135

Racial ghettos
  conditions in, 372–73
  formation of, 370–71
  housing in, 387–89
  immigrant ghettos and, 373–74
  See also Negroes
Racism, 272, 339–40
  institutionalized, 350, 358–59
Radburn, N.J., 392–93
Railroads, 129–38
  See also Pre-Industrial cities
Railton, George, 220
Rauschenbusch, Walter, 224–25
Regional Planning Association of America, 392
Relief, *see* Great Depression; Welfare programs; *and specific cities*